PORCUPINE AS PRIEST

THE
CHEYENNE INDIANS
THEIR HISTORY AND
WAYS OF LIFE

BY

GEORGE BIRD GRINNELL

*Photographs by Elizabeth C. Grinnell
and Mrs. J. E. Tuell*

VOLUME TWO

NEW HAVEN
YALE UNIVERSITY PRESS
LONDON · HUMPHREY MILFORD · OXFORD UNIVERSITY PRESS
MCMXXIV

CONTENTS

v

35375

ILLUSTRATIONS

WAR AND ITS WAYS

THE Cheyennes have a tradition of a golden age when war was unknown and universal peace prevailed. All strangers met in friendship and parted on good terms. Such a far-off time, when hostile encounters were unknown, is told of by many of the tribes of the northern plains.

No doubt there were fightings and wars long before the coming of the white man, but these were probably the results of more or less temporary quarrels, and were not bloody. The only incentive likely to have caused such fightings was the desire for revenge, and this desire, unless promptly gratified, was apt soon to be forgotten. The introduction of the horse, however, furnished to all the Plains tribes a new and strong motive for war, for by war men might acquire something of very great value. Until the coming of the horse, the only possessions of the Plains tribes, except food and clothing, were their dogs, and their arms and implements of stone and wood. When the horse came its usefulness was at once recognized, for here was an animal whose possession added immensely to the comfort and freedom of the people. On its back they could carry loads which hitherto they had borne themselves; it carried them and their families where they pleased, and revealed to them a means of discovering and venturing into new countries of which they had known nothing; it permitted the pursuit and capture of food and its transportation for long distances to the camp. Since everyone desired to possess horses, all men would exchange desirable things for them; thus no one could have too many horses.

Only two ways of procuring horses in any numbers were known—by capturing those running wild on the prairie and

I

those which were in possession of neighboring tribes. I have elsewhere pointed out that among most of the Plains tribes the practice of taking horses from the enemy became a regular profession.

When we read of wars by the Indians, we think chiefly of surprises and battles, and the killing and scalping of enemies; but while such imaginings would fit many war journeys, there were many brave and successful warriors of the Cheyennes who never went on war-paths of this description, who on their war journeys tried to avoid coming in close contact with enemies, and had no wish to kill enemies. Such men went to war for the sole purpose of increasing their possessions by capturing horses; that is, they carried on war as a business—for profit. Some of these—men who possessed high reputation for courage, success, and general well-doing—made it their boast that they had never killed a man, and perhaps had never counted a coup. Such men specialized in capturing horses: their interest in war lay in that alone. An example is Big Foot, who, when with two companions he came upon a mounted Ute Indian and the Ute was shot from his horse, paid no attention to the wounded man—toward whom his two companions were racing, each wishing to have the glory of the first coup—but rode off as fast as he could to capture the enemy's horse.

On another occasion a war-party, of whom Big Foot was one, charged a body of the enemy, who fled. Big Foot was riding a very fast horse and noticed that one of the enemy was riding a particularly fine horse. Instead of taking part in the fight, he followed this man, and, when he overtook him, did not try to kill him, but threw his rope over him, dragged him from his horse, and, letting the man go, caught the horse and went off with it.[1]

Men famous for success in this particular field of war were Old Yellow Wolf, who lived in the first half of the nineteenth century, and was killed at Sand Creek; Big Foot, who died

[1] Indians of Today, p. 10, Chicago, 1900.

about 1901, and Elk River, who died about 1908. All these men lived to great age; all were successful in war, and all had great reputations as being most skillful in dealing with enemies and in securing horses. One of the achievements of Old Yellow Wolf has been already recounted.[2]

Elk River had a remarkable life. He was never a doctor; never was in a sweat-house; never took part in ceremonies. He just lived his life, took care of his family, and held the respect of the whole tribe. He was a most generous man, and at the same time a man with a remarkable sense of justice. He was a skillful catcher of wild horses, and it is said that on several occasions he rode up beside a wild horse and put a hackamore on it before stopping it.

EARLY WARFARE

The old people say that it was long after they had begun to journey westward that they had their first battle, and that the Hohe (Assiniboines and Crees, or possibly Ojibwas) were those with whom they fought. This early fighting took place long before they saw the first white man, and before they had reached their plains home.

Of this first battle it is said that during their journey westward, the people went out to kill buffalo, and that while engaged at this the Assiniboines came up and tried to surround the same herd.[3] The encounter caused a dispute, and soon afterward, in the night, the Assiniboines attacked the Cheyenne camp. The Assiniboines already possessed guns, while the Cheyennes had never seen any, and did not know what they were. The noise and effect of these strange weapons frightened the Cheyennes, and they ran away. The Assiniboines killed some of them, and cut off their hair; that is, scalped them.

The Hohe often attacked the Cheyenne camp at night. They

[2] The Fighting Cheyennes, p. 36.
[3] The Fighting Cheyennes, p. 5.

carried horns made of the hollow stems of some plant, by blowing through which they made a sound like the call uttered by
the buffalo in spring, and made this sound as they approached
the camp, so that, if the Cheyennes heard them, they might
suppose buffalo were coming, and should not suspect the approach of enemies. One day a camp of Cheyennes heard this
sound, and while some thought it was made by buffalo, others
feared that enemies were coming, and said, "Those are Hohe
coming; we had better get away!" Some ran and hid themselves, but others said, "No, those are only buffalo!" and did
not go.

The Hohe came and killed those who remained. Those who
had run away went to another camp farther down the river.
When the fugitives came to the stream, their dogs ran to the
bank to drink, but stopped and turned away without lapping.
The water looked red. The Cheyennes drank, however, and
afterward learned that they had drunk the blood of their own
people.

The fighting between the two tribes lasted for many years,
and the Cheyennes say that it was the Hohe who drove them
away from homes they had established, and forced them south.
Lewis and Clark mention the story of their flight southwest-
wardly, but attribute it to the Sioux.[4] They tell many stories
of attacks made on them by the Assiniboines before they
reached the Missouri River, where, according to tradition, they
obtained their first guns through the cunning of an old woman,
who led the enemy into a trap.[5]

Afterward, when the Hohe again attacked the village, the
Cheyennes with their guns defeated and drove them off.

The Cheyenne men were all warriors. War was regarded as
the noblest of pursuits, the only one for a man to follow; and
from earliest youth boys were encouraged to excel in it. They
were taught that no pleasure equaled the joy of battle; that

[4] Lewis and Clark, vol. vi, p. 100.
[5] The Fighting Cheyennes, p. 7.

success in war brought in its train the respect and admiration of men, women, and children in the tribe, and that the most worthy thing that any man could do was to be brave. It was pointed out that death in battle was not an evil, and that such a death, besides being glorious, protected one from all the miseries which threaten later life and are inevitable to old age.

This training, and the public opinion which supported it, guided the Cheyenne youth and gave them their motive for that hardihood and readiness which were essential to success in war. Bald Faced Bull, who was born in 1835 and died only a few years ago, showed how these boys felt and acted, when he said:

A party was going to war, and I wished to go with them, but my people thought I was too young to go. I told my family what I wished to do, but they said, "No, you are too young." The day before the party started, I took my horse from the camp and tied him in the timber a long way off, and the next morning took my bow-case and bow and arrows, and left the village on foot. I went to my horse, mounted him, and followed the party. I was then ten years of age.

The party traveled on for ten days, and at last found a Pawnee camp. The leader of the party chose the ten men that had the fastest horses, and sent them to make a charge on the camp; I was one of those selected. Before we reached the camp we met two Pawnees. One of them dismounted and ran into the brush; the other stayed outside to fight. He had a gun, and all the Cheyennes were afraid to go near him. One of the Cheyennes, a Crazy Dog Soldier named Bear Appearing Over The Hill, was coming up, and the other Cheyennes called out to him, "Look out for that man; he will kill you!" He charged down on the Pawnee to strike him, but the latter jumped back, and shot him in the breast. Then three or four Cheyennes jumped on the Pawnee, and cut him up alive.

After this, the Cheyennes went to look for the other Pawnee. He had hidden himself under a pile of weeds, but as he breathed, the weeds moved a little, and one Cheyenne, who had a lance, saw the weeds move and said, "Aha, it looks as if here were a Pawnee!" He thrust his lance down into the weeds and struck the Pawnee in the

5

back; he jumped up and ran, and another Cheyenne shot him with a gun. After this we returned to our village.

Among a people whose chief occupation was war, a large part of the oral literature naturally consists of stories of battles and the achievements of heroes. I have elsewhere set down some of this tribal history, and others of these tales are found in this book.

Their bravery led the Cheyennes to take risks in war not commonly faced by Indians, with the result that they lost many men in proportion to their numbers, and at the same time made their name a terror to their enemies. If injured by people of another tribe, they were eager for revenge. If people belonging to the village had been killed in some recent fight, the women in the camp went about and begged the young men to go to war, to take vengeance on their enemies. They passed their hands over the men, imploring them to take pity on them, while through the village old men shouted advice to all men to go to war, and kill some of the enemy, that the lamentations of the mourners might cease. The killing of enemies brought comfort and consolation to those whose relations had been killed by those of that tribe—it wiped away their tears. In the same way, a man who had lost a relation in war might carry the pipe about through the village and offer it to warriors, asking them to help him; meaning that they should assist him to revenge himself on his enemies. If they accepted the pipe and smoked, they promised to do what he asked. War-parties often set out from this motive alone. On some occasions, when the injury was great, the whole tribe broke camp and moved toward the enemy, seeking vengeance. When such a general move took place, the medicine arrows and the sacred hat were carried with them and into battle as war medicine. Such a tribal war journey was made in 1838, preparatory to the fight between the Cheyennes and Arapahoes, and Kiowas and Comanches; and again in 1853[6] against the Pawnees.

[6] The Fighting Cheyennes, p. 80.

6

CUSTOMS AND CEREMONIES

The motives which led the Cheyennes to go to war were thus a desire for glory, a wish to add to their possessions, or eagerness for revenge, but the chief motive was the love of fighting, which was instilled into them from early youth. From their earliest days boys were taught to long for the approbation of their elders, and this approbation was most readily to be earned by success in war. The applause of their public was the highest reward they knew.

The Cheyennes were always active, and even in severe winter weather the men were usually out and about, hunting, chasing buffalo, or even going on the war-path. Late winter or early spring was, in fact, considered a very favorable time for going to war on foot; that is, to take horses. The reason is obvious. At that season, after the long, hard winter, the ponies were thin, and little able to carry riders for great distances. The small raiding party, with its long start and many remounts, had every advantage over the pursuers, whose horses were likely to become exhausted before the enemy could be overtaken.

Parties returning from such expeditions often reached home at the time the swelling cottonwood buds were about to burst. It was the practice to use these brown, gum-covered buds to paint records of their deeds on their robes, making pictures that did not wear off for a long time. Hence the saying, "I have painted my robe seven times in the spring," came to mean, "I have gone on foot to war [so many times]." Another fashion of robe-painting will be noted later.

In old times—say up to about the year 1850—war-parties usually went on foot. Such excursions were made for the purpose of taking horses. It was not until somewhat later that trips for the purpose of attacking and killing enemies became usual. On the other hand, when some grave injury had been

7

inflicted on the tribe, the general movement to revenge this injury was made on horseback.

On the foot parties, the men who carried the war-pipe—the leaders—were usually middle-aged men. Young men very seldom led a war-party. They were satisfied to gain experience by following their elders, until they had reached a point where they thought themselves competent to carry the pipe.

When this time arrived, and a man determined that for the first time he would lead a party—carry the pipe to war—he called into his lodge some older man of great experience, and offered him the pipe and asked him for help. When the elder had accepted the pipe, the younger man explained that he wished to lead a party to war, and asked advice as to what he should do to insure success. Very often he was recommended to make an offering to the medicine arrows. The most acceptable gifts that could be offered to the arrows were the tail-feathers of eagles, but blankets, cloth, and calico were more often offered. After the young man had smoked with his adviser, he put on his buffalo-robe with the hair side out, took his gift for the arrows and a filled pipe, and left the lodge. Wailing and mourning so that everyone in the village might hear him, he walked toward the arrow lodge, carrying his pipe, and his offerings held with the pipe. He walked very slowly, and when he had reached the door of the arrow lodge, stood there and wailed. If the arrow-keeper was absent, in some other lodge in the village, he was told that a person was going to the arrow lodge, and went there to receive the visitor. The man who was carrying the pipe and the offerings entered the lodge and placed the pipe on the ground in front of the arrow-keeper, and then stepped back around the fire to the other side, for, of course, no one might pass between the arrows hanging at the head of the arrow-keeper's bed and the fire.

The young man presented the offerings to the arrow-keeper, who took them in his left hand, placed the palm of his right hand on the ground, and passed the right hand down over the offerings. This he repeated. Then he transferred the offerings to his right hand and rubbed his left hand on the ground and passed it over the offerings, and repeated this. He then handed the gifts back to the young man and directed him to tie them to the arrow bundle. While doing this the young man prayed to the arrows aloud, for the arrows hear everything that is said to them. He told the arrows that he intended to go out with a party to get scalps and horses; begged that none of his young men should be hurt or killed; that he himself might count a first coup, and that his men might return home happy, with blackened faces. The arrow-keeper then lighted the pipe, and they smoked together, and if there were others in the lodge they also smoked with them. Any man who was going with this party might make an offering such as the leader had made, or might make other sacrifices.

Men were sometimes advised to go out on the hills and remain there all day, swinging to the pole by a rope tied to skewers which pierced the skin of the breast on either side. Others might go away from the camp and lie on a bed of sage for one or four days, without drinking or eating. These sacrifices were made to bring good fortune. Similar sacrifices might be made to insure good fortune in any other matter. They were by no means peculiar to war, but were often made by partisans under certain special circumstances.

A man who had already led parties to war and contemplated another trip made less formal preparations. He called into his lodge his friends and some older men to discuss the matter. After they had eaten, a pipe was filled and the intending leader spoke, saying: "My friends, I wish to go to war. I wish to make up a party to follow me, and I have called you here to ask if any of you will join me." If he was a successful man—one who had been fortunate in leading war-parties—a number of young men always smoked, thus signifying that they wished to accompany him. Those who did not care to join let the pipe pass without smoking.

9

When a number had agreed to go, a pipe was filled but not lighted, and they went to the lodge of some priest or doctor, and after entering, the leader said to the medicine man, "We wish to go to war," and offered him the filled pipe. The man took the pipe—thereby agreeing to perform the necessary ceremonies—it was lighted and he smoked, and then sang a medicine war-song. Then he was likely to say to them, "It is well, my friends; you are to go to such and such a place, on such a stream; there you will find people—your enemies"—mentioning the tribe.

Before starting, the party sometimes went into a sweatlodge with this priest, who prayed over and consecrated some special war implement that someone was to carry. This might be a war-bonnet, a shield, or a lance, and prayers were offered asking that the one carrying this implement might be fortunate and that neither arrow nor bullet might hurt him. The good influence of these prayers extended over the entire party. During this ceremony the young men cut bits of skin from their arms and legs, and left them as sacrifices in the sweat-lodge, or, perhaps, put the bits of skin or flesh under the buffalo-skull which rested on a heap of earth just before the sweat-lodge. This sacrifice was to gain the help of the spiritual powers. It has not been practiced for many years, but was common in the middle of the last century, and no doubt was offered more or less frequently up to the end of the old wars.

Mooney[7] explains what he calls "giving the pipe" as a ceremonial manner of enlisting recruits for a large war-party. The practice was common among the Cheyennes and other Plains tribes, but Mr. Mooney's definition is not broad enough. The offering of the pipe was not confined to war matters; it was the ceremonial method of requesting *any* favor of importance. The acceptance and smoking of the offered pipe was a favorable answer to the request. Thus, if a man wished to ask some of his tribesmen to accompany him to war, he might possibly

[7] Kiowa Calendar, p. 282.

take the pipe to them. If the chiefs of one tribe wished the assistance of another tribe in war, they sent the pipe to that tribe.[8] If a young man wished to make an offering to the medicine arrows, he first offered a pipe to the arrow-keeper. If he wished an older man to paint him for the suffering of the medicine lodge, or to consent to make a shield for him, or to doctor his sick wife, or, indeed, wished any rather unusual and important favor, he went to the man to be appealed to with a filled pipe, offered it to him, and said, "Accept this pipe; I ask you to help me." Usually the old man knew pretty well what favor was desired by him who offered the pipe. The old man was free to smoke, or not, as he pleased, but it was unusual for a man to refuse, though sometimes he accepted with reluctance.

In the same way, if the tribe wished a priest or a doctor, or a man possessed of some special spiritual power, to perform certain ceremonies or to exercise his power in certain ways, someone was sent to offer him the pipe. Stories are told of cases where some man possessing miraculous power had been implored to bring food to the camps during times of starvation, and such a request was always accompanied by the offer of the pipe. In other words, this offering the pipe was the general ceremonial way of asking an important favor.

Certain matters might interfere with the starting out of a war-party. If it had been announced that anyone had made a pledge to renew the arrows, no war-party might start out until the ceremony had been completed. Sometimes, if people were in great haste to start out, the ceremony was greatly shortened and the arrows were merely wiped off. If the arrows had just been renewed, new feathers were not put on when another person promised to renew them. It often happened that while war-parties were out some member of the tribe would pledge himself to renew the arrows, not knowing that they had recently been renewed. In such a case the arrows were merely wiped off.

[8] The Fighting Cheyennes, p. 174.

If someone had pledged himself to renew the arrows, just after a war-party had set out—if it had been gone only a few days—the chiefs would send out a runner to recall the war-party. If anyone had been killed by his own people, or anyone had committed suicide, then the war-parties that were out were in great danger, for some of their number were certain to be killed, or perhaps the whole party might be destroyed by the enemy.

After the arrows had been renewed, however, war-parties were likely to start out in every direction, for the renewing of the arrows gave war-parties great power to succeed in their raids.

Before the war-party started, they supplied themselves with a little food, put their arms in order, and provided themselves with extra moccasins. Sometimes, during the night before leaving camp, they marched about the circle, stopping in front of certain lodges and singing wolf songs. Sometimes women went with them—generally relatives of the young men. From some of the lodges before which they sang, little presents were often handed out—moccasins, tobacco, arrows, small packages of powder, a few balls, or some caps.

On the appointed day, the leader, alone, or with one or two companions, left the camp on foot; and afterward, at different times through the day, others set out, all meeting before night and camping together. Each man carried his personal belongings—arms, food, clothing, robe, and a rope. It was common for men to take with them dogs to carry a portion of their load, especially their extra moccasins. The pack was lashed on the dog's back as a pack is lashed on a horse. The food carried was usually dried meat, in sheets or pounded fine. This was to be used only in case of need, for they expected to subsist on the flesh of animals which they killed on the way.

The leader of the party bore the pipe, and went in advance. The others followed in single file, no one going ahead unless so ordered. When camp was made at night, the pipe was formally filled, lighted, and offered to the sky, the earth, and the four cardinal points. The leader talked to his young men, giving them good advice, and telling them how they should act. They ate, smoked, and perhaps sang, and made a prayer. Perhaps they did not pray. At this time they seldom made a sacrifice. After all had lain down and were probably asleep, the leader sang to himself a spiritual song—a prayer for help and for wisdom. At this time also he very likely made certain vows, about which he said nothing until the time came for going into battle.

The leader might not ask for, or help himself to, food or water—they must be offered to him; he must be invited to eat or to drink. Yet, even as long ago as the earlier half of the last century there were Cheyennes who did not conform to this old custom. Old Yellow Wolf (killed at Sand Creek in 1864) did not believe in this practice, and refused to follow it. He served himself.

On the occasion in 1828 when Yellow Wolf took a great band of horses from the Comanches under Bull Hump, he told his young men that he did not wish to have the usual customs as to the leader observed with him on this trip. Neither would he carry the pipe.

"These ceremonies," he said, "oblige us to avoid too many things. If we should fail to observe some law or some custom we might be obliged to turn back. On this trip I will get my own water and cook my own food, and in these matters will be just like any of you. But I wish you to remember that I am still the head of this party."

Yellow Wolf was a great general, a great planner. He seldom, or never, went to war for scalps, but was a noted taker of horses. He was very successful in catching wild horses and in capturing horses from the Kiowas and Comanches. He seemed to know always where the Comanches would be at certain times of the year, and would set out to get horses from them. Elk

13

River, also very successful in such enterprises, discarded these ceremonies in the same way.

In old times the leaders of war-parties were not permitted to skin or cut up any animal that had been killed.

On a war journey the young men and boys did all the work. They carried the leader's load, mended his moccasins, and served him with food and water. It was always understood that the harder physical labor was to be performed by the young men. On the other hand, if a little boy had stolen off and joined the war-party, they were likely to be very tender of him and not to allow him to do any work. This practice is made clear in the stories of their first war journeys told by aged men.

In the enemy's country, or when the weather was bad, that is, rainy or snowy, or cold, a war-party usually built war-lodges. These were conical shelters formed of poles, covered with boughs, grass, or bark, which kept out the weather and hid the light of the fire that burned within. When the enemy's country had been reached—or a territory where enemies might be looked for—the leader sent young men ahead, usually in pairs, to act as scouts and to look over the country. These scouts traveled cautiously, in ravines and low places, where they might escape observation. Climbing to the tops of the highest hills they scanned the country minutely, to see if people were about, if smokes could be detected, or if the wild animals of the prairie showed signs of alarm. If buffalo were running, if antelope were seen to be watching from the top of a hill, if wolves were noticed sneaking off and looking back, the scouts waited with the utmost patience to learn the explanation of these actions.

On the other hand, if all the animals of the prairie were feeding quietly and no signs of people were observed, the scouts came down from their post of observation, and signaled the party that was watching them far behind to come on; while the scouts themselves, with the same caution they had used before, advanced to some other point of observation.

If no mischance occurred and a camp of the enemy was found, the party went as close to it as seemed safe, and waited. When the circumstances were favorable, at night, when they supposed all the enemy were sleeping, they crept down into the camp and took what horses they could. At the point where they had waited, they left all they had been carrying—their extra moccasins, robes, any food that they might have, and perhaps some of their arms, but not their ropes. To this place all were to return when they had collected what horses they could, and from it they would start on their return journey.

When approaching the camp, they usually separated and entered it in pairs. It was the work of the older men—those who had much experience on the war-path—to go about through the camp, cut loose the more valuable horses which were tied in front of the lodges, and lead them out. While this was being done, the younger men and boys gathered up the loose animals feeding on the prairie near by and drove them to the meeting place. Of the men who went into the camp to secure the war-horses and buffalo horses tied before the lodges, the most persistent, daring, or acquisitive would sometimes return several times in order to take as many as possible of these desirable horses.

The horses taken by each man belonged to him; and at the meeting place, and when they started on their flight, these captured horses were, so far as possible, kept apart until day came, when each could look over those he had taken and thus recognize the animals that were his. It is difficult for white men to understand how an Indian by simply looking over the little herd of from five to forty horses could so fix in his mind the appearance of each that he would certainly know them later. Yet this is just what the Indians did, and it was unusual for any difference of opinion to arise among members of a war-party about any horse. This keenness of observation and memory for details is to be seen in other more or less primitive

15

peoples. Mr. George L. Harrison, Jr., tells me that he has seen examples of it among the goat herders in northern Africa.

The men who first reached the meeting place might be obliged to wait some little time for the others, but usually the leader kept them there until all were assembled, when they started off at a good pace, driving the horses in separate groups. As soon as day came and each man could look over his own horses, all were thrown together in one herd, and they were driven hard, most of the men following them, but one or two riding on either side in order to direct the herd. As they had plenty of remounts, they kept the horses going at a high rate of speed, for they were eager to put as many miles as possible between themselves and the camp they had raided. Very often they drove the horses constantly for twenty-four hours or more. Toward the end of the first afternoon, the leader was likely to leave behind him two young men on fast horses to watch the back trail in order to learn whether or not enemies were pursuing.

During this fast drive, many of the horses that were old, slow, and weak, and so unable to keep up, dropped out of the herd and were abandoned.

When the people of the plundered camp discovered that their horses had been taken, a force of pursuers often set out to overtake the raiders. Sometimes they succeeded in doing this; more often they failed. Those who were driving the horses had so many fresh animals to choose from that they had a distinct advantage over those following them, each of whom had only a single horse to ride in the pursuit.

If the raiders were successful and reached their village with many horses, sometimes they gave them all away. Usually the young men gave away some of them. A young man who was courting a girl might drive all his horses up to her father's lodge, and leave them there. On the return to the camp, no religious offering was made, nor any special present to the priest, though any man might make an offering to him.

16

OLD LITTLE WOLF AND WIFE

When starting out on foot for the purpose of capturing horses, men often carried with them pieces of buffalo-robe, and when they had come near an enemy's camp and seemed to have a good prospect of taking horses, they made of these buffalo-hides saddle-pads, with stirrups, and used these on the horses they had taken instead of riding bareback. The robes were cut into pieces, which when sewed up formed long, narrow bags, in which an opening was left through which the bag might be stuffed with dried grass.

When a party started to war on horseback, each carried on his horse his moccasins, a sack of pemmican or dried meat, his arms, and his rope. In winter he had a blanket coat and a robe, and in summer a single blanket or a summer robe. Usually a man rode a common horse and led a running horse—his war-pony—which he would mount when going into battle.

When they had come near the place which the medicine man had indicated, the leader sent out one, two, or three scouts to go to this place and learn if the people were there that he had been told they would find. Usually the people were found, they tell us, just as the medicine man had indicated. After one set of scouts returned, they were relieved by others, who at once went out. Scouts who discovered enemies or signs of enemies came running back, and when they had come near to their party they began to howl like wolves. If, however, the enemy were so near that they might hear the howling and suspect something, the scouts did not howl, but stood with their sides to the party, holding their heads down, and barked like dogs. Then they hurried on to join their fellows. If the enemy were moving, the scouts, by riding in circles, signaled the party that they should come on.

Among a number of Plains tribes a scout or spy was called a wolf, and when he had discovered enemies he howled as he returned, to let his people know that the "wolves" were coming back with news. The meaning is, "We wolves are returning to tell something," and this was perfectly well understood by everyone who heard it.

When the scouts were seen returning, their party built up a little mound, perhaps of earth or of buffalo-chips, and the members of the party sat down a little behind it in a half-circle. The scouts came on, ran four or five times about the mound, and then sat down near it, in front of and facing the war-party. The pipe was filled and offered to them, with a caution that the report they were to make must be true. They smoked, and reported, the formal smoking being a pledge that what they were about to tell was the truth. After the scouts had reported, all the party sat in a circle and sang a song which had been specially taught them by the priest before they left the camp. But if the enemy were close at hand, the ceremony accompanying the report was omitted.

A common piece of simple strategy practiced by the Cheyennes, as by other Plains Indians, was to send forward a small party on swift horses to charge a camp or a party, in the hope that those attacked would set out in pursuit of the few enemies seen, who, retreating, might lead them into an ambuscade. Sometimes this plan was successful, and one or two important defeats of white troops—notably that at Fort Phil Kearny in 1866—have resulted from it. Often, however, the people hidden in ambush could not restrain their eagerness, but rushed out and showed themselves too soon, so that the stratagem failed.

If a party returning from war had been successful, had taken horses, killed an enemy, or counted a coup, and had lost no men, they stopped at a little distance from the village to prepare for their entry.

It was at this place that they often painted their robes—"painting the war robes," they call it. The edges of the buffalo-robes were trimmed off evenly, strips of wolf-hide about two inches wide were prepared, and some man who had before had his robe thus ornamented was called on to sew a border of wolf-skin all about the robes. Someone went out and killed a buffalo, and taking off a large piece of its hide, tied up the end of one of the large intestines, filled this with fresh blood, and carried hide and intestine to the camp. A number of forked sticks were thrust in the ground in a circle about three feet in diameter, and by holes cut in its border the piece of green hide was hung over the prongs of the sticks, flesh side up, to make a sort of kettle or vessel, into which they poured the blood. Rye grass was now collected and tied in bunches, which were lighted and burned, and the ashes allowed to fall into the blood. This was stirred continually, and the ashes mixed with it by the hands. When a sufficient quantity of ashes had fallen in the blood, it became dark in color, and they tested it, and if when it dried it was quite dark, it was ready for use—a black paint. The robes to be painted were now spread on the ground; a short stick was used as a ruler, and either with the fingers dipped in the blood, or with a sharpened, flattened stick, straight lines were drawn on the robes' flesh surface from one side of the robe to the other, and between these parallel lines were painted the tracks of wolf, or fox, or rabbit, or bear. Since the Cheyennes wore the robe with the head on the left side of the body, the tail on the right, the lines drawn across the skin ran vertically when the robe was worn. The robes were not all painted alike; there were various designs.

This paint did not come off; it clung to the dressed skin like glue. Anyone might have his robe painted, if he could persuade someone to do it for him. In the spring the buds of the cottonwood, instead of the ashes, were sometimes used to mix with the blood to make it black. They call these buds, and the tree as well, *mohk wi hio mohk tut tuts*,[9] which means "robe painters." The instructor did the work of painting, and the young men looked on and listened to the old man's instructions.

When the successful war-party that had killed an enemy drew near to the home camp, and after they had painted their robes—though often they did not paint them—two scouts were

[9] Petter, English-Cheyenne Dictionary, pp. 193, 924, and 1067.

19

sent out to learn exactly where the main camp was. The leader told these scouts just where the war-party would camp, so that on their return the young men might readily find it. When the scouts returned—usually in half a day, or at longest in a day—and reported the situation of the camp, all the young men uttered the war-cry. Now they took willow branches and burned them, and painted their faces with the powdered charcoal, each according to his own fancy. Some used vertical stripes, but most men blackened the whole face. Meantime some members of the party made drums.

When all was ready, they set out for the camp. If they approached it at night, they waited until daylight before giving any sign of their presence. No one in the camp knew that the war-party was coming in; they took it by surprise. They tried to get close to the camp—near enough so that they could hear the dogs barking. Here they dressed themselves in the attire which they had worn in the fight.

At daylight the leader, who carried the pipe, mounted his horse and first set out, closely followed by the young men who carried the scalps on the poles. The others had loaded their guns, and stayed a little behind. The leaders went forward slowly until close to the camp, and then rode fast, shooting off their guns to awaken the sleeping people. Those who had been left behind on the hill, as soon as they heard the guns, formed in line and began to beat their drums and yell. If the people were camped in a circle, the leaders rode into it and around it. If they were camped along the stream, they rode along the border of the camp.

Sometimes advance notice of the return was given. After the party had stopped at a short distance from the village, the men dressed themselves in the attire they had worn in the fight. A party of men—from eight to fifteen, if the war-party was a large one—was sent forward to announce the return, so that all might know what had happened. These messengers approached the village as closely as possible without being seen, and then charged through the camp, shooting off their guns and waving the poles on which were the scalps that had been taken. The people were excited, and welcomed them with shouts and yells. All was joy. The women sang songs of victory, and prepared to welcome the main party, which came on not far behind, riding side by side in two lines. In the front rank were those who had shown the greatest courage, who had counted coups, or had performed any specially creditable acts. A man who had performed a deed of noteworthy bravery might be sent to ride ahead of the first line, which might number two, or three, or even ten or fifteen warriors. In the second line were the others of the party.

The whole camp came out a short way from the village and welcomed them. As they rode into the camp, the women and the people standing about to watch them called out: "Here they come! We have heard that they were coming and now they are here!" Some threw their arms about the successful warriors. Old men and old women sang songs in which their names were mentioned. The relatives of those who rode in the front rank—their fathers, and mothers, and aunts—testified to their joy by making gifts to friends or to poor people. The whole crowd might go to where some brave man lived, or to where his father lived, and there dance in his honor. The members of the party went directly to their own lodges, and turned out their horses. Their women blackened their faces, and sometimes the little children, and even near relatives, did the same. Then they were likely to prepare to dance all night, and perhaps to keep up this dancing for two days and two nights.

When a war-party which had lost men came within sight of the village on its return, they signaled by waving robes or blankets the number of their men that had been killed. In later times they conveyed this information by signaling with mirrors. If a member of a victorious war-party was killed, his companions sometimes left him on the ground on the battlefield, or perhaps carried him off to a distance and left him unburied.

Sometimes a young man asked that this might be done, but even if nothing was said about it, he was likely to be placed on his robe on the prairie and left there. Sometimes the dead warrior was wrapped in his robe and put on a platform in a tree, this being regarded as the same thing as leaving him on the prairie, since his body would soon fall down and his frame be torn to pieces by animals. The Cheyenne warrior wished to be killed, if at all, on the broad level prairie, where everyone could see him. When he died he did not wish to be covered by earth, but preferred to lie out on the prairie where the birds and the animals might devour his body, and his remains might be scattered far and wide.

There were a great number of customs and definite ceremonies connected with the war-path. When starting out, all the members of the party abstained from food and drink during daylight of the first day, but after the sun had gone down, food was cooked, meat roasted, and set before the leaders, and all ate. The leaders of a war-party might not eat any part of a buffalo's head, not even the tongue; nor any part of the hump, nor the sirloin—the best parts—nor any portion of the back. This tabu is believed to bear some relation to the sacred hat, called issiwun. If the leaders ate any of these parts of the buffalo before anything was accomplished on the war-path, they would have no luck. After they had killed an enemy, however, they might eat the hitherto forbidden parts.

On the war-path they sometimes boiled meat in a hide kettle, supported on forked sticks, usually eight. The meat was put in cold water, and a man armed with two forked sticks took from the fire the hot stones and put them in the water. As they grew cold he removed the stones, while others kept up a supply of hot stones. When the water was boiling, the forked sticks trembled. The bottom of the kettle did not rest on the ground, but was unsupported. The buffalo's paunch was also used for boiling meat on the war-path.

During the first meal, just after the party had started out, if no dipper carrier was with the party—and often there was none—a young man went down to the stream and brought water in a skin, a bowl, or other vessel, and offered it to the leaders, beginning at the right of the line, until all had drunk.

To procure water easily, a dipper called *histāh'hēvĭk'ŭts* ("heart bladder," *i.e.*, pericardium) was used. This consisted of a straight pole, six feet long, forked at one end, nicely trimmed and seasoned. A bull's pericardium was softened, and was kept open by a hoop, which was tied with four strings close against the forks of the stick; the butt of the pole was sharpened, and when the implement was not in use was thrust in the ground. A young man without leggings or blanket would take this, run to the stream, dip up a bladder full of water, and run back to the war-lodge and offer water to the leaders. After they had drunk, others of the party might drink, the water-carrier making perhaps several trips to the stream, until all were satisfied. He might go to several war-lodges with water, if there were so many in the party. A dipper might not be made or carried by everyone. He who had it must have been instructed in its making and use by someone who himself had been taught to make one. To carry one of these dippers was likely to bring a young man good fortune in war. The man who carried it was called *sīhĭvĭk'otŭmsh*, "owner of the pericardium." When the party had returned from the war-path to the camp, if they had killed any enemies, the owner of the dipper, at the dance which they held in celebration of the event, would sometimes go to the river, fill his dipper, and, returning, would pass it around to the members of the war-party.

He who carried the dipper must be the first one to get up in the morning, to go and get water for his fellows. If, while traveling, they crossed a stream, he was likely to reach down with his dipper, get water, and ride up to offer it to the leaders.

There were several kinds of vikuts. One of these had crow-feathers tied to the ends of the prongs, which in this case formed the handle. In this type the cup was tied, not to the prongs of the stick, but to the butt end. From the fork, lying in a groove (called "wolf road") cut for it, a bowstring ran down into the cup, and was tied to it at the bottom. Four strings hung down from the thick butt of the staff and supported a hoop to which the pericardium was fastened. On the staff, about halfway down its length, was carved the figure of a wolf. Near the cup was carved a round sun, and still nearer the cup a crescent moon.

The purpose of the bowstring was to carry out a practical joke. If in the war-party there was a young man whose sweetheart was reported to have run away from him in the village, the man who was offering the water might, when this young man was drinking, pull on the bowstring. The effect of this was to throw the bottom of the cup up, and to dash the water into the drinker's face.

In another kind of vikuts, sinew strings ran from the bowstring along the prongs to their extremities, and to each prong a buffalo-tail was tied. A fourth sort had a straight staff without forks at the end, while still another had four prongs, and eagle-feathers and strips of otter-skin and wolf-skin hung down from these prongs.

When a young man wished to have one of these things made for him, he filled a pipe, and sought a man who knew how to make the kind of vikuts he wished. When found, he offered him the pipe, saying, "Friend, take pity on me; I wish to have one of the vikuts made." Sometimes men were obliged to beg hard, and to throw their arms about the man, trying to persuade him to help them. The implement was made while on the war journey. The young men in the war-lodge were likely to contribute property to enable this young man to pay for the making of the vikuts. The young man had prepared beforehand all the parts of the dipper, and when the instructor consented to make it, the pieces were speedily put together.

When the maker consented to manufacture the dipper, the young men gathered wood and made a fire outside the lodge.

While this was being done, the instructor painted himself and the young man red, on the hands from the wrists down, and on the feet below the ankles. A narrow strip of wolf-skin was tied about the wrists and ankles. The faces were painted red, on cheeks, mouth, and chin. A narrow strip of wolf-skin was tied about the neck. Sometimes the hair above the forehead was tied in a bunch with wolf-skin. The instructor and pupil now went out of the lodge, and danced about the fire, moving the hands as a wolf moves his fore paws. The older men sang for them as they danced. Both men were entirely naked. They danced four times, receding toward the end of each song, and returning when the next one began. At the end of the fourth song, the instructor howled like a wolf, and made a sign under his arm that they were going to kill an enemy close by. The young man imitated this sign.

When the dipper had been made and handed to the young man, the older man said to him, "Give water first to those men." He carried water to the man who had counted the most coups. The man to whom it was offered took the staff, held it out, counted his most important coup, and then gave it back to the young man, who took it to three other men, one after another, each of whom did the same. Then he carried water all about, giving drink to all. If on any morning he should happen to oversleep, another young man might take the dipper to the stream and use it.

If, on this war-path they did not kill anyone, they left the dipper behind them; but if they killed, they blackened the staff, took it home and used it, as stated, and after the dancing was over, hung it up in some tree, and left it.

In large war-parties different groups of men cooked on different fires. A man belonging to one fire might pass by another fire and see cooking there a piece of meat which attracted him. He might take this piece of meat from the fire and carry it to his own. Then the men who belonged to the fire from which the meat had been taken might choose their best wrestler and go over to the other fire and challenge the best wrestler who belonged to it. The winner in the contest would take the meat which was in dispute. This was not done seriously, but as a joke, the meat being taken for the purpose of bringing about the contest.

VARIOUS BELIEFS

Dreams and other portents had much influence on people who were going on the war-path, and an unfavorable dream might cause one man or a whole party to abandon the journey and return to the village. In old times—especially in the earlier half of the nineteenth century—a method of divination was practiced in which the badger—an animal that possesses mysterious power—was employed. When men went afoot on the war-path, a badger was sometimes killed, the belly ripped open, all the entrails removed, but all the blood saved, and the animal left lying on its back on a bed of white sage on the ground with head toward the east till next morning, the blood remaining in the visceral cavity.

Next morning, the men who wished to do so unbraided the hair and, naked, walked by the badger, one after another, and each looked down at his reflection in the smooth surface of the blood. If in this mirror a man saw himself aged, wrinkled, and with white hair, he knew that he should live to be old; if he were soon to die the reflection would have its eyes closed. If the looker was to die of disease, he saw himself much emaciated. If he was to be killed and scalped, the reflection appeared without scalp, and with bleeding head. It was like a looking-glass. No man told another what he had seen. Usually the men who saw themselves scalped seemed downcast, turned back from their war-path and returned to the village. The others went on. Not every member of the war-party looked into the blood; it was not obligatory.

Hawk Nose, who on such an occasion saw himself as an old man and who was eighty years of age when he died, in the year

26

1862 gave George Bent this advice: "If ever you go out with a war-party and they kill a badger, do not go near it; if you see yourself with your eyes shut or scalped, you will always feel badly."

Old Whirlwind, a famous warrior, told what he saw on an occasion when he looked into the badger's blood. He recognized his own face, but it was changed, wrinkled and withered, and his hair was gray. Thus he knew that he would not be killed in war, but would live to old age.

In later times the Cheyennes became afraid to practice this mode of divination, and abandoned it.

The associations of the war-path seem to have fostered intimacies and to have made this a propitious time for young men to ask favors of one another. Of these favors, some had to do with love and marriage.

In old times, when they went on the war-path, if a man wanted a girl for his wife, he might cut from a tree a slab of wood, draw on it the figure of a girl, and also whatever he wished to give for the girl, such as horses, bridles, a war-bonnet, and other articles. Having completed the picture, he sent it by another young man to the war-lodge in which the girl's brother or cousin slept. The messenger handed it to the brother, and after he had looked at it, he was likely to send for any of his brothers who might be with the party. To them he showed the slab of wood, and told them who had sent the offer for this sister. If all agreed to the marriage, another picture of the girl was drawn on the slab, with figures of whatever they were willing to offer in return for his presents, and the piece of wood was returned to the suitor. After the party had returned to the main village, he sent to the girl's lodge the things represented in his drawings, and the young people of the other war-lodge sent what they had drawn, with the girl, to his lodge.

If a member of a war-party saw a horse that he desired, he might perhaps send to ask the owner for it, in the same way— by a drawing. If the owner of the horse did not accede to the request, the occupants of the war-lodge from which the message came might express their dissatisfaction by tearing down the war-lodge in which the owner of the horse slept.

In old times, when young men were on the war-path they sometimes made what they called a mysterious (or "medicine") sausage. When they were about to set out on the war-path some young man who was in love with a girl in the camp pledged himself to cook this food. A four year old bull was killed, and the tenderloin brought into the camp. The young man who was to cook the food was painted over his whole body with white clay, and a ring of red was painted about wrists and ankles. His face was painted white, with a horizontal black bar over each eye. At the side of each wrist and ankle was tied a bundle of white sage, and on his head was put a wreath of sage. White sage was spread on the ground, and the large intestine of the buffalo, reversed and washed, was stuffed with the finely cut-up tenderloin, and when full, the end was tied up with a sinew. The man had hot coals to roast the food over, and while roasting it he was obliged to stand; he might not sit down. When cooked, the food was put back on the white sage; then, when cool, the young man called his fellows to eat. A young unmarried man might step up to the bed of sage and, saying, "I wish to marry a certain girl in the camp," take one bite. Another might do the same, until all had announced their wishes. The maker of the sausage was the last one to speak, and after he had said what it was that he desired, he ate the food that was left.

People say that men eating this food usually got the woman they longed for. The custom has long been obsolete.

No one can now tell why they painted their faces black when they had killed an enemy. It is said that in old times people who had killed enemies painted the whole body black. They even painted the flesh side of the robe black.

Mr. Petter says black signifies peace, or cessation of hostilities.

A long time ago someone had prophesied to the Cheyennes that in the future they would fight and kill people, and when they did so they would take the hair of the enemy and put it on a stick and look at it, and it would make them glad. When they saw how the Assiniboines had cut off the hair of the people they had killed, they supposed they must have done it for this purpose, and when they began to fight they also commenced to scalp the killed. For a long time after that, however, they did not scalp all the dead.

A man who had been scalped, and still lived, lost nothing of honor or prestige. He was not—as with the Pawnees—regarded as dead; he came back and was looked on as just as good a man as ever.

So much that is erroneous, and much more that is misleading, has been printed relative to certain war acts that some years ago it seemed desirable to try to explain something about the way in which the coup and scalp were regarded among the Plains Indians. The essential parts of some paragraphs from this article[10] are here included.

ACTS OF BRAVERY; SCALP AND COUP

The quality most highly esteemed among the Indians of the plains was courage, and the warrior who displayed the greatest courage was he who brought back most glory from the warpath. It has been said that in former times the most notable achievement of an Indian was the taking of a scalp; and again, that to kill an enemy, to scalp an enemy, or to be the first to strike an enemy alive or dead, were three brave deeds, which impliedly were equally creditable. My experience does not confirm this implication.

Among the Plains tribes, to kill an enemy was good in so far as it reduced the numbers of the hostile party, but otherwise the act was regarded as relatively unimportant. Likewise to scalp an enemy was not a notable feat and in no sense espe-

[10] *American Anthropologist*, vol. XII, no. 2, p. 296, 1910.

cially creditable. If scalped, the skin of the head was taken merely as a trophy, something to show, something to dance over—a good thing, but of no great importance; but to touch the enemy with something held in the hand, with the bare hand, or with any part of the body, was a proof of bravery—a feat which entitled the man or the boy who did it to the greatest credit.

When an enemy was killed, each of those nearest to him tried to be the first to reach him and touch him, usually by striking the body with something held in the hand—a gun, bow, whip, or stick. Those who followed raced up and struck the body— as many as might desire to do so. Anyone who wished might scalp the dead. In many instances no one could be certain who killed a particular enemy, while some boy might be told to take off a scalp. The chief applause was won by the man who could first touch the fallen enemy. In Indian estimation the bravest act that could be performed was to count coup on—to touch or strike—a living, unhurt man and to leave him alive, and this was frequently done. Cases are often told of where, when the lines of two opposing tribes faced each other in battle, some brave man rode out in front of his people, charged upon the enemy, ran through their line, struck one of them, and then, turning and riding back, joined his own party. If, however, the man was knocked from his horse, or his horse was killed, all of his party made a headlong charge to rescue and bring him off.

When hunting, it was not unusual for boys or young men, if they killed an animal, especially if it was a dangerous one, to rush up and count coup on it. Where young men chasing a black bear on the prairie killed it with their arrows, they raced up to it on foot to see who should count the first coup.

It was regarded as an evidence of bravery for a man to go into battle carrying no weapon that would do harm at a distance. It was more creditable to carry a lance than a bow and arrows; more creditable to carry a hatchet or a war-club than a lance; and the bravest thing of all was to go into a fight with nothing more than a whip, or a long twig—sometimes called a coup-stick.

It was not unusual for a man, if he had been long sick and was without hope of recovery, or if some great misfortune had happened to him and he no longer wished to live, to declare his purpose to give his body to the enemy. In practice this meant committing suicide by attacking enemies without suitable means of offense or defense, doing some very brave thing, and being killed in the act. This was a most honorable way of dying, far more so than to kill one's self by shooting, by the knife, or by the rope, though there was no disgrace in self-destruction. Suicide by hanging, however, was usually confined to girls who had been crossed in love.

There is still living in Montana a man who, when seventeen or eighteen years of age, after a long illness from which there seemed to be no hope of recovery, declared to his father that he wished to give his body to the enemy. The father assented, fitted out the son with his strongest "medicine," and sent the boy off with a party to the south, armed only with a little hatchet. After the party had reached the country of the enemy, two of these, who were Utes, were discovered returning from the hunt. Both had guns. The Cheyennes charged on them, and the boy, Sun's Road, having been provided with his father's best war-horse, led. He overtook one of the enemy, who turned and tried to shoot at him, but the gun snapped. Sun's Road knocked the man off his horse with his little hatchet, and riding on overtook the other man, who turned and shot at him; but Sun's Road dropped down on his horse, avoided the bullet, and knocked the Ute off his horse. Both enemies were killed by the Cheyennes who were following Sun's Road. The young man had now fulfilled his vow. He received from the members of the war-party, and from the tribe when he returned to the village, the greatest praise. He recovered his health.

The Cheyennes counted coup on an enemy three times; that is to say, three men might touch the body and receive credit,

31

according to the order in which this was done. Subsequent coups received no credit. The Arapahoes touched four times. In battle the members of a tribe touched the enemy without reference to what had been done by those of another allied tribe in the same fight. Thus in a fight where Cheyennes and Arapahoes were engaged, the same man might be touched seven times. In a fight on the Rio Grande del Norte, where Cheyennes, Arapahoes, Comanches, Kiowas, and Apaches defeated the Utes, the counting of the coups by the different tribes resulted in great confusion.

When a Cheyenne touched an enemy, the man who touched him cried *"Ah haih'!"* and said, "I am the first." The second to touch the body cried, "I am the second," and so the third.

It is evident that in the confusion of a large fight, such as often took place, many mistakes might occur, and certain men might believe themselves entitled to honors which others thought were theirs. After the fight was over, the victorious party got together in a circle and built a fire of buffalo-chips. On the ground near the fire were placed a pipe and a gun. The different men interested approached this fire, and, first touching the pipe, called out their deeds, saying, "I am the first," "second," or "third," as the case might be. Some man might dispute another and say, "No, I struck him first," and so the point would be argued and the difference settled at the time.

Often these disputes were hot. I recall one among the Pawnees about which there was great feeling. A Sioux had been killed, and Baptiste Bahele, half-breed Skidi and sub-chief, and a young man of no special importance were racing for the fallen enemy to secure the honor of first touching him. Baptiste had the faster horse and reached the body first, but, just as he was leaning over to touch it, the animal shied and turned off, so that what he held in his hand did not actually touch the body, while the boy who was following him rode straight over the fallen man and struck him. Baptiste argued plausibly enough that he had reached the body first and was entitled to be credited with

32

TANGLE HAIR AND GRANDCHILD

the coup, but acknowledged that he did not actually touch the body, though he would have done so had his horse not shied. There was no difference of opinion among the Indians, who unanimously gave the honor to the boy.

Once two young Cheyennes were racing to touch a fallen enemy. Their horses were running side by side, though one was slightly ahead of the other. The man in advance was armed with a saber, the other, almost even with him, was leaning forward to touch the enemy with his lance. A saber being shorter than a lance, the leading man was likely to get only the second coup, but he reached down, grasped his comrade's lance, and gave it a little push, and it touched the enemy as they passed over him. Although the owner of the lance still held it, yet because his hand was behind his fellow's on its shaft, he received credit only for the second coup. If a man struck an enemy with a lance, anyone who touched or struck the lance while it was still fixed in or touching the enemy's person, received credit for the next coup.

A man who believed he had accomplished something made a strong fight for his rights, and was certain to be supported in his contention by all his friends, and especially by all his relatives. When disputes took place, there were formal ways of getting at the truth. Among the Cheyennes a strong affirmation, or oath, was to rub the hand over the pipe as the statement was made, or to point to the medicine arrows and say, "Arrows, you hear me; I did (or did not do) this thing." The Blackfeet usually passed the hand over the pipestem, thus asseverating that the story was as straight as the hole through the stem.

With the Cheyennes, if there was a dispute as to who had touched an enemy, counting the first coup, a still more formal oath might be exacted. A buffalo-skull, painted with a black streak running from between the horns to the nose, red about the eye sockets, on the right cheek a black, round spot, the sun, and on the left cheek a red half-moon, had its eye sockets and its nose stuffed full of green grass. This represented the medicine lodge. Against this were rested a gun and four arrows, representing the medicine arrows. The men to be sworn were to place their hands on these and make their statements. Small sticks, about a foot long, to the number of the enemies that had been killed in the fight which they were to discuss, were prepared and placed on the ground alongside the arrows and the gun.

In a mixed fight where many people were engaged there were always disputes, and this oath was often—even usually—exacted. A large crowd of people, both men and women, assembled to witness the ceremony. The chiefs directed the crier to call up the men who claimed honors, in the order in which they declared that they had struck an enemy; first, the man who claimed the first coup, then he who claimed the second coup, and so on. The man making the oath walked up to the sacred objects and stood over them, and stretching up his hands to the sky said, *Mā ĭ yūn ăsts′ nī āh′ tū*, "Spiritual powers, listen to me." Then, bending down, he placed his hands on the objects, and said, *Nā nĭt′ shū*, "I touched him." After he had made his oath, he added, "If I tell a lie, I hope that I may be shot far off."

He narrated in detail how he charged on the enemy and how he struck him. Then were called the men who counted the second and the third coup on the same enemy, and each told his story at length. Next the man who touched the second enemy was called, and he was followed by those who had counted the second and the third coup on the same individual. In the same way all claimants told their stories.

If, under such circumstances, a man made a false statement, it was considered certain that before long he or some one of his family would die. The Cheyennes feared this oath, and, if a man was doubtful whether he had done what he claimed, he was very likely not to appear when his name was called. On the other hand, each of two men might honestly enough declare—owing to error—that he first touched an enemy. Or, a man might swear falsely. In the year 1862, a man disputing with another declared that he had first touched the enemy. The next year, while the Cheyennes were making the medicine lodge on the Republican River, this man died, and everyone believed, and said, that he had lied about the coup of the year before.

When two men were striving to touch an enemy and others were watching them, and the contest was close, the spectators might say to one of the two, "We did not see plainly what you did, but of what he did we are certain." In this way they might bar from the first honor the man concerning whose achievement they were doubtful.

If enemies were running away and being pursued, and one fell behind or was separated from his party, and was touched three times, if he escaped serious injury and later succeeded in joining his own people, the coup might again be counted on him up to the usual three times.

As an example of the odd things that have happened in connection with the practice of touching the enemy, according to Cheyenne rules, the curious case of Yellow Shirt may be mentioned. In the great battle that took place on Wolf Creek in 1838, between the allied Kiowas, Comanches, and Apaches, on one hand, and the Cheyennes and Arapahoes on the other, coup was counted on Yellow Shirt,[11] a Kiowa, nine times. When the charge was made on the Kiowa camp, Yellow Shirt was fighting on foot and was touched three times, but not seriously injured. Later, he reached his village, mounted a horse, came out to fight, and was touched three times on horseback. Almost immediately afterward his horse was killed and his leg broken, and he sat on the ground, still fighting by shooting arrows, and was again touched three times and killed. So in all nine coups were counted on this man, all of which were allowed. In another case coup was counted nine times on a Pawnee, who was not killed and finally got away.

[11] So called by the Cheyennes from the color of his war shirt. His Kiowa name means Sleeping Bear.

If, through oversight, the third coup had not been formally counted on an enemy, the act of taking off his moccasins as plunder has been decided to be the third coup, because the man who removed them touched the dead man's person. Coup, of course, might be counted on man, woman, or child. Anyone who was captured would first be touched.

Among the Cheyennes the capture of a horse or horses was a brave deed, and if the man who had touched an enemy took from him a shield or a gun, the capture of this implement was always mentioned. The drum would be sounded for touching the enemy, sounded again for the capture of the shield, again for the capture of the gun, and—if the man had scalped the dead—for the taking of the scalp.

I believe that the high esteem in which the act of touching the enemy is held is a survival of the old feeling that prevailed before the Indians had missiles and when, if they fought, they were obliged to do so hand-to-hand with clubs and sharpened sticks. Under such conditions only those who actually came to grips, so to speak, with the enemy could inflict injury and gain glory. After arrows came into use it may still have been thought a braver and finer thing to meet the enemy hand-to-hand than to kill him with an arrow at a distance.

The general opinion that the act of scalping reflects credit on the warrior has no foundation. The belief perhaps arose from the fact that, when an enemy was killed or wounded, brave Indians rushed toward him. White observers have very likely inferred that those who were rushing upon an enemy were eager to take his scalp. As a matter of fact they cared little or nothing for the scalp, but very much for the credit of touching the fallen man. Most people are untrustworthy observers, drawing inferences from their preconceived notions rather than from what actually takes place.

As already said, among the Plains tribes a scalp was not highly valued. It was regarded as an emblem of victory and was a good thing to carry back to the village to rejoice and dance over; but any part of an enemy's body might serve for this. Scalps were used to trim and fringe war clothing (shirts and leggings) and to tie to the horse's bridle in going to war. Usually the scalps taken were only a little larger than a silver dollar, but like any other piece of fresh skin they stretched greatly. Occasionally the whole skin of the head was taken.

When, on the war-path, a scalp had been taken by a young Cheyenne who had never before scalped an enemy, it was necessary that he be taught how to treat the scalp, how to prepare it for transportation to the village. Instruction in this ceremony was given by some older man familiar with such things, who in times past had himself been taught by a man older than he how the scalp should be handled. Before any work was done, the pipe was filled, lighted, and held toward the sky and to the ground; then the stem was held toward the scalp and a prayer asking for further good fortune was made. The instructor lighted the pipe and offered the prayer.

Previous to this a large buffalo-chip had been procured; this was placed on the ground before the instructor, and between him and the fire. The instructor took in his mouth a piece of bitterroot and some leaves of the white sage, and masticated them a little. The learner stood before the instructor and held his hands out before him, palms up and edges together; then the instructor spat ceremonially on the palm of each hand, and the young man made the ceremonial motions.

The scalp was now placed on the buffalo-chip, flesh side up. The instructor sat close by the young man and directed each of the various operations. The learner took from the fire a bit of charcoal and rubbed it over both sides of a knife, from hilt to point; he held the knife over the scalp and said, "May we again conquer these enemies; and, if we do so, I will cut this again in the same way." With the point of the knife he now made a cross-cut over the scalp from north to south, and another from east to west, always beginning at the edge of the skin away from himself, or toward the fire, and drawing the

37

knife toward him. The point of the knife passed through the flesh still remaining on the skin and down to the skin, dividing this flesh or fascia into four sections. The learner now took the scalp in his hands, and, beginning at the outer side of the circle, shaved off the flesh from the quadrant toward the east and placed it on the buffalo-chip. Next he shaved off from the skin the quadrant toward the south, and the flesh so taken was put in its place on the buffalo-chip. The quadrants toward the west and the north were then taken off in order and placed on the chip. Thus, the four sections of flesh trimmed from the scalp lay on the buffalo-chip in their proper relations.

Now some young man was called and was told to carry the buffalo-chip away, and leave it on the prairie. Before he started, the learner told him that he must ask the maiyun (the mysterious ones, the spirits) to take pity on him, that he might be aided to count a coup.

The young man now bent a willow twig, already provided, into a hoop, lashing the ends together with a sinew. Then with sinew and awl the margin of the scalp was sewed to the hoop to stretch it. If the hoop was too large and the scalp did not reach it, the scalp was made larger by cutting short holes about the margin and parallel to it. The sewing was done from east to south, to west, to north, and to east. A slender willow pole six feet long, trimmed and peeled, and sharpened at the butt, with a notch cut in the other end, had already been prepared. By a string tied to the hoop the scalp was fastened to this pole, the sharpened butt of which was then thrust into the ground. If convenient, all this was done on the day the scalp was taken, at all events as soon as possible. When traveling, the willow pole to which the scalp was attached was carried on the left arm. The scalp was taken back to camp on this pole and remained attached to it during all the dancing that took place.

Among the Cheyennes the scalp dances of modern times have not been at all the same as those of earlier days. The last of those, I am told, took place in 1852.

SCALP DANCE

Anyone familiar with Indians and Indian ways will understand that the various dances that they practice are not merely haphazard jumpings up and down and posturings, to the music of chance singing. The ceremony of the various dances is perfectly well defined, and the songs are well known and as unvarying as if they had been printed. There was an established ceremony about the practice of the old-time scalp dance. While in a sense a triumph dance, it was also very largely social in character. The account which I give of it came to me from George Bent.

These old-time scalp dances were directed by a little group of men called *Hēē măn ĕh'*, "halfmen-halfwomen," who usually dressed as old men. All belonged to the same family or group to which Oak (Oumsh) belonged. This family was called *Ŏttŏ- ha nĭh'*, "Bare legs." Of these halfmen-halfwomen there were at that time five. They were men, but had taken up the ways of women; even their voices sounded between the voice of a man and that of a woman. They were very popular and especial favorites of young people, whether married or not, for they were noted matchmakers. They were fine love talkers. If a man wanted to get a girl to run away with him and could get one of these people to help him, he seldom failed. When a young man wanted to send gifts for a young woman, one of these halfmen-halfwomen was sent to the girl's relatives to do the talking in making the marriage.

The five men above referred to were named Wolf Walking Alone, Buffalo Wallow, Hiding Shield Under His Robe, Big Mule, and Bridge. All these men died a long time ago; but in more recent times there were two such men, one living among the Northern Cheyennes and the other among the Southern. These men had both men's names and women's names. The one among the Northern Cheyennes was named Pipe and his woman's name was Pipe Woman. He died in 1868. The one

39

who lived with the Southern Cheyennes was named Good Road and Good Road Woman. He died in 1879. These were the last two of these people in the Cheyenne tribe.

When a war-party was preparing to start out, one of these persons was often asked to accompany it, and, in fact, in old times large war-parties rarely started without one or two of them. They were good company and fine talkers. When they went with war-parties they were well treated. They watched all that was being done, and in the fighting cared for the wounded, in which they were skillful, for they were doctors or medicine men.

After a battle the best scalps were given to them, and when they came in sight of the village on their return they carried these scalps on the ends of poles. When they neared the village the men who carried the pipes—the leaders of the war-party— and the halfmen-halfwomen carrying the scalps went ahead of the party and ran along outside the village, waving the scalps tied to the poles. This took place usually in the early morning, so that the village should be taken by surprise. The old men, the women, and the children rushed out to meet the war-party. If the members of a war-party had their faces blackened when they came in, this showed that the party had not lost any of its members. If one of the party had been killed, the scalps were thrown away and there were no scalp dances on the return. If a person had counted a coup and had been killed, the scalp dance went on just as if no one had been killed. It was a great honor for a person to count coup first, and then afterward to be killed in the same fight. His relations did not mourn for him, but, instead, joined in the scalp dance performed that night.

The great scalp dance took place in the evening in the center of the village. The halfmen-halfwomen went to each lodge and told the owner to send some firewood to the center of the village for the big dance that was to take place that night. As the people brought the wood, the halfmen-halfwomen built it up in a conical pile, in the shape of a lodge, by standing the sticks on end. All about and under it was put dried grass ready for the fire at any time. This pile of wood was called "skunk" (*hkā́ ō*). The "skunk" was lighted when a majority of the good singers with their drums reached the place. The singers were chiefly middle-aged men, all married. Then the singers and drummers began their songs, and everybody came to the dance, all of them painted red and black. All the older persons had their faces and bodies painted black. The men wore no shirts, and the old women had their bodies blackened from the waist up. In the center of the village the drummers stood in a row, facing the opening in the circle. The young men stood in a row facing the north; the young women stood in a row facing the young men, and so looking south. The old women and the old men took their places down at the lower end of the young people, and faced west. The halfmen-halfwomen took their places in the middle of this square and were the managers of the dance. No one was allowed in the middle of the square except these persons.

The performance now commenced. The women began to dance in line toward the center, and the young men all walked around behind the drummers to the girls' side of the square, placed themselves behind their sweethearts, and each put one arm through an arm of one of the girls and danced with her in that way. This was called "the sweethearts' dance."

After dancing for a time they returned to their places and stood in rows as before. The halfmen-halfwomen danced in front of the drummers, holding the poles to which scalps were tied and waving the scalps while dancing. At the other end old women danced, also carrying scalps tied on poles. The old men whose sons had counted coup also danced at the lower end. These old men and old women often acted as clowns, trying to make the people laugh. Some of them were dressed like the enemies that had been killed.

The next dance was called "the match-making dance," and the songs sung were different from those sung in the one before.

41

If in this dance there were two of these halfmen-halfwomen, one went over to the line of young men and one to the line of young women and asked the different dancers whom they would like for partners. Then the two halfmen-halfwomen came together in the center and told one another whom to select. All this time the singers and drummers were making their music. The halfmen-halfwomen then walked to the young men and took them by the robes and led them across to where their sweethearts were standing, and made the men stand by the girls. In this dance no one might begin to dance until every woman had her partner. Two men might not stand together. Men always stood between women.

After all the women had their partners, all those in this row danced toward the center and then danced back, not turning at all. Several times they danced back and forward; then the halfmen-halfwomen said to the young men, "Go back to your places."

If the night was dark the big fire was kept up by the boys, but if the moon was full less firelight was needed.

After a time the halfmen-halfwomen called out the third dance, telling what dance it was. The young men and young women danced toward each other in two long rows, and then danced back again. After a time the halfmen-halfwomen called out, "Select your partners," and each man crossed over to get his sweetheart as a partner, and the young women when told to select their partners also crossed over and met their sweethearts. After all had partners—for the men and the women were equal in number—they formed a ring around the big fire and danced about it. In this circling dance the drummers and singers also joined the circle, and the whole ring danced to the left about the fire. The old women and the old men were in the center of the ring, holding the scalps which they waved in the air. The halfmen-halfwomen danced around outside the ring, always toward the right. With the scalps tied to poles they kept the young girls and the boys away from the dancers, for the boys and girls were afraid of the scalps. In this way they kept the children from crowding close to the dancers.

After dancing for some time in this way, the halfmen-half-women told the drummers and singers to put the women inside in this round dance. While the young men were going around the ring, now and then one of them would step inside and put an arm around his sweetheart's neck. After this had gone on for some time, all fell back as before into their old places—the drummers and singers to their places, and the young men and women to theirs.

Soon the fourth dance was called by the halfmen-halfwomen, and the singers started up a different song for this. This dance was called "the slippery dance." In this only women participated, and in pairs. These women danced up to their sweethearts and took hold of their robes and then danced back to the center, leading the young men out. The young men walked after those who were holding them and were held by their sweethearts until the men's sisters had presented to the sweethearts a ring or a bracelet. This process was called "setting them free." Sometimes a young fellow went up and presented a ring or a bracelet to have his friend set free.

After this dance the halfmen-halfwomen told the dancers to rest for a time and asked that someone should bring water for the dancers. The assembly partly broke up. Women would go away to tie up their legs, for, as they wore long deerskin dresses, and the next dance was to be a stooping dance, the dresses might get in their way, be stepped on, and trip them. This was the last dance, called "the galloping buffalo-bull dance."

When all had returned the halfmen-halfwomen told the people to sit down, and all took their places. The drummers and singers also sat down. When the singing and drumming began three or four women arose and danced toward the men, and when they were close to them stooped down and turned their backs toward the men and danced before them. Then just as many men as there were women stood up and danced, joining the women; the men stooped also, just like the women. More women danced out and men joined them, and at length all the men and women came together and the whole party danced in a long row, all stooping down, dancing like a bull galloping. The halfmen-halfwomen would then say, "Go round in a circle," and all the dancers stood erect and began the circle dance, or round dance, while the drummers and singers joined them in the circle. In this round dance everyone sang as they went around. By this time it was nearly morning, and the dance at last broke up, the people returning to their homes.

These were all scalp dances.

WOMEN AND WAR

While it was not common for women to go on the war-path with men, yet they did so sometimes, and often showed quite as much courage and were quite as efficient as the men whom they accompanied. I have already mentioned the achievement of the sister of Chief Comes In Sight, who during Crook's battle on the Rosebud, June 17, 1876, charged down against the white troops and brought off her brother, whose horse had been killed, and who, except for his sister's courage, would very likely have died on the field.[12] This woman became the wife of Black Coyote, a man belonging to a very distinguished fighting family among the Northern Cheyennes, who was captured by the soldiers, in 1878, and committed suicide in prison.

In an attack on the Pawnees, the wife of White Frog charged down with the Cheyennes, was attacked by a Pawnee who carried a hatchet, and wrenched the hatchet from his hand, knocking him from his horse.

One of the last war women in the tribe died in August, 1915. She took a prominent part in an important battle between the Cheyennes and the Shoshonis in 1868, at which time she counted coup on one Shoshoni and killed another. This woman's name was Ehyophsta, commonly translated Yellow-

[12] The Fighting Cheyennes, p. 324.

head Woman, or Yellow Haired Woman. She was the daughter of Stands In The Timber, who died in 1849, at the time of the big cholera, and a niece—as we would say—of the old Bald Faced Bull. Her husband, Walking Bear, was killed in 1867 by the accidental discharge of his own gun.

The year after his death an important battle took place between the Cheyennes and the Shoshonis on a little stream[13] between Lodge Pole (Clear) Creek and Powder River, near the foot of the Big Horn Mountains, Montana. Sixty-two Shoshonis were killed by the Cheyennes, fifty on the first day, six on the second, two on the third, and four more on the fourth. The last two groups seem to have returned to the battlefield under the impression that the Cheyennes had moved away.

Some time before this some Shoshonis had come to a small camp of Cheyennes—seven lodges—at this place and had taken all their horses. After having returned to their own camp with the Cheyenne horses, the Shoshonis told their people of this little camp that now had no horses and so could not move. A large party of Shoshonis started out to kill all these Cheyennes. Meantime, however, the whole Cheyenne camp had moved in and camped with the seven lodges. In all there must have been two or three hundred lodges in the camp.

The night before the fight some Cheyenne young men discovered signs of the war-party, and very early the next morning, the Shoshonis came close to the camp and sent a man up on the hill near it. He called out to the Cheyennes: "We have come here for your women and children. If you can keep them, it is good. If not, we shall take them home with us."

In the Cheyenne camp there was a man named *Min's shĭ o-tăns'*, Gives Birth In A Willow Patch, who could talk Shoshoni. He called back, saying: "It is good. You have come to a camp of Cheyennes. No other tribe is with us. After you have killed all the men, you shall take the women and children." While

[13] This stream is now known as Beaver Creek. The scene of the fight was about two miles below the house now occupied by Mr. L. R. A. Condit.

these two men were talking, the Cheyenne men had left the camp and were secretly surrounding the Shoshonis, who were on a high hill, the ascent of which was long and sloping. When the Cheyennes charged, the Shoshonis ran away through the thick timber. If they had stayed in the timber they might have saved themselves, but they ran on and made their breastworks in a big ravine.

On this first day, when the Cheyennes killed fifty, they found that six men had thrown themselves over a cliff and killed themselves. One of them lodged in some bushes growing out of the side of the cliff. Gray Thunder counted coup on him with his reata, which was just long enough to reach the Shoshoni.

In the afternoon the Cheyennes chased the Shoshonis out of their breastworks and followed them, fighting. A Shoshoni met Wolf Ear face to face and they clinched. Ehyophsta rode up to them and dismounted, and as they were wrestling drew her butcher knife and stabbed the Shoshoni twice. After the fight they went about looking for wounded men, or those who had hidden. They found a number hidden in clefts of the rocks and shot them and dragged them out. A young man was dragged out of a hole, and after he had been pulled out he sat up. Some one suggested that it would be well to ask him some questions. Ehyophsta said, "If you people will stand aside, I will question him." She stepped forward and lifted up his arm and thrust her knife into his armpit. She took one-half of the scalp of his whole head.

On the third day Big Foot discovered two men coming back to the scene of the fight and reported to the camp, and they went out and killed them.

On the fourth morning Ehyophsta and her daughter and some others went out from the camp and looked about. A dog that was with them pointed his nose, and seeing that he smelt something, they followed him. He led them to a place under the high bank, where were three Shoshonis who had built a fire and were drying their clothes. Rain had been falling, followed by a soft snow, and the ground was wet. The Cheyenne men made a charge and killed the three. The last three killed looked as if they had been out for a long time. Their clothing was worn and they were thin.

The Shoshoni war leader, who was also a medicine man, carried on his left arm a shield and in the left hand his walking-stick, while in his right hand he had a six-shooter. He would come out of the breastworks and walk about, and all the Cheyennes would shoot at him. Then he would go into the breastworks and his men would come out and form in line and begin to shoot.

It must be understood that at this time practically all the firearms of the Cheyennes and other Indians were muzzle-loaders, which it took some time to reload, and after a volley had been fired the enemies might expose themselves for a while without danger.

The Shoshonis say now that only a single man of this war-party escaped.

Women who had been to war with their husbands formed, it is said by some, a guild or society and held meetings at which no one else might be present, but, of course, the number of these women was very small.

WARRIOR SOCIETIES

SOLDIER ORGANIZATIONS

THE soldier bands of the Cheyennes are six in number; of these four are ancient, and are foreshadowed in the Culture Hero stories of the people, while the other two are modern. Besides these, a seventh band consisted merely of the forty-four chiefs of the tribe who had their own organization, and certain dances peculiar to themselves. These soldier bands are as follows:

1. *Wōhksēh'hetăniu,* Kit Fox men; commonly called Fox Soldiers.
2. *Hĭm'ōwēyŭhk'ĭs* (Meaning uncertain); commonly called "Elk Soldiers" or "Elk-horn Scrapers"; possibly "Fingers." A modern nickname for this band is Blue Soldiers (*Tŭtăwēnŭt'kiū*), from a comparatively recent securing of blue coats —*i.e.,* old-fashioned soldier overcoats.
3. *Hōtă'mĭtă'niu,* Dog Men.
4. *Măhōhē'wăs,* Red Shields; also called Bull Soldiers, *Hotu'anŭt'kiu.*
5. *Hotă'mi măssāu,* Crazy Dogs.
6. *Hĭm'ă'tăno'hĭs,* Bowstrings.
7. *Wĭh'iu nŭt'kĭū,* Chief Soldiers.

These soldier bands included a large number, but not all, of the able-bodied and ambitious men of the tribe, from youth to old age. They were the organized military force of the camp, and acted as its police force. To them was intrusted the enforcement of the orders of the chiefs. Since, in the Indian camp, public opinion was the ruling force, and since the soldiers constituted a majority of the bravest and most influential men in the tribe, the soldier bands were often consulted by the chiefs

48

WIND WOMAN

on important matters relating to peace or war. Sometimes one or more of these societies, acting unitedly, might force the tribe to adopt some certain course of action that it was not generally desired to take, or might even oblige some priest or important man to perform an act that he felt to be wrong or to threaten harm to the tribe. Such a case occurred about 1836, when one of the soldier bands forced White Thunder, the keeper of the medicine arrows, to renew them at a time when the spirits were unfavorable.[1]

Long ago, it is said, there were only four of these bands. The Crazy Dogs and the Bowstring Soldiers are recent bands which have not existed for many generations.

Boys from thirteen to sixteen years of age might elect to join almost any of the soldier bands. The two or three growing sons of a member of one of the bands would be likely to join the father's band. The father and mother of the candidate usually accompanied him to the first dance of the society that he attended, and two or three horses were then given away by them, or by some relative of the boy, perhaps to the chief of the band, or to some one of the dancers, or even to a person entirely unconnected with the society—it might be to some poor woman. A gift must be made on the occasion. The candidate was received without special ceremony. He was dressed for the dance before he left his own lodge.

There were always some young and active men who belonged to no soldier society.

In old times a man might belong to one society only, and must leave it before he could join another. There was keen rivalry among the soldier bands; and even today one may sometimes hear old men boasting about these matters, each declaring that the society to which he belonged was the best. The Kit Fox Soldiers always claimed superiority over the others, and—among the Northern Cheyennes at least—when a list of the bands is given, that society is usually mentioned

[1] The Fighting Cheyennes, p. 42.

first. It is suggestive that of the Blackfeet secret societies or soldier bands, the most important is also named after the kit fox (*sĭn' ō pāh*).

To each soldier band belonged four young women, usually girls—though some might be married—of good family. They joined in the dance, and sometimes sat by the singers and sang with them. If the soldiers made a dance, or went from one place to another, feasting, the women were with them, but if the camp was moving the girls traveled with their families. Their duties were chiefly social; that is to say, they were present at meetings of the band, took part in the singing and dancing, and sometimes cooked for the soldiers. They were not necessarily related to anyone in the band, but were supposed to be girls of the best families in the camp. If one of them resigned, or for any reason fell out, another was selected to fill her place by the soldier chiefs. When a girl had been chosen, two young men were sent to her lodge to bring her. The position was an honorable one.

Such a girl was spoken of as *nŭt ūhk e â,* female soldier. Usually a good-looking girl was chosen, who devoted herself to the position in much the same spirit that a nun gives herself up to her vocation. The girl was not compelled to retain this position; if she wished to marry, she might resign, and often did so.

Sometimes a soldier band started off to war as a body. The members did not leave the camp together, but went off by twos and threes and met at some designated place on the road. They might be joined by other young men who did not belong to the organization. This may have happened in 1837, when the forty-two Bowstring Soldiers were killed.[2]

A man might resign from one soldier band and afterward join another. If the chief of one of the soldier bands should be appointed one of the four principal chiefs of the tribe, and

[2] The Fighting Cheyennes, p. 42.

accepted the appointment, he then ceased to be a member of the soldier band.

If a man was elected chief of a soldier band and declined to accept the election, he did not by this declination forfeit his place in the soldier band, but remained a member and another man was chosen as chief. The chief of a soldier band occupied a position of great responsibility, which some men felt to be too serious a burden to assume.

The position was understood to be one of such danger that death was always to be expected—a soldier chief was chosen to be killed. Only a man at all times ready to face death could be selected for this office. The soldier chief possessed a high sense of the dignity of his position, and if he thought he was not treated with the consideration due him, he was ready to demand his rights. His position was always respected, partly because people generally feared to quarrel with him.

The fact that they had been soldier chiefs did much to make Dull Knife and Little Wolf noted men in the tribe. Both were brave and good fighters, but they were very different. Dull Knife was a brave man and a good fighter, but fought merely as an individual leader of men. He was not an organizer, and did not plan his battles.

Little Wolf, when a soldier chief, always led his men; he never sent anyone ahead of him. So he always counted the first coup. But besides fighting himself, he made a plan for each battle. During the progress of a fight Little Wolf constantly called out words of instruction and encouragement to his warriors, telling them to fight hard and advising them how to fight efficiently. He thought not merely of his individual deeds, but of the battle as a whole. In other words, he was what few Indians have been—an organizer. His march north from the Indian Territory in 1878 showed him to be a great general.

Little Wolf always considered a situation in advance and planned what should be done. He possessed great foresight, tried to think of and to provide for every contingency, and to leave nothing to chance. It is reported that on more than one occasion when planning a fight and directing his men what to do, someone interrupted him and proposed a different course of action. Little Wolf walked up to the man and struck him, ordering him to cease talking, and saying that he was interfering with his plans.

After Little Wolf had been chosen one of the principal chiefs, his manner became much milder.

Tangle Hair, a former chief of the Dog Soldiers, who had many times been with Little Wolf in situations of danger and difficulty, where other men were very much alarmed, said that Little Wolf was never seen to show signs of fear. Little Wolf's death in battle was predicted for many years, but he died of old age.

A soldier chief might commit an act which automatically removed him from his office, as happened in the year 1837, when Porcupine Bear, the chief of the Dog Soldiers, took part in the killing of a tribesman. This act of itself caused him to cease to be the chief, and no formal action by the soldier band was required. In a short time the place held by Porcupine Bear was filled by the choice of another man.

The lodge of that soldier of any band who was chosen to carry the drum was headquarters for the members of his band. For this office, therefore, they usually selected a good-natured man, with a kindly, friendly wife.

If, as often happened—for the soldier bands were composed of the bravest warriors in the tribe and were constantly losing men in battle—the number of any soldier band became greatly reduced, a meeting was called, for which a large, double lodge was put up, and it was heralded through the camp that recruits were needed for this particular band. Then very likely many young men joined it.

The Crazy Dogs were said to be considered the "toughs" of the soldier bands, by which I suppose is meant those with the least feeling of responsibility.

Two important duties of the soldiers in the camp had to do with the renewing of the arrows and the building of the medicine lodge. When the arrows were to be renewed, the soldiers were sent about over the country to the different camps to notify the people and to ask them to gather at the place appointed for the ceremony. The arrows were renewed on the occasion of the killing of a tribesman by a member of the tribe. The ceremony was thought to insure the health of the people and an abundance of buffalo, cherries, berries, roots, grass, and all animals for the coming year, and was helpful to the people. All desired to share in its beneficent influence, and it was unusual for anyone to refuse to come in—all were eager to be present. If any little camp of people failed to come in when ordered, there would probably be much sickness among them, and some might die.

While the arrows were being renewed, a guard of soldiers was stationed about the camp. No noise was permitted; no one was allowed to do anything that was bad. No one might be cross, speak angrily, or dispute with anyone; all must be good-natured and friendly. After the ceremony, the people separated and went their several ways. Now all would have good fortune, health, and plenty of food.

Among the common everyday duties of the soldier bands was the work of seeing that the camp moved promptly, according to the orders of the chiefs, and of leading the marching column. If the camp was to move next day, the chiefs came together the evening before, and called into the lodge with them the chiefs of the band of soldiers then in charge of the camp. The chiefs, who had talked the matter over and decided what should be done, announced to the soldier chiefs: "Tomorrow we will move camp; every lodge must go. We will camp at such and such a place." That night the order was cried through the camp, and in the morning the soldiers rode about through the village and saw that every lodge was taken down. Then they started toward the camping place, marching ahead of the others, and when they reached the spot, they sat on the ground in a line just beyond where the camp was to be, and no one passed them.

If on any day orders were given that there should be no hunting, the soldiers saw to it that no one hunted. If anyone started out for this purpose, he was followed and brought back, and if he did not submit promptly, he was likely to be well whipped, and perhaps even some of his property might be destroyed. An example of the power of the soldiers, and of the way in which they treated men who neglected or disobeyed orders, is shown by an incident of many years ago. Tall Bull and Spotted Tail, two of the men mentioned, afterward became well-known chiefs of the Cheyennes and Sioux, respectively.

A large party of Cheyennes and Sioux was out looking for the Pawnee camp. Tall Bull, Wolf Mule, and White Antelope—Cheyennes—with Good Bear, Spotted Tail, and Yellow Eyes—Sioux—were sent out as scouts, to search for it. They had been ordered to find the Pawnee village, and then to come in and report, but were told that if unexpectedly they came upon a Pawnee on the prairie, they should kill him; they must not let him go away, to report to the enemy's camp.

The scouts failed to find the Pawnee camp, but they discovered a single Pawnee going along on foot, carrying something on his back. They charged on him, and he dropped his pack and his robe, but instead of running away, he ran toward them. Good Bear rode up to him to touch him, but the Pawnee shot his horse through the body with an arrow, and the horse ran a little way and fell. White Antelope rushed toward him, and the Pawnee shot his horse in the breast. He turned off. Wolf Mule then charged, and the Pawnee ran toward him. Wolf Mule turned to ride away, and the Pawnee shot him in the back, but the point of the arrow struck one of his silver hair plates in the center, piercing it so that the point of the arrow went an inch or two into the muscles of the back. The Cheyennes and Sioux then stood back and did not attack the

Pawnee any more. He made signs to them, saying: "Come on! Kill me! I am a chief; it will be a good thing for you if you kill me; if you do this, you will have killed a chief. I am like the sun," and he pointed toward it.[3]

The Pawnee had fought so well that the Cheyennes and Sioux feared to continue the fight, and when he made these signs they drew off and left him.

When the scouts returned to the main war-party of Cheyennes and Sioux, it was seen that something had happened. Good Bear had no horse, and was riding behind another man; and White Antelope's horse was lame. The scouts did not wish to tell of the fight with the Pawnee, and how he got away. The leaders said nothing, but some of the young men in the camp got hold of Wolf Mule, who was stiff from his wound, and he told them what had happened. Then the Sioux soldiers quirted Spotted Tail and Yellow Eyes unmercifully, and the Dog Soldiers whipped the Cheyennes—all except Wolf Mule—for their disobedience of orders—letting the Pawnee get away. Wolf Mule was spared because he had told what had happened.

The war-party went on and found Good Bear's horse, dead. Later they found where the Pawnees had been camped, nearly a day's journey from the place where the fight had taken place; so that the Pawnee must have been a long way from his camp. They did not follow the Pawnees, but went home without accomplishing anything.

When a soldier society was to have a dance, every member was expected to bring the ribs and hump ribs of any buffalo he might have killed to the center of the circle for their feast. The servants, generally four in number, who sat at the lodge door, did the cooking and brought the water.

The informal or social dances of all the soldier bands were

[3] A person who is very handsome is said to be like the sun. Also a very brave man may boast to his enemies that he is like the sun—a big chief. If they kill him they will have done a good thing, and can dance a great deal. Cheyennes, Arapahoes, Arikaras, Kiowas, and Pawnees, all use this figure.

55

similar, except in the number of men who rode in the dance. The practice is described under the head Himoweyuhkis.

Only two bands of the soldiers were permitted to fire their guns while dancing. These were the Elk-horn Scrapers and the Red Shields.

Soldier Wolf, a middle-aged and well-informed Northern Cheyenne, believed that the names of the soldier bands were changed at regular intervals. Every four years, he said, they came together for the purpose of changing the names of the soldier bands. On the occasion of the change, while all the bands were dancing, an old man would get up and call out to the soldiers, "Now, all you people, from this day forth you will call the Wolf Soldiers the Elk Soldiers, and you will let the old name lie right here on the ground." He called this out to the Sutaya, to the Sandhill People (Tsistsistas), to the Arapahoes, and to the Sioux. If Soldier Wolf is right in this, it would account for certain other names of soldier bands which are sometimes heard, but which do not appear to be generally known. Such names are *Ĭmo' yŭk he' tăn iu,* translated "Strongheart men," and *Wōhk pōhŭm he tăn iu,* "White-horse men."

Fox Soldiers (Wohksehhetaniu): When the Fox Soldiers were about to hold a dance, their lodge was pitched in the center of the circle. When the ceremony began, they came out of the lodge and walked around the circle, singing and shaking their rattles. In going around the circle they stopped four times: once when they reached the southeast, and again at the southwest, the northwest, and northeast. At each stop they sang, and when they had passed completely around the circle, they entered their lodge and began to dance. Their large rattle —its globe painted red—was carried by a certain chosen popular man. When they entered the lodge, the rattle was smoked over sweet grass burned on a coal. Then a song was commenced, and during the singing the rattle was shaken in the four directions, and then placed on the ground. This was

56

repeated four times, four songs being sung. This opened the dance, which often lasted for four days.

West of the fire a small circle, called the earth, *hoh* (?), was smoothed on the ground. In this circle was placed a coal taken from the fire, and back of it lay four pipes, filled, which were to be lighted from the coal. The stems of the pipes pointed to the north.

In front of the lodge, and fifty or sixty yards distant from it, was piled up a mound of earth or of buffalo-chips. Early each morning an old man shouted out a call to the soldiers, and all in the lodge jumped out of bed, ran to this mound and around it, and then back to the lodge.

For these four days the dancers did not go home, but remained at the lodge, eating and sleeping there. Two special men, noted for their bravery, were chosen to cook. They sat on either side of the door and did the cooking. Next to each of these sat another young man, selected to serve food to the dancers. They served first the men who did the cooking.

The Kit Foxes painted the trunk from neck to waist, and the arms down to the elbows, black. One of them carried the skin of a kit fox.

Among the ceremonial objects of the Fox Soldiers were four lances of wood about six feet long, the shafts painted black. A large bunch of feathers was tied near each end, and smaller bunches at intervals along the shaft. These lances were carried by chosen brave young men.

Besides the kit-fox skin which the Kit Fox men carried, they also had with them stone arrowpoints as a part of the soldier society belongings. From this they were sometimes called *Mŭt sō ūn ē tăn' iu*.

ELK-HORN SCRAPERS (Himoweyuhkis): To the Himoweyuhkis belonged two crooked lances—shaped at one end like a shepherd's crook—and two straight lances. These were carried by the bravest men in the society. The shafts of these lances were wrapped with strips of otter-skin, and at four different points along the shaft of each, two eagle feathers were tied. These lances were carried in the dances, and to war.

Each one of the Himoweyuhkis carried in the hand a piece of elk-horn, carved to imitate a snake and notched on one side, over the notches of which they rapidly drew a piece of bone. This elk-horn rattling instrument was painted yellow below and dark blue above, with a snake's head carved on one end and the tail on the other. These rattles represented the blue racer (snake) which came from the sun. It is from this instrument that they received the name Elk-horn Scrapers. The instrument is said to have been devised after the dance was established, under the following circumstances:

Once there was a very beautiful girl in the camp, and all the young men wanted to marry her, but she would have none of them. The Dog Soldiers and the Kit Fox Soldiers had a dance, and each young man tried to do his best, but the girl would look at none of them. Then it came the turn of the Himoweyuhkis, and they felt discouraged, because they thought they could do no better than the other societies had done. But a man who possessed spiritual power spoke to them, saying: "That girl will be here to see you dance, and she will fall in love with one of you, and he will get her. Now go and bring me the horn of an elk—a yearling—one that has no prongs on it, and the shank-bone of an antelope." The young men brought him what he had asked for. He carved the elk-horn in the shape of a snake, and on it cut forty-five notches. Then he made from the shank-bone of the antelope an implement to rub over the horn; and this device was used in the dance.

The girl was there to see the dance, and fell in love with and married one of the young men.

The meaning of the name Himoweyuhkis is obscure, and I have found no one who knows its significance. It contains the sound *mō'ē'*, which means elk, but the word may have another

58

derivation. It is said that after the dance had been named the elk dance, a certain man had a dream. He was told by his dream to make a rattle of antelope-hoofs strung on a deerskin string, and fastened in four bunches at different points along a stick about four feet long, to the end of which were tied the tail-feathers of a bald eagle. For most of its length the stick was wrapped in porcupine quills, colored white, red, yellow, and black, in bands. As they danced, the men shook the sticks so that the hoof sheaths rattled. Some men say: "From this they called it the finger dance. It sounds like elk, from *mōwē'*, but perhaps really it is from *mōwĭshkŭn'*, meaning 'fingers'— of the antelope. Perhaps the meaning may be 'his fingers.' "

A trivial name for the society was Blue Soldiers. It is said that years ago the Himoweyuhkis used to visit and stay in the lodge of a trader on the creek Where They Strike The Drum (Brown Creek, Wyoming). One day when a number of them were in the lodge, the trader knocked out his pipe, and a spark fell into an open keg of powder. The explosion burned a number of the soldiers on the breast and belly, and particles of the powder were driven into the skin. From this, the soldiers of the other bands, in derision, called them Blue Bellies.

Afterward, on the Lodge Pole Creek this band had a fight with troops and killed about sixty. They took the clothing of the soldiers and dressed in it. Then one of the Himoweyuhkis said to the people who had made fun of them, "You have called us Blue Bellies; now, from this time on, we will call ourselves Blue Soldiers, from this clothing we are wearing." They did so, and used to ride two-by-two like soldiers.

The killing of these soldiers took place one or two years after the first railroad was built into the country, and was no doubt the so-called Fort Phil Kearny massacre.

The Himoweyuhkis seemed especially to reverence the thunder. Soldier Wolf's father used to tell him that a long, long time ago, a person came to the camp and told the people that he had come to establish a band of soldiers. This person had his hair cut short, and wore on his head a down-feather painted yellow. He got the people together and taught them this dance.

During this dance they shot off their guns, to represent the sound of thunder, and the dancers acted like birds flying before a coming thunderstorm—they were all in confusion.

In the formal dances of the Himoweyuhkis, the announcement was usually made in the morning that certain members of the band would dance that same night. About the middle of the day the soldiers of the band assembled at the lodge of the member who was to give the dance, and partook of a feast. Then certain members of the band, who in earlier life had been important men but now were too old to go to war, and who acted as singers and drummers for the society, selected the men who were to be the leaders in the dance. They chose eight men —of the bravest of the society—to ride in the dance, and said to each: "Friend, you are to ride. Get your horse, paint yourself, and make ready."

The members went to their homes and dressed themselves in their ceremonial clothing and, at a signal given by drumming, all repaired to the lodge of him who had given the feast, and stood there before it. Then the drummers spoke to some brave man, and said to him, "You are to lead the line"; to another, who in some fight had been the last one to turn and retreat, they said, "You shall bring up the rear." Presently the dancers started, the leader going ahead, the others following on foot in single file, the eight horsemen riding one after another, four on each side of the line. Behind the footmen walked some of the girls belonging to the society, behind whom the drummers followed immediately.

From the lodge of the giver of the feast they marched to the entrance of the circle, turned south, and perhaps stopped in front of some lodge belonging to a well-to-do member of the Hivistsinihpa, who did not belong to the Himoweyuhkis. In front of this lodge they swung out, and stopped in a half-circle.

The drummers left their position in the rear, marched into the half-circle, and stood in the line, the young men making room for them. Then, after drumming for a short time, one of the old men handed his drum to a neighbor, stepped out into the circle, and taking from one of the soldiers some weapon with which years before he had struck an enemy, he held it up and told what he had done, saying that when he had struck the enemy he had used this implement. As he finished telling of each coup, he turned toward the drummers, and the drums sounded.

After the old man had danced and related his deeds, one of the horsemen—or sometimes two together—rode into the circle, and each recounted a coup, and as each man finished speaking, the drums sounded. The horses were often painted with symbols of the coups that their riders had counted. White horses were usually painted with red paint, dark-colored horses with white or yellow paint. If one of the men had had his horse shot under him, he painted his steed with a round dot to show where the ball or arrow had entered, generally using red paint.

After the young men had related their deeds, they rode out of the circle, and then all the young men who were on foot stepped forward from their places, and danced to the singing and drumming of the older men. If anyone did not dance forward, the horsemen who were now behind the line rode up to him and pushed him into the circle.

Now the lodge owner appeared at his door, leading a little child who held in its hand a small stick which it presented to someone, perhaps a dancer or a drummer, or even to someone not connected with the dance. The stick represented a horse, which the lodge owner presented to the person who received the stick.

The dancing in front of the lodge was a compliment to the lodge owner—a high honor.

After the society finished dancing before this lodge, it passed on, in the same order as before, to another, where the dancing was repeated. So the soldiers proceeded about the circle until they reached the end, where the Dog Soldiers and Omissis were. Here they stopped dancing. During their march they might stop before twenty or more lodges, receiving a present at each. After the dancing was over they repaired quietly, and in a loose body, without any order, to the host's lodge, where most of them had left their robes and blankets, and when they had taken those they returned to their homes.

The Himatanohis, Bowstring Soldiers, danced as did the Himoweyuhkis, but with them only four men rode. With the Fox Soldiers, the Dog Soldiers, and the Red Shields, only two men rode. Except for the number of horsemen in the dance, the performance for each society was substantially the same. In these dances the company moved from the opening of the circle south, west, north, and east, about the circle, as was the invariable practice in any formal passing about the camp.

Before the formal dance of the society began, the young men who carried the elk-horn rattles purified them by passing them four times through the smoke of sweet grass sprinkled on a coal taken from the fire.

RED SHIELDS (Mahohewas): The Red Shields, or Bull Soldiers, were for the greater part elderly men. A man once a member of this society was always a member. The members seem to have been elected. Occasionally a young man might be chosen to membership. Such young men were selected from among the best and most promising of those in the camp, and to be chosen a member of the Bull Soldiers was a great honor.

In their dancing the Red Shield Soldiers imitated bulls, grunting and butting one another. Sometimes, also like bulls, they charged upon a crowd of onlookers at the dance. In this way they afforded much amusement to the people. They wore hats or bonnets made of the skin of a bull's head, with the horns attached. A Red Shield who had counted a coup painted the right horn of his bonnet red; if he counted another coup, he painted the other horn red. This paint was left on until it wore off. Some Red Shields danced naked except for the breech-clout; others wore leggings, and still others, fine, fancy leggings and moccasins. Some of them painted their bodies red, striped with white, and others painted their bodies white all over.

All carried red shields, some with buffalo-heads painted on them, some with buffalo-tails hanging from the middle. All the shields had raven-feathers attached to the borders. This was the only soldier band, so far as known, that carried a shield peculiar to the organization.

This band had two special lances, straight and finely orna-mented with raven-feathers. When the people camped, and this band was in charge of the camp, these lances were set in the ground, butts down, the points inclined in the direction the camp was to move. In the morning, if the camp was not to break but to remain where it was, the lances were brought in; but if the camp was to move, they still stood there. People would come out of their lodges and ask if the lances had been brought in. If the answer was "Yes," they would say, "Well, we shall lie over a day longer."

Dog Soldiers (Hotamitaniu): In speaking of the tribal groups it has been explained how the Dog Soldiers came to have a camp of their own in the circle of the lodges, and that this soldier company really represented a small division of the tribe whose existence has been almost forgotten.

Since the Dog Soldiers came from different groups, the mem-bers of this band might marry among themselves, although in ancient times care was taken that relatives should by no means marry. A man who joined the Dog Soldiers did so with the full knowledge that he must leave his own clan and with his whole family go to camp with the Dog Soldiers. The origin of the Dog Soldier band is accounted for in the following story:

The people were camped in a circle, and a man had it cried out that he had had a dream, and he wished to establish a

63

society of soldiers to be called Dog Soldiers. He asked anyone who wished to join this society to come to his lodge at a certain time. No one cared about joining this new band of soldiers, and no one went to this man's lodge.

When he saw that no one was coming to him, he went out into the middle of the circle, about the time the sun was setting. In his hand he held a rattle, such as the Dog Soldiers use now, and all night long he sang the Dog Soldiers' songs and shook his rattle. At the end of each song he would mourn and cry.

When he began to sing, all the dogs, even the pups, in the whole circle began to howl. Before day had come, the people had all gone to sleep, and in the morning when they awoke and looked out of their lodges, every dog in the village, even down to the little puppies, had disappeared. The man too had disappeared, like the dogs.

From this time on they could find no buffalo; it seemed that the buffalo too had gone away. As food began to get scarce, they sent out two young men to try to find something to eat—buffalo or elk or deer. These young men traveled far over the prairie, and at length from the top of a hill they had climbed they saw below them a stream, and on it a big village. In the center of the circle was a large lodge.

The young men watched the camp until the sun went down, and then from the lodge which was in the center of the circle they heard sounds of drumming. People were singing and dancing. When it was dark they went to the lodge and peeped in, and there they saw the man who had disappeared from the Cheyenne camp, and on each side of him, all around the lodge, men were sitting. All these men were nicely dressed, with feathers in their hair, and all held Dog Soldier rattles. Some were dancing and all were having a good time.

The young men left the camp, returned to the Cheyenne village, and told what they had seen; and next morning at daylight the whole village moved over to the newly discovered camp. When they reached the hill from which the young men

WALKING SPIRIT

had first seen it, the people saw no camp, but the man was walking about in the circle, and all the dogs were lying by bands. Those which belonged to the people of each band were lying where that band should camp. The people moved in and set up their lodges and their dogs knew them, and were glad to see them.

When they reached the place, the man told the people to put up a large lodge, using two coverings. Then he told a man to go out and cry through the village, saying that whosoever wished to join his band of soldiers should come to this great lodge. Now young men came from every group and made up the largest band of soldiers that the Cheyennes have ever known. The man made rattles and different ornaments, and taking one of the rattles he hit himself with it on both sides of his body, and then he pulled out from his mouth a small dog rope about fifteen inches long. This, he told them, was the pattern on which all dog ropes should thenceforth be made. He placed it on the ground by him, and, as before, hit himself with the rattle on both sides of the body, and pulled out another dog rope. Twice more he did this, and got a third and a fourth. All these he placed on the ground.

Then he said to them, "Now, my people, the first two of these dog ropes are to be used by unmarried men." He took them up and handed them to certain women, and said to them, "You shall make two ropes like these," and he showed them how to do it, telling how long the ropes must be, and pointing out that they were ornamented with quills. "These two other ropes," he said, "are pretty strong. If anyone desires one of them he must ask me for it. I cannot give them away; they will have to be paid for." Then he opened his mouth and swallowed these two ropes.

The women made two dog ropes after the pattern that he had given them. The man chose two young men who should wear these, and after the young men had put them on, he painted all the young men, each in a different fashion. Then they

65

loosened the pinnings of the lodge coverings, and pulled them part way back so that all the people might look in under the lodge-skins.

An old woman, named Dying Woman, looked in. Her son, named Crooked Neck, had joined the Dog Soldiers. She looked at him and saw that he had been adorned with paint mixed only with water, and that the painting was not well done. She called out to him, "My son, why did you not get better paint than that?" This made the boy ashamed, and he held down his head and began to cry. But the old woman kept talking to him, and said, "You are so badly painted that I am afraid you will never see your father, the Whooper, any more." Then Crooked Neck raised his head, and spoke to the head of the Dog Soldiers, saying: "My friend, what this woman has said is true. I wish to have one of those dog ropes that you swallowed." When the people heard him, they all said, *"Haho'! haho'!"*

The man said, "We will dance here for four nights," and they did so; and at the end of four nights he said, "Now, we will move the camp." He sent out some of the Dog Soldiers to look for a leaning tree that pointed north. When they found it, the whole camp moved and camped around that tree. They took lodge-poles and leaned them against the tree. This was the Dog Soldier lodge. After it had been set up, all the Dog Soldiers went in, and the man pulled out from his mouth the dog rope that Crooked Neck had requested. He sent for one of the women who could do the best quilling, to put quills on the dog rope, just as they were seen on this pattern.

Dying Woman said to him, "I will give you five dogs." One of these was a wolf; three were male dogs. The next morning when the women began to make this dog rope, they saw buffalo scattered all about the camp on the prairie. When the dog rope was finished they put it on Crooked Neck; and now they painted him red, with grease mixed with red paint, all over his body. This satisfied his mother. Meantime many of the Cheyennes were out killing buffalo. Some of them brought in a piece of backfat and put it in a pot of water. After it was cooked they passed it along the circle of Dog Soldiers sitting in the lodge, and each took a bite of it.

The man said, "Two of the bravest take the lead, and two other brave ones come behind." He also chose two men to ride horses; they were to go on either side of the line of the dancers. At sundown they went to the lower end of the village, and danced about it all night long, until daylight.

Certain customs and ceremonies observed by the Dog Soldiers deserve special mention.

If a mounted Dog Soldier dropped anything, he did not pick it up. Each member of the society wore on his breast a whistle made from the bone of a bird's wing, and if he dropped an article—even if, when coming in from hunting, the load of meat slipped and fell off his horse—he might not dismount to put it on again, but must blow on his whistle, and ride on. This was the law. Anyone who saw him riding off and blowing his whistle might go to him and strike his horse over the head with his whip, and then catch the horse and lead it back to where the article had been dropped. When this had been done, the man who had lost it might dismount and recover his property. Another man—if he wished to do so—might pick up what the Dog Soldier had dropped and carry it to camp.

In certain ceremonial parades the column of the Dog Soldiers was usually followed by a horseman not a member of the society, who picked up and carried with him any article that might have been dropped by a member.

Two members of the society were known as Black Dogs. When the Dog Soldiers wished to have a dance, and had no food for the feast, it was the custom for one of the Dogs to paint his whole body black, dress in his dance costume, and start out through the camp. Two servants followed him. He went first to the lodge of the nearest chief, and sat down in the door, turning his body from side to side, imitating the motions of a dog as it wags its tail when it desires something to eat, and at the same time blowing his whistle. The people in the lodge gave him whatever they had for him, and from there he went to the next chief's lodge, the servants carrying what he had received. When sufficient contributions of food had been given him, he returned to the lodge where the society were assembled, and they had their feast. The society was made up of young and middle-aged men.

Many of the Dog Soldiers were half-breed Sioux, and the group was sometimes called the Cheyenne Sioux. They wore bonnets of raven-feathers, standing upright in a chaplet, but the bonnet had no tail. To the tips of the feathers were glued—in later years—tiny red down-feathers procured from traders. In their dances the Dogs wore these headdresses, and each carried a small, short rattle—a hollow ring of rawhide with a short handle. The outer border of the ring was ornamented with fur or with deerskin fringe or with red cloth.

The formal dances of the Dog Soldiers continued during four days and four nights. At the beginning of the dance they dug out in the back of the lodge a hole in the ground, about a foot deep. The best part of the meat of a buffalo was chosen, and cut up into pieces about an inch square, there being as many pieces as there were men in the band. A wooden dish holding these pieces of meat was put in the hole, and the meat was then tightly covered with the lining of a buffalo's paunch, stripped off in one piece, which was tucked in about the sides of the dish. Near this hole sat a drummer who with a stick tapped constantly on the covering of the dish. On the last day of the dance the cover was taken off the meat, and each man in the dance ate one of the pieces. By this time the meat was usually tainted.

Hō tăm' tsĭt, the dog rope (from *hō'tăm'*, dog, and *tsĭtŭs'*, rope), spoken of in the story just given, was peculiar to the Dog Soldiers. It is also called among the Northern Cheyennes *Ĭs tu tăm' tsĭt*, meaning "back dog rope." This was a strip of dressed buffalo-hide as wide as the hand and eight or ten feet long, handsomely ornamented with feathers and porcupine quills. Often it was a strip of cow-hide cut from the top of a lodge. Usually a loop at one end passed over the right shoulder and under the left arm of the wearer, and at the other end was a short braided string, to which was tied a red-painted, sharp-pointed wooden pin, like a little picket-pin. The dog rope did not always pass over the wearer's shoulder; sometimes it was attached to the owner's belt by a string.

In battle, the man who carried the dog rope, if he dismounted to fight, might stick the pin in the ground, and by doing so he pledged himself not to retreat from the spot unless some one of his own party pulled up the pin. He himself might not pull it up, on penalty of proving himself a coward—losing his man-hood—and being thenceforth the laughing-stock of the camp. His own people might free him, but if they did not, he must die on that spot. Only brave men carried the dog rope, for he who had one must use it, and to use it might mean death.

In a hard fight, if the man who wore a dog rope saw his party about to retreat, he might stick his pin in the ground and blow his whistle to encourage the others and to show that he would not yield. Then, if his party was driven back, unless one of them pulled up the pin and set him free, he died there. After a comrade had thus pulled up the pin, he struck the man with his quirt, and so literally drove him from the field.

The Kiowas also had a society whose members wore the back rope or dog rope into battle. The manner of wearing this rope and of fixing it to the ground differs in detail from that prac-ticed by the Cheyennes, but the custom is essentially the same. The Kiowas also had the crooked lance, similar to that carried by the Elk Soldiers of the Cheyennes, beyond which, after it had been thrust in the ground, the owner could not retreat. It is said that the owner of a back rope or a crooked lance among the Kiowas might be degraded if suspected of coward-ice. Nothing of this sort is ever suggested of the Cheyennes, for a man who had proved himself worthy to carry either of these notable medicines never could be suspected of cowardice.

The custom of the dog rope may be compared with a practice of the Hurons, noted by Paul Ragueneau,[4] who says:

> It is the custom of these captains, when they find themselves on the verge of combat, to draw forth sticks, which they purposely carry with them, and to present these to their men, that they may fix them in the ground, that they may protest by this act that these sticks will sooner leave their place than they will retreat.

Tall Bull, a Northern Cheyenne, was present on an occasion when the dog rope was used. Little Man was at the front, leading the charge, and when the Cheyennes began to retreat, he sprang off his horse, thrust the pin in the ground, and stood fast. Then all the Cheyennes stopped running, and began to fight harder, and to yell and struggle. They were slowly pushed back, however, and presently a Cheyenne, wearing a warbonnet, sprang from his horse, pulled up Little Man's pin, and struck him two or three times with his whip, whereupon Little Man jumped on his horse and rode off.

As told in the story, there were but four dog ropes—in two grades of importance. Those with pins about four inches long were the more important. The Cheyennes, Arapahoes, Kiowas,[5] and Kiowa-Apaches all used these, with essentially the same customs.

When a Dog Soldier had carried a dog rope as long as he wished, he began to think of handing it over to another, and let it be known he was now ready to part with it. At some dance, when all were present in the lodge, the eight principal men of the society chose one of the bravest of the young men to be the successor of him who had worn the rope. He who was chosen to receive it was obliged to pay heavily for it. All his relations were likely to contribute to help him. When all was

[4] Des Hurons, Jesuit Relations, vol. xxix, p. 229, Burrows Brothers ed., 1898.

[5] Mooney, Kiowa Calendar, pp. 284-285.

ready, singing was begun, and the man who had carried the dog rope placed it on the ground in the lodge, and the relatives of the one who was to have it piled up near it robes and blankets, guns, ammunition, sticks—representing horses—and other property. The owner of the rope might then take it up and put it down in another place, and the relatives of the other young man might pile up more things there. The owner might even move it a third time.

When, however, he thought sufficient had been given, he put the rope over the purchaser, and the dancing began, the seller leading off, by taking hold of the rope which was around the purchaser, and leading him about.

A Dog Soldier who possessed a dog rope, like one who owned a scalp shirt, ignored the whole matter if his wife ran off with another man. In old times, it is said, the owner of a war-bonnet acted in the same way. Yet sometimes the eloper—who perhaps was a little uneasy as to what might happen—might persuade one or more chiefs to take a pipe, with two or three horses, to the injured husband. They entered the lodge, turned to the right, placed the pipe on the ground before the man, and said to him, "There are your horses." If he lighted the pipe and smoked, the incident was closed.

In breaking camp, the clans generally moved out by individuals, whenever the women found themselves ready to go; but the Dog Soldiers might not move out individually: they waited for one another, and all moved out in a body. Thus the Dog Soldiers always brought up the rear, and were in fact the rearguard of the marching column.

The Dog Soldiers were under more severe discipline than the other soldier bands, and usually kept very much by themselves. Made up largely of especially brave men, and on this account looked up to by the tribe, they were often arbitrary, and not infrequently insisted that the whole camp should do as they wished. They were also more disposed to war against the whites than the others, and when the rest of the tribe was quiet and peaceful, they often started out on raids and war-parties, and were joined by other young men who did not belong to the band, but who wished to make names for themselves. This was the case in 1869, when the main tribe had no thought of war, but suddenly learned from fugitives of the attack on Tall Bull's village of Dog Soldiers and its destruction, and of the killing of Tall Bull himself.

This episode, which occurred at Summit Springs,[6] Colorado, broke the power of the Dog Soldier band and practically put an end to it. Scattered remnants were left, but it never regained its old prominence and prestige. Some of the Cheyennes who escaped fled southward and joined the Hevataniu, and others went north to the Omissis. Previous to this the band had been large—perhaps seventy-five or a hundred lodges. They were never so numerous as the Omissis, the largest group of all.

BOWSTRINGS (Himatanohis): The Bowstring Soldiers wore skins of animals, used somewhat as ponchos. A slit was cut in the hide, through which the head was passed, and the skin hung down over the shoulders, the head resting on the wearer's chest and the tail on his back.

The Wolf Soldier band, known in later times as Bowstring Soldiers, was established by *Mist' ai măhăn'*, Owl Friend, the uncle of Elk River's father. Elk River was born about 1810, and Owl Friend may have been fifty or sixty years older, so that this soldier band may be more than one hundred years old. In the story of the establishment of the society mention is made of Northern and Southern Cheyennes, but the narrator may actually have said Omissis and Hevataniu, which today would mean Northern and Southern Cheyennes, but anciently meant only the two bands. People recently living remembered Owl Friend, and his powers and peculiarities. The story of the founding of the society, related to me by Elk River, is as follows:

[6] The Fighting Cheyennes, p. 299.

The Northern Cheyennes and the Southern Cheyennes were apart, and the two camps were traveling to meet each other. Runners had been passing between the two camps, and it was understood where they were to come together. A certain man named Owl Friend started from the Northern Cheyenne camp to go to the village of the Southern Cheyennes, for he had heard where it was going to camp. After he had traveled for some time, just as he came to a stream, a heavy thunderstorm arose. Owl Friend was nicely dressed; he had on a pair of deerskin leggings, cut in a fork at the side and beaded at the knees, and a red-painted robe, and after it began to rain hard he sat down under a cedar tree for shelter, but his robe got wet. The rainstorm passed, and changed to heavy snow, when it grew cold. Seeing that the storm was not going to cease, he said to himself, "I must go on; if I stop here I shall freeze." It was snowing heavily, and he could see only a little way before him; all he could do was to follow the timber down along the stream. He kept on walking, and the trees grew thicker. He did not know where he was, and began to think that he was lost. Presently he came to a place where the stream made two bends, and there he saw a fine large lodge with a red light in it.

"Why," he said, "here is the camp now. I might have stayed up there on the creek and frozen to death." He went up to the lodge, and at the door stamped the snow from his feet, and as he did so he heard within the young men talking with one another.

He lifted the door and went in, and one of the young men said: "Hello! here is our friend! Where did you come from? You might have frozen to death in this storm. Hang up your robe to dry, and sit down over there and pull off your moccasins and leggings, and get warm and dry."

Owl Friend said: "I heard the village was going to camp above here, but I did not find it, and came on down here looking for shelter. If I had kept on much farther, I should have been lost."

73

One of the young men said, "Cook him something to eat, while some of you dry and soften his robe and moccasins and leggings."

He sat down, and one said: "Lie there and rest, while we are cooking. Here is a robe."

Owl Friend lay down, and soon said: "I am getting pretty warm now. Will one of you hand me a cup of water?" A cup of water was passed him. Soon they gave him some food, and he drew his knife and began to eat.

While he sat there eating, he could hear people passing to and fro outside the lodge—children playing, young men calling to one another and yelping, and now and then a girl laughing. Once or twice someone came into the lodge and stood by the door looking at him.

After he had eaten, they gave him his robe and moccasins, dry and softened, and he put them on. He looked about the lodge and saw many curious things; among them four pipes, four lances with red shafts and scalps tied to them, and four drums. There were also rattles ornamented with feathers and weasel-tails; on one side was painted the moon, on the other the sun. Once he stepped outside the lodge and looked about, but it was still storming, and he went in again.

Occasionally a man would come in and say: "Hello! our friend has arrived! It is lucky he got here; he might have frozen to death."

He stayed in this lodge four days, hardly going out at all, for the storm continued. On the fourth day, the young men in the lodge told him to look around carefully and see what was there. Besides the things that he had already noticed, they showed him two hawk-skins, two otter-skins, two swiftfox-skins, a bear-hide, and a wolf-hide. The wolf-hide was slit at the neck, so that it could be slipped over the head and worn on the back, and on the middle line of the back were tied eagle-feathers. After he had seen all these things, they showed him four other lances, with bunches of feathers tied to them and

74

with single eagle-feathers tied at different points along the shaft.

On the evening of the fourth day the young men began to dress for a ceremony, and to put on all these things that he had seen. Owl Friend looked out of doors again. It was still storming.

While the young men were dressing, they sent out one of their number to ask an old man to call to the Wolf Soldiers to assemble, saying that they were to have a ceremony. The young man went out, and soon returned, saying that the old man was getting ready, and would soon call out. Then the young men in the lodge said to Owl Friend: "You see us? This is the way you shall dress." Besides the things that he had already seen, they got out, while they were dressing, two war shirts, and two pairs of leggings trimmed with scalps.

Soon the old man could be heard coming, calling out for the Wolf Soldiers to gather; that they were going to have a dance; and soon he came into the lodge, wearing his robe hair side out. When he entered, he said to Owl Friend, "Hello! friend; you were nearly frozen to death, were you not?" Soon the young man told the old crier to go out and to call for certain men to come and sing for them. Those whom they wished were Wears His Robe Hair Out, White Wolf, High Wolf, Black Wolf, and Big Wolf. Before long these singers began to arrive. White Wolf was a fine-looking man, well dressed. Wears His Robe Hair Out did not come with the others; it took him a long time to dress, and several times the old crier went out and called for him. While they were preparing for the dance, the four principal lances were stuck in the ground in the middle of the lodge. Still Wears His Robe Hair Out did not come, and at last they sent a messenger for him to the lodge where he stopped. When the messenger told him that they were waiting for him, the man said, "I am all ready, and was just about to start." When he reached the lodge and entered, he said to Owl

75

Friend, "Hello, friend! I heard you came near freezing to death."

When Wears His Robe Hair Out came in, they filled the four pipes from a big tobacco sack ornamented with porcupine quills; then they told one of the servants, who sat in the door, to get some sweet grass and burn it; and when he had done so, Wears His Robe Hair Out took the drums and held them over the smoke, and smoked them, so that they should be pure; and then he hit one of the drums four times, *Poom, poom, poom, poom!*

After this, they said to Owl Friend: "Friend, this is what you will have to do; all this you must imitate. Watch closely, therefore, and see what we do. Now it is going to stop storming."

Now Wears His Robe Hair Out sang two dance songs, then said to Owl Friend, "These are the two songs that I am going to give to you." Then he sang two more wild songs, beating on the drum as he sang, as he had done before. As he sang the first of these two, Wears His Robe Hair Out stood up and danced, taking one of the lances and counting a coup, telling of where he had killed an enemy; and then gave the lance to someone at the back of the lodge; and others did the same, until four men had danced, each man using a different lance.

Then they did the same thing with the pipes, and after each danced, the pipe the man had held was smoked, and then put away, until four men had thus danced and smoked. During the dancing, occasionally a man went out, and when he returned, said: "It is clearing off nicely. You can see stars shining everywhere."

They danced for a long time, and when finished they had a feast, and then the young men undressed, put away their fine clothing, and some of them went to their homes. After the dance was over, the young men said to Owl Friend: "All of these things you must do yourself. You have seen this dance, and now we give it to you. You must dance four days and four nights. One thing you must remember: you must never let the sun find you in bed when he rises. Through the day you may lie down and sleep, but you must rise early in the morning." After they had said this, Wears His Robe Hair Out said to him, "This is the Wolf Soldier dance, but I am not one of these people; I am a different person." Afterward, in a dream, Owl Friend learned that this man was the Thunder.

They told Owl Friend that now he could go to bed, but before doing so he went outside and saw that it was fine weather. In the morning he awoke from a sound sleep, and his robe felt hot over his head. He thought to himself, these men must have built a big fire in the lodge. He pushed the robe from his head and looked about him, and, behold! he was lying out on the prairie and the sun was high in the heavens, and all about him were beds where wolves had lain. All around him on the hills were wolves, some of them howling; and on one high hill there was a great white wolf, and not far from him three other large wolves. Owl Friend could understand the howling of the wolves, and knew what they said, so he went over toward the four big wolves, and found that they had killed plenty of buffalo and young calves. As he went toward them, he could hear the white wolf calling the other wolves, and they went to meet him. The wolves talked to him, and told him that they had taught him all they knew. They said: "After you have danced four days and four nights, take this medicine which we give you now, and rub it over all your body. Now, friend, the camps have come together, and you can go to your home."

Now, when the camps came together, the people of the Northern Cheyenne camp asked the others if any of them had seen Owl Friend. No one knew where he was, and all the people thought that he must have frozen to death. They supposed that they should see him no more. But one day, as Owl Friend was journeying toward the camp, he overtook four men who were traveling along, and they were surprised to see him, and asked him where he had been. He told them that he had been caught

77

in a storm, and had crept under a rock cliff, and so had saved himself.

Owl Friend established this dance among the Cheyennes, and so originated the Wolf Soldier Band. He made for the dance all the clothing and ornaments, such as the wolves had had, and the dance was performed just as they had danced it. The people danced in the lodge four days and four nights. To each of the lances was tied some of the "black medicine" (*Balsamorrhiza sagittata*). On the fourth day the lodge was taken down; a big fire was made, and the Wolf Soldiers danced around the fire, as the wolves had instructed him. Owl Friend danced into the fire from the four directions—east, south, west, and north. He and his soldiers danced in the fire until it was put out, yet neither they nor their clothing was ever burnt.

After he had lived with the wolves, Owl Friend always wore his robe hair side out. The name of the Wolf Soldier dance was afterward changed to *Hēmătōnō'*, the meaning of which is unknown.

All through his life Owl Friend obeyed the wolves' injunction about rising early. Once, when he was quite an old man, his wife got up early one morning and went out somewhere, and stopped there talking. After she had been there for a little while she noticed that the sun had risen. She said, "Why, there the sun has risen, and the old man is not yet up; I must hurry and wake him!" She ran to the lodge and shook him by the shoulder, but he did not get up; he was dead.

Owl Friend always slept on wolf or coyote skins. They say that he had eyes like a coyote, and was always watching, and seeing everything that happened.

Crazy Dogs (Hotamimassau): The Crazy Dogs had special customs and costumes. The brave ones wore short robes cut above and below into strings nearly two feet long. The upper strings were flung back so as to hang down over the back. They wore hats or bonnets ornamented with antelope-horns, and with a tail of eagle-feathers extending down the back. All the Crazy Dogs carried small rawhide rattles. They had special straight lances, the shaft of each wound with red cloth, and a long row of eagle-feathers hanging down from it. There were about ten of these lances, carried by braves of good families.

When the Crazy Dogs began their dance they were obliged to continue to go forward in whatever direction they might be headed. They might not turn unless the director of the dance drove them to one side, or faced them about by striking them with his whip. This director rode a horse, while the others were on foot. He was one of the bravest men in the society, and was chosen for the express purpose of directing them.

If, when they were dancing, they came to a river, they were obliged to continue to go forward, into and through the water,[7] no matter how finely ornamented their moccasins and leggings might be. They turned aside only by direction of their leader. When they were dancing, they ran forward for some distance, then stopped at some lodge and danced, and then ran on again.

CONTRARIES

Among the Cheyennes there were certain men known as *Hohnŭhk'e,* a word which conveys the idea of doing precisely the reverse of what is said. They were called Contraries. There was no band or guild of these: they were merely individuals bound by certain beliefs. They were, however, braves of much importance, and were often intrusted with serious duties—even with leadership—in battle. For this reason it may be proper to speak of them in this place. There were usually two or three Contraries in the tribe. On occasions there may have been four, but this is regarded as doubtful.

These Contraries acted by opposites. If they wished to signify assent, they said "No." If one requested a Contrary to go away, he came nearer. If asked to ride, he walked. If he called

[7] Compare the account of Yankton soldiers walking into an airhole, by Lewis and Clark, Original Journals, vol. I, p. 130.

out to his woman, "Do not bring any more wood, we have plenty," she knew that the wood in the lodge was exhausted and that more should be brought.

A man became a Contrary because he feared the thunder. He carried a peculiar lance which was the especial property of the Thunder, and a Contrary had no fear of being struck by lightning.

My old friend, Brave Wolf, for many years a Contrary, became one through fear. For years, whenever a heavy thunderstorm was approaching, he always believed he saw, standing on the clouds, a man holding a Contrary lance in his raised left hand. This vision caused him to fear the thunder—the lightning—and as from time to time it appeared to him more and more frequently, his fears grew stronger, so that, as he said, his fear of thunder became so great that he was foolish. At length, in a dream, the man that he had seen in the clouds told him that if he carried one of these bow-lances, he need no longer fear the Thunder. When the man told him this, he determined to have one.

Brave Wolf asked a Contrary in the tribe to give him his lance, and the Contrary did so. For it Brave Wolf paid eight horses and much other property, and from that time felt no fear of the Thunder. The spiritual power of this lance was very great; it was one of the most potent medicines of the tribe, handed down from long ago. A man who possessed one of these lances, and did what he ought to do, need not fear the Thunder; yet if he failed to treat the weapon reverently, the lightning might kill him.

Brave Wolf carried this lance for about ten years (1866 to 1876). While carrying it he was always painted red, and wore leggings, moccasins, and a blanket made of old lodge-skins. When he lay down, he had no bed to rest on. The Contrary might not even sit on a bed. If he entered a lodge, the host or hostess at once moved things out of the way and the Contrary sat on the naked floor of the lodge. When he rose to go, the

PUTTING UP POLES FOR LODGE

Contrary passed white sage over the ground to purify it, for he always carried with him a bundle of the plant for use in the ceremony of purification.

The Contraries were not chiefs, they were merely braves. They bore the usual weapons carried by warriors, but besides, each carried one of these lances—*Hōhnŭhkawo'*, Contrary bow —shaped like a bow strung with two strings, but with a lance-head on one end,[8] and adorned with various mysterious symbols. The lance was about five feet in length, and near one end was tied the stuffed skin of a bird (*maivĭsh*, an oriole), in the South. In the North the Louisiana tanager, which has some red on the head instead of merely yellow or orange, was used for this purpose. The name came from the North. The red painting of the person and clothing of the thunder-bow bearer is said to have been in imitation of the color of this bird, which represents, they say, the body of the man who carries the thunder-bow. At each end of the lance, tied on with a white string of bear intestine, was a bunch of the feathers of owls, hawks, and eagles. When not in use, the lance was wrapped in a piece of tanned buffalo-hide. Its owner wore a cap or fillet of owl-feathers, and to the heel of each moccasin was attached the beard of a buffalo-bull. The braids of his hair were wrapped with strips of dressed buffalo-hide, each strip split at the end so as to make two little tags, something like those at the heel of a moccasin. A whistle of ash wood hung about the neck by a string of dressed buffalo-hide. It was five or six inches long and as thick as a man's finger.

Lashed to the lance outside of the buffalo-hide wrapper was a short, forked stick, sharpened at the butt, painted red, and with two prongs of unequal length. When the lance was unwrapped for use in a fight, or for other purpose, the sharpened end of the forked stick was thrust in the ground, and the lance was rested on it, the point up, so that the point should not touch

[8] Compare Morice, Western Denés, Trans. Canadian Inst., vol. IV, p. 60, March, 1894.

the ground. When the Contrary took up his lance to go into the fight, he might hand this stick to any young man to carry. It was supposed to give the young man good luck in battle, because it was one of the belongings of a great medicine. When the lance was first taken out of the wrapper, sweet grass was burned over a coal and the lance held over the smoke, and as this was done it was lightly shaken four times.

Only the Contrary himself might handle the lance; not even his wife might touch it. Occasionally, if a Contrary was obliged to leave his lance, to do something, he might give it to a man to hold, but after the Contrary had taken it back, a ceremony of purification must be performed on the one who had held it.

If in a fight the bearer of the thunder-lance was shot, or if his horse was shot, so that he was out of the fight, he might hand his lance to any man, to be used in the fight in counting coup. If he did this, the user must be purified after carrying the weapon. These bow-lances were sometimes called thunder-bows, because they had the power to influence the thunder—that is, the lightning. Anyone who was careless about the possessions of a Contrary, or showed lack of respect for him, was likely to be killed by lightning.

In the camp, the Contrary lance was usually hung, by day, upon a pole which stood in the ground behind the lodge, and when the sun set, the pole was brought close to the back of the lodge and was leaned up against it. If, by any chance, the lance touched anyone, the person so touched must be rubbed off with a brush of white sage; or if, in riding a horse, the lance touched it—as it was quite sure to do—the horse, before being turned loose, must be wiped off with white sage and prayed over. If children playing about the camp knocked against the lance, or against the pole on which it hung, or if a horse did the same, the lightning was likely to kill them, unless they were thus purified.

In the lodge of a Contrary, no one slept at the back of the lodge; at night or in stormy weather this place was reserved for the thunder-bow. No one, not even the Contrary himself, might pass between the bow and the fire; only the pipe could pass there. No dogs were allowed in this lodge—the Contrary might not own dogs.

When going into a fight, the Contrary carried his thunder-bow in the hollow of his left arm. So long as he held the lance in the left hand, he might advance and retreat, fighting like anyone else, but if he shifted his lance to his right hand, and blew his whistle, then he might not turn back, but must rush upon the enemy, no matter how many guns were being shot at him; he was obliged to press on until he reached the enemy. When he passed the lance to his right hand, blew his whistle, and cried like a burrowing owl as he rushed toward his enemy, these various acts were thought to cause the bows of the enemy to break, if they were armed with bows, or, if they carried guns, they would cause them to miss fire. The thunder-bow was used to touch the enemy in counting coup; it was not a fighting weapon.

When transferred from left hand to right, the lance was not passed in front of the body, that is, before the face, but behind it, over the back of the neck. The point of the lance might not be turned toward the ground, except when the owner passed it from left hand to right behind his back; then he threw the point down slantwise toward the ground.[9]

When a charge was made, the Contrary must be off to one side by himself. If he rode behind or before anyone, it would bring bad luck to that person—perhaps his horse might break down. In the same way, on the march, the Contrary might not follow the trail made by the others, but must travel off to one side.

As no one might step in the tracks of a Contrary, nor he in those of anyone else, lest that person should become footsore and lame, so it was the duty of the Contrary to step in the tracks of enemies, in order that they might become exhausted

[9] The Fighting Cheyennes, p. 232.

and be overtaken. If an enemy stole horses from the tribe, it was part of the duty of the Contrary to pierce the tracks of the stolen horses with the points of his lance, for the same reason.

In the old days when the Cheyennes traveled chiefly on foot, if a man became exhausted by running or marching, the possessor of a thunder-bow might put sprigs of white sage in the moccasins of the person to renew his strength. Scouts who were about to be sent out often went to the bearer of the thunder-bow and asked him so to treat their moccasins that they might not become tired out on their journey.

Contraries have sometimes been killed in battle. Bear Foot was killed by the Crows, on the Little Big Horn River. His people hung his lance up in a big tree near where he fell. No one would have dared to take it away.

It was proper for the Contraries to repair and renew their lances at the time the medicine arrows were renewed. When this was done there must be no noise whatsoever. The old men who went into the lodge to see the thunder-bows renewed, did not wear good clothing; their garments were old and worn, and the men were painted red. While they were in the lodge, it was not permitted to scratch the head with the fingers; a little pointed stick must be used for the purpose.

The roots and herbs used by the bearer of the thunder-bow are said to have been peculiar to this office and quite different from all other medicines used by priests or doctors in the tribe.

In late years the point of the Contrary lance was made from the bottom of a frying-pan. It was notched or slightly barbed, just above where it entered the wood. Black Bear, *Mōhkstă-mō'ăhts*, long ago dead, was a noted maker of such lancepoints.

In the old times the men who carried thunder-bows were usually single men, or, at least, men who at the time had no wives. The case is cited of Gray Head, who in 1865 had a thunder-bow made for him, and because he had been married the occurrence created a scandal, and his power was not highly regarded. In later years married men had these thunder-bows made for them, but they were not considered real thunder-bows, and the power of the owners was not very highly esteemed.

When a man felt that he must become a Contrary, he tried to take over the position from someone who held it. For this he was obliged to pay a large price—horses, arms, clothing, and robes. Though carrying with it much hardship and many responsibilities, the office was one of great power and importance.

Anyone who might dream of the thunder-bow, or of the thunder, might ask a Contrary for his lance, the symbol of his power. Until someone did this, the Contrary could not escape from his office. It had come to him as an order, and if no one asked for the thunder-bow, the Contrary was obliged to keep it. Thus a man might be a Contrary for a long time. Men have carried these lances so long that they felt they could no longer endure the responsibility, and having made a rawhide sack, they have put the lances away for a time.

A Contrary might not associate on terms of equality or familiarity with the rest of the camp. He might not joke, nor have a good time, but was obliged always to be alone and apart. People might visit his lodge, but they were expected to do so with dignity and decorum, moving slowly, and not remaining long. The Contrary's lodge, and most of his possessions, were painted red. He ate and drank from a special dish, made from the horn of a mountain sheep, which no one else might use, or even touch. After the owner had used it, the dish was wiped out with sage, and was put away.

Thus the ownership of a thunder-bow involved not a little hardship. The care, responsibility, and loneliness which went with it were not pleasant. A Contrary might be in a crowd only during a fight, when all were charging. In the camp he was always alone—often on a distant hill by himself. If there were two Contraries in the camp, they might be together, but no one else might associate with them, and a single one led a lonely life. No one became a Contrary by choice; but from the warning which came to him there was no escape.

The possession of an implement which possessed spiritual power, and was to be handled always with great respect and continually to be watched over, carried with it, to a man of tender conscience, or one who greatly feared the spirits, a feeling of responsibility which became oppressive. Men who for many years had been Contraries have spoken to me with great feeling of the hardships of their office, and in the same way it sometimes happened that a man might feel the possession and care of a shield too great a burden for him.

Stories are told of men who have abandoned the Contrary bow, leaving it hanging in a tree, and never returning for it. At the time of the Mackenzie fight, in November, 1876, Brave Wolf, who died about 1910, was a Contrary, and when the village was attacked, sprang from his bed and rushed out of his lodge, forgetting his Contrary bow, which no doubt was destroyed when the village was burned.

RELIGIOUS BELIEFS

NO subject is more difficult of treatment than one which deals with the beliefs of any people concerning abstract matters. It is not easy to learn from men and women of our own kin and kind just what are their beliefs concerning religion, and what we term superstitions. If this is true among civilized people, whose language we speak, whose education and whose experiences are essentially our own, it is obviously much more difficult to determine the beliefs of an alien race, speaking an unknown tongue, and with a wholly different inheritance, training, and viewpoint.

The Indian's life and experiences dealt wholly with material things, and he saw going on about him operations of nature which he did not understand, for the causes of which he sought explanation. Mysterious happenings were constantly coming under his observation, and he was as constantly striving to learn why they took place and what they meant. Like other peoples of the plains, the Cheyennes personified the elements; to certain birds, animals, and natural objects they attributed mysterious powers, and believed in the transference of such powers from the birds and animals to man. Prayers were offered to these natural objects; yet, as has been said in another place, not to the actual animals, but rather to the qualities, or forces, which these animals typified, or which took their shape. They had the same respect and reverence for war birds —birds of prey—and for flesh-eating birds—buzzards, crows, ravens, and jays—as well as for certain quadrupeds, as was felt by other tribes of the plains, especially by other western Algonquians.

Yet in the Cheyenne community, as with civilized people,

there was great individual diversity of faith and feeling. Some men believed firmly in spirits, birds, and animals; others were almost skeptics. It is thus possible to receive from two individuals in the tribe quite divergent opinions concerning the same matter.

DEITIES

The Cheyennes say there is a principal god who lives up above—Heammawihio—and that there is also a god living under the ground—*Ahk tun o' wihio*. Both are beneficent and they possess like powers. Four powerful spirits dwell at the four points of the compass. In smoking, the first smokes are offered to these six powers. The stem of the pipe is pointed first to the sky, then down to the earth, then to the east, to the south, west, and north. The smoker prays, using his own form of words, mentioning each power by name, and asking him to smoke. Ordinary people use no set formula in addressing these spirits. They call them by name and ask for what they want— for health, for abundance of food, or that their children may not be ill. The man setting out on a war-party asked that he might not be wounded or killed, and that he might count a coup.

Heammawihio, the Wise One Above, was the chief god. He was the creator; he first of all was addressed in prayer, and to him the first smoke was offered. The man who prayed looked upward, and perhaps held his hands toward the sky, saying, "I am poor, and in need; help me"—to food, health, long life, success in war, or whatever it might be that he especially desired.

The dwelling place of Heammawihio is denoted by his name, which is composed of the adverb *hē'ămmă*, above, and *wī'hio*, a word closely related to *wī'hiu*, chief. Wihio also means spider, and white man, and appears to embody the idea of mental ability of an order higher than common—superior intelligence. All its uses seem to refer to this mental power. To the Indian the white man appears superior in intelligence to other men.

88

He has great knowledge, wonderful implements, and clever ways. When he came, he knew more than the Indians, and taught them how to do things they had never done before or, indeed, had ever thought of doing. On account of his ability they called him wihio. The spider spins a web, and goes up and down, seemingly walking on nothing. It is more able than other insects; hence its name.

The Arapaho word for spider is *nĭa'tha*, which is also the word for white man. Niatha is given as meaning "the wise one."[1] I believe that wihio has the same significance. On the other hand, I have been told that the word wihio conveys the idea of being enclosed in something. Of water in a keg, and of a saddle tied up in a sack, the same word would be used. It has been said that when Wihio left them to go up into the sky, he was clothed in a garment woven of grass, which entirely covered him.

Next after Heammawihio the power of the earth is named in prayer. It is implored to make everything grow which we eat, so that we may live; to make the water flow, that we may drink; to keep the ground firm, that we may live and walk on it; to make grow those plants and herbs that we use to heal ourselves when we are sick; and to cause to grow also the grass on which the animals feed.

"The great power put the earth here, and must have put us on it. Without the earth nothing could live. There could be no animals nor plants. The father of life taught us this."

Such reverence for the earth is general among western Indians.[2] It was said by one man that he believed the sun, the moon, and Heammawihio to represent the same person.

[1] According to Wautan (an Arapaho) Chiva Niatha means Niatha above, or the good God. They asked blessings from him; he is the owner of all the land. Niatha below he thinks is the same; he is also called the Owner of the Ground. When they smoke, they say, "Owner of the Ground, smoke," meaning the underground God; there is no name for him. The medicine men in smoking point the stem of the pipe to the four points of the compass, then up and down, but other people make only the last two motions.

[2] *American Anthropologist*, vol. IX, p. 3, Jan.-Mar., 1907.

The sacrifice to the four directions, called nivstanivoo, is offered that the owner of the lodge may live long, and that his lodge may be firm on the ground and may not blow down. It is believed by some that the four spirits who live in the four directions (possibly, as some say, the winds which blow from the four directions) exercise a potent influence over the lives and fortunes of people. These are all well disposed and friendly. Nevertheless, they are to be propitiated.

When Heammawihio first made people, he made them to live. When they died they were to be dead for only four nights, and then they would live again. After a little time the Creator found that this would not do. It would have made people too brave, and they would have done too much killing. That is why now people die forever. If it had continued as at first, people would have been like the bald eagle. You may go out and kill a bald eagle, and take him home and use his feathers, and in four days, if you go back to the place where you killed him, you will again find the bald eagle on or near its nest.

At one time Heammawihio was with the people on the earth. He it was who taught them how to make stone arrowpoints, and knives of stone and bone for cutting. He instructed them how to take the arrowpoints he had taught them to make, and to put them on shafts, showed them how to make a bow, and how to use the arrows for shooting. He told them that the animals, the buffalo, the elk, and the deer—all the animals that are on the earth—and the birds of different kinds, were for them to kill and subsist on. They made their fire, as he taught them, with two sticks rubbed together till the fire started, and also by knocking together two hard stones.

In those days Heammawihio told them that there existed many other peoples that they had never seen, and that after a time they would meet them; they would find all these people armed as they were, with stone arrows, and stone and bone knives; he had taught all the people on the land the same way to live.

Heammawihio showed them the corn, and told them to plant, and cultivate, and eat it, saying that after a long time all people would learn to plant and raise grain, and to grow other things for their subsistence. On the other side of the big water, he said, a different people were living, and a day would come when these people would cross over to this side of that water, and they would see them. A time would come when there would be wars, and many people would be killed.[3]

After Heammawihio had been long with them and had taught them how to live, he told them that he was going up to the sky, that he would watch over them, and that when they died they should come to him; while they were on earth they might have much trouble, but when they died all would go up into the sky and live with him.

PLACE OF THE DEAD

✷ *Sēyăn'* (?),[4] the place of the dead, is above, where Heammawihio lives. Those who die are with him, excepting only those who have killed themselves. Brave and cowardly, good and bad alike, go there. All who have died are equal. After death there is neither reward for virtue nor punishment for sin. The spirit of the one who has died goes up above to Heammawihio. Seyan is reached by following the Hanging Road, the Milky Way (*Ē kŭt sĭ hĭm' mī yo*). There the dead live as they lived on earth—they chase buffalo, hunt other game, and go to war. Occasionally people who have been very sick believe that they have died and gone to this country, and then have returned again, but they seem never actually to reach these camps of the dead. They perhaps come within a short distance of the village, and may meet and talk with people coming from and going to it, but they never quite reach it. Before doing so they return to life. They describe the camps, and tell of the white lodges hand-

---

[3] By some men these acts and prophecies are credited to the culture hero Mŏtsĭ ĭ" ŭ ĭv.

[4] *Sehăn'*, "dead," Petter Dictionary, p. 344, Kettle Falls, Wash.

somely painted, the people passing to and fro, the scaffolds hung with drying meat, the women tanning robes, all the sights and sounds of a camp, just as they know it here.

Picking Bones Woman—sister of Red Eagle, a Northern Cheyenne doctor—when eighty-four years of age (born about 1818) told me of her experience about fifty-four years earlier (1848) when she had died and gone to the place of the dead.

Not very long after she had been married, she was very ill on the South Canadian. One morning, just after the sun had risen, she was sitting, bent over, when someone called to her: "Picking Bones, they want you over there! Your mother wants you!" Her mother had long been dead.

She arose and left the lodge and went straight north. She did not walk on the ground; she was running, but her feet did not touch the ground—they seemed to move a little way above it. She looked neither to the right nor left, but straight before her. She felt as if she were flying. As she looked down, the grass appeared yellowish-red before her. All at once she came to the top of a hill, and looking at the ground before her, it seemed green. Then just in front of her she saw a big bluff, and in it a door. She ran right up against the door, and when she struck it, it opened and she fell through the door on her left side. She felt the unevenness of the ground against her body as she lay there.

Someone spoke to her, and said, "Your mother has gone back." She did not see the face of the person who spoke, but she saw his legs from the knees down; he wore blue striped leggings. As she rose to her feet, she saw old men sitting all about her. They had their hair dressed in different ways, according to the old-time fashion, some of them having it tied up in great bunches on the forehead. The bodies of all were naked, but all wore buffalo-robes about their waists and legs. One man who sat nearest to her she recognized; it was Red Water, who had been dead a long time. The person who had spoken to her, spoke again, saying, "You must take this baby

92

back with you; it is your husband's child." She stretched out her arms, and he put into them the naked child, which she held.

She then went out the door and came back to her lodge just as she had gone from it, but carrying the baby before her. While she was going back she did not touch the ground, but went just as if she were flying. She remembers reaching her home and going in, holding the baby. Her husband was sitting there, and she said to him, "Here is your child; take it." She handed it to him. Then she turned and looked at her bed, and saw there her body lying on the bed. She does not know how her spirit went back to the body, but when she came to herself she was sitting up. She rose to her feet, and when she did so she felt well.

Her body had not been gone from the lodge. No baby had been in the lodge.

SOUL OR SHADE

A man's spirit or living principle is called his shade or shadow, *tăsŏōm'*; that is, the soul, mind, or spiritual part; not the body, the immortal part. Tasoom is also the shadow of any animate thing, as a man, horse, bird, or dog. It is not the shadow of a tree, a rock, or a building. Of a dying person who has lost consciousness and merely breathes, they may say, "His tasoom has been gone a long time; he is only just breathing."

Those who die become shadows, or spirits. If a man sees his shade, it is a sign that he will soon die. A sick man may send for a friend to come to him, and say: "Well, my friend, I have sent for you that I may see you once more, for I am about to die. I have seen my shadow."

Women saw their shadows more often than men, and with them the vision was not certainly followed by death. If an old woman had been badly frightened, she might say, "I was so badly frightened that I saw my shadow." The idea seems to be that her life was literally frightened out of her body, and for a moment stood before her. The shadow is a mere shape, seen

93

for an instant, and then gone. It is like a shadow in having no detail; no clothing, no features—a silhouette.

Years ago Indians commonly refused to be photographed, because they believed that when the picture was taken away the life of the subject was taken away too, and the actual man would die. They regarded the photographic print as the man's shadow. In the same way, in early days when little trade mirrors were first received, many people refused to look into them, because they would see their shadows, and bad luck would follow.

CARDINAL DIRECTIONS

The wind comes from the west, from the quarter whence the snow comes. A great whirlwind coming up from the ground always blows there, and from this comes the wind. Whenever a great windstorm passes by, it never comes from any direction except from the west; it never comes from the south, east, or north.

The cardinal points are:

Nōtŭm' (?), Where the cold wind comes from—the North.
Nŭm' hāisto (?), Where the cold wind goes to—the South.
Ĭsh' ĭ tsĭs ĭss' ĭ mĭ ĭs', Where the sun comes up—the East.
Ĭsh' ĭ tsĭs' tā kĭt ā ĕs', Where the sun goes over—the West.

The Cheyennes believe that toward the north the ground slopes upward, and thus being higher, is colder. Toward the south it slopes down, and is lower, and so grows warmer.

NATURAL PHENOMENA

A place is told of, far to the north, where there are always clouds, and the sun can never shine through them to heat anything. From this place comes a being known as *Hō ĭm' ă hă*, who brings the winter. Hoimaha appears as a man, who is white. He comes in a white cloud from the north, and when he approaches he says to the Sun: "I am coming. I am coming. Back away now, because I am going to make it cold all over the

94

land!" As he comes on, he spreads this cold all over a wide country, and it is cold everywhere.

When Hoimaha came in winter, and it snowed, and it was thought that too much snow was likely to fall, the people used to be called together and to have a feast. Then they filled the pipe, offered it to Hoimaha, calling him "Father," and "Grandfather above," and prayed to him, asking him to stop the snow from falling so that they might be able to kill their food animals, and eat and live.

In the spring, as the Sun gets higher and higher, he says to the cold: "Go back now whence you came. I wish to heat the earth, and to make the grass and all things grow." Then the cold goes back.

So it is that each one has its power. At one time that person overpowers, and again the Sun overpowers. They follow each other back and forth.

The Thunder often appears as a great bird, somewhat like an eagle, but much larger. Sometimes he is seen riding on a white horse. Old men have said that it was Heammawihio who made the Thunderbird; it was his bird. In the ancient days, if they lost their arrows which had been given them by Motsiiu, or if they forgot how to make them, then this bird would instruct them.

The Thunderbird makes the thunder and lightning and storm. It goes south at the approach of winter, and returns from the warm country with the Sun, bringing the heat and the rain. It shoots an arrow, but they never see it. Sometimes it kills people and animals, but they do not see the arrow. Rarely, however, they find one of the old stone arrowpoints, which some people think is the head of the Thunderbird's arrow.

A certain species of butterfly, gray in color, with blue eyes, and with rounded and black striped wings, is called the thunder parasite (*nā' nō mī' hĭs tĭ ĭm*). These butterflies are oftenest seen just before or after a thunderstorm, and while the report of thunder is heard, hence the name. The belief seems to be that

95

the Thunderbird, when angry, shakes himself, and his parasites fall from him.

When the Thunder began in spring, they used to fill the pipe, offer a smoke to the Thunder, and ask him to take pity on them. They sang and prayed, saying: "Far back, many of our people have died and are gone. We are now a poor people. Take pity on us. Give us food of all kinds on the earth, and we will all eat together and be friends." They prayed to the Thunder because he was bringing the warmth, and asked him to make the berries and all things grow. This ceremony is described as much like the Blackfoot ceremony to the Thunder.

When the Thunder, bringing the rain from the south, brought too much rain, they went through the same ceremony as to Hoimaha in winter, addressing prayers to the Thunder, calling him "Father," and "Grandfather above," and asking him to stop the rain. This was long ago.

The rainbow, *no nŭn' o*, is regarded as a device for catching something, a trap. The same word is used for fishing line, or for any other device by which animals are caught. When the rainbow appears, the rain almost stops falling; hence the rainbow is regarded as having caught or trapped the thunder, that is, the rain, and caused the storm to cease.

WATER SPIRITS AND MONSTERS

Spirits or powers dwell in the springs, in the rivers, in the hills, and in certain high bluffs. Sacrifices are offered and prayers made at such places—for example, at the Painted Rocks, on the west side of the Rosebud, six or seven miles below Lamedeer, Montana, where pictures have been painted, and in a similar place, with pictures, in the Big Horn Mountains. The spirits are in no respect harmful, but there is a possibility that they may become offended and then may work injury to human beings. As their power is great, it is important that they be propitiated with sacrifices and gifts, and made

BRAVE WOLF
ONE OF GENERAL MILES' SCOUTS

favorable, so that this power may be exercised in one's behalf. Usually spirits are not seen, but they may take material form.

Like the Blackfeet, the Cheyennes believe in under-water people and under-water monsters. The under-water people were not unlike those who live on the prairie; they possessed buffalo, and led a life similar to that of ordinary people. These under-water people, however, appear to have had the power of changing their form; but this may not have been a characteristic of them as under-water people; rather it may merely have been evidence of their unusual powers.

Under-water monsters were of various sorts, and, whether harmful or not, they were alarming.

In some bodies of water there are said to live great snakes.

One under-water monster was the *mĭh'n'*,[5] described as somewhat like a very large lizard, with one or two horns on the head, and often covered, or partly covered, with hair. Sometimes these monsters caught people who went into the water, and swallowed them. The Thunderbird has been known to kill these monsters.[6] Usually but a single one lives in a lake, or in a considerable stretch of river. The mihn is not necessarily harmful. If people pray and offer sacrifices to it, they are likely to have good fortune, but if they treat it disrespectfully, they will have bad luck.

Although in these days no one professes ever to have seen these monsters, many stories are told of the mihn. This animal is said sometimes to have seized, or overturned, a bull-boat when people were crossing the Missouri River, and those in the boat were not seen again.

A story referring to this monster resembles in some respects a Pawnee tale:[7]

A long time ago, when we still lived far to the north, two young

[5] *Mĭh'*, singular; *mĭh' nĭō*, plural, applied to a mythical animal inhabiting water, and sometimes to a very large snake.
[6] A concept perhaps borrowed from the Dakotas.
[7] Pawnee Hero Stories and Folk Tales, p. 171, "The Snake Brother."

men wandered away from the camp to search for eggs. They separated, but were to meet on the shores of a lake not far off.

When they came together, one of them showed his companion two eggs that he had found, unlike any eggs that they had ever seen; they were white and large. The young man who found them said to his friend, "Let us eat these eggs here; they seem to be nicer and better than the other eggs, and I feel like eating them."

The other said: "No, those are strange eggs. I have never seen any like them, and I am afraid to eat of them."

The one who had found the eggs ate one of them, and again offered the other to his friend, saying that the one he had eaten tasted good. The other again refused to eat. His friend was about to eat the second himself, but before he did so he began to feel strangely, and his desire to eat left him. He said to his friend: "Come, let us go on. I am feeling very strangely. I never felt like this before. Something must be the matter with me." The two young men started toward camp.

After they had walked some distance, the man who had eaten the egg said to his companion: "I am feeling more and more strangely. I must soon find water into which I can plunge. Let us go out of our way to reach some water. My desire for it grows stronger and stronger. I can no longer control it. I must get to deep water." The two turned aside from their way to go toward a lake not far off.

Now his companion noticed that the young man who had eaten the egg was changing in appearance. His head was growing larger, and very ugly and terrible. As they came near to the water, the one who was in trouble said to the other: "You must go back to the camp without me; I shall not be seen there again. I know now that I am changing into a mihn, and I shall always remain in the water."

By the time they reached the water, the young man had changed into a fearful-looking animal, with a big head and a mouth large enough to swallow a person, and a short horn. The mihn person plunged into the water and disappeared. The other young man went to the camp and told the wonderful story.

Āhke[8] is another under-water monster, which lives in springs.

[8] *Āh'ke,* singular; *āhkī'yo,* plural, a four-legged monster which lives in water, but also comes out and walks about over the land. Compare the water bull of the Blackfeet.

It is described as being like a bull. Offerings are made at springs supposed to be inhabited by such a monster. The word ahk means "of stone," "petrified," and the large fossil bones sometimes found along streams or on the prairie are said to belong to ahk.

A harmful creature of great power was the so-called double-toothed bull (*hĭ'stōwŭnĭnĭ'hōtū'a*), that is, a buffalo-bull with incisors in both the upper and the lower jaw. It is described as a small, humpless buffalo, with small, sharp, polished horns, and a short snout. This animal was supposed to come into the camp and eat people. The Shoshonis are said to have been the last people to have been visited by this monster. In some way they killed it, though it had always been supposed to be invulnerable.

GHOSTS

Ghosts are greatly feared. As a rule these do not seem to work much actual harm, but they come about and whistle and frighten people. If a person should be where there were too many ghosts, they might draw his mouth down on one side, and it would remain so. Such things are said to have happened.

Mĭs'tāi, ghost (not usually of a person), is very rarely seen, but is often felt or heard. Sometimes when one is walking at night through the timber, where it is very dark, a ghost may seize robe or blanket and give it a tug. Ghosts sometimes scratch or tap on the lodge-skins, or make strange and mysterious noises just outside the lodge. People who are walking through the timber at night are likely to sing loudly, or to utter loud calls, to frighten away the ghosts; and generally when the ghosts show that they are near at hand, anyone who possesses spiritual power will sing a medicine song to drive them away. Ghosts are believed to be from the dead, but there is scarcely anything in common to mistai and tasoom, except the fact that both are from the dead. Mistai is always alarming, but never,

99

so far as known, does any actual harm. It seems to take pleasure in frightening people, and to be somewhat like the white man's idea of a hobgoblin, or malicious elf. On the other hand, mistai may take various forms, or perhaps there may be several kinds.

Mistai also means owl, sometimes a mysterious one, and sometimes just an ordinary owl; usually the great horned owl (*Bubo*), but sometimes the little screech owl (*Megascops*). They say that the owl is not a natural bird, and that some owls are the ghosts of people. People who hear an owl cry may be able to tell whose ghost it is that is speaking.

The ghost of a person is called *sī'yŭhk*, which appears to mean rather the skeleton of a person. A pile of human bones would be called siyuhk. Some people declare that it is the siyuhk that taps on the lodge-skins, whistles down the smoke-hole, and makes queer noises near the lodge; nevertheless, when they hear these noises, people usually say: "What is that? It must be a mistai."

As might be supposed, there is much confusion in the popular mind as to the qualities and relations of these different kinds of spirits.

Wolf Chief was once camped at Colony, Oklahoma, where Foster's store stood in 1905. It was a moonlight night and he was feeding his mules near his lodge; after feeding, he led them to the hill to picket them. As he was returning, he passed by the lodge of a very old woman, named Root Woman, and saw someone peeping in through her lodge door. Wolf Chief did not know who it was, but stopped when opposite her lodge. While he stood there, this person turned and came toward him. Wolf Chief paid no special attention to him till he saw him stand in the path, with his head and shoulders partly bent over. Wolf Chief then thought that someone was trying to play a trick on him, and reached his hand out and tried to touch the person, but could not do so. Every time he reached out his hand, the

person would disappear and then reappear again. By th
Wolf Chief knew that it was a ghost and went back t
lodge as fast as he could. The ghost then went back to R
Woman's lodge and dragged her out, dislocating her arm. Sh
crawled up to Wolf Chief's lodge and told him about it. Her
arm after that was always weak and loose at the shoulder.

In 1852 there was a large camp on Smoky Hill River, Kansas. One moonlight night several young men came into the
lodge of Wolf Chief's mother, and Wolf Chief asked her to
cook food for them. She said, "I have no water; wait until I go
and get some." His mother and another woman and five boys
went off after water. It had been raining and there was a pool
near the edge of the camp. They dipped up the water and
started back toward the lodge, when the dogs, which had gone
with them, began to bark and looked toward the pool. They
listened and heard someone coming toward them shaking his
robe, but could see no one. The person was making a noise,
"*Hŭn, hŭn, hŭn!*" The women dropped the buckets and ran
toward the lodge; when they got there, they declared that a
ghost had chased them and they had dropped their buckets and
run. Wolf Chief said that he and the young men would go back
with them and get the water. One of the young men, named
Bear Shield, took a gun. They all went out, picked up the
buckets, and got some more water. The young men said to the
women, "Which way did the ghost come from?" The women
pointed to a dark place near the pool. After the women had got
the water, they went back to the lodge, but the young men
stood there and presently heard the same noise. Bear Shield
started to run, but one of the others stopped him and said,
"Give me your gun." They crouched down to look, and could
see something like a person walking, but he seemed up in the
air, above the ground. The man who had the gun fired at the
thing. After he had fired, the ghost called out "*E-e-e-e-e!*" and
went off in the direction of the timber. They all said, "He calls

out just as if some man was calling to another." They walked back very fast to the lodge and went in.

Little Big Jake—Man Above—had his lodge down near the timber. After everyone had gone to bed, the ghost began throwing buffalo-chips against Little Big Jake's lodge, and then against all the other lodges. All were afraid to go out. The ghost kept the camp awake all night. In the morning, the whole village moved as early as possible. They did not even wait for breakfast. Long before the date mentioned there had been a fight at this place between the Cheyennes and Pawnees, in which all the Pawnees were killed. It was thought that the ghost was the spirit of one of the Pawnees.

When Wolf Chief was very young, one winter long before the big cholera year (1849), the Hair Rope People moved to the South Platte. Yellow Wolf was their leader. When they arrived, they found a large camp of Cheyennes already there, and they made camp not far off. The women from this camp came to meet them, and said: "Why don't you camp closer to us? There is a ghost here, which comes every night and chases all the people into their lodges. No one dares to go out after sundown." That evening the other village invited the men of the Hair Rope People to come to a feast, and soon after dark, all the dogs in their village began to bark, but they could find no reason for it. Someone said, "Maybe that is the ghost"; but others said, "No, they are probably barking at the wolves and coyotes." Wolf Chief was in his father's lodge, the door of which was a Mexican blanket hanging in front. The dogs began to run into the lodge. As all the men were away, the women crowded together at one side of the lodge and they could hear a robe being dragged around the lodge on the snow; it was moonlight. As the ghost went by, it threw open the door of their lodge and did the same to all the other lodges. Again they heard it coming, and this time the ghost tore the blanket off the doorway. Then they heard nothing more. Wolf Chief's mother went out and hung another door on the lodge. After a time the men came back and the women told them what had happened. Wolf Chief's father said, "I think some young fellow has been playing ghost to frighten you." Next morning they could not find the Mexican blanket, but some people who were driving horses to water saw, out on the river, the blanket spread open on the ice and on it a human skull. They told of this and both camps went down to see it. One of the men was cutting a hole in the ice to water his horses, when a medicine man said to him, "Give me your axe." This medicine man went up to the skull and cut a hole in the ice near it; then wrapped the skull in the blanket and pushed it into the water and under the ice. The ghost never again troubled the camp. Wolf Chief's father and mother saw the skull, but he was afraid to go down and see it himself.

A person once saw a mistai which was like a gigantic human being, with bristling hair standing on end on the head. It made a grunting sound as it walked—a sound like the hooting of a great horned owl.

When camp is made near the timber or mountains, and rocks on which lichen grows are at hand, ghosts—if any are about— may be driven away by burning this moss in the fire at night.

ANIMAL BELIEFS

As with most prairie tribes, the buffalo was greatly reverenced. Before the entrance of every sweat-lodge, propped up against a sagebrush, a pile of stones, or a mound of earth, stands an old buffalo-skull. A very long time ago, a medicine man's dream told him to make a sweat-house, and then to take the skull of a bull—one that had been killed for a long time—and to put it in front of the sweat-house, and then to go in and take a sweat. When he came out, he should fill the pipe and hold the pipe to Heammawihio, and ask him always to keep plenty of buffalo on the earth for the people to eat. He must present the pipe to the skull also, and smoke to it, and must ask the skull to rise to its feet, clothe itself with flesh, and come to life, so that the people might have its meat to eat, and its skin to make their lodges. At the same time they prayed to the buffalo in general, asking them to travel over smooth ground, not to run where it was rough and where there was danger that the horses might fall and break men's limbs.

Sometimes the buffalo-bulls talked to them, and sometimes the elk and the bear. It was always a male that talked. Not everyone could understand their language. Only now and then a person understood.

The deer has much power, which may be used for good or for evil. The mule-deer is a great spiritual helper. From the cavities beneath the eyes, it possesses the power to shoot disease-arrows at a man; or, if a doctor carries the tail of one it will help him so to afflict a person whom he may wish to harm. On the other hand, if favorably inclined, the mule-deer may help a person in many ways. As elsewhere pointed out, the white-tail deer is a powerful helper in love affairs. While the deer's power may be used for good or for evil, the power of the antelope is all good. To dream about an antelope is fortunate.

Elk have great power, and are hard to kill. They can endure a great deal. If a man dreams of an elk, it will be a great help to him. The elk has power like that of the mule-deer, but it is stronger.

The beaver was reverenced to some extent, no doubt because of the intelligence which was attributed to it, from the fact that beavers built dams to raise the waters in streams, and houses to live in. It is said that in very old times beavers were not often killed, and that no Cheyenne woman would dress or even handle a beaver-skin. There was no such feeling about the otter —regarded by the Blackfeet as related to the beaver. The Cheyennes have always killed the otter, using its skin to make bow-cases and quivers, and also to wrap about the braids of the hair.

The skunk possesses power. Doctors used its hide to hold their medicine. Men tied its tail to their horses' tails in war.

It is engraved in ornament on the seeds employed by women in gambling, and is painted on robes and lodges.

The Cheyennes still consider the badger very powerful. In ancient times it talked to people, if they met it on the prairie, and advised them what they ought to do and how they should live. They still pray to the badger and smoke to him, and often offer him a portion of the food when they eat, saying as they offer it, *"Mā' āh kū tsĭt o mǐss' ĭ"*; that is, "Badger, eat." When the pipe is offered to the earth, it is thought to be offered in part to the badger.

The bear possesses power—spiritual power. He can heal himself, and can heal other bears. He is a great medicine animal. In old times no Cheyenne woman might dress a bear-skin.

Eagles, ravens, hawks, owls, and magpies are birds which possessed power in matters concerning war. This attribute was no doubt assigned to them because they capture their prey and subsist on flesh. Because of this power, their feathers were used to attach to shields. While on his war journey a man sometimes wore the stuffed skin of a raven tied to his scalp-lock, and this skin often warned him of danger by talking to him. All birds of whatever kind had some power.

In ancient times no one killed wolves or coyotes, and women would not handle their skins. Even today some women will not handle a wolf-skin or a coyote-skin. Coyotes have always been more sacred than wolves, possibly because they are more intelligent. The people used to pray to the coyotes, asking them to lead, guide, and warn them. Some men could interpret the howling of wolves and coyotes.

If the sun rises on a wolf asleep, it dies. It must have lain during the night and slept until the sun rose. During the day it can lie down and sleep in the sun.

A man who could understand the speech of the wolves would turn back if a wolf or a coyote were killed by any member of a war-party with which he was journeying. These animals were seldom killed by the Cheyennes in old times, possibly because the medicine arrows were always wrapped up in the skin of a coyote.

Once, in 1858, Dives Backward, who could understand what the coyotes said when they howled, was with a war-party to the south, which had just reached the Rio Grande del Norte, when a coyote was heard to howl close to the camp.

"Hold on," said Dives Backward. "Across that big river are some lodges of people whom we ought to attack." They crossed the river and went on. Before they reached the place, they joined a war-party of Arapahoes, and a little later a coyote howled again, telling them that the enemy were close by. They found the camp,—six lodges of Utes,—attacked it, and captured Yellow Nose, then four years of age, and his mother, who afterward escaped.

Once some young men who were on the war-path captured some young wolves, which they were going to eat. Before they killed them they heard someone singing, not far off. They did not know who this might be, and listened. The purport of the song was that if the young men would spare her children, and take pity on her, they would not have bad luck. They kept looking all about to see who it was that was singing, and at last discovered that it was a she-wolf. They set her children free, and next morning had gone only a little way farther when they killed a Pawnee.

About 1854 or 1855, William Rowland was in the Cheyenne camp in the late autumn. About nine or ten o'clock at night a coyote near at hand set up a great howling. Soon after this an old man went around through the camp and announced that the wolf had been talking to him, and that it had told him that a war-party of Pawnees was near, and was about to attack the camp; that all must be prepared. The next morning the camp was attacked by Pawnees, who were driven off.

Gentle Horse once told me of an old man who declared that the wolves advised him what to do, and gave him medicine so that he could turn himself into a wolf. He could understand what the wolves said when they howled. A wolf would come on a hill and howl, and the man would understand what it said. Perhaps the wolf would say to the people, "Just behind this hill that I am standing on there are enemies." They generally found the enemies just where the wolf told them they were. In old times there were men who understood the talk of various animals, and of different birds, as crows and magpies.

I shall later refer to the gift of prophecy derived through the wolves by Horn and transmitted by him to his son, Brave Wolf.

As with all other Indians, a high value is set on eagle-feathers. They prize chiefly the feathers of the gray eagle (*H. leucocephalus*). The speckle-tailed eagle, that is, the golden eagle (*Aquila chrysaëtos*), seems to have been the least esteemed of the three kinds which they knew. They secured many eagle-feathers by finding an eagle's nest in spring, and taking the young and rearing them in captivity. After the eagles had reached full size they pulled out the tail-feathers three times. After they had been pulled out the first time they grew again, and the second and third time; but after that they would not grow again. They thus obtained thirty-six feathers from an eagle. If secured soon after they were hatched, the young eagles were easily reared. They were kept tethered by the legs to a pin driven in the ground.

As before mentioned, two or three generations ago the Cheyennes caught eagles as did other Plains tribes, but of late years they have not used these eagle traps.

Eagles possessed great power. Once a young man went out and found a nest, and took from it two eaglets still covered with down. He reared them, killed them, and took the feathers. The next year he did the same thing. No matter where the camp might be, at the proper time of the year this young man went back to this nest to get the eagles. The third year he did the same thing; and the fourth time he went he brought two eagles from the nest.

There was a big camp of Cheyennes, and these eagles, staked out near this young man's lodge, used to make a good deal of noise whistling, as eagles do. This young man was well-to-do, and had a large, fine lodge. The eagles were tied behind it, able to fly only the length of their ropes. One day the young man was sitting in his lodge when he heard eagles whistling up in the air. He went out and looked up, and saw many eagles flying about, high above his lodge, and whistling, as if calling to their young. The young birds in the camp were excited, and kept flying and whistling, and at last, as they flew backward and forward, the ropes became loosened from their feet and they escaped, and flew upward toward the others. As the young man watched the eagles flying, his hands began to move up and down, and to flap like wings, and presently he began to move upward, flying toward the eagles. He kept going higher and higher, until at last he disappeared. The young man was never seen again.

The bald eagle is the strongest bird that flies. Once a young buffalo-calf was found in a bald eagle's nest. The eagle must have carried it thither, which shows its great strength.

Owing to the protective power of the bird, a man wearing a war-bonnet of gray-eagle feathers believed that he would not be hit by either bullets or arrows. These bonnets were worn, therefore, not merely because they made a man look fine, but for protection as well. Some men, however, would not wear war-bonnets, because they made one conspicuous; and the enemy was more likely to shoot at a man wearing a war-bonnet than at one without the decoration. War whistles were often made from wing-bones of eagles.

Another bird that possesses strong power to keep one from being hit in battle is the blue hawk—perhaps the duck hawk. Small swift hawks—sparrow-hawks—possess protective power. The belief seems to be founded on their swiftness and activity.

A famous example of the protective power of this hawk is cited in the well-known case of old Whirlwind (died 1891), who in the celebrated fight with the Sauk and Fox[9] had every feather of his war-bonnet shot away, but was not himself hit, nor was the hawk on his war-bonnet touched.

The little prairie owls are believed also to have protective power, and the Contraries wear them on the head. The night owl was a great medicine helper, especially strong in matters connected with lightning. Owl-feathers were worn on the head and on the arms, giving to the wearer certain powers possessed by the owl, as silence in moving about and the power to see at night.

Woodpeckers likewise possessed great powers. Parts of their bodies were used in the ceremony of the Medicine Lodge, and their feathers were often worn as helpful talismans and ornamented war-charms and war-clubs. They were much used on war implements, not merely because they were pretty, but because of the bird's spiritual power. This power had, perhaps, some relation to the birds' life in trees and hence indirectly to growing vegetation.

According to the Cheyenne small boys, the meadow-larks, when they return in spring, say in their whistling, *Wĭt ăn ī' yo-he năn hē' ŭhkt*, meaning, "I have come from Tallow River" (the South Platte River).

The sandhill crane was also believed to possess strong protective power. As before remarked, its feathers and the skin of the head were used as ornaments for shields. The heads were fastened on the center of the shield. A long time ago a man dreamed about the cranes, the dream telling him that when he went into a fight he should imitate their cry. It was generally believed that if in a fight a man imitated the call of a sandhill crane, he would not be hit by a bullet. Carrying out the same idea of the crane's protective power, war-whistles were often made from the wing-bones of the crane. This bird was believed

[9] The Fighting Cheyennes, p. 99.

to take pity on everybody. It also had special power in matters connected with lightning.

They consider the chickadee (*Penthestes*) a meat-eater. The chickadee is called "the bird that tells us that summer is coming." It is a wise bird and knows that summer is coming, and it goes about and tells the people. Its cry is *mehnew'*, with a rising inflection. The Cheyennes would say, *mehaniv'*; that is, "Summer is coming." The chickadee's name has thus precisely the same meaning as with the Blackfeet.

Sometimes a magpie would fly up close to where men sat, and would alight on a tree, and make a noise, talking. If anyone in the party understood the speech of the bird, he would say to the rest: "Now, watch this bird. Whichever way he flies, from that direction enemies are coming."

In the old days, sometimes when the buffalo had disappeared a raven would come to the camp, and fly over it calling, and would say to the people: "Now watch me, and the direction in which I go. Follow me, and you will find buffalo close by."

The little, quick-moving lizards seen among the rocks were helpers. Figures of them cut from rawhide were frequently worn to bring good luck, and quite generally in the Medicine Lodge. A man who was enduring suffering to pay a vow or to obtain power, was likely to wear one of these figures. They were made by medicine men, and sold, or given away. The Cheyennes did not like to kill these little lizards, and if by accident a man did so, he made some little gift to it as a propitiatory offering. Perhaps before going away he would tie a bit of red string about its neck. This lizard typifies activity and swift motion. It is never long quiet. It is a powerful war-charm and gives courage to one who wears its image, the power to get about quickly and to avoid arrows and bullets.

The little deerskin charms containing the dried fragments of the umbilical cord, and tied to the clothing of children up to the age of six or seven years, often have the shape of a lizard or a turtle. This charm has wide currency. It is common to the

Sioux, Cheyennes, and Arapahoes, and more than a hundred years ago Mackenzie observed the same thing among the Chipewyans in the North. He says, "The women have a singular custom of cutting off a small piece of the navel string of new-born children, which they hang about the neck. They enclose it in a case made of buckskin, which they decorate with porcupine quills and beads."[10]

It is believed that one of the swift lizards, or a horned toad, can kill any snake instantly by running across its body or along its back.

Newts, water-dogs, or mud-puppies, have power, too. If a person has leg-ache, and sets his bare foot on one, he will be cured. Women greatly fear these animals, however, dreading lest they get hold of the skin of the breast and draw it all into their bodies. Almost exactly the same fear exists among Blackfeet women. Nevertheless, a woman may kill one of them, and taking her little child up to it, may cause the child to put its bare foot on the animal, in order to cure leg-ache. Sometimes, with the same purpose, the figure of a lizard or a newt may be sketched with charcoal on the sole of the foot.

Most aquatic animals possess some mysterious power.

A spider is a "medicine" animal.

In old times, when there were buffalo, the Indians sometimes captured the great black prairie cricket, and asked it where they should go to find buffalo. The cricket was held lightly in the hand and, after it had become quiet, the direction in which its antennæ pointed was noted; and usually, by following that direction, buffalo were found. If one antenna was pointed backward, this indicated that in that direction there were a few buffalo. The belief in this sign is still held by some of the Indians.

Two other sorts of insects are frequently tied to the hair for charms in war—the dragonfly and the butterfly. The butterfly

[10] Mackenzie, Voyages from Montreal, on the River St. Lawrence, through the Continent of North America, 1801, p. cxxii.

is used because it is light and irregular in flight; it makes the person wearing it light and active. The dragonfly, called whirl-wind (*tē wō wītŭs'* ?), because it makes a little whirlwind—though it is not seen in the whirlwind, only the dust being visible—will make the man wearing it hard to see and hard to hit. Neither of these creatures is ever long motionless. Both typify swiftness and activity, and give the wearer ability to move about swiftly, and to escape bullets and arrows. Both are painted on shields. Some men when going into battle paint on their bodies the figure of a dragonfly. The war-bonnet worn by Roman Nose, who was killed in the Beecher Island fight (1868), had dragonflies painted all down the strips of buffalo-hide that supported the feathers.

PROPHETS OR SEERS

Anciently there were believed to be prophets or seers—men or women who could announce what was about to happen or could tell what might be occurring at the time at a distance. Persons possessing this gift of prophecy received their knowl-edge in different ways, from birds or animals, as already sug-gested, or from their dreams or secret helpers. Horn, later named Blind Bull, formerly had this power in high degree. He was born toward the end of the eighteenth century and was the father of Brave Wolf, also known as Box Elder or Maple (died about 1885), and to Brave Wolf the father had taught all that he knew. This knowledge came to Horn, and later to his son, through the wolves, though they did not give him his power; they were only the messengers who brought it. His power came from the maiyun. The wolves with whom these two men communicated told Brave Wolf that he would die of old age; he would not be killed in battle; yet he was much on the war-path and often in danger.

His power was such that he always knew what was going to happen. Before starting on one of his early war-paths he pre-dicted that he would bring back captives, and he returned with

A SWEAT LODGE

WITH BUFFALO SKULL, SAGE, AND FORKED STICKS

four captured Pawnee women. A second time he foretold that he would bring back captives; he did so. His predictions are reported always to have been realized.

The warnings conveyed by dreams greatly influenced these people. Most of them were encouraged by favorable, or depressed by bad, dreams, though there were some who did not greatly regard them. As a rule, however, an unfavorable dream would divert a man from any enterprise.

Helpful spirits appeared to them in dreams. A man who went out on the hills to suffer might have some maiyu appear to him in his sleep, and thereafter the spirit which appeared was his special protecting power, or secret helper. Such helpers did not usually appear to men before they were twenty years of age; often not until after they had been to war, and perhaps been through the ceremonies of the Medicine Lodge. The power which appeared might have the form of bird, mammal, or person. It advised the man how to act, and might promise to help him. Such a helper is called *mā ĭ yŭn a hŭh' ta,* "a spirit told me in sleep."

Some men had the power to call to them this secret helper, from whom they might ask advice or information. This was not always done in the same way, for different men employed different methods. Usually many people were present, and singers were always asked into the lodge. The man unwrapped his sacred things; the singers chanted their spiritual songs, and the fire was permitted to die down, until the lodge was dark. Before the fire was out, the man who was calling the spirit was tied with four bowstrings. Each finger of each hand was tied separately to the next finger, in a hard knot, and the ends of the bowstrings on each hand were tied together, behind his back, so that his hands were tightly bound there. His feet were tied together in the same way, each toe being tied to the next one in a hard knot, and the feet bound together by the bowstrings. Thus tied, he sat at the back of the lodge, and sometimes was tied to one of the lodge-poles. At times a little shelter, shaped like a sweat-lodge, was built in the middle of the lodge, and the man was put in that.

After the fire had gone out, in some interval of the singing, the lodge was shaken as if by a strong wind; the poles creaked, and suddenly in the lodge a strange voice was heard, talking to the man. The secret helper was perhaps called to ask where there were buffalo; or where there were enemies; where missing people were; or even where lost horses might be found. Sometimes the secret helper told what was happening at a distance; or perhaps warned the camp of enemies near at hand. After the spirit had gone, and a light had again been made, the man was found to be untied, and the bowstrings were lying in the door, tied in innumerable knots. It was believed that the spirits untied him.

In what is now Oklahoma lived a man who possessed this power in an unusual degree. His name was Stone Forehead. He could call to him his maiyu, and sometimes while he was talking with the spirit, it would call out, "Make a light!" and when the fire had blazed up it would be seen that Stone Forehead had disappeared, although sometimes his rattle would be seen and heard moving alone through the air, as if shaken by a person. Sometimes this man would dance through the camp, carrying in one hand a pole and in the other a drum. Often he threw the drum in the air, and it would fly a long way, then suddenly turn and fly back, come to the end of the pole, and slide down the pole to his hand. He possessed a little ball which he could make fly about in the same way.

Among the Northern Cheyennes, Crazy Mule had strong mysterious power.

During the Medicine Lodge celebration in the summer of 1902, a ceremony was held at which a man was tied with bowstrings and then covered up and the light extinguished. Under the covering was placed a whistle and a pipe. The whistle sounded during the period of darkness. In a few moments the light was renewed, and the man was found to be untied. Dur-

ing the ceremony two young men drummed on two beaded parfleches about one foot wide and eighteen or twenty inches long.
These young men were supposed to represent the male and the
female badger. The ceremony on this occasion was undertaken
for the purpose of learning who had picked up some property
lost from a wagon a few days before. The spirits came in
response to such an invocation, and talked with the man who
was tied up; last of all might come the badger to talk to the
man and answer his questions. The badger was known by his
voice.

The story of a remarkable happening in which White Bull
figured has been current among the Cheyennes ever since it
took place in 1867. White Bull had determined to call to him
his secret helper, which was done in an unusual way. A hole
deep enough for a man to sit in was dug in the ground. The
soldiers went up to the hills and brought down a slab of sandstone, which they placed over the hole in which the man was
to sit. It took a number of men to move this stone. It was too
large to be carried, and could be brought only by being turned
over, end over end. White Bull, tied as above described, was
put in the hole. After the slab had been put over the hole, large
stones were piled on the slab and a lodge was pitched over it.
The singers entered and began to sing their songs. After a time
White Bull's voice was heard down in the hole, talking to a
strange voice. Presently the voices ceased, and nothing more
was heard; but not very long after White Bull walked into the
lodge through the door.

White Bull himself told me the story of this event as he
remembers it:

When I was fifteen years of age I went out into the hills to starve
myself and to pray for power. While I was doing this, there appeared
to me in my dreams a little man whose face was very handsome. He
said to me: "Friend, some day I wish you to dig a big hole in the
ground, and get into it, and then put a big rock over the hole in
which you are. Let the rock be a big one, even if it should be so big

that it would take a number of people to lift it. I will be with you and help you, and will bring you out safely."

It was a long time afterward that we were camped on the Rosebud. There were four camps, three of Sioux and one of Cheyennes. This was thirty-four years ago [in 1867]. It was then that I made up my mind that I would now do what the little man had told me, and I instructed the people to dig the hole, and sent a great crowd of them to go out and bring in a big rock. The Cheyennes were grumbling greatly about it, and said among themselves, "He can never get out of that hole, and the stone is so big that very likely we cannot get it off the hole, and he will die there."

Over the hole there was pitched a lodge so large that three lodge coverings were needed to cover the poles. There was a great gathering and a great feast, and the people ate buffalo-meat and dog-meat and dried fruit. The Cheyennes kept talking about what I was going to do, and said to each other: "Let no one go away who has helped to bring this rock here. He can never get out of this hole, and we shall have to take the rock off again. Since we can remember, nothing of this kind has been attempted—it is foolish!"

A complete buffalo-robe was to be spread over the hole, the head pointing to the rising sun. On the hair-side this robe was painted with a red spot on the right shoulder, a black spot on the right hip, a white spot on the left hip, and a yellow spot on the left shoulder. On the rump was painted the yellow figure of the moon, and on the hump, the red sun, and a red stripe ran down the back—the sun's road or path through the sky.

I was put in the hole, tied hand and foot, just at night. The robe was spread over the hole, and with great labor the stone was put on the hole. On the four corners of the big stone were placed four other stones, each one as large as a strong man could lift. Then over the rock was built the frame of a sweat-house, and this was covered with robes. There were many people in the lodge—three rows deep—and they were beginning to sing their medicine songs.

I sat in the hole under the rock; my hands were tied behind my back by the wrists, and my fingers were tied together with a bow-string. The rope from my wrists ran over my shoulders and tied my feet together at the ankles. My upper arms were tied tightly to my thigh bones. All the ropes were tied tight—by people who did not believe that I could do this thing. I sat there, with my face toward the rising sun [east]. For a little while, after I was put in the hole, I seemed to know nothing that was happening. Then I heard something moving by my side, and I looked, and there was the little man. He patted me on the back and sides, and said to me, "Why have they got you here?"

I answered him, "The people think they are going to be in trouble, and they want help."

The little man said, "Shut your eyes." I did so, and the little man slapped me on the sole of my right foot, and then on the sole of the left, and took me by the hair and seemed to pull me up a little. Then the little man said, "Open your eyes." I did so, and found myself standing on the ground in front of the big lodge.

Standing just in front of me was a woman, who at that very moment called out to the people in the lodge, "Why do you not hurry and sing a medicine song before he gets smothered under that big rock?"

"Who is to be smothered?" I said to her, and she looked back at me and was astonished to see me.

"Let them finish their song," I said, "and then ask them to make a light, and let us have something to eat, for I am hungry."

Soon the news got about outside that I was there, and at length those in the lodge heard of it—they could hardly believe it.

Someone said, "Look in the hole." My wife was the first one to push her head into the sweat-house. She called out: "The rock is moved off the hole. He is not there." The rocks were found piled up on one side of the hole, the robe on top of them, and the ropes and strings, with which I had been tied, on the robe.

AMULETS AND CHARMS

Amulets and charms of many descriptions are carried and worn, and the various reasons for the belief in these protective articles suggest something of the mental processes of the people. Many of these things are put on very young children by their mothers for the purpose of insuring good health, and protecting them from evil influences.

Men very commonly wear stone arrowheads tied in the hair

or about the neck, and usually to the shank of the arrowpoint is tied a little deerskin bundle containing some medicine, usually a part of some plant. They wear these stone arrowpoints in order that they may have long life. This is a part of the general belief as to the endurance, permanence, and perhaps even immortality of stone. When the culture hero, Motsiuiiv, went into the lodge of the maiyun, and was given the medicine arrows, he saw there four men, two of whom afterward proved to be stone, and two, plants. The chief spirit in the lodge told him that he might choose one of these four men whom he desired to resemble. The culture hero chose the wrong man—a mere plant—and was told that if he had chosen either of the stones he would have lived forever.

When going to war men wore certain charms or amulets, which protected them from harm, or warned them of impending danger, or endowed them with qualities of the person or thing represented by the charm. Gentle Horse, who was born in the year 1800, and died at the age of ninety-five, possessed a protector—a lock of hair cut from the head of the son of his father's brother. When his uncle, who had made this charm, gave it to Gentle Horse, he told him that if he would always keep this lock, it would warn Gentle Horse when danger was near. The charm might be carried by one not the owner, if the owner had instructed him in its use. On one occasion Gentle Horse lent this medicine to Stiff Finger, and told him its secrets, just as he was starting off to war. Flocco and Brave Wolf were of the party.

One day while they were going on, Stiff Finger heard something whistle close to his ear, and felt something brush against his head. From what he had been told by Gentle Horse, he knew that danger was near, and told his companions that he intended to turn back. Stiff Finger was a brave man, with an established reputation, and his advice carried great weight. Nevertheless, there was a difference of opinion in the company.

Finally, Stiff Finger and some of his companions turned

back. Others, who laughed at the warning and went forward, were attacked next day by Utes, and two were killed and two wounded.

When the famous warrior Roman Nose[11] was killed, in the Beecher Island fight in 1868, he was wearing a war-bonnet made for him many years ago by White Bull, one of whose earlier names was Ice. Several imaginary descriptions of this war-bonnet have been given by writers who have described this battle, but the story of how it came to be made, of two of the tabus connected with it, and of its various protective influences, was given me by the maker, White Bull.

On one occasion during a storm, when it was raining and thundering, White Bull looked up into the sky and had a vision of a person there on horseback wearing a war-bonnet such as this, and by the side of this person was a hawk carrying in its feet a gun and a saber. The Thunder instructed White Bull to make a war-bonnet like the one he had seen, but it was not until long after this vision that he did so.

Once, however, while it was thundering, Roman Nose spoke to White Bull and asked him, "Do you ever see anything [*i.e.*, that will protect from lightning]?" White Bull replied, "Yes, once I saw something." Roman Nose continued: "I once saw something too. Make that for me"; meaning, make that which you saw to protect one from the thunder.

When making this war-bonnet, White Bull first prepared a paint. He pounded to a powder many different colored stones, certain metals, black and yellow, yellow earth, some of the grass and other plants that sometimes come down from above, apparently frozen in hailstones, as well as the powdered stone bones of great animals. This powder was mixed with clay. Before dressing,—*i.e.*, painting,—black paint must be used, made of charcoal from a tree which had been set on fire by lightning, and yellow earth must be put on the body in spots, like hail. In the front of the war-bonnet, close to the brow-band,

[11] The Fighting Cheyennes, pp. 276-277.

and over the warrior's forehead, stood a single buffalo-horn. Immediately behind this horn, on top of the bonnet, was the skin of a kingfisher, tied to the hair. At the right side of the head was tied a hawk-skin. This hawk represented the person who in White Bull's vision had held in its claws the gun and the saber. From the headpiece, on either side, two tails of eagle-feathers ran down toward the ground, the feathers on the right side being red, and those on the left side white. At the back of the head, part way down on the war-bonnet, was the skin of a barnswallow, while to the right side of the war-bonnet, where the feathers were red, was tied a bat, so that the warrior might safely fight in the night, for a bat flies at night and cannot be caught. The bat flies high up, and you may throw things at him, but you will not hit him. Sometimes he will fly down, pursuing what is thrown at him. In a battle an enemy may shoot at the person who is wearing this charm, but the one at whom he shoots is not really there in the flesh, as he appears to be: the real person is up above—the bat. The swallow often flies close to the ground, working back and forth. The enemy may be shooting at the person on horseback, but what he is shooting at is not actually the person: the real person is the swallow, down below, flying close to the ground. The kingfisher which is tied to the head behind the horn was worn for the purpose of closing up holes which might be made in the body by bullets, because when the kingfisher dives into water, the water at once closes over it.

When the bonnet had been prepared, and was to be given to Roman Nose, White Bull warned him, saying: "After I have finished this and you put it on your head, you must never shake hands with anyone. If you do so, you will certainly be killed. If you get into any fight, try to imitate the call of the bird you wear on your head—the kingfisher." Besides this, one of the laws of this war-bonnet was like a law of the Contraries —that the wearer might not eat food that had been taken from a dish with a metal implement.

The man who wore this war-bonnet must have his horse dressed—*i.e.*, painted—in a particular way. First a large scalp was tied to the horse's jaw, and zigzag lines, representing lightning, were drawn down the front of the horse's legs. To paint a white horse, blue earth was used for these lines; for a black horse or a bay, white earth was used. A cream-colored horse, with white mane and tail, would have no lightning marks on his fore legs, but on both shoulders and both hips rainbows must be painted, four rainbows in all.

Roman Nose had entire faith in this war-bonnet, and it was believed that it had always protected him in battle. He had worn it in many fights, especially in the year 1865, when on several occasions he rode back and forth within twenty-five or thirty yards of lines of white troops, all of whom shot at him without effect.

As elsewhere told,[12] it is believed that he was killed because he unwittingly violated one of the laws of the war-bonnet.

Soldier Wolf possessed a war-charm, made for him at the time he first went to war, when he was only about thirteen years of age. In the old times he wore it in battle, tied on his breast. He so wore it in the Custer fight. He was never wounded.

This charm is a naked human figure of deerskin, three or four inches long, with the long hair of the buffalo hanging down from its head. When worn in battle, the charm became the real Soldier Wolf, and the wearer, Soldier Wolf, could not be wounded unless the charm was hit. This charm might have been made from the hair of the person's scalp; but, on the other hand, the protective power of the buffalo is very great.

In the Custer fight, Soldier Wolf rode at a man who tried to shoot him, but the gun failed to discharge, and Soldier Wolf rode over and knocked down the man. Turning his horse, Soldier Wolf came back again. The man had now regained his

---

[12] The Fighting Cheyennes, p. 276.

feet, and again tried to shoot, but once more his gun snapped, and Soldier Wolf shot him in the chest.

The same man possessed a luck charm, one against accident and sickness. This was a tiny bundle of medicine tied with a beautiful agate arrowhead, on a twisted deerskin string, to wear about the neck. From the medicine, eight short strings hung down; four of these were ornamented toward the end, each with an old, rather large, red bead; two carried larger dark blue beads, one a large pale blue bead, and one a large white bead.

A dream and war-charm which belonged to Spotted Wolf is the stuffed skin of the belted kingfisher (*Ceryle alcyon*). The eyes are two brass beads; the feathers about the bill are painted with a little red band. Across the back of the stuffed skin is a "saddle" of deerskin, ornamented with old-time blue moccasin beads. This saddle, passing across the back and shoulders, binds the wings to the sides. At the back of this saddle is tied a little deerskin bundle of medicine. Back from the saddle runs a long deerskin string carrying a gray eagle's tail-feather, and a shorter string with a gray eagle's down-feather. The longer string is about two feet and the shorter one eighteen inches long. Under the bird's breast are the strings to tie it to the head. The strings about the bundle, in which the "dream" is tied up, are wound with porcupine quills.

This dream, or charm, was made by Spotted Wolf's father (born about 1800), also named Spotted Wolf, and later Whistling Elk. It was a powerful protection in war.

Sections of baculites are worn as charms. Sometimes a small section may be tied in the hair, but usually they are worn on a string of deerskin or of buffalo-hide, tied about the neck. When worn by men on the war-path, such charms will often indicate to a man where enemies are to be found, and when men are fleeing and being pursued, the stones if prayed to and shaken in the air will bring a heavy storm so that the tracks of those who are running away will be effaced; thus acting like the "storm eagle" of the Pawnees.

White Bull had one of these sections wrapped with beads and adorned with weasel-tails, which he used to wear as a necklet. When he abandoned scouting and fighting, he addressed the stone, telling it that he had now given up fighting and killing people, and from this time forward the stone would be obliged to live as best it could, and that he was going to war no more. Then he put it away in his house.

Armlets, in pairs, made of the hoof and skin of the shank of a white-tail deer, were sometimes worn in the dance or in medicine-making, or in war, tied about the naked arm. They conveyed to the wearer some of the great power of the deer, making him swift to run, and light and active in all his movements.

A protective charm to be tied to the scalp-lock, close to the head, consists of a brass ring to which is tied a bundle of medicine. Two twisted deerskin strings hang from the ring, and on the end of each are two white beads. The two strings represent each an arrowhead, and the ring, the muzzle of a gun. When going into battle the bundle of medicine is untied; a spear of grass is plucked, the end wet in the mouth and touched to the medicine in the bundle. The man then spits ceremonially on his hands and makes the ceremonial motions, and sticks the spear of grass in his head. The effect of this is to protect him from the arrows and the bullets, making him as slender and as hard to hit as the spear of grass is.

A necklet, owned by Crazy Head, has protective power. A long string of twisted buffalo-hair supports a flat, oval stone, perhaps an inch and a quarter by an inch and a half, bearing a general resemblance to the human face. The two holes drilled in it allow the passage of buffalo-hair strings. These holes perhaps represent eyes, and above each is a curved line, the eyebrows. Somewhat below the eyes a representation of teeth is scratched in the stone. Behind the stone is tied a little bundle of medicine, consisting in part of the heart of a swift hawk. To two strings hanging from the bundle are tied the feathers of the hawk.

This bundle has protected Crazy Head in battle. Several times when wearing it he has just been scratched by bullets. Once he was shot in the body, the ball grazing the edge of the stone and chipping a little flake from it. The ball penetrated the flesh not more than an inch. In the fight with the Crows on the Big Horn River, where he received his name, he was wounded—scratched—in the palm of the hand, in the leg, in the body, and was knocked off his horse, and coup was counted on him—by people who beat him about the head—five times. From all these wounds he was laid up only about one day.

A doctor's necklace, from Calf, shows oddly shaped stones above and below, an eagle's claw on either side, a pair of hawk's talons, a stone spearhead and knife, and two bundles of medicine. A deer's tail hangs from the necklace, and below the deer's tail a down-feather. Sweet grass is tied to the uppermost stone. All these things are protective—to bring help. The medicine is for use; the deer's tail is protective in war; the bird's claws inspire dash and courage; the stones above and below are for health and long life, because stones do not change or wear out.

An old-fashioned headdress, from Little Crow, resembles many of those figured by Catlin, and by McKenney and Hall. It is a deer's hair crest worn lengthwise like a roach, the hairs falling down on the outside, all about. This headdress came to Little Crow in a dream, as did also a magpie to be tied to the scalp-lock as a protection in battle. Before being tied on the head, the stuffed magpie-skin is moved four times about the head, and then fastened to the scalp-lock.

A Crazy Dog Society rattle given to me by Little White Man shows on one side the sun and the sun's road, and on the other side the moon and stars; in other words, it gives protection day and night. The rattle was made by Little White Man, who was taught to do so by Beaver Claws and Bob-tailed Horse.

In old times there were sixty or seventy men in the Crazy Dog Society at Tongue River.

TABUS

There are certain tabus or beliefs which should be mentioned.

While on the war-path, it was forbidden to point at a wolf with a knife. This no doubt had reference to the supernatural power of the wolf and its generally friendly character.

To point at the sun, moon, or any particular star, will result, it is believed, in causing a felon on the pointing finger, and the loss of at least a part of the finger.

Women feared to handle or touch a golden—speckle-tailed—eagle, believing that if they did so patches of paler color would appear on their hands and body. Pipe Woman, of Colony, Oklahoma, killed a speckled eagle and now is spotted all over, because, as she believes, she handled the eagle.

Women believe that if they touch a gray eagle they will turn gray.

Some women—perhaps all Cheyenne women—might not burn owl-feathers; if they did so they became deaf. When doctored for this trouble, if the doctors took owl-feathers from their ears, they could hear again.

DISEASE, HEALING, DEATH

NO one knows how disease first came into the world, nor always what causes it. Often it is believed to come from invisible arrows, shot into the person by various hostile agencies. Certain spirits, or personalities, which inhabit springs, may shoot such arrows at people who visit the springs. These arrows remain in the person and cause sickness. If they are not removed, the person dies. One who carelessly jumps across a spring, or across the water near its source, may be shot with such an arrow. These spirits must be propitiated, and gifts made to them. Such offerings are often seen lying on the ground about springs. Where doctors cure such sick people by taking out the cause of the disease, this cause sometimes appears as a small stone. These spirits are called Ground People: *Ho ho' ta ma ĭtsĭ hyo' ist*—"live in the ground." They are particularly active at night. If offended, the supernatural powers, maiyun, which often dwell in peculiar-looking bluffs, or hills, or peaks, may cause sickness. They are not necessarily malignant, and may be made favorable by prayers and sacrifices, or if neglected or ill-treated, may be rendered ill-disposed, and may cause sickness or even death.

I have elsewhere told of the case of Sun's Road, who, about the year 1890, built a cabin on Muddy Creek, and soon after moving into it, became sick, and for a long time was in bad health. Nothing seemed to help him, though the tribal doctors and the agency physician did what they could. At length, however, he discovered the cause of his illness. In the hills on the north side of the Muddy, standing out a little from the higher bluffs, is a peculiar conical peak, odd in shape and color, and on the south side of the stream is another odd-looking peak. Sun's Road's house was in the line between these two peaks, and thus was on the trail traveled by the spirits dwelling in them, when they went from one peak to the other to visit. Since the doors at the front and back of the house faced up and down the stream, it appeared evident that when the spirits passed to and fro they could not pass through the house, but were obliged to climb over it. This obstruction in their trail annoyed them, and to punish Sun's Road for troubling them, they made him ill. When Sun's Road awoke to the situation, he at once moved his house out of the line between the hills, and also turned it half round so that if they wished, the spirits might pass through the house, instead of climbing over it, if it still stood in their way. He became better at once, and in a short time recovered his health. Sun's Road often expressed astonishment that he could have been so careless as to build his house in such a situation, and so to have subjected himself to danger.

TREATMENT; DOCTORS

Since disease is believed to arise from supernatural as well as from natural causes, the work of healing is a mingling of natural and supernatural remedies. Many people—men and women alike—have the power to heal sickness. They do this by administering roots and herbs, or by the exercise of spiritual power, often employing both methods on the same person, either in succession, or both at the same time. The priests or doctors give medicines and pray to friendly spirits, asking them to cause the patient to recover, and as they seek the aid of those who are favorable, they also by threats and alarming manifestations try to frighten away the evil influences which afflict the patient.

When a man is to become a doctor, after he has thought and prayed much about it, some power—perhaps Heammawihio—comes to him, or sends to him a messenger in sleep, to teach him what he shall do in doctoring, and what herbs and roots—

which the messenger describes—he must search for in the hills. The messenger usually takes the form of a person, but may appear as an animal.

A young man who wishes to become a doctor and to obtain the special power possessed by some doctor in the tribe, may go to that man and offer him the pipe, begging for the special power desired. The doctor may be reluctant to give this power to the seeker, yet even so may accede to the request.

In 1885 someone told Red Eye (a doctor and the stepfather of Standing Out Woman), then camped near Darlington, Oklahoma, that Rearing Bull was coming to offer him a pipe and ask for his medicine. Red Eye did not wish to give anyone his power, so he crossed the creek and went away to hide. He told his wife and stepdaughter that if Rearing Bull came to the house with the pipe, they should not tell where he was. Later in the day Rearing Bull followed Standing Out Woman into the lodge and offered her his pipe, holding it toward her with the bowl down. Standing Out Woman's mother said, "Take it quickly or it may bring us bad luck!" The young woman took it. Her mother said to her, "Bring it around in front of the bed and place it on the ground with the stem pointing to the door." Then the mother said to Rearing Bull, "Sit down and I will go to find my husband." After a time Red Eye came in, took up the pipe, and smoked it, after which he touched the pipe twice to each shoulder and returned it to Rearing Bull. Later he gave Rearing Bull his power.

A man cannot become a doctor by himself; when he receives the power, his wife—who afterward is his assistant—must also be taught and receive certain secrets. The doctor who imparts his powers and secrets to another receives a property consideration therefor—horses, saddles, clothing, robes, or arms. If the wife of the man who is receiving the power does not wish to become a doctor, the man must find another woman to act with him. A man may become a doctor through a dream, thus receiving spiritual power directly from above, but even in this

LODGE WITH MEDICINE BUNDLE

case he must have a woman to help him. Even though he receive his power through a dream, he must still go to another doctor to be taught certain things. The doctor who gives power to a young man does not part with his own power, nor abandon his office as a doctor; he still practices healing as before.

Among other things, the instructor indicates to the novice what roots for healing he shall gather; but the novice may dig only four roots in one day—either four roots of different plants or four of the same kind of plant. These medicines the older man prepares for use, and tells the novice their properties and how they shall be employed. Of the medicines brought in by the novice, the doctor retains a part for himself. Thus, if he gives instructions to many persons, he is never obliged to collect medicines for himself.

As the medicine seeker knows what kind of healing power he desires, he offers the pipe to a doctor who possesses the medicine that he wants. If friends or relations contribute to assist the medicine seeker to pay the man whose medicine he receives, the contributors will be repaid if and when the medicine seeker in his turn is paid for giving his medicine to another.

The doctoring of human beings was elaborate and full of ceremony. If a person was sick, and his relations desired treatment for him by a doctor, one of them, or a messenger, went to this doctor, carrying a filled pipe, and entered the lodge and sat down. He placed the pipe on the ground, with the stem directed toward the doctor, and pushed it toward him, at the same time saying, "I wish you to come and doctor my child." If the doctor was unwilling to act, which was unusual, he declined to accept the pipe. If willing to go, however, he held the palms of his hands toward the sky, and then placing them on the ground, took up the pipe with both hands, and holding it in his left hand, again held the right palm upward; then placed it on the ground, and finally rubbed the hand over the pipestem, from left to right, away from the bowl. Then he lighted the pipe and smoked—thereby consenting—and after the pipe was smoked out, accompanied the petitioner to his lodge.

Before the doctor treated a patient, he purified himself and the sick man. The word *măt to' ho wăt* means to burn the leaves of sweet pine (or sweet grass, the needles of the ground juniper, dried and pulverized mushroom or toadstool, or powdered bitterroot) on a live coal. A coal was taken from the fire, and the herb was sprinkled on it. As the smoke and fumes rose, the doctor held his hands over the smoke, so as to receive on the palms the heat and the odor. He then pressed the palms of his hands on the affected part of the patient's body. This process of purification was preliminary to the ordinary treatment for any kind of illness.

While treating a sick person in a lodge the doctor held in his hand a rattle, and sang, shaking the rattle in rhythm with the song. The song was an invocation or prayer, while the rattle was used to drive away the bad spirit which caused the sickness. At intervals the doctor stopped singing, and prayed in a few words. Sometimes he stood up and walked about the lodge, singing and rattling, in order to expel the bad spirits from every part of the dwelling. Throughout the active treatment of the patient the praying and laying on of hands continued. The hands were frequently passed through the smoke, the palms held up to the sun, and then rubbed on the ground, and afterward placed on the patient, while prayers were made to the Great Power, asking that he would help to cure this sick person.

The rattles used by the doctors were usually made of buffalo-skin, and filled with little stones. Some doctors used rattles made of gourds, especially when treating wounds where blood had been shed; and no doubt in old times, when agriculture was more a part of the tribal life than recently, such rattles were more common. When a person was sick, it was thought that the cause of the disease existed in a certain place in the body. Over this place the doctor shook the rattle, to drive out the evil influence, and then with the mouth strove to suck out the cause of the disease. He appeared to draw out from the patient's body buffalo-hair, stones, and even lizards, which were thought to be the cause of the sickness. When the cause was removed, the patient would recover. Different doctors had different methods. In addition to the rattle, some used the wing of a hawk or an eagle, to fan and cool the sick person. Some used a whole bird of some kind.

Porcupine, a famous doctor and once the leader of the "ghost dance" cult in the North, explained to me his method of using a rattle long employed in his doctoring, and told how he healed the sick.

A braid of sweet grass was always tied to the handle of the rattle, and of this sweet grass a little was burned on a coal, and the rattle passed through the smoke to purify it. A small piece of a medicine root was bitten off and chewed, and spat or blown on the hands in the ceremonial way, and the ceremonial motions made.

As the rattling began, three songs were sung. If the patient was very weak, dull, and sleepy, and the doctor wished to rouse him, he struck the ground four times with the rattle.

When the three songs had been sung, the doctoring stopped for a time, and a pipe was smoked. After it had been smoked out, sweet grass was again burned on a coal, and the pipe, having been cleaned, was filled and placed on the ground before the doctor, the stem pointing toward the door and the bowl to the back of the lodge. The doctor now gave medicine to the patient.

Now five different songs were sung, one after another, and without intermissions. Sweet grass was burned again, and the patient treated further, the afflicted part being sucked, or, as the Cheyennes call it, "bitten." Then a tea was administered —a warm drink suited to the disease. The doctor bit off a piece of the medicine root, chewed it, and spat it on various parts of the patient's body, which were now cooled by patting and fanning with an eagle's wing. Then the pipe was smoked

131

again, and after it had been smoked out was again filled and placed as before. The rattle was now taken up, another pinch of sweet grass burned, the rattle passed through the smoke, and seven different songs were sung, again without intermissions. At the conclusion of the singing, the pipe was smoked before the doctoring was continued. The doctor now mixed medicine with deer fat and rubbed the mixture on his hands, and held them over the fire until they were warm, when the hands were placed on the part of the body where the pain was felt. If the pain was in the body, both hands were placed over it; if in the head, first one hand was pressed on the head and then the other.

Before singing again, the rattle was once more held over the smoke of burning sweet grass. Then nine different songs were sung, without interval, and before the nine songs were finished the patient had begun to sleep.

After the nine songs were sung, the doctor, grasping the pipe in his right hand, held it up to the south, west, north, and east, to the sky and to the ground. The pipe was then changed to the left hand, and they smoked. This ended the doctoring.

Food was now brought in and from it five little pieces of meat were cut or pulled off and put ceremonially on the doctor's right palm. He put his left hand on top of them, and turning over the hands transferred the pieces of meat to the left hand. Then he went out the door and to the south of the lodge, and standing, back to the lodge, took one piece of the meat in his right hand, held it to the south, and then placed it on the ground at the edge of the lodge. At the west, north, and east of the lodge he did the same, and then entering, he held the fifth piece to the sky, and put it on the ground at the edge of the fire nearest the door. This is the usual offering—nivstanivo. Then he returned to his place, and they ate.

Of the food offered to those in the lodge, enough was served to each man so that he could take some of it, even if only a mouthful, to his home, that each member of the family might taste thereof. The ceremonies performed had in a sense consecrated the food.

Some doctors have names for the cardinal points—to be addressed in prayer—which differ from those in common use. Thus, north is *notum;* east is *ho shĭn'*, in ordinary language *ishi tsis issimi is;* south is *hŭn' sō wŭn*, the same as *num haisto;* west is *so wŭn'*, the same as *ishi tsis tahkata es*.

The sweat-lodge—the vapor bath—was used in medical treatment as in religious ceremonies. The sweat-lodge was made, in the usual way, of willow shoots, of any number, according to the view of the man who made it. The number was seldom fewer than twelve, and might be much greater. Sixteen was a common number—six each at the sides and two each at the ends. The shoots were generally from six to eight feet in length, and the lodge was from three to four feet in height. Any number of people, from one to eight, ten, or twelve, or as many as the lodge would hold, might take the sweat together. The doctor or medicine man went in with the patients. Women might take the bath as well as men. Stones were heated in a fire outside the sweat-house, passed in by a woman, who handled them with two forked sticks, and placed in a shallow rectangular hole dug in the center of the lodge. Water was then sprinkled on them from the mouth or by means of a brush made of a buffalo-beard, creating dense steam and heat, which were confined by a covering of skins or canvas or blankets spread over the framework. While the sweat was being taken, the doctor prayed, sang, and used his rattle. After the sweat a plunge in the river followed.

Added to the spiritual side of healing—that is, exorcising or frightening away of the spirits or evil influences which cause disease—was, and still is to some extent, the practice of medicine by administering remedies. For the greater part these remedies were herbs, many of which unquestionably were more or less efficacious, and in not a few cases the Indians appear to have some practical ideas of the medicinal properties of

133

certain plants. Healing by the administering of herbs was practiced by men and women alike. Almost every old woman had a
bundle of medicines peculiarly her own, the secrets of which
were known only to her. These were usually carried about in a
little buffalo-skin sack, often one of those so commonly used
for carrying the stakes for gambling, or for sewing materials.
To each little bundle was usually tied some mark of identification, so that the owner might readily recognize it. Thus, to one
bundle might be tied a blue bead, to another a white one, to a
third the claw of a badger, to a fourth a part of the beard of a
turkey. Sometimes these articles, which at first were attached
to the bundles solely to identify them, came at length to possess
a sacred character and to have a close connection with the healing power of the medicine; so that in some cases it was a part
of the administration of the remedy to stir (before the patient
drank it) the water in which the medicine had been mixed, with
the claw of the animal, or with the beard of the turkey, or perhaps with the little stone arrowhead which was tied to the
bundle.

Tied to the necklet or to the shoulder-girdle, or perhaps to
the hair, most men carried about with them one or more little
bundles of medicines, some spiritual,—*i.e.*, effective by their
mysterious power,—others with curative properties. Some men
had vegetable medicines of which they alone possessed the
secrets: these might be what we might term drugs, or they
might be merely maiyu—might possess spiritual power. The
old stories tell us that people learned of the various medicinal
plants, and of the uses to which they were to be put, by means
of dreams, or that certain mythological heroes went out with
them on the prairie and pointed out various plants to be used
for treating diseases.

Red Eagle, born about 1810, was a noted doctor. His drinking vessel could be only of wood, horn, shell, or pottery, not
of metal. This instruction was given him in a dream. He owned
a shallow wooden cup or small bowl about eight inches in

diameter, with five incised figures of water animals on the inside, and pierced near the margin for attachment of a string. It was made long ago by his mother's mother, for Red Eagle's uncle, and was finally given to Red Eagle. Such cups were formerly carried on war journeys for use as drinking vessels, but of late years this one had been used by Red Eagle in administering medicine to the sick. The figures cut in the cup are those of water animals, because the cup was intended to be used for fluids, and water animals have much power as to water. The figures are frog, fish, turtle, otter, and, on the bottom, a siredon or mud-puppy. When the doctor put medicine in the cup, he dropped it in over each one of the four animals, in the four directions. The cup stood on the ground in front of the doctor, the turtle pointing north, the otter east, the frog south, and the fish west. The doctor put in a pinch of medicine each over the turtle, the otter, the frog, and the fish, in that order, and then one over the siredon in the middle. The patient took a sip from the cup opposite the head of each animal, in the same order in which the medicine was put in. The dish was then turned completely around to the left four times, and when the fourth turn was completed the patient took the cup and drank all the medicine.

A long time ago the Cheyennes had ceremonial stone pipes which possessed special power and which on occasions were used in treating the sick. The bowls of these were straight, not bent at a right angle like the modern stone pipes. One or two such pipes still exist, and are used in some important ceremonies—those of the Medicine Lodge and the Massaum. The stems of some of these pipes are said to have been ornamented, wrapped with skins, painted, and with pendent feathers. Other stems were perfectly plain, without ornament or painting. It is not known how these pipes were first received, but a story is told of how the first one came.

It is said that a long time ago an old doctor met a person who had come out of a cave in a big hill. This person advised the doctor to go to the top of the hill, and to remain there four days and four nights, saying that at the end of this time he would again come and see him. The doctor did as advised. After four days the person came to him, and said, "Come with me; we will go in." They went down from the hill and entered the cave, and there the person taught the doctor how to make a medicine pipe, and what to do with it; four days must be occupied in making and finishing the pipe, and the doctoring with it must occupy four days. Then the doctor came out of the cave and returned to his village. He is thought to be the first man who made one of these pipes.

These pipes were given only to men who possessed spiritual power for healing. Such an one sometimes made a feast, and calling in many of the old men and chiefs, told them that he needed a medicine pipe. The chief men and the doctors of the village were called together, and a great feast was made. To the lodge where these people were assembled a number of horses were sent by the doctor who had asked to have the pipe made, and tied before it. After all had eaten, those present discussed the matter, and perhaps it was decided that the pipe should be made and given to this doctor.

After the pipe had been made, and it was first shown to the old men, they looked at it very carefully, for they were men who knew how a medicine pipe should be made. Perhaps one or another suggested that it should be changed a little, that it ought to have some different painting, or to be ornamented with other feathers. After it had been finally approved, another man might caution those who were handling it, saying: "Be careful how you handle it. Do not move it too quickly." When all the changes had been made, and the pipe was finished, they all sang. Then the pipe was presented.

When they had given this pipe to the doctor, it was wrapped up and put away as sacred, and was used only on certain special occasions. But if anyone in the camp became sick, he might send word to this doctor that he wished him to bring his medi-

cine pipe to him, that he wished to smoke. The doctor unwrapped the pipe at home, filled it there, took it to the man's
lodge, and entered. If, in filling the pipe, which sometimes
was done by another than the doctor, the finger touched it, this
would cause death. Even he who owned and carried it, when
he took it from its wrappings, had spread on the ground before
him white sage stems, to keep the pipe from the ground. On
this sage rested a piece of buffalo-chip, on which the bowl of the
pipe was supported. When the owner was about to fill it, he
did not touch the pipe with the naked hand, but took a handful
of sage, which he held in his hand between his thumb and
fingers and the bowl of the pipe. When he filled the pipe, he put
in seven pinches of tobacco: one for each of the four points,
one for the rising sun, one for the setting sun, and one for the
sky. When it had been done in that way, they might smoke. No
one but the doctor who owned it might handle the pipe bowl.

When the doctor reached the sick man's lodge, the pipe was
lighted, and pointed to the sky and to the earth. Then the
doctor held the stem, and let the sick man smoke; but before
he might smoke, white sage was laid all over the floor of the
lodge. All day long the doctor remained with the sick man, and
during all the day he drank no water. The next morning they
had a feast, at which all the men concerned in the giving of
the pipe were present.

Not every sick person smoked one of these pipes; only those
who asked to do so. Those who did not smoke were doctored,
and the doctor smoked, holding the pipe over them.

A doctor might not sell one of these pipes. If he did so he
lost his power.

The stem of a medicine pipe, as it was passed along, might
be held by anyone, but no one might touch the bowl. When
the smoking was finished, the doctor placed the pipe on the
ground. It was necessary that this should be done very slowly
and carefully, and his hand drawn away from the pipe without
haste. When he lifted it up, the same slow motions must be

used. If he moved his hand quickly, this would cause a storm or a high wind. In cleaning out the pipe he must be slow and careful, and touch it lightly.

Now the first person who had one of these pipes had been told that he must occupy four days in doctoring with it, and for a long time all who had these pipes obeyed this instruction. Ultimately, however, the people grew careless, and began to employ only three days in doctoring, and then two days, and sometimes only one day. So the power to heal with these pipes was lost, and at last they were given up; hence for a long time there have been none in the tribe. Even the memory of them has almost passed away.

Many men had their own special medicine, which they used to doctor themselves when they became ill or were wounded. Bull Head, now dead, but a contemporary of Two Moon, and other recent men, doctored himself for rattlesnake bite by eating the flesh of the rattlesnake. Many years ago Bull Head was wounded by the Utes, the ball passing through the lower part of his side, making a wound that never healed. For this wound too he doctored himself by eating the flesh of the rattlesnake.

A Sioux named Sitting Bull, who had long lived with the Northern Cheyennes and was called by them Short Sioux, while retreating in a running fight with the Crows, was shot in the back. The ball had gone through his body; blood was flowing from the wound in the back and in the breast, and from the man's mouth. After the Crows had left them, Sitting Bull said to those near him: "I must find an ant-hill. Look for one." When an ant-hill was found, Sitting Bull dismounted, collected a handful of ants, and put them in his mouth and swallowed them. "Now," he said, "I shall be well." He mounted and rode on all through the night, and at last recovered.

Certain medicines, before being boiled, must be offered to the four directions, a very little each to east, south, west, and north; and, while heating, the medicine was to be stirred with some special thing, usually tied to the bundle.

Horse-doctoring. The very great usefulness of the horse in all aspects of Plains Indian life, but especially in war, gave an extraordinary importance to the work of curing injured horses or—by means of mysterious power—enduing them with an added measure of activity, speed, strength, and endurance. The doctor who possessed the power to heal men exercised this power as well on horses.

When a doctor instructed a young man how to cure sickness, he usually taught him also the secrets of doctoring horses. If he did not do this, the young man might ask him for this instruction and it was given. There was no separate guild of horse doctors.

The doctors administered to horses by the mouth a certain root which made them long-winded and renewed their force when they became tired. This root does not grow in the country of the Northern Cheyennes, but came from the South, from a people known as *Mōhk stē e ŭn is' tăn e,* the Kiowa-Apaches, who now live in Oklahoma. This root may still be administered by anyone who can procure it and has been taught how to give it.

In a doctor's lodge, when the woman rose in the morning, it was her duty to strike the important lodge-pole four times with a stick. Before this was done no noise must be made in the lodge, but afterward dishes might be rattled and the bones of animals broken. This act of striking this pole four times nullified, for that day, the tabu against knocking or tapping things in this doctor's lodge.

If the pole had not been struck as described, and a marrow-bone was broken in a horse doctor's lodge, it was certain that one of the horses belonging to that family would break its leg. To break a buffalo-rib presaged that the horse, or its owner, would be tossed by a buffalo.

A doctor never struck a horse on the head with a whip,

bridle, or reata. Presents of horses were the payment usually received by a horse doctor for his services, and it was believed if he struck a horse on the head he would receive no more horses.

In a horse doctor's lodge all the members of his family were expected to hang up their bridles, reatas, and whips, and not to leave them on the ground; they were generally hung on a forked stick at the head of the bed. To throw a whip or a rope on the ground presaged that the owner would be thrown from his horse and hurt. A woman might hang her whip on the high pommel of her saddle. The doctor carried a bundle of horse medicine tied through the hole in the handle of his whip; it was thus always at hand in case a horse fell sick and he was obliged to doctor it. His other medicine he always carried with him on a line passing over the right shoulder, the medicine bag hanging on his left hip. On buffalo hunts the doctors attended to the men who were thrown and hurt, and also to injured horses. The women doctors carried their horse medicine tied to their whips and their doctoring medicine on a deerskin belt about the waist.

If the Cheyennes were going to race horses against another tribe, those who were backing the horse might take a pipe, and, generally, also some arrows, as a gift, to ask help from the horse doctor. To do this in ordinary tribal races was not admissible. The horse doctor then sought and found the track of the opponent's horse, and taking a handful of dirt from the track, he put this earth in a gopher's hole. This, it was believed, would cause the horse to step in a hole and fall or get hurt. The opportunity to do this was often found when the doctor was sitting with his robe around him near where the horse was being led up and down before the race. This custom was later adopted by the Kiowas, Comanches, and Apaches.

When a pipe was offered to the horse doctor, he accepted it and smoked, and then returned it to the owner, who touched the stem of the pipe to his right shoulder, and to his left shoulder, and then repeated the motions. He then puffed at the empty pipe, blew in his hands, and made the ceremonial motions.

A large war-party was usually accompanied by one or more doctors. Just before charging the enemy, the pipe bearer—the leader—offered the pipe to the oldest doctor, who smoked and returned it. The pipe bearer then asked the horse doctor to exercise his power behind the line, so that the horses should not fall or be hurt; and the doctor walked up and down over the horses' tracks and sang his mysterious songs. Often the same ceremony was performed on a buffalo hunt, so that none of the riders or horses might be hurt. The man who asked the doctor to exercise this power was expected to present him a good fat buffalo. If this was done, the doctor cut up the meat and called aloud the name of the man who gave it to him.

In doctoring a horse, the horse doctor opened the bag carried on the handle of his whip, held it in his left hand, and with his right hand put a pinch of the medicine in the right-hand side of the horse's mouth; then with the same hand he took another pinch, put it in his own mouth and blew it against the horse's body behind the right shoulder and rubbed his hand over it, and then blew another pinch on the horse's right flank and rubbed it. Passing behind the horse he put a pinch of medicine on the left side of the horse's mouth, and then blew a pinch on the left shoulder and flank, as he had done before on the right side. While working on the right of the horse he carried the bag in his left hand, and used his right hand to take out the medicine and rub it on; and on the left side he reversed the use of the hands. He walked behind the horse to the right side again, holding the bag in his left hand; took from the bag and put in his mouth a pinch of medicine; blew it out on the right hand four times, and rubbed the hand up the horse's head from the nostrils over the ears. The horse was then turned loose, and, if it rolled, the medicine was good and would have the desired effect. If the horse did not roll, the ceremony was useless.

Not all men followed precisely the same methods. Some held the bag containing the medicine in the left hand, and put the first pinch of medicine on the right corner of the mouth, and then rubbed the medicine down the right fore leg with the right hand. Then a pinch of medicine was put on the right hip and the hand rubbed down over the right hind leg. The doctor passed behind the horse, put the medicine on the left hip, and rubbed it down the left hind leg, and then on the left side of the mouth and rubbed down the left fore leg. He then stood in front of the horse, put a pinch of medicine in his mouth, blew it out in his right hand, and starting at the horse's nose, passed his right hand down over the animal's head, mane, and spine, to its tail, walking down on the left-hand side. Then he put more medicine in his mouth, blew on the hand twice, and pulled . the horse's tail four times. If the horse shook itself or rolled, the medicine was good.

There were two kinds of medicine—two different plants— one carried in a bag tied with plaited horse-tail hair, the other in a bag tied with deerskin. Both medicines were used in the same way. They revived and strengthened a horse when it was tired.

In doctoring for ordinary diseases, the horse medicine was used in water. Five pinches were put in a vessel of water—one in each of the four directions and one in the middle, forming a quincunx. The medicine was then shaken and given to the horse to drink.

In doctoring men wounded in battle, a pinch of the medicine mixed with buffalo tallow was placed on the wound. The songs sung over the wounded man were the same as those used in doctoring a horse.

A charm for protection in battle was made and given to people by a horse doctor named Willow. It was of deerskin strings twisted like a bowstring, and small bags of horse medicine were tied to it at intervals of about six inches. It was worn over the right shoulder. Such a charm might be borrowed from its owner for use by another.

The Cheyenne terms for those who treat horses are *moi' nu-enu' itan,* horse doctor (man), and *moi' nu-enu' itane,* horse doctor (woman).

A story is told of an old-time horse doctor, who, when engaged in his practice, would spit horse-dung from his mouth; a colt's hoof sometimes came part way out of his mouth and then drew back. He was named *Mănhǐk'* (Golden Eagle Bone). When his favorite horse was out on the prairie and he needed it, he took his medicine bag in his hand and began to sing. If within the sound of his voice, the horse always came to him. He was celebrated as a horse doctor, and declared that the horse helped him in his doctoring. In 1862 there was a very old horse doctor named Gland, who said he possessed the original medicine which had been given him by Manhik. When he wished his horse to come, he did not call out loud, but simply held up his medicine bag and sang.

No horse doctor would eat horseflesh, and no horse doctor would shoot a horse, wild or tame.

Fees for Services. The Cheyenne doctors did not usually set a price for their services; they did not take advantage of a man's necessities. When they first entered the lodge they were told what would be given them—it might be a horse or a blanket—and they doctored the patient, taking what was offered.

In old times doctors were paid with property of any sort, as blankets, arrows, robes, saddles, or horses; but in recent years they have sometimes been paid in money. As long ago as the year 1900, Tall Meat, a doctor, received five dollars each for doctoring two patients. One was a man who, from a description of his symptoms, seems to have had dropsy, and whom Tall Meat frankly said he could not cure. The other was a woman.

Magic Power. The mysterious powers possessed by some medicine men were believed to make it possible for them to kill persons by blowing on them, or to afflict them with disease or death. Such power, however, might react on the one who exercised it, and he often took steps to protect himself against the agency that he himself had set in motion.

One who had dreamed that he possessed a certain power might determine to make trial of this power on another by merely exercising his will. His motive might be jealousy or anger or mere curiosity—to see if he could really do this. Perhaps he took some medicine or some small object, even a hair from his robe, and rolled it into a little ball and held it up toward the sun, and wishing something bad for him, threw it toward the person. The object disappeared and went to the one about whom he was thinking. The man need not be near the person he was thinking of, yet he had the power to harm him.[1] A man who had done this knew that he had done wrong, hence to make atonement and to protect himself from evil consequences he might go into the sweat-house and have two strips of skin taken from his arms or from his breast. The little ball which he had sent away might cause illness to the one to whom it had gone, or might even cause his death. After a time the person to whom the ball was sent might perhaps, in a dream, see the one who had sent it, in the act of dispatching it. If a doctor who had been called in to heal the sick person succeeded in getting the ball out of his body, it might be sent back to the one who originally dispatched it. Unless the sender had sacrificed a part of his body, the returned missile might do him the same kind of harm.

If the man who had sent the ball had reason to think that it might be returned to him, he went to a hilltop at daylight in the morning and watched for the return of the ball, which, when it came back to the sender, wherever he might be, looked like a little spark of fire. If the sender had protected his head by

---

[1] *Ē ēhyō'm*, signifying, "he has power to harm at a distance."

BOW, BOW CASE, AND ARROWS

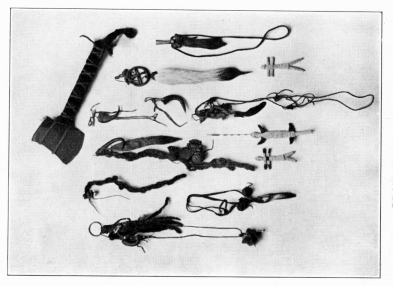

PROTECTIVE CHARMS

rubbing a special medicine on it, he caught the spark in his hand and the medicine prevented the ball from entering his flesh. When he extinguished the spark, the power of the ball was gone. That ended it.

· Men possessing strong spiritual power have been known to take a flicker's tail-feather, worn in the hair, and this, if sent into a person's body, caused lingering illness and death. He who performed such an act took one of the rectrices from the tail and darted it, quill forward, in the direction of the person he wished to injure, at the same time stamping the right foot on the ground and uttering a deep, low grunt. The feather or its power was believed to fly through the air and to enter the person's body. It did not kill at once, but acted slowly and surely, causing death unless the afflicted man suspected the cause of the trouble and through the aid of some power secured relief.

It is said that in ancient times certain doctors used to make drums called beaver drums, which implies beaver songs and a beaver worship. These doctors are said to have had beaver cuttings which they shot into people whom they did not like, and which caused diseases which were fatal. The Blackfeet have a similar belief.

Crazy Mule, a famous medicine man, who died years ago in the South, stated that at one time he had the power to kill by looking at a person, and was obliged to use great caution to keep from injuring his friends; but before his death he relinquished this power.

Often a doctor possessing great spiritual power might give exhibitions of it, either for his own glorification or to strengthen people's faith in him, or even for the entertainment of those present. These mysterious exhibitions were not uncommon in old times, but the power to perform them has now passed away. My old friend, Gentle Horse, who is no longer living, gave me the following account of the power of a relative:

My uncle, Bear On The Ridge, my mother's brother, was a great doctor. He had a skunk-hide and a badger-hide. He used to keep the skunk-hide where he kept his medicine; it was made up like a sack, and was an old hide, much worn, the hair all coming off. When he made medicine he often took that hide, holding it with one hand by the head, and with the other by the back, and threw it over by the door, and when it struck the ground the skunk was alive, with its hide fresh and clean. Then he took a robe and threw it over the skunk, and when he took the robe away, there was the old dead hide. He often did the same with the badger. It was alive and growling; then when he threw the robe over it, it became the dead hide again.

When making the medicine he sometimes took a tin cup and partly filled it with water; he wet some earth, and modeled the mud into the shape of a turtle. He put the piece of mud in the cup, covered it, and went on making the medicine. Presently something was heard, a sound of scratching against tin, and when he took the cover from the cup, there was seen in it a living water-turtle trying to get out.

The mysterious medicines which came to the doctor by the help of the spiritual powers were known only to him. They were kept carefully wrapped in a bundle or a pouch. The medicine sack of the doctor hung above the lodge owner's head, and so opposite the door, in stormy weather; but—as much as possible—it was felt it should be out of doors so that the sun might shine on it, and the wind blow over it, and it might be kept pure. It was often hung up over the door, tied against the lodge outside; or a lance was set in the ground in front of the door, or to the south of the lodge, and the medicine-bundle tied to it. The spiritual power of these medicines might be weakened, or even destroyed, if the laws regarding them were not observed. A number of tabus were connected with these, some of which are mentioned elsewhere.

Tabu. When the medicine was in the lodge, if wood was lying by the fire no one might knock against it, or knock or tap anything in the lodge. On entering, no one should pass in front of other persons; one should pass behind them to his place. All would lean forward. Children playing outside might not throw anything against the lodge. If any of these things took place—unless appropriate ceremonies were performed to overcome the evil effect—the power of the doctor's medicine was impaired—he would have bad luck, and could not cure anyone.

Surgery. The Cheyennes never practiced amputation. No man was willing to lose arm or leg or finger, nor would any doctor take the responsibility of cutting off a limb. Yet more or less cutting was occasionally required to remove an arrowhead. Shell gave the following account of taking an arrowhead from a wound:

In a certain fight a Cheyenne was shot in the shoulder blade with an arrow, the head of which entered the bone, and the shaft broke off. His friends took a pair of bullet molds and tried to extract the head, but could not get hold of it. They cut away the flesh on either side of the arrowhead, until the bullet molds could grip the iron, and then, while four or five men held the patient down, another gave two or three strong pulls on the head, but failed to start it. They then took a sharp bladed knife and ran it down into the bone close to the iron on either side of the arrowhead, working the knife from side to side to loosen the arrowhead, and at last succeeded in pulling it out. During the whole operation the young man did not flinch.

Cheyenne doctors were skillful and successful in treating such injuries as broken bones, gunshot wounds, and arrow wounds. In the treatment of wounds—*i.e.*, where blood had been shed—rattles made from gourds were thought to be especially useful.

Broken legs were often set, and made excellent unions, so that no evidence of the injury remained. On the other hand, sometimes when a leg was set, if the wounded man was obliged to ride a horse, or to be jolted in a travois, during flight from a pursuing enemy, a vicious union of the bone resulted and the man was perhaps a cripple for life. Under favorable circumstances, however, astonishing cures were sometimes made.

There was recently at Pine Ridge a man who in the winter of 1876 was shot in the leg, the ball entering at the shin, and coming out halfway between the knee and the thigh, smashing the knee and shattering the bones above and below it. He was taken to the hospital at Camp Robinson, where the doctor said the leg must come off if the man's life was to be saved. The Indian declined to consent to this, and was taken away. An Indian doctor took charge of and cured him, so that he walked on the leg, though it was stiff.

Rattlesnake Bites. A very few men can cure the bite of a rattlesnake. It is not known what medicine they use, for this is their secret.[2]

If a horse is bitten by a rattlesnake, it is never good for much afterward, even though cured. If it has been a fast horse, it loses its speed; if it has had great endurance, it is deprived of this; the same may be true of a man. Elk Shows His Horns used to be a great foot-racer. He was bitten in the foot, doctored and cured, but henceforth could never run fast. In the same way the Pawnees believed that a horse bitten by a rattle-snake is thereafter worthless.

When Arapaho Chief was about twenty-eight years of age (say 1864), he was bitten by a rattlesnake at the Painted Rocks on Box Elder River, a tributary of Powder River, Montana. This place is mysterious because there pictures appear on the rocks "without anyone having painted them." It is a place where sacrifices are made, and at the time this happened many people had gone there to pray, but most of them had already gone home.

Arapaho Chief was one of the last to go. He was near the middle part of the cliffs on which the pictures are, and threw up his hands toward the pictures and bent his head and prayed, asking that he might be helped, in his next fight, to count a coup and to capture some horses. The snake was at his feet, but he did not see it until just as it struck him. He felt no pain from the bite, but felt a glancing blow, as if the side of his leg had been struck. He went on and felt no inconvenience at

[2] See the list of plants, Vol. II, p. 169.

all until he had waded the stream. Then his leg began to swell, and presently he could not move it. He was in great pain. He called to his friend, Pipe, who was not far off, and told him his trouble, and Pipe took him on his back and carried him to his lodge.

Doctors were called in, and Arapaho Chief gave them what he had to give, and his sister gave all her property—two horses and whatever else she could spare. These doctors could do nothing to help him.

At last came a sister of Turkey Leg, who had some medicine which she moistened and wrapped on the wound. It ceased to be painful almost at once. The woman took hold of the patient's right great toe and shook it; then she took hold of the right little finger and shook it, and of the left little finger and of the left great toe in succession, and shook each; then she said to the young man, "Now, you will see all sorts of snakes." Arapaho Chief felt very sick, as if he were going to die, and he did see many snakes, more than he had supposed were in the whole world. The woman began to rub his leg from thigh to ankle, and soon the swelling commenced to subside. The pain left him, and before long he was able to stand on his feet.

Since that time, however, Arapaho Chief's leg has been bad, and not so strong as the other.

Once White Shield was bitten in the thick of the left hand. Bird Bear, who was with him, jumped on his horse and brought Young Bird, a doctor, who tied a string around White Shield's arm above the elbow. In the meantime the arm was swelling, and the pain extended up the under part of the arm and to the patient's heart, making him sick and dizzy. The hand became numb. Young Bird asking for a deerskin string, they gave him one about a foot long, and he painted it black on one side and yellow on the other. He then held one end between his left thumb and finger, and pulled it through the thumb and fingers of the right hand four times. When he stopped pulling the string through his fingers, it writhed and twisted about like a

149

snake. He said afterward, "A hawk taught me this when I saw him flying over me with a snake in his claws."

While doing this, Young Bird told those standing about to find him a horned toad. A boy ran and caught one, and brought it to him. They now had White Shield lie on his face on the ground, with his arms outstretched by his head, and Young Bird placed the deerskin string on his arm, reaching from where the string was tied about the arm above the elbow to the place where the wound was.

Meantime, White Shield's aunt and his sisters had come. They placed their hands on either side of the deerskin string which lay on White Shield's arm, so as to form a little chute or channel, fenced in on either side by the women's hands. The horned toad was placed in this chute on the upper end of the deerskin string, its head directed toward the patient's hand. At first the horned toad tried to climb out on one side or the other of the channel formed by the women's hands, but being prevented, at last it ran down the chute, off the hand, and away. This ended the doctoring. Young Bird said to White Shield, "Get up now, you are cured." White Shield rose to his feet. The pain was much eased. By night the swelling had partly subsided, and by morning it had disappeared, and his arm no longer pained him, but a little later all the skin peeled off the forearm and hand.

Some time afterward, while White Shield was washing his hands, he felt a little roughness where he had been bitten, and looking carefully, saw something, which he picked out, and which proved to be the point of a snake's tooth. The snake which had bitten him was a large rattlesnake.

The painting and twisting of the string was perhaps to imitate a blue racer, one of the constrictor snakes, commonly regarded as an enemy of the rattlesnake. The blue racer is said to have come down from the sun, and so to have great power. The running of the horned toad along the course of the blood from the wound reminds us of the Cheyenne belief that if a horned toad runs over a snake it at once kills it.

Power of Animals. An example of successfully doctoring under animal tutelage was related by Spotted Wolf—later called Whistling Elk—who was born about the year 1800. The account was given me by his son, Spotted Wolf. The older Spotted Wolf once accidentally shot himself in the hand, and was apparently bleeding to death and already very weak. Doctors were present, trying to help him. He called his children to come and sit by him, saying that he was about to die. After the children had seated themselves, he dismissed all others present. He asked them to make two little smokes, or fires, one on each side of the door—one of big sagebrush and one of a little weed that bears a yellow flower.

This was in the middle of the day, and the camp was a large one. Not very long after the fires had been lighted, a coyote walked through the door and up to the man's side, and sat there looking at the door.

After the coyote had been there a short time a badger entered, went over to the man, and lay down on its belly beside the coyote. Both were to the left of Spotted Wolf. A little while afterward, a kingfisher flew in the door and alighted on a backrest, chattering and making a great noise. When the bird made this noise, Spotted Wolf understood its cries. It said to him: "Get up now, and go to the stream and act as I do, diving down into the water. Also, you must promise to make a medicine lodge, and then I will save you." But the coyote said, "No, my friend, instead of making a medicine lodge, I should like to have you make a horse dance."

After a time the bird flew out through the smoke-hole of the lodge. Then the badger walked out, and all the women who were watching outside kept calling to one another, saying, "Look out for the dogs; do not let the dogs chase it!" Then the coyote also walked out, and they kept the dogs from chasing it.

After the animals had left the lodge, Spotted Wolf rose and went down to the stream, and all the people followed him to see what he should do. Before he went into the water, he said that first he would dive upstream and then would dive downstream. He asked the people to watch the water below him, and if they saw anything living appear, he would not die.

Then he went into the water, and did as he had said he would. The fourth time he dived downstream, and while he was under the water a big fish leaped out of the water and on the bank. When the people told him of this, he came out of the water and said, "Well, I shall live." He returned to the lodge and recovered. Afterward he made the horse dance as the coyote had requested, and after this he came sometimes to understand in part the speech of the wolves.

About the year 1850 there were two young men who were great friends. One was named They Pass Each Other; the other, Little Head. They Pass Each Other was the son of Old Frog and a brother of Mrs. William Rowland. At a time when these two young men were in different camps, Little Head died. A messenger went to the other camp and said to They Pass Each Other, "Your friend is dead, and has been buried on a scaffold for one day." When They Pass Each Other heard this he mounted his horse and set out for the village, traveling that day and night. Early in the morning he reached the camp, and went to the lodge of the dead man's father. When he entered and they saw him, all the dead man's relations mourned and cried. They felt sorry for the young man. He said to them, "Do not cry, I am going to see my friend."

He went out to the tree where his friend lay, climbed up among the branches to the scaffold and opened the robes in which he was wrapped, and looked at his friend's face. When he did so, he found that the body was not stiff and it did not seem cold. Nevertheless, the young man did not breathe, and was dead. Presently They Pass Each Other returned to the village and said to the dead man's relations: "Now pitch me a big lodge in the middle of the village, and have it stand so that it shall face the rising sun. Also fix up a bed at the back of the lodge. I am going to bring my friend here, and take him into the lodge. You must fetch him from where he lies now, and carry him in at the door, and put him on the bed at the back of the lodge, and I will try to make him live."

Everything was done as they had been instructed. Then They Pass Each Other and his brother, Big Ribs, went into the lodge together to doctor. The people could hear them singing their medicine songs; and after they had been thus singing for a long time, a buzzard came flying over the camp, circling round and round, and slowly coming nearer and nearer to the lodge, and at last it came down through the smoke-hole and flew about the men while they were singing; and while still they were singing and the buzzard was flying about in the lodge, the dead man sat up. Then the buzzard flew out through the smoke-hole. This happened in the afternoon.

Then They Pass Each Other went out and called the young man's father, and took him into the lodge. He said to the father, "When you see your son, do not show that you are sorry or surprised, but speak quietly to your son, as if you had just left him." The father went into the lodge and saw his son sitting there, and did as he was told. Then They Pass Each Other went out and got the young man's mother, and took her in, advising her as he had the father. Then he went out again and told all the young man's relations that they might come in to see him, and they did so. Little Head lived long in the camp, and at last was killed by the soldiers.

A long time ago a war-party of nearly a hundred warriors went out to attack the Pawnees. They traveled for many days, and at last came near to a Pawnee village, but before they discovered the village they saw some Pawnees on the prairie. The Cheyennes had separated, and were traveling in two bodies a little apart, and not in sight of each other. One of these parties chased a young Pawnee who was on foot, and the young Cheyenne who had the fastest horse overtook and struck the Pawnee. Just as he turned his horse after doing this, another Pawnee a little way off shot at him and killed his horse. The young Cheyenne jumped up, and as he turned to run to his people, the Pawnee shot again, and the bullet went through the young man, from side to side, just at the short ribs. White Bull (born 1834) was close to the man who was shot, and saw it all.

The fight then stopped. The Pawnees returned to their village, and the Cheyennes took the wounded man and set out for their home. That night they went quite a long distance and camped. The other party of their people had not yet come to them. The next morning they continued their journey, carrying the wounded man, and during the day the other party joined them. This party had gone to the other side of the Pawnee camp, where they had a fight, killing three Pawnees, and had among their number many wounded men, but none hurt so badly as the first one. The Cheyennes traveled on and reached their village. Some young men were sent ahead and gave the news, and some of the people of the camp went out to meet them.

The night after they reached their camp, White Bull heard people singing, and was curious to see what it was about. He went toward the place of the singing, and as he approached he saw a large fire burning in front of a large lodge, and when he reached the fire he learned that the young man who had been so badly wounded was being doctored. While White Bull stood there listening to the singing, someone came out of the lodge and said, "The young man cannot live long; he is dying." After a little while White Bull went nearer to the lodge, and presently he heard the wounded man say to the people: "My friends, I am growing blind; I cannot see. I want you to send quickly for my friend Buffalo Chips." A young man at once set out to get Buffalo Chips, who was in another village, so far away that the messenger did not arrive there until daylight the next morning.

Buffalo Chips was a doctor, a young man, and a close friend of him who had been wounded.

The next morning, when White Bull went out, he saw a great crowd about the lodge where the wounded man had been, and walked there to see what was going on. The women about the lodge were all wailing; they told him that the young man was dead. Toward the middle of the day, two men were seen coming over the hills, and about half a mile from the lodges they stopped and sat down. A young man who had just come in with some horses galloped out to where they sat, and saw that the two were Buffalo Chips and the man who had gone to fetch him. The young man rode up and said to Buffalo Chips, "You have arrived too late; your friend is dead." Buffalo Chips answered, *"Ohohyaa!"*[3] Then for a few moments he held his head down, looking at the ground between his knees. Then he looked up, and said, "Let us go into the camp."

To the young men who had ridden out he said: "Go back to the camp as quickly as you can, and tell them to move that lodge out to the middle of the circle where it is level and smooth, and to pitch it with the door to the rising sun. Have them make a bed at the back of the lodge, and let them carry my friend into the lodge and put him on that bed. Tell all the people that no one must go near the lodge, and no one must make any noise. Let all keep quiet."

White Bull sat in the camp and saw the lodge moved. Buffalo Chips remained where he was until all had been done as he had directed, and then started down the hill. The hill was steep, and at its foot there was a low place, in crossing which he passed out of sight of the people. After he had crossed the low place, just as he came in sight again, the people saw great flocks of birds of all sorts flying over his head and seeming to follow him. He went straight to the lodge where his friend's

---

[3] An exclamation of grief, about equivalent to "Oh, that is terrible!"

body was, and entered, and the birds followed him; some went in behind him through the door, and some at the smoke-hole, and some alighted on the lodge-poles. Soon Buffalo Chips looked out of the lodge and saw some of the dead man's relations—his brother, mother, and sisters—standing near, looking on. He spoke to them and said: "Make no noise. Do not mourn or cry. Tell all the people that no one must go near the lodge, and no one must make any noise. Tell the people in the camp to keep still all through this night. All night long birds will be coming in and out of the camp, and after a time there will be a fire here in the lodge."

Soon after it grew dark the people heard far off a moaning or a grunting sound. It seemed to draw constantly nearer, and at last it sounded like an owl coming and calling. When it had come close to the lodges, every now and then there seemed to be in the air a flash of light from this bird that was coming, flying. It flew straight into the lodge where the dead man was, and twice after it went into the lodge White Bull heard it make this noise, like an owl, and with each noise there was a flash of light, and the second light made did not go out; and there was light in the lodge all night long. After a time this bird went away into the hills, and as it went the people heard it make this noise, and every time it made the noise the light appeared, until the bird was hidden in the hills.

The close relations of the dead man sat in front of the lodge, at a little distance, and with them a number of the others, among them White Bull, some smoking, but no one talking. Pretty soon White Bull saw the lodge door lift and the light shine out, and then a man appeared. He called out, "Are you close by here?" He spoke no names, but all knew that he meant the dead man's relations. They answered, "We are here, close by." He said to them, "I want you to get some more robes, so as to make a better bed for my friend in here." While he was saying this, they all heard someone in the lodge make a slight noise, as if clearing his throat. The relations went away and got the robes, and brought them to the lodge. While they were at the lodge door, Buffalo Chips said to them: "In the morning, at daylight, a bird will come and bring water to my friend. I do not wish it to be disturbed."

Just before sunrise a bird came flying over the camp to the back of that lodge, making a rough, harsh, croaking noise. It was flying high when it came into the camp, and it flew over the lodge, turned and alighted in front of the door, and walked in.[4] Soon this bird came out of the lodge and flew off in the direction opposite to that from which it had come.

Presently Buffalo Chips came out of the lodge and said to the father and mother of the dead man, "I wish you to bring me something to eat, and something for your son." They brought food for two persons, and when the father and mother came in with the food, they found their dead son sitting up on the bed.

Buffalo Chips said to the father and mother, "I wish you to get a black horse and a blue horse. Let there be no white spot on either one. Have them ready for me in four nights. They are for me and for your son to ride. In four nights we will come out of this lodge, and we will both ride."

After four nights, in the morning, these two horses, saddled ready for riding, were led up and tied in front of this lodge. It was afternoon before the men came out. The wounded man wore in his head a white feather, and Buffalo Chips a black one. The wounded man got on the blue horse, and Buffalo Chips on the black. They rode to the right and all around the lodge. Then they passed outside the camp-circle and rode slowly around the village, and all the men and women came out and shook hands with the young man. Then they rode back to the lodge, dismounted, and went in. Then Buffalo Chips called out and said, "Now any of you people who wish to come in here may do so."

For two days more, until the camp was moved, these two

---

[4] As described, it seems to have been a great blue heron.

men lived there alone in that lodge. When the camp moved, the young man was seen riding alone, well.

During all this doctoring, Buffalo Chips never sang once. There was no sound in the lodge. It might have held only dead men.

Other Healing by Magic. Another account of healing a wounded man, in 1864, was related a few years since. In a fight with the Pawnees, a young Cheyenne named Belt was shot, the bullet passing through his head above the ears. He was carried back to the village, but could not speak nor recognize anyone. When the war-party reached the camp, his mother, Antelope Woman, took a pipe and visited two well-known gourd doctors, *Hōhk'ovo* (Bridge) and *Nōmōn'evoo* (Sleeping Rabbit), doctors who used gourd rattles to treat the wounded. These two men were Northern Cheyennes, known for their skill and success in stopping the flow of blood. They came to the lodge where the wounded man lay and sat down to the left of the entrance, near Belt.

After a time Bridge said to Sleeping Rabbit, "Wash all the blood from his head and I will cure him." Sleeping Rabbit asked Antelope Woman to bring him the largest wooden bowl she could get, half full of water. She placed the bowl before Sleeping Rabbit. Both doctors began to sing and shake their gourd rattles. While singing, Sleeping Rabbit struck himself on each side with his rattle. Then he put it on the ground and, with his right hand, pulled a fresh green cornstalk from the right-hand corner of his mouth and placed it in the bowl, and from the left corner of his mouth took another green cornstalk. He explained that when he struck his sides, he forced these stalks out of his body. He crushed the stalks in the bowl, held Belt's head over it, and washed the wound clean; then he rubbed the wounded man's head with medicine taken from a medicine bag in front of him. When he had done this the doctors asked for a skin pillow. When it was brought, Bridge directed Sleeping Rabbit to rub medicine all over it. Belt's sister was sitting near the door, and Bridge told her to sit by Belt's head. Sleeping Rabbit lifted the pillow, held it to the four points of the compass, raised it toward the sky, and, as he brought it down, put it in the lap of Belt's sister, telling her to sit still. Then they laid Belt's head on the pillow.

Bridge then told Antelope Woman to go out and get a young girl who had never known a man; to bring her in and let her make the print of her right foot on the right side of the lodge door as she entered. The girl did this and went away. Bridge took a coal from the fire, dropped a little medicine four times about it at the four directions, and the fifth time put a pinch on the coal and, with both hands, held his rattle above the smoke.

Then he walked over and struck the rattle on the ground on the girl's footprint, and it broke to pieces. During all the time he was doing this he was singing. Leaving the pieces of gourd lying there, he went to his place, took up his robe, held it to the four points of the compass, raised it high in the air, and, as he brought it down, dropped it over the broken rattle. Then he stepped back and continued singing. After a few moments he lifted the robe, and the gourd rattle, unbroken, lay on the ground under it. Bridge then spoke to those present, asking them not to move or to go out, and he and Sleeping Rabbit continued to sing and to shake their rattles. The young man went to sleep, and Bridge motioned to everyone, except Belt's sister, to leave the lodge. She was to stay with her brother, and, if he awoke soon, she should call Bridge again. Her brother slept all day and toward evening awoke.

They did not then wash the wound again, but used root medicines. In two days Belt could recognize people and talk. They doctored him for four days, then renewed the treatment for four days again, and the young man was cured. About a month later Belt's horse stumbled with him while riding and hurt his spinal cord. He went back to camp, and, as it was in the summer, sat down outside the lodge door. After resting there awhile, he tried to rise and fell over dead. This account was given in 1878 by Dull Knife, Little Wolf, and Bushy Head, who were in the Northern Cheyenne camp when it happened.

DEATH CUSTOMS AND BELIEFS

When a man died, anyone who would undertake it, usually his close relations, men and women, sometimes assisted by a comrade or a close friend, if the man had one, prepared the body for burial. It was dressed in its finest clothing, and sometimes friends and relatives brought their own best clothing for him to be buried in. The body, extended at full length, hands at sides, was placed on robes or blankets, which were then folded closely over it, and the bundle was lashed with ropes passed many times about it. The bundle was then taken out of the lodge, lashed on a travois, and carried to the place of deposit, the immediate family following.

With the man they placed his war implements—his gun, bow and arrows, and axe and knives—and also his pipe and tobacco, and anything he especially valued. If the dead man had a bow and arrows in a cougar-skin case, this was perhaps not left with him, but might be given to his comrade or close friend, if he had one very dear to him. This was done by the relatives, even if the dead man had not mentioned it. His shield and his "medicine," which usually hung outside of the lodge, were not always deposited with him. If the dead man owned horses, his best horse was saddled and bridled, and shot near the grave. Sometimes several horses were so killed. If the body was put in a tree or on a scaffold, the horses were shot under it. This was done even though a man had killed himself, but in this case the dead man did not go to Seyan.

The spirit of the dead man found the trail where the footprints all pointed the same way, followed that to the Milky Way, and finally arrived at the camp in the stars, where he met his friends and relations and lived in the camp of the dead.

On the death of a person of some importance, an old man

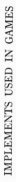

IMPLEMENTS USED IN GAMES

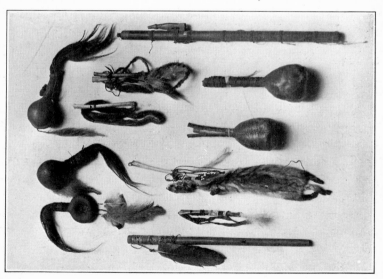

MUSICAL INSTRUMENTS

RATTLES, FLUTES, WHISTLES

sang over the dead an old-time song, and prayed to the Great Spirit that created people—*Ma' kă mă i yō' tsĭm ăn' stōm ai,* "Great spirit making maker." This ceremony, still performed, is a funeral service. The song is sung and the prayer made before the dead man is taken from the lodge or house in which he lies. The ceremony is short, occupying but a few minutes.

The burial took place soon after death. Because of the fear of ghosts, dead bodies were not kept about. The dead person having become a ghost, his spirit was likely to linger near the body, and might take away with it the spirit of some person still living. This fear was felt especially as to little children. A ghost might easily take away with it the spirit of such an one, and would be likely selfishly to do so, in order to enjoy the child's society. The power to do this was believed to be especially strong so long as the body was not removed.

Relations testified to their grief by cutting off the hair. The wife, the mother, and often the sisters, cut their hair short, gashed their heads, and sometimes the calves of their legs, with knives. Sometimes they cut off a finger. Male relations did not cut their legs, but they unbraided their hair and let it hang loose.

Women gashed their legs in mourning only when some young male relative was wounded or killed in war. If his blood had been shed, they shed theirs; but if he died from sickness, they did not cut themselves. Sometimes after the death in war of a young man with many relatives, a long line of mourning women was seen marching around the camp, their legs bare and bleeding. If the young man owned a war-bonnet, the first woman might carry it; another might carry the lance; his horses might be running loose near by, some painted as for war, with tails tied up, and feathers in manes and tails.

Women did not wash the blood from their legs and faces for a long time, and sometimes went bare-legged for months. The man's relations, male and female, mourned at the grave by wailing, as did also his close friends. A wife or a daughter or mother might remain at the grave mourning for twenty-four hours. Sometimes a wife or a mother remained at the grave, mourning and refusing to eat, until her relations went out and took her forcibly away. At intervals for a considerable time, whenever they passed the grave—even if it were twenty years after the death—they cried for the dead.

Among the Northern Cheyennes it is said that persons who at the loss of a relative did not cut off the hair or gash the person, were expected to mourn—that is, to wail—for a long time; while those who cut the hair or mutilated themselves were not obliged to wail. Some people did not like to wail and escaped the duty by having their hair cut. A woman who lost a member of her family by disease showed the outward signs of mourning for at least a year.

When a man died, all his property not placed with him—and often that of his father and even of his brothers—was given away, and to people who were not his relations. As soon as his death became known, the whole camp was likely to gather near the lodge. All the relatives were crying. The widow herself, or perhaps one of her sisters, began to carry out the property within the lodge, and to throw the things down on the ground before the various people standing about who were not relations. Then the lodge was torn down and given to someone, and soon everything was gone, and the widow perhaps retained only a single blanket with which to cover herself. This distribution took place immediately after the body was removed from the lodge, and this was always as soon after death as possible.

Thus, if a man died leaving a widow and two or three growing children, they retained nothing. They went to their grandfather or uncles, and for a year or two lived about with such relatives. In the course of this time, however, some one of her relatives was very likely to have given a lodge to the widow, and she camped near a brother, who supplied her with meat; and after a time she began to get her children back, one by one, until at last all were living with her again. If she had growing boys, they learned to hunt, and assisted in supporting her and the sisters. Such a family always got along somehow. Often widows married again. A widow decided for herself whether she would marry, or whom she would marry. When a man asked a widow to marry him, she might—after stipulating for the support and good treatment of her children—tell him to give a horse to her father, or to one of her brothers, and she would marry him.

The bodies of men, women, and children were placed on scaffolds in trees, on scaffolds on poles on the prairie, on scaffolds or on beds in a lodge, and in caves or crevices in the rocks, or were placed on the ground and stones piled over them.

Sometimes, if several people died at the same time, as often happened in epidemics, or after a battle, two or three might be placed on the same scaffold in a tree.

The body of a man who died in battle, however, was left lying on the prairie, sometimes covered with a blanket, oftener not covered. Men thought it well that the wolves, coyotes, eagles, buzzards, and other animals should eat their flesh, and scatter their bodies far and wide over the prairie.

Alights On The Cloud and his companions, who were killed in the great fight with the Pawnees in 1852, were not buried, but their fragments were gathered up and left in a little low place on the prairie covered with blankets. Persons who saw Alights On The Cloud after he had been killed, state that besides being scalped, his head, hands, and feet had been cut off, and his body ripped up. It took some time to gather up the pieces of the body and put them together, but they were at last propped in place and left as mentioned.

When a Cheyenne or an Arapaho was killed wearing a warbonnet and scalp shirt, it was considered an honorable thing to leave him untouched to be stripped by the enemy. They did not take away his fine clothing. Just what the motive was for this is doubtful; perhaps the dead man was so left in order that

163

he might present a good appearance when the enemy reached him. On the other hand, if the young man killed in war had not taken with him his war-bonnet, or had left a good horse in the camp, these were usually given to some member of the soldier band to which the dead man belonged.

When a man wounded in battle was being transported to camp, and died on the way, they made a little house, somewhat like a sweat-lodge, and placed him in it, wrapped in blankets on a bed of white sage. The shelter was covered with grass, over which the bark of trees was laid, and over all a sheet was spread and pinned down all around.

People who sang songs of mourning for the dead were likely to sing the songs of the soldier band to which the man belonged. His father, mother, sisters, or aunts might sing these. If he was a chief, they sang songs of the chief soldier band, Wihiunutkiu. There were no words to these songs.

The older Cheyennes formerly had much to say about the new diseases introduced by white men, which were very fatal. The cholera of 1849 was perhaps more fatal to the Cheyennes than any other of these epidemics, for it is said to have killed half the tribe. When it appeared, half of the Cheyennes were camped on the Smoky Hill River, in present Kansas, and half in the Kiowa camp on the Canadian River, where the Kiowas were holding their Medicine Lodge.

Porcupine Bull, the son of White Face Bull, chief of the Oivimanah, was present at the Kiowa Medicine Lodge when the cholera broke out there. It killed a Kiowa dancer in the dance lodge; and then an Osage, sitting outside watching the dance, was struck. White Face Bull shouted to the Cheyennes to run to their camp and flee. They broke camp at once and fled north all night, reaching the Cimarron in the morning. As soon as they made camp, people began to die, among them Owl Woman, the mother of Colonel Bent's wife. Little Old Man, a very brave man, donned his war-dress, mounted his war-horse, and rode through the camp with a lance in his hand, shouting,

"If I could see this thing [the cholera], if I knew where it came from, I would go there and fight it!" As he was doing this he was seized with the cramps, fell from his horse, and died in his wife's arms. Again the people rushed away in terror, and all night fled through the sandhills to the Arkansas. It was on this flight toward the north from the Kiowa camp that the Hevhaitaniu crossed the Arkansas and met Gentle Horse coming south with cholera in his camp.

USEFUL PLANTS

IN an earlier chapter I have referred to the use of various plants by the Cheyennes for food and other purposes. The roots or fruits were eaten in addition to corn, beans, and squashes, which they cultivated in early times. Many plants were and are used for medicine, and almost every doctor employed some whose virtues he believed himself to have discovered. These constituted a part of his own secret medicine.

The gathering of the crops was the work of the women. They watched the growth of the plants, and when the time came for harvesting them, women and girls in little parties spent much time searching for the roots which were in season, and unearthing them with their digging-sticks. Again, in the later summer, when the buffalo-berries, choke-cherries, and plums ripened, parties of women set out to gather these. Often with such berrying parties went a few men, young or old, whose chief purpose was to stand guard and scan the country in order to detect the possible approach of strangers, or, if enemies unexpectedly made their appearance, to wait behind and fight them off, so that the women might escape.

In administering plant medicines, two methods are commonly used. Either an infusion is made, to be taken internally or used as a lotion; or occasionally poultices of the pulverized plant wet with cold water are applied and renewed as frequently as may be. The methods of administering the remedies described below have been given me by various doctors, many of them women, for, as already stated, women practice healing quite as frequently as men.

Some years ago I enumerated a few of the medicine plants used by the Cheyennes and, because of the interesting comments made on them by Dr. H. H. Rusby, which suggested that in a few cases experience appears to have given the Cheyennes some notion of the therapeutic value of these plants, I repeat the substance of these notes.

The Indian medicine of today is perhaps not very different from that of our forefathers six hundred years ago. It is a mingling of charms and herbs. If occasionally the administration of a plant remedy appears to be followed by good results, they try it again, and presently come to have faith in it. On the other hand, many of the plants are used less for their material than for their spiritual effect; in other words, in the treatment of the sick, as with many other things about which they feel they know very little, the Indians depend on the doctrine of signatures. A plant which possesses some property that the doctor wishes to have transferred to his patient to produce certain results, is steeped in cold or hot water and the fluid is administered to the patient with due ceremony, in the belief that this will bring about the desired result. In the same way a variety of things, organic or inorganic, are thought to transfer to the individual possessing them the special attributes or powers that they possess.

In the names of some more or less common plants that English-speaking people use today, we find remnants of this idea which persisted among our forefathers long after the time when the administration of medicines was only a part of the effort to cure, and when spells, charms, incantations, amulets, and talismans were in the common estimation as potent as they still are among most Indians.

Aside from the uses to which various woods were put in the manufacture of implements, the mechanical uses of plants were not many. In ancient times mats were woven from rushes, and baskets made for carrying loads and other purposes, from a common grass which grows in wet places. Of late years this art of weaving has passed out of use and has been almost forgotten; but Mrs. Willis Rowland, a middle-aged woman, knows how to weave baskets, having been taught by her grandmother, who told her that in her young days—early in the nineteenth century—every woman understood the art of weaving baskets from this grass. The mats of tule were used to sleep on, and were often placed on the willow mattress to make a softer bed. Of late years the common gunnysack in which grain comes is used for this purpose, and from this similar service has received the name of the plant from which the old-time mats were woven.

I owe to the kindness of the Rev. Rodolphe Petter, of Lamedeer, Montana, the etymology of the different Cheyenne plant names herein given. No one knows so much of the Cheyenne language as Mr. Petter, whose dictionary, which he has published, and whose manuscript grammar (now, I believe, in the Newberry Library in Chicago) constitute the final word on this language. Mr. Petter has very kindly read over this list of plant names, and whatever linguistic material it contains is due to his erudition.

Most of the species here enumerated, but not all of them, were identified at the Bureau of Plant Industry in Washington, through the courtesy of Dr. F. V. Coville, the botanist of the Bureau, and Mr. O. M. Freeman. To their patient kindness I owe several most helpful suggestions.

Without attempting to name the families, it is a general fact that fungi are used as food and in other ways. Various mushrooms are eaten, and several kinds of food fungus are described. There is a large fungus, spherical above and flat below, which grows on cottonwood trees, that was boiled and eaten with grease, or was cut up and boiled as an ingredient in soups. A toadstool or mushroom which cannot be identified, after being dried and reduced to powder, was used to sprinkle over the burning coal in certain ceremonies to make a purifying smoke. A fungus which grows on trunks or limbs of trees, and which often has somewhat the shape of an ear, is called "one's ears." This looks somewhat like old-fashioned dried apples, and these are called by the same name.

A story is told of a bad being who used to enter the lodges at night and bite off people's ears, which he wore on a string about his neck. The hero who finally deceived and overcame this person gained his confidence by making for himself a necklet of these fungi, which he wore.

(1) *Evernia vulpina* (L.), made yellow by heat, *ē ōv′ a ōh′ a* (*heōv′*, yellow; *howa*, implies heat).

This lichen, when boiled in water, makes a deep yellow dye used in coloring porcupine quills. The water must be cool before the quills are put in it, and then they should be left in the dye for at least a day.

(2) *Equisetum arvense* (L.), horse medicine, *mō ĭn′ ă ăm ĕs sē ĕ-ohk* (*mo ē′*, elk, domesticated; *ĕs sē ĕ ohk*, medicine).

This medicine is used, as its name implies, for horses only. An infusion is made of the stems and leaves, and the fluid poured down the throat of a horse that has a hard cough.

(3) *Abies* sp. with fungus, *Melampsorella elatina*, sweet pine, *mē ē mī′ ă tŭn* (*mē ē′ mī*, smell, fragrance; *ă tŭn*, denotes incense smoke).

This is believed to be the common fir of the region, but is a diseased form. Only on an occasional tree is a twig or two of this yellow color found growing. The leaves are used in ceremonial purifying and are burned with or without sweet grass on a live coal. It is used in sickness to purify and make stronger the medicine used by the doctor, and to make the patient more receptive. Found infrequently, it is considered important and desirable to mix with other plants burned over a coal for purposes of purifying.

(4) *Juniperus sibirica* Burgsd., hollow evergreen, *wī′ ĭv tsĭs′ tŏ tŏ″* (*wī′ ĭv*, refers to something hollow, as depressions or ravines where ground cedars grow; *tsĭs′ tŏ tō*, any coniferous tree).

This is a cedar or juniper growing close along the ground and common in the higher hills. A tea made by steeping the leaves in hot water is used to help a cough or a tickling in the throat. If the cough

169

is bad, the patient may chew one or two of the berries and swallow the juice.

(5) *Juniperus scopulorum* Sarg. (a tall tree), *wĭ' ĭv tsĭs' tŏ tō'*, as above.

A tea made by steeping the leaves and drunk will relieve constant coughing or a tickling in the throat.

(6) *Typha latifolia* (L.), flag, *wĭ' tăn ōts* (*wĭtăn*, tongues; *ōts*, plant).

This is the ordinary cattail flag. The dried pulverized root and white base of the leaves are steeped in hot water and given as a drink to relieve cramps in the abdomen—"belly-ache."

(7) (?) *Sagittaria* sp., *hō hăst' sōh'* (*hō hăst'*, shining, glistening; *sōh'*, stalk).

I have not been able to secure a specimen of this plant, which is described as growing at the edge of water, an arrow-shaped leaf with a tall stem above the leaf. The blossoms at the end of the stem are said to be pink, and the stalk below the blossom is peeled and the inside eaten raw. It is tender and, when young, is slightly sweet to the taste. It may possibly be a Sagittaria.

(8) *Torresia odorata* (L.) Hitchc., sweet grass, *vīh" ō ŏts* (*vī*, refers to sweet; *ō*, grass plant; *ōts*, bunch of).

Dried sweet grass is burned over a coal in many ceremonies. It is also used as a perfume, and when so used is wrapped up with articles to which it is desired to give the odor. Its fragrance is very noticeable at some distance, as one is walking or riding along.

(9) *Eleocharis* sp., interpreted as: smooth chips or scrapings of the buffalo-hide, *sōhk' ā nă wŭhk' tsĭt* (*ē sōhk*, smooth (pl., *ē sōhk-e ne*); *nŏ wōhk ts ts*, chunk, chip, lump).

This spike rush was formerly used in basket-making. The baskets made were large and small. The small ones were sometimes used as dishes in which to serve food, and those still smaller were made for children's playthings. Another sort, when fastened at the head of a baby's board, formed a shade for the face. The large baskets were used to hold small utensils and for carrying loads on the back.

(10) *Scirpus nevadensis* S. Wats., pretty plant, *mō ūm' stăts* (?), stately shaped (plant) (*mō ōma*, stately).

"Pretty plant," in allusion to its shape and manner of growth. In old times women wove of these tule stems mats to be spread like blankets on the primitive wooden mattress. They now call the gunny-sack which is often used as the foundation of a bed, *mō ŭm stăts*.

The roots of these rushes are eaten. They are white, six or eight inches long, and are easily pulled up. The outside sheath is removed and the root eaten raw. Two or three roots would serve for a meal.

(11) *Acorus calamus* (L.), bitter medicine, *wĭ' ŭhk ĭs ē' ĕyo* (*wĭ-ŭhk*, bitter; *ĭsē' ĕ yo*, root (pl., *sēē ohk ts*, bunch of roots), remedy, medicine).

An infusion from a little of this root boiled in water is drunk for pain in the bowels, while the root chewed and rubbed on the skin is good for any illness. A bit of the root tied to a child's necklet, dress, or blanket, will keep away the night spirits.

This plant does not grow in the northern country, but is obtained by the Cheyennes from the Sioux. In former times they mixed a little of the pulverized root with red-willow bark, and used it for smoking.

(12) *Juncus balticus* Willd., for robe ornamenting, *hō ōmā' wĭshē-mēn ŏh' to wĭts* (*hō ōmā'*, robe; *wĭshē*, wherewith; *mēn ŏh' to wĭts*, ornamenting with quills, or other things to be applied).

From the rootstock, from which the stems grow, are developed very slender, fine rootlets which in earlier days were used in the ornamentation of robes or other leather, being sewed in patterns on the leather.

The stems of this rush are said to have been used in old times for weaving baskets, which are no longer made.

(13) *Allium sibiricum* (L.), *Allium nuttallii* S. Wats., skunk testes, *khā ā' mŏt ōt kē' wăt, khā ŏhk tsĭ mē' ĭs tsē hĭ*, skunk it smells (*kha*, urine, and is a usual prefix for weasel, skunk, mink, and similar animals which have a strong odor; *ma tah ke wăt*, testes; *e me e nōts*, it smells).

These two species of wild onion are extremely abundant in damp meadows of stream bottoms, but they are seldom eaten at the present day. Formerly they were boiled with meat, especially when the Cheyennes lacked salt and wished to flavor the food.

(14) *Allium brevistylum* S. Wats., *păt sē' wŏts* [unrecognized].

For use as a relief for a carbuncle both before and after it opens. The roots and stems of this onion are ground fine and applied over the place as a poultice. After the sore is opened, the medicine is boiled and some of the infusion poured into it, to loosen and clear out the pus which clings within the cavity.

(15) *Calochortus gunnisonii* S. Wats., *ĕhkā' ĭ nĭ'' kăn* (etymology uncertain; *hkā' ĭ nĭ*, means straight face).

The long, sweet-tasting bulbs of this species of mariposa lily are gathered, dried, and stored for use in winter. After they are dry, they are pounded fine and the meal boiled alone makes a sweet porridge or mush. When cooked fresh, these bulbs are very tender and likely to fall to pieces.

The showy white red-centered flowers are sometimes called *tsāĭmĭt' ăn*, war-bonnet.

(16) *Eriogonum subalpinum* Greene, medicine, *hĭssē' ĕ yō* (*ĭssē' ĕots*, roots).

This is considered very scarce, and very desirable; but this applies only to the lower plains where the Cheyennes live at present. In the Big Horn Mountains it is extremely abundant, and grows everywhere in the open. When full blown, the flowers are yellow.

If a woman's menses run too long, a strong tea made from the powdered stems and flowers will stop the trouble. A tablespoonful or two of the tea drunk will act at once. The medicine is so desirable that a man of family would often give a horse for a small portion of the prepared medicine.

(17) *Rumex venosus* Pursh., red maker, *mā' ĭ tŭk ŏhē'* (*mā' ĭ*, red; *tăhk kō ē'*, refers to steeping in water).

From the roots and dried leaves of this dock, yellow and red dye is made. The roots are cut in small pieces and boiled. After the infusion has cooled, the feathers, quills, or hair to be dyed are put in the water to be dyed yellow. If a deep color is desired, the materials are left all night in a covered vessel; immersion for a shorter time produces a paler color. If a red dye is required, ashes are put in the yellow dye liquid, which is boiled again and allowed to cool, when it becomes red. The strength of the color is varied by longer or shorter immersions. If a black dye is needed, the bark is taken from red-willow shoots, scorched and pounded fine, and put in the red or yellow dye and boiled again.

(18) *Rumex crispus* (L.), red medicine, *māh ĕsk ō ē'* (*mā' ĭ*, red;

USEFUL PLANTS

ĕsh ko ē' refers to steeping); *māh ē tsē' ĭ yŏ* (*mai*, red; *ĭs sē' ĕ o*, blood-root, *i.e.*, remedy against bleeding).

This species of dock is a dye, and also a remedy. The leaves and stems are boiled together; and after the liquor has cooled, the porcupine quills to be colored are put in the fluid and left there for twelve to twenty-four hours, when they come out bright yellow in color. The women who are dyeing the quills watch them carefully to see how the operation is progressing.

Used as medicine, the dried root is pounded until pulverized, and a pinch of it put in boiling water. After it has become cool, the infusion is drunk as a remedy for hemorrhage of the lungs.

It is also used externally, some of the pounded dried root being wetted and placed as a poultice on a wound or sore. The dried root is almost without taste.

(19) *Bistorta bistortoides* (Pursh.) Small., tasteless, *ā ĭs' tō mĭmĭs' sĭs* (*ā ĭs tōm*, for nothing, vain, false; *mĭs' sĭs*, from *mĕsĕ*, to eat).

This is very abundant in stream bottoms in the Big Horn Mountains. It produces one or at most two roots from the size of a pea to the size of a man's thumb. In places where it is plentiful, a woman might gather a pint or more of these small roots in a morning. The roots are usually boiled fresh with meat; and in old times, when the Cheyennes ranged where it grew, it was a most highly esteemed food plant.

I have heard it called also *āi' ĭs tŏm ĭ mĭ sĭs' tŭk, toco*, diminutive; and also *hō wāi' ĭs tŏm ĭk*, which means "entirely for nothing" (as to taste—tasteless).

(20) *Nymphea polysepala* (Engelm.) Greene, spongy, *hēh păn'* ? (interpreted as spongy, soft, with the sense of being water-soaked, from the character of the root's flesh. Mr. Petter thinks the word probably adapted).

Though not often seen in Montana, this spatter dock grows freely in favorable situations to the east and also to the south. The roots, from which it takes its name, were eaten raw or cooked. They are of varying size, sometimes not larger than a hen's egg, and at others, long and thick. When cooked, they were usually boiled.

(21) *Thalictrum sparsiflorum* Turcz., horse medicine, *mō ĭ' na-*

173

mē ĭt sē' ĕ yo (*mō ĭ' nă ăm,* horse (domesticated elk)); *ĭs sē' eo,* root (medicine).

Dried and ground to fine powder, this meadow rue is used for the purpose of making a horse spirited, long-winded, and enduring. The detail of its administration is given elsewhere, page 141.

(22) *Actæa arguta* Nutt., sweet medicine, *mŏtsī' ĭŭn* (the name of the culture hero; *mŏtsī* is a prefix used to denote male of large animals, like bull, buck, ram).

The roots and stems, after they have been dried, may be pounded up to make an infusion to be given to a woman after childbirth, to make the first milk secretion pass off quickly. It is considered generally a good medicine for the blood. Often it is boiled with the blue medicine (*Mertensia*). Either of the two may be used alone, but better results are thought to be had by mixing them. The roots of sweet medicine need not be pounded fine to make the infusion, but may merely be cut in small pieces before being steeped in the hot water; in this respect it differs from most other medicines. It is believed that the roots of sweet medicine lose some portion of their strength in drying, and to prevent this loss they are commonly scalded in water in which a little fat has been boiled; this often leaves the roots covered with a whitish coating of grease.

Sweet Medicine, or Sweet Root, the Cheyenne culture hero, after he had returned to the tribe, is said to have named this plant for himself, telling the people that this would help them to save and to bring up their children.

(23) *Bursa bursa-pastoris* (L.) Britton, blue medicine or headache medicine, *ho tăt' wĭ sē' ĕ yo* (*otă tăv',* blue; *wĭ sē' ĕ yo,* medicine); *mĭk ōn ĭv tsē hĭsts* (*mĭ kōn ĭva,* with, on, or for the head (*mĕ ko*); *tsī hist a,* having to do with).

The powdered leaves and stems put in a little cold water are allowed to stand for awhile and the infusion is then drunk. This speedily relieves a pain in the head. The powder may be taken in small quantities without the water; but used in this way it burns the tongue. The plant is called either blue medicine or headache medicine.

(24) *Arabis glabra* (L.) Bernh., yellow medicine (but not the same as *Senecio triangularis*), *ē hyōv' ĭ sē' ĕ yo* (*ē ōv',* yellow root or medicine).

This is used to check a cold when it first appears, and also, they say, as a general preventive of sickness; and is "given to children when sickness is about." An infusion is made and drunk in varying quantities. It may also be used as a beverage.

(25) *Grossularia setosa* (Lindl.) Cov. & Britt., *ēshko' vǐ tǎ sǐ'-mǐns* (*ěsh kōv*, thorny; *hǐs tǎ ǎ tsi*, heart-shaped; *mǐns*, berry).

This gooseberry is the earliest fruit to ripen that the Cheyennes know, and is most commonly eaten, cooked or uncooked, just after gathering. In old times it was used as a winter food, dried and formed in little cakes, as currants were once treated.

(26) *Ribes lacustre* (Pers.) Poir., elk-berry, *mō ě' ětǎ tsǐ' mǐns* (*mō ě*, elk; *hǐs ta a tsi*, heart-shaped; *mǐns*, berry. The notion is not that the berries are shaped like the heart of an elk, but that they are of the heart-shaped berries known as elk-berries).

This berry is usually eaten fresh, though if gathered in sufficient numbers it may be dried and used as are dried sarvisberries.

(27) *Ribes inebrians* Lindl., red currants, *māh' kī mǐns* (*mā' ǐ*, red; *kǐs*, little; *mǐns*, berry).

The fruit of this plant is gathered in quantity, like sarvisberries. The fresh berries are pounded fine between stones, and the pulp is formed into little round cakes and dried. These cakes were often stewed with the chips, or scrapings, from buffalo-hides.

(28) *Ribes aureum* Pursh., yellow currant, *ē hyō' wā tā sǐ' mǐns* (*ē hyō' wā*, yellow; *tā sǐ'mǐns*, heart-shaped berry).

Yellow currants are few in the present range of the Cheyennes. Formerly they were pounded up, dried, and made in cakes for winter use, somewhat as choke-cherries are pounded and dried. From lack of the fruit, this is no longer done.

(29) *Ribes ?* [*aureum* Pursh.], black currants, *sōh'k ō tā sǐ' mǐns* (*sōh' kōm*, slender; *tā sǐ'*, heart-shaped; *mǐns*, berry).

The Cheyennes knew large low-growing black currants, which may be a black-berried form of *R. aureum* or still another species.

(30) *Saxifraga jamesi* Torr., red medicine, *māh ǐs sē' ě yō* (*mā' ǐ*, red; *ǐs sē' ě yō*, medicine).

The dried plant should be rubbed in the hands until finely powdered, and then boiled. A patient who has hemorrhage of the lungs should drink of this tea as much as he may care to at one time, and this will speedily relieve the trouble.

(31) *Heuchera ovalifolia* Nutt., rheumatism medicine, *ē hyō′ ĭs-sē′ ĕ yō* (*ē ōv*, yellow; *ĭs sē′ ĕ yō*, medicine).

A remedy for rheumatism, or generally for sore muscles. The roots are ground fine and the powder rubbed on the skin. This powder of the pulverized root feels gummy, and tends to cling to the skin. The top is powdered and made into a tea with hot water, to be drunk by the patient.

(32) *Parnassia fimbriata* Konig., for children to drink, *kăs kūn′ ĭ-sĕstĭ măn ĭ′ wăts* (*kăs gōn*, children; *măn owă′ tots*, a beverage; *măn-owa′ to*, to give drink).

From the powdered leaves of this plant a tea is made, which is administered to very small babies when dull or when sick at the stomach.

(33) *Amelanchier alnifolia* Nutt., male berry, *hē tăn′ ĭ mĭns* (*hē-tăn′*, male; *mĭns*).

When the opportunity occurs, sarvisberries are gathered in quantity, dried, and stored for winter use, when they are stewed and become an important article in feasts. I have not learned that among the Cheyennes they have a sacred character as they did among the Blackfeet, but the name suggests that they possess strong qualities. Dr. M. R. Gilmore has told me that he finds this name in use among several Plains tribes. A tea made from the leaves is used as a beverage.

Also, a tea made from the leaves of this tree is used in healing. The fluid is red in color and has a flat taste. Some informants say it tastes like green tea.

(34) *Cratægus douglasii* Lindl., haw, *nāh′ kō tăsĭ′ mĭns* (*nāh′ kō*, bear; *tăsĭ′mĭns*, heart-shaped berry).

The berries of this haw, gathered late in the fall when ripe, are pulverized, dried, and saved for use in winter. The berries cling to the trees all through the winter, and may be gathered at any time and cooked fresh. "Pack-rats" (*Neotoma*) gather these berries and store them, and sometimes the Indian women find their caches.

(35) *Fragaria glauca* (S. Wats.) Rydb., strawberry, *wĭs′ kē ē-mĭns* (*wĭs′ kē*, small (when many are implied, *i.e.*, the visible seeds in the fruit); *mĭns*, berry).

(36) *Dasiphora fruticosa* (L.) Rydb., Contrary medicine, *ō nŭhk′-ĭs ē′ ĕ yo* (*ōh nŏhk*, contrary, opposed, + medicine).

MEDICINE LODGE
BRINGING THE OFFERINGS

During the Contrary dance this plant is used to protect the hands from injury when they are thrust into the kettle of boiling soup. The leaves, after having been dried, are ground to a fine powder, which may be rubbed over the hands, arms, and body; or an infusion of the powder may be made by soaking it for a time in cold water, and the infusion may be rubbed over the whole body. It is said perfectly to protect the parts exposed to a severe temporary heat.

(37) *Rubus occidentalis* (L.), black raspberry, *mŏhk" tāh wis-kē ē' mĭns* (*mŏhk" tāh,* black; *wĭs kē ē' mĭns,* as above).

(38) *Rubus melanolasius* Focke, raspberry, *wĭs kē ē' mĭns.* (See above, *Fragaria glauca.*)

The red raspberry is always eaten fresh.

(39) *Rosa fendleri* Crep., rose-berry, *hīh' nĭn* (*hīh' nĭn,* to pour out (as water, flour, grain); also the name for tomato).

Rose-berries must not be eaten too freely.

(40) *Prunus americana* Marsh., big berry, *māk ū mĭns'* (*māk u,* in composition, great, + berry).

Near the camps the wild plums seldom ripen because the children pick and eat them green; but in places at a distance many plums were gathered by women, and were stoned, dried in the sun, and kept for winter. When ripe plums thus dried were cooked by boiling, they became almost like cooked fresh plums. They were a great and rather unusual delicacy. The plum bushes do not always produce a crop, and sometimes for several successive seasons, as a result of late frosts or from some other cause, no crop of plums is had.

(41) *Prunus besseyi* Bailey, *mŭh' kō tă' mĭns* (*mŭhk ho tsi hi,* to smell from a distance; interpreted as: *mŭh' kō tā,* it "winds," or actively smells or scents people (the word would be used of game catching the scent of persons), + *mĭns*).

In picking these cherries, if the scent of a human being reaches them, their taste is spoiled, hence they must always be picked from the leeward side. Dr. Gilmore states that this belief is held by other Plains tribes.

(42) *Prunus melanocarpa* (A. Nels.) Rydb., *mĭns* (berry; a general term, but usually applied to the choke-cherry).

This is perhaps the most abundant and important fruit that the Cheyennes have; it is "the berry" *par excellence*. It is gathered in quantities, pounded fine—pits and all—on stone anvils, and the pulp made into flat cakes which are dried in the sun and saved for winter use. Pounded choke-cherries were used in making fine pemmican—berry pemmican. These cherries, fresh or pounded and dried, are not separated from the pits.

(43) *Psoralea lanceolata* Pursh., *mŏhk' tā ēn'* (*mŏhk" ta,* black; *ēn,* face).

The well-known Indian turnip, so called—or, as the French termed it, white potato (tipsen of Gilmore), was a very important root to the Cheyennes, as it has been to many tribes. The roots were gathered by women in early summer. They are still harvested, and are unearthed by means of an iron bar, for the old-fashioned root-digger has entirely passed out of use, and now appears only in certain ceremonies.

(44) *Psoralea argophylla* Pursh., "to-make-cold medicine," *tō'-wăn ĭ yŭhk ts* (*tō,* cool; *wăn ĭ o nots,* ingredients to).

This is used to reduce fever. The leaves and stems are ground fine and boiled in water, and the tea is drunk. To cure a high fever, the leaves and stem ground to powder are also mixed with grease and rubbed all over the body. Dr. Rusby has said that the medicinal properties of this plant are not known to science, but it is a near relative of species having active and important properties, though not much used in medicine. Its use as a febrifuge is of great interest and very suggestive.

(45) *Psoralea hypogeæ* Nutt., *mā ĭm mŏhk' tā' ĕn* (*mai,* red; *mŏhk ta,* black; *ĕn,* face).

This is similar to *pomme blanche,* and is eaten fresh or is dried for winter use. The flesh of the root is red. It does not grow so large as mohktaen, perhaps only to the size of a hen's egg; while *pomme blanche* may be four times as large. It is more tender and to the taste more delicate than *pomme blanche,* and is highly esteemed. The whites call it "red turnip."

(46) *Glycyrrhiza lepidota* (Nutt.) Pursh., yellow-jacket, *hăht' nō-wăssŏph* (*hăh nōm,* stinger (bee, wasp); *wa,* suffix with stative meaning; *ŏ,* plant or growing like a plant).

The shoots of this wild licorice, when it starts in spring, are cut off close to the ground and eaten raw. They are good to eat until they are a foot high and begin to leaf out. The name wasp, or yellow-jacket, is thought to be given the plant from the color and burs of the fruit. These burs stick to the clothing, and the Indians say yellow-jackets (wasps), when they get about one, stick to him like these burs.

(47) *Astragalus nitidus* Dougl. F., poison-weed medicine, *māhk-hă' nōwăs* (*māhk*, big or large; *no*, poison, seemingly only in connection with eating or drinking; *wa*, stative suffix).

This plant is used in cases of poisoning by ivy or other noxious plants. The leaves and stems are ground fine, and when the poisoned skin presents a watery appearance the powder is sprinkled on the afflicted parts.

The use of this plant is also interesting, and if a really efficient and reliable remedy could be found for ivy poisoning (and it is possible that this plant might be such) it might become a very important article of trade. This plant is closely related to the famous loco weed.

(48) *Oxytropis* sp., sweet (literally) medicine, *wĭ' kē ĭssē ĕ yo* (*wĭ' kē*, sweet, + root or medicine).

The powdered root of this plant, mixed with motsiiun, is given to a woman who is suckling a child, to increase her flow of milk. If the milk is becoming reduced, or if the mother has not enough for the child, this medicine will increase the flow. It is also given in the same form to a woman whose milk does not seem to agree with the child. If they lack the motsiiun to mix with this, the blue medicine (*Mertensia*) is used.

(49) *Alycine apios* (L.), *aĭ' ĭs tōm ĭ mĭ sĭs' tŭk* (*ho wāĭ' ĭs-tōm ĭk*, nothing as to taste, tasteless; *mĭs ĭs*, eating).

I have no specimen of the potato bean, but from the Indians' description, conjecture that it is this species. The older people speak of red-skinned tubers on the root of a climbing vine, which taste and look like a potato. The rounded leaf is shaped like a teaspoon and somewhat cupped. The plant grows on the North Platte, Missouri, and Laramie rivers. The largest tubers may be the size of a hen's egg. The plant with the same Cheyenne name found in the Big Horn Mountains has a root only as large as the end of the thumb, and produces one or two tubers. This is *Bistorta*. On the vine there may be half a dozen tubers on a single root.

(50) *Geranium richardsonii* Fisch. & Trautv., nose-bleed medicine,

179

măt′ o mĭn ĭs tō′ a (*măt o min,* to bleed from the nose; *ĭs sē′ ĕ o,* root).

In the case of nose-bleed, the pulverized leaf is to be rubbed on the nose and the powder snuffed up the nostrils. This will stop or check the hemorrhage. Besides this, the dried roots are powdered and an infusion made to be drunk by the patient.

(51) *Rhus glabra* (L.), *nō′ ănĭō nī maĭ′· kĭ mĭns* (*nō′ ănĭō nī,* mixing ingredients; *māh,* red; *kĭs,* small; + *mĭns*).

Sumach leaves are sometimes mixed with tobacco for smoking. The term "mixing" refers to this use of the leaves.

(52) *Rhus trilobata* Nutt., name of bush, *hō ă tō′ ŏ nŭts* (*hō ă- tō′ va,* smoke issues; refers also to prayers in ceremonial); name of leaves after being gathered and prepared; *hōh kō mē ē nŏ ăn ĭ ŏn* (*hōhk,* clean, pungent; *mē ē,* smelling; *nŏ ăn ĭ ŏ nŏts,* mixing ingredients).

The dried leaves of this plant are mixed with tobacco for use in smoking; the berries are not used. If the Indians were quite out of tobacco, they often mixed this plant with larbe (65) and red-willow bark, and this made a useful smoking mixture.

(53) *Vitis vulpina* (L.), *hōh pāh tsī nă′ mĭns* (*hōhp,* juicy, + *mĭns;* interpreted as sticky or gummy berries).

The wild grape is eaten fresh but never dried.

(54) *Malvastrum coccineum* Pursh., gray, *wĭ kĭ issē′ ĕ yo* (*wĭkĭ,* sweet, + medicine).

The plant is ground up fine, leaves, stem, and roots, and is steeped in water, the infusion to be mixed with other medicines. The tea, having a sweet taste, makes other and sometimes bad-tasting medicines more palatable.

(55) *Opuntia polyacantha* Haw., prickly fruit, *māh tā′ o mŭnst* (*măh tă′ o,* spiny, full of thorns; *mŏ nŏts,* pl. animate of *mĭns*).

The fruit of this cactus is eaten raw and is dried for winter food as well. In the South, in former days, before the occupancy of the country by white people, the gathering, drying, and storing of the fruit of the cactus was one of the women's important duties at the proper season. The fruit was collected in parfleche sacks and was then put on the ground in little piles and stirred and swept over by small brushes, made of the twigs of the sagebrush, until most of the thorns had been removed. The women, having first made little finger tips of deerskin to protect the ends of the fingers, then went over the piles and removed the last thorns from the fruit. When this had been done, the fruit was split, the seeds removed and thrown away, and the flesh dried in the sun. This was used to stew with meat and game, and made a gelatinous thickening to the soup. This fruit was still gathered as above as late as 1915.

(56) *Lepargyrœa canadensis* (L.), or more likely *L. argentea* Greene, *măt' sĭ tă sĭ' mĭns* (*măi*, red; *hĭs ta sĕ*, hearted, + *mĭns*).

The buffalo-berry—often called bull-berry—does not grow very freely in the present country of the Northern Cheyennes; but so far as they collect it, this is done much as the Indians of the Missouri River gather bull-berries. When the berries are ripe, robes or skins are placed on the ground, and the thorny bushes are beaten with sticks so that the berries fall from the twigs and may be gathered up on the skins. It would seem as if the buffalo-berry were worth attention by residents of the country where it grows, for excellent preserves may be made from it.

(57) *Chamœnerion angustifolium* Scop., red medicine, *mā hĭss ē'-ĕ yo* (*māĭ*, red (blood); + root, medicine).

A remedy given when a person has hemorrhage of the bowels. The dried and pulverized leaves are separated from the roots, and an infusion of each may be drunk. That from the leaves is much milder than that from the roots.

(58) *Osmorrhiza longistylis* (Torr.) DC.; *Osmorrhiza obtusa* (Coult. & Rose) Fernald, both species are used, *mă tā mhāo ē'* (*mă tă*, spiny; the last part of the word implies infusion by heat).

A remedy for one who feels "tight" or "bloated" in the stomach, and generally for disordered stomach. The leaves, stems, and roots are pulverized and an infusion is made of each. Before powdering the leaves and stems, the seeds must be removed and thrown away. They are very sharp-pointed and are likely to stick in the skin. The drink made from the leaves is weak, while that from the roots is much stronger.

The root, which smells like anise, may be used alone for a disordered stomach. After it is pulverized, a tea is made of it—a pinch or two of the powder to a pint of water.

This is also given if a man's kidneys do not function as they should. The root, stem, and leaves are pulverized and an infusion made which is given, not too frequently, but freely at one time.

(59) *Carum gairdneri* (H. & A.) A. Gray; "soon there will be four" (roots), *ăn'o nĭv ĭ ĭ tĭs* (having four (*nĭv*) connected elongated points).

The roots are gathered in May or June, soon after the plant starts, and a little later the roots cease to have a food value. The two to four roots are as thick as the little finger and may be eaten fresh, or are dried and saved for winter use. The roots are scraped fine and dried, or are dried without scraping, or are cooked, dried, and later pulverized, and used as a mush by pouring soup over them.

The Cheyenne name refers to the progressive increase in number of the branches of the root. At first there is but a single root, but somewhat later it has four branches.

This plant is used as a medicine, as well as for food, and is mixed with what is known as bark medicine (*Balsamorrhiza*), the roots, stems, and leaves being boiled together.

(60) *Cogswellia orientalis* C. & R. Jones; bears' food, *nāhko' hĕs-tăm' ōka* (*nāhko*, bear; *matăm*, food).

Bears are fond of the root of this plant, and dig and eat it; hence the name. As a medicine it is helpful given as a tea—both roots and leaves pounded up and steeped—or eaten dry, to relieve pain in the bowels, or diarrhea. It is used chiefly for little children, but if made stronger may be given to older people.

(61) *Cogswellia* sp., *mō tsĭns' tăhn* (meaning uncertain; presumably related to *mŏtsē*, term for male, or breeder, among large animals).

A tea made from the dried pulverized root of this plant is applied to reduce a swelling. It is cooling to the skin. When pounded fine and wet, the mixture has a greasy feeling.

(?) No specimen; No name; *stăm' ōk ăn* (same as *nāhko' hĕs tăm ōkan*, bears' food).

The root of this plant is collected, dried, pounded into meal, and saved for winter. For food it is used like *Psoralea*. It is gathered when *Psoralea* is ripe; that is to say, late in June or early in July, in Montana.

(62) *Leptotænia multifida* Nutt., *mō tsĭn' ĭsts*. Meaning uncertain; see *Cogswellia* sp. above.

This seems to be a tonic or stomach medicine. The roots, after having been dried, are pulverized and a pinch of the powder is boiled in about a pint of water and the infusion drunk, much or little according to the condition of the patient. It is taken for pains in the stomach, or for any internal disorder. It has no effect on the bowels. A weaker infusion is made from the pulverized stem and leaves, boiled as above.

(63) *Cornus stolonifera* Michx., red-willow, *măh' kōm ĕ hĭs* (*mai*, red; *kōm ĕ hĭs*, diminutive form of bark).

The plant commonly known as red-willow, or kinnikinnik. The red outer-bark is removed and thrown away, and the white under-bark dried, pulverized, and mixed with tobacco for use in smoking.

(64) *Pterospora andromeda* Nutt., nose-bleed medicine, *mātŭ'-mĭnĭs' tō ĭs sē' ĕ yo* (*matŏ men*, to bleed at the nose; + root or medicine).

Used to prevent bleeding of the nose or from the lungs. The stem and berries are ground together and an infusion is made in boiling water, which is allowed to cool. When cold, some of the infusion is snuffed up the nose and also put on the head for nose-bleed; and is drunk for hemorrhage of the lungs. This drug is moderately used as an astringent, but is not of commercial importance.

(65) *Arctostaphylos uva-ursi* (L.) Spreng., smoke leaves, *nō'ăn-ĭ ŭn ots* (*nō ăn*, to mix).

Used for persistent pain in the back, and especially for sprained back. The stems, leaves, and berries are boiled together and the infusion drunk. The wetted leaves are also rubbed on the painful place.

This is the well-known bear-berry and is a standard officinal drug. It is effectively used as a diuretic in cases of congested kidneys. In view of the qualification as to its persistence, the pain in the back to which the Indians allude is undoubtedly referable to disordered kidneys, so that we have again a confirmation of the keenness of these people in appreciating the properties of certain drugs.

The leaves are used to mix with tobacco or red-willow to smoke in a pipe, and the Cheyenne name refers to this. The well-known larbe (*l'hérbe*) of the North.

(66) *Vaccinium scoparium* Lieberg, little red berry, *măh' kĭ mĭns* (*mā'i*, red; *kĭs*, small; *mĭns*, berry).

This is the common tiny red whortleberry so widely distributed in the high Rocky Mountains. The berries, dried and pulverized, are given to a child that has a poor appetite. The dose is small—a pinch merely before the first meal of the day.

The leaves and stems, dried and pulverized, are given in about two tablespoonfuls of warm or cold water to one who is nauseated or has little appetite.

(67) *Frasera speciosa* Dougl., hard turnip, *ē kŏn ĭ mōhk tā' ĕn* (*hē kŏn*, hard, strong; *mōhk tā*, black; *ĕn*, face; *i.e.*, hard *pomme blanche*).

The leaves of the plant are dried and pulverized, and an infusion made from them is drunk by one suffering from diarrhea. The root is stronger than the leaves, and is used in the same way, if the complaint is more severe. The remedy is an efficient one.

(68) *Asclepias speciosa* Torr., milkweed, *mă tăn āī' māhkst* (*mătăn*, milk; *mătăna*, of milk, milky; *māhk*, wood; *māhkst*, pieces of wood; pl. form).

Just before the flowers open, the buds are eaten, being boiled whole in water as an ingredient of soup or with meat. After the fruit has formed, but is yet green, it is gathered, the outer skin is peeled off, and the inner layer or covering is eaten. The inside, the part that would afterward be the seeds, is rejected. This pod is called *mĭs' tā ĭ hăm' skŏn*, "owl-spoon."

When the plant is in flower, by breaking down the sessile leaves from the stalk and allowing the exuded milk to dry and harden, a chewing-gum that is much esteemed is procured.

(69) *Phlox multiflora* A. Nels., rubbed on, *ĕsk o wăn ī' o* (*eshkowa*, rough, thorny, gritty).

This appears to be a mild stimulant. The leaves and flowers are pulverized and an infusion made of them in warm water. The fluid is then rubbed over the body of a patient who is numb—has no feeling in his body. This will restore his light and natural feeling. A little of the tea may be drunk at the same time.

(70) *Mertensia ciliata* (Torr.) Don., blue medicine, *tăt' ā wĭs ē'-ĕ yō* (*otă tăw*, blue; + medicine).

This is thought to be useful in cases of smallpox and measles. An infusion is made of the leaves and the fluid drunk. In cases of smallpox, drinking an infusion of the powdered root relieves the itching.

An infusion made of this plant is given to drink to women who have just borne children and have an insufficient supply of milk, for the purpose of increasing the flow. With this is often used the sweet medicine, and also the milk medicine, *mătăna ʾissē' ĕ o*.

(71) *Lithospermum ruderale* Lehm., whiteweed, *wōh" pō ĭt* (*wōhkp*, whitish; *o'sts*, pl. form of plant, growth).

Used chiefly to relieve rheumatic pains. The leaves and stems, having been dried, are finely pulverized, a portion of the powder is wet and applied externally. It is thought it would be better if this could be kept on the painful part constantly; but since usually this is impossible, frequent applications of the poultice are made. This relieves the soreness of pain from any cause, where the skin is not broken.

(72) *Lithospermum linearifolium* Goldie, paralysis medicine, *hōh'-āhĕă nō ĭs' tūt* (from verbal root *hō ă hē*, to revive, to quicken the life).

Recommended for paralysis, and also in cases where the patient is irrational from any illness.

For paralysis, the leaves, roots, and stems are ground fine, and a very small quantity of the powder is rubbed on the paralyzed part. It causes a prickling sensation of the skin. It is said also to be sometimes used green, the doctor wrapping some of the leaves in a cotton cloth, then crushing them with her teeth, and rubbing the affected parts, when the same prickling or stinging sensation is felt.

Where the person is irrational by reason of illness, a tea is made of the roots, leaves, and stems, and rubbed on the head and face. The plant is also employed when a person is very sleepy—hard to keep awake. It is chewed fine by a doctor, who spits and blows the medicine in the patient's face and rubs some of it over his heart.

The prickling sensation referred to is probably largely mechanical and is due to the extremely fine hairs of the plant which will account for the counter-irritant effect. Beyond this the borage family is very little understood, though many of its members are used as diuretics.

(73) *Onosmodium occidentale* Mackenzie, big rough medicine, *māk ĕsk ō' wă nĭ' ā* (*mahk*, large; *ĕshk ō wă nĭ' a*, thorny, rough, gritty).

If a patient's skin is without feeling—is numb—the leaves and stem of this plant, after being pulverized and mixed with a little grease, are rubbed on the afflicted part and sometimes over the whole body. This seems to restore life to the skin. The remedy is used to advantage in cases of lumbago.

(74) *Agastache anethiodora* (Nutt.) Britt., elk mint, *mō ē'-ēmŏhk' shĭn* (*mo ē*, elk; *mŏhk' shĭn*, mint).

Used as tea by boiling the leaves, it makes a pleasant drink. An infusion of the leaves when allowed to become cold is good for pain in the chest (as when the lungs are sore from much coughing), or for a weak heart.

(75) *Monarda menthæfolia* Benth., bitter perfume, *wī' ŭs kī-mŏhk' shĭn* (*wī' ŏhk*, bitter; *mŏhk' shĭn*, mint or perfume); horse perfume, *mō īn' ă mŏhk' shĭn* (*mō īn' ă*, horse, + *mŏhk' shĭn*).

This plant is in part ceremonial. Its stems and flowers were employed to make pillows used by young girls from puberty to marriage. The pillow was made of deerskin and was filled with antelope-hair. One side was embroidered with porcupine quillwork for show and ornament during the day; but when the pillow was in use, the head rested on the unornamented side. The stems and flowers of the plant were used in the pillow, next to the ornamented deerskin, for the purpose of lessening, "killing," the odor of the antelope-hair.

The plant was used also by young men to perfume their favorite horses, especially as to the manes and tails. The leaves were chewed fine and blown on the animals from the mouth. A lad who was particularly fond of his sister might occasionally perfume over its whole body the horse she was to ride. Sometimes a young man used the plant to perfume his body, clothing, and robe. Usually the dried leaves of this plant were mixed with the needles of a sweet fragrant pine; and both, pulverized, were kept in a little bundle for use in burning over a coal at any time. Sweet pine is very rare on the Tongue River Indian Reservation.

(76) *Mentha canadensis* (L.), vomiting medicine, *hē hēyŭts'-tsĭhĭss' ōts* (*e hĭ' he ots e' ots*, he vomits); *māhpĕ mŏk' shĭn* (*mapi*, water; *mŏhk' shĭn*, mint or perfume).

To prevent vomiting, grind the leaves and stems fine, boil them in water, and drink the tea slowly.

One of the varieties of this plant is a source of menthol, which latter is largely used as an antiemetic; hence interest attaches to its use by these Indians.

(77) *Pedicularis grœnlandica* Retz., red (pink) medicine, *māh-ōm' ăts* (*ma ōm a āhkts,* reddish, pinkish).

An infusion of this medicine is drunk to stop or to loosen a cough which has run for a long time. The leaves and stems are rubbed to a powder, and a pinch put in the water and boiled for a long time. It is considered a useful medicine.

(78) *Chrysopsis foliosa* Nutt., chickadee plant, *mĭs' kă tsī,* or *mĭs-kă hĕts'* (from *mesh,* hairy).

An infusion made of the top and stems of this plant is given to one who is feeling generally poorly. The drink tends to put him to sleep. From the description, it appears to be a soothing, quieting medicine.

The name is given it because the chickadee—titmouse—commonly eats the seeds of the plant.

(79) *Chrysothamnus nauseosus* (Pursh.) Britt., scabby medicine, *ō' ĭv ĭs sē' ĕ yo* (*ō' ĭv,* skin scabby—itch).

This is used to heal eruptions or sores on the body. The leaves and stems are boiled together, and the affected parts are washed with the infusion. If this does not soon effect a cure, the fluid must be rubbed on hard. In severe cases some of the tea must be drunk; it is used in this way to cure smallpox. The plant has no medicinal properties known to science.

(80) *Aster cusickii* (?), ear medicine, *stō' wāhts ĭs sē' ĕ yo* (*hĭs'-to wō ōts,* one's ears; + root).

To relieve earache, an infusion is made of the dried stems of this plant and a little of it dropped in the ear.

(81) *Erigeron salsuginosus* (Richards) A. Gray; pink medicine, *mā hōm' ă ŭts ĭs sē' ĕ ao* (*mā ōm' ă ŏhkts,* reddish, pinkish, as above).

This remedy is used for one who is dizzy, or who has a backache, or who tends to be drowsy. The roots, stems, and flowers are dried, pulverized, and put in hot water so as to make a hot infusion. A blanket is put about the patient, and he sits over the vessel containing the steaming fluid and sweats himself. If a patient has an ache between the shoulders, the painful part should be kept wet with the infusion. A little of it may be drunk.

(82) *Anaphalis margaritacea* var. *subalpina* A. Gray, strong medicine, *sīhy'ā īnŏ ē ĭs sē' ĕ o* (*tsi o,* that which; *o hāā,* highly; *ī nŏ,* flavored, seasoned—of taste).

If a gift, to be left on a hill, is to be made to the sun or to the spirits, this "strong medicine" is used to smoke and purify it before it is taken out. The leaves of the medicine are dropped on a burning coal, as sweet grass or sweet pine is used in smoking other things.

In one of his little medicine-bundles, each man carries some of the dried and powdered flowers of this plant; and formerly, when going into battle, he chewed a little of it and rubbed it over his arms, legs, and body, for the purpose of imparting strength, energy, and dash, and thus protecting him from danger.

A man still puts a little of the powder on the sole of each hoof of the horse he is riding, in order to make it enduring and untiring, and he blows a little of the powder between the animal's ears, also for the purpose of making it long-winded. The medicine is rubbed on the body so that the warrior may be hard to hit by the missiles of an enemy. After this medicine has been rubbed on him, no woman may touch the man. To do so nullifies the power of the medicine.

The dried flowers of the plant may be rubbed into a very fine, light dust, which is easily blown away or moved by any force, and the qualities that it is believed to impart to one treated with it probably have reference to this readiness with which it is moved.

(83) *Ambrosia psilostachya* DC., black sage, *mōhk tāh' wānōtst* (*mōhk tā*, black; *wānōtst*, sage, pl. form).

For cramps in the bowels and to stop bloody stools. Grind the leaves and stems fine and make a tea, using a pinch of the powder to a cupful of water. Drink this, and the pains and bleeding will cease. A tea made from the plant will help a cold.

(84) *Echinacea angustifolia* DC., black medicine, *mŏhk tā' wĭ sē'-ĕ yo* (*mŏhk tā*, black; + root).

This is a remedy for sore mouth, gums, or throat. The leaves and roots, when powdered, are used to make an infusion which is drunk. Moreover, the patient may be given a piece of the unground root to hold in the mouth and chew a little, letting the saliva run down the throat. A toothache, resulting from a hollow tooth, is relieved if some of this juice can be got on it. The infusion, rubbed on a sore neck, will relieve and finally remove the pain. This root has a distinct and unusual taste,—salty, and somewhat cool,—and stimulates the flow of saliva.

(85) *Ratibida columnaris* (Sims.) T. & G., rattlesnake medicine,

shĭ' shĭn o wŭts' tsē ĭ yō (*shĭ' shĭn,* rattle; *shĭ shĭn o wŭts,* rattle of flesh, *i.e.,* rattlesnake).

The leaves and stems are boiled and make a yellow solution, an external application of which relieves the pain and, it is believed, will draw out the poison of a rattlesnake's bite. The same fluid gives quick relief in cases of poisoning by ivy (*Rhus toxicodendron*). This is a yellow cone flower, very common on the high prairie.

(86) *Balsamorrhiza incana* Nutt., or *B. sagittata* (Pursh.) Nutt., bark medicine, *ē tŭn ĕ hĭss ē' ĕ yō* (*ē tŭn eŏ* (inside) bark); *kătstsŭn' ĕ ĭs sē ĕ yō* is the name of the young of the same plant.

This is a remedy for a cold, for stomach trouble, and for headache.

For pains in the stomach, the leaves, roots, and stems are boiled together and the infusion drunk. For headache, the face is steamed over the boiling tea, the head and the vessel containing the fluid being covered with a cloth. Some of the tea is rubbed on the part where the pain is felt.

Dr. Rusby says: "This is not a highly important medicinal agent, yet at the present time it is attracting considerable attention as a carminative, anti-spasmodic and alterative. It is interesting to note that these are the very properties indicated in the Cheyenne uses."

(87) *Helianthus tuberosus* (L.), *hōh ĭ nōn',* brought back by scouts.

Grows in damp places. Tubers grow on the roots of the plant. The artichoke, which is a species of sunflower, is scarcely found in the North, *i.e.,* Montana, but is abundant to the south—say southern Wyoming, Colorado, and Oklahoma. Also called *hō ĭ nŏhk' kŏn.* Both Cheyenne names are now applied to the sweet potato.

(88) *Achillea lanulosa* Nutt., cough medicine, *ĭ hā' ĭ sē' ĕ yō* (*i iyha,* to cough; *ĭs sē ĕ o,* root, remedy).

A remedy for a cough or to relieve tickling in the throat. The plant, either freshly collected or dried, is pounded fine, and put in hot water so that an infusion is made. It is then drunk little by little for the relief of the trouble. It may be used at any time of the year.

Tea made of the leaves, green or dried, is good for anyone having slight nausea. The same tea is useful in case of a cold.

(89) *Matricaria matricarioides* (Less.) Porter, prairiedog perfume, *ŏ'nŏnĭ wōnskĭ ă mŏhk' shĭn* (original meaning of *ŏ'nŏnĭ wōnskĭ*

was "not well known or seen (buffalo) heifers"; *ŏ'nŏnĕ*, not well known or recognized; *mŏk'shĭn*, mint or perfume).

The flowers and leaves of this little plant, mixed with two other plants, make a favorite perfume. These plants are sweet grass and horse-mint (*Monarda*), and sometimes sweet pine. The different plants are dried, pulverized, and the powder mixed.

The Cheyennes say that ononiwonski means Ree beans, and also means prairie-dog (*Cynomys*); that the beans used by the Rees all look alike. When they first came out on the plains and reached the range of the prairie-dogs, those animals all looked alike to them; and from this similarity of appearance they were called Ree beans. *Ŏ' no nio* = Arikara Indian.

(90) *Tanacetum vulgare* (L.), yellow medicine (not the same as others similarly named), *ē hyō' ĭs sē' ĕ o* (*ē ŏvĕ*, yellow).

This remedy is used for a patient who is weak and feels dizzy. The stems are not used, but the leaves and blossoms are pulverized and an infusion made which the patient drinks.

(91) *Artemisia gnaphalodes* Nutt., man sage, *hē tăn' ĭ wān' ōts* (*hētăn'*, man or male; *wān' ōts*, sage).

This is a ceremonial plant used for many purposes. On ceremonial occasions it is spread about the borders of a lodge in a special way. Other uses are to wipe off ceremonial paint; or to purify, by wiping off, with a bundle of the sage, the body of one who has committed some fault—violated some tabu. It is used by Contraries to wipe off the ground in a lodge where a Contrary has been seated. There are frequent references to these uses elsewhere in this book.

The dried leaves are burned on the coal to make a smoke used in purifying implements or utensils used in ceremony; or to smoke, and so purify, the body of an individual. This is to drive away bad spirits, and particularly to drive away a bad or ominous dream had by a sick person, which dream may remain in the mind of the person and trouble him. It may be mixed with motsinists—a small pinch of each in about the same quantity—for the same purpose. The patient who is being smoked sits over the coal on which the sage is being sprinkled, with a blanket over the body and the coal in order to confine the smoke.

(92) *Senecio triangularis* Hook., yellow medicine, *ē hyō' vē sē ĕ yo* (*ē ōv'*, yellow).

Given to a patient who has a pain in his chest, this will relieve the pain. It acts also as a sedative. The roots and leaves are used separately. An infusion is made, in hot water, of the pulverized leaves or of the roots, which the patient drinks.

(93) *Cirsium edule* Nutt., a thistle, *ĕsk kō' wāts* (refers to something thorny; *ĕsh ko,* tapering to a point; *wets* implies collectively).

The stalk of this thistle when young, say a foot or eighteen inches high, is cut off; and after the thorny skin has been peeled from it, the stem is eaten as a great luxury. This peeled stem is sweet and soft, and is greatly relished. The plant does not grow in the plains country, but is found in the Big Horn Mountains. It is often spoken of as a fruit, the Indians comparing it to a banana.

(94) *Lygodesmia juncea* (Pursh.) D. Don., blue medicine, *tăt' ā-wĭs ē' ĕ yō;* milk medicine, *mătă'nă ĭs sē' ĕ ō.*

See description of No. 70.

CEREMONIAL

THE Cheyennes have much ceremonial accompanied with extended and varied ritual. I have been present at many of these ceremonies, and have recorded what I saw and secured such explanation as I could. Yet, after all, this gives little idea of the actual meaning of what takes place, and since the various acts are but imperfectly under- stood—either as to meaning or to motive—the full significance of these ceremonies cannot be comprehended. Some of them are extraordinarily detailed and wearisome in their repetition. I believe that many of the acts performed are meaningless to those who perform them; in other words, they are part of a routine which has been handed down from generation to gen- eration, with only minor changes, until at last their primary significance has been lost.

Yet, even though we may not understand them, it is im- portant to record all these operations; for someone may here- after find a clue to the meaning of one act or another, and many things now obscure may then be made clear.

In another place[1] I have written at some length of the two great mysteries of the Cheyennes. The medicine arrows and the buffalo hat are the two cherished talismans handed down to protect the Cheyenne and the Suhtai, to give them health, long life, and plenty, and strength and courage to conquer their enemies. The ceremonies of renewing the arrows and of un- wrapping the sacred hat are two of the most important prac- ticed by the tribe. The ceremonies of the Medicine Lodge and of the Massaum are others of great importance. These four

[1] *American Anthropologist*, vol. XII, p. 542, October-December, 1910.

Mrs. J. E. Tuell

MEDICINE LODGE
PAINTING THE RAFTERS

sacred performances stand out, I think, above all others of the Cheyennes.

There are minor ceremonies without number, but only a few of them may be noted. As has so often been said, the Indian is intensely religious, and by prayer and sacrifice continually endeavors to protect himself from the evil threatened by hostile powers, and to entreat the continued favor of those that are beneficent.

On the spiritual side, the Cheyenne's life was hedged about by a multitude of barriers of ritual and custom. If his beliefs demanded that he should do things that were worthy, it seemed quite as important that he should abstain from things forbidden and believed to bring bad fortune. The Cheyenne prayed constantly and offered many sacrifices to propitiate the unseen powers and to enlist their help. He practiced charity, for from earliest youth he had been taught to be kind to his fellow men, to feel sympathy for the unfortunate and to make efforts to assist them. It often costs civilized man a struggle to carry out the precept to love his neighbor, but the Cheyenne did kindly, friendly, or charitable acts of his own free will, and took no credit for them. Yet he lived in constant fear of doing some forbidden thing which would bring him bad luck.

The list of the proscribed acts is a long one. They had to do with the most ordinary operations of life: with his eating, drinking, and sleeping, with the members of his family, his life in the lodge, his hunting, and his war journey. In all that he did at home and abroad he was closely bound by custom which had become law.

TABUS

Certain things might not be done in the lodge, others were forbidden to the owner of a particular weapon or of a particular medicine. Men holding special positions were obliged to act with circumspection. Leaders of war-parties were not free to ask for food and water: these must be offered to them.

The same was true of the owner of a medicine war-pipe; until someone offered him food and water he must go hungry or thirsty.

A man might not address, nor in some cases even look at, certain of his close relations. Here, as in other tribes, the mother-in-law tabu existed;[2] and a man might not speak to his adult sister. Leaders of war-parties might not eat of certain parts of animals until after an enemy had been killed or property had been captured, nor might they skin or cut up any animal until after certain events had taken place.

The Contraries were restricted by a multitude of tabus and customs which made life a real burden to them.

Tabus connected with shields were many, for the shield was a spiritual protection of great power and the laws connected with it must be strictly observed. A shield owner was constantly on the alert to avoid committing acts that were proscribed.

To some shield owners the eating of entrails was forbidden; to others the neck; and to others still the ham of the buffalo. Some might not take food from the fire with an iron implement; a sharpened stick must be used.

The tabu of the protective war-bonnet worn by Roman Nose when he was killed, has already been described.[3]

In certain lodges and under certain circumstances people might not scratch the head with the finger nails. A little pointed stick must be used.[4]

In the case of some tabus the performance in advance of a special ceremony permitted the otherwise forbidden act without evil consequences. In other cases a subsequent ceremony averted the ill fortune.

[2] For early note on this tabu and one as to the father-in-law, see Cabeza de Vaca, Hodge ed., Spanish Explorers in the Southern United States, p. 51, Scribner's, 1907.

[3] The Fighting Cheyennes, p. 276.

[4] Compare, for the Pimas, J. William Lloyd, Aw-Aw-Tam, p. 94, Westfield, N. J., 1911.

Many of these tabus having to do with a great variety of circumstances have been mentioned under other headings. I shall refer to certain tabus for women a little later.

SACRIFICE

In times of difficulty and danger a vow or promise was often made that, if the higher power would give help, the individual would offer some sacrifice or perform some ceremony. To make such a pledge and to fail to carry it out was a serious fault, one certain to be followed by misfortune. The promise ought to be performed with reasonable promptness. If, for example, a man in the autumn pledged himself to make a medicine lodge, this lodge should be made during the following summer and not a year later.

In 1903 a Southern Cheyenne named Turtle pledged himself to make a large sweat-house and to offer to the Great Power a painted cloth. He had made the vow to bring about the recovery of his elder son, who was very ill. The boy recovered, but up to the end of 1905 the pledge had not been fulfilled. Two years had elapsed and Turtle had not paid his vow! Meantime, both his sons died, one in the winter of 1904 and the younger one about November 1, 1905. It was generally believed that these deaths took place because Turtle had not fulfilled his obligation, and that unless he did so something bad would happen to him or to his wife.

In 1858, while a member of a war-party against the Pawnees, Mad Wolf, a Southern Cheyenne, who died not long ago, pledged himself to renew the medicine arrows. No enemies were found on this war journey; the party was not successful, and on his return to the camp Mad Wolf did not renew the arrows. Until he had done so no one would go to war in his company and he was not allowed to join any war-party. It was felt that the failure to fulfill his pledge would bring bad luck on himself and probably on the other members of the party— he had become a dangerous companion. After vainly trying to join three or four different war-parties, Mad Wolf carried out his pledge, and renewed the arrows.

In the offerings of the body, some sacrifices were made without ceremony, while others were accompanied by a certain ritual. Women quite often cut off joints of their fingers in sacrifice for the recovery of a sick husband or child, and with no ceremony beyond the usual prayer by a priest. Medicine Woman, formerly the wife of Wolf Chief, when one of her children was sick, promised to sacrifice to the sun the terminal joint of the little finger of her right hand, if the child should get well. It recovered, and at the proper time Medicine Woman went to a priest, who raised her right hand to the sun, made a prayer, and then, with a sharp knife, cut off the joint.

As already explained, men going to war often sacrificed bits of their skin or flesh, at the same time praying for success in their undertaking. On a war journey in 1866, in which about eighty Southern Cheyennes took part, Eagle Head, the pipe bearer, made a vow that every man in the party should have a piece of skin cut from his arm, in order that all might have good fortune and secure a scalp without injury to anyone. The pledge was made while they were on the march, and Eagle Head stopped and announced it.

That evening, after they had camped, a sweat-house was built, a little mound of earth heaped up before it, and a buffalo-skull leaned against this. Each man then came forward and had one or more pieces of skin cut from his arm. The line where the skin was to be cut was marked with a bit of charcoal from the fire. Big Wolf cut away the skin, held the piece toward the sun, and then with a prayer put the skin under the buffalo-skull. To cut the skin, a bit of sharpened tin was used; in earlier times a flint was employed. A knife was not used.

In this ceremony each man decided for himself and announced how many pieces of skin he wished cut from his arm. One man in this party had two pieces taken from each arm.

Two well-known men of this party—Red Moon and Tejon—

objected to having this done, but were told that the promise had been made, and that they must either make the sacrifice or leave the party and go back. To have declined to have a part in the sacrifice would have brought ill fortune. After the sacrifice had been made all the older men took a sweat.

Two days afterward, on Smoky Hill River, a Kaw Indian was met, killed, and scalped, and the party returned successful, with faces blackened, showing that a scalp had been taken without loss of life to the party.

In the prayers which accompanied these various sacrifices mention was often made of the gristle rope which was sometimes used, and of the four ridges. The gristle rope means a rawhide rope often braided, but in old days sometimes a mere flat softened rawhide line cut from the hide of a buffalo or even from the hide of a horse. Such ropes were commonly used by men who felt obliged to pay their vows by swinging to the pole, and the same ropes were used over and over again by different persons in the payment of such vows. I have no doubt that in time they acquired a certain sacred character of their own which made them more desirable for these purposes than an unused rope would have been. They were readily lent by their owners to other people who wished to use them in sacrifice.

The four ridges referred to represented four trials, four sacrifices to be made, which were the performance of important ceremonies. It was believed that the Great Power would be pleased with one who should go through four such ceremonies, and one who wished to obtain the special favor of the Great Power might strive to cross these four ridges—to perform these four difficult ceremonies during his life. There was no special order in which the four ridges were to be crossed, nor need the four ceremonies always be the same. We may conceive that a man who had passed through all the mysteries of the Medicine Lodge was thought to have crossed one of the ridges. The unwrapping of the medicine arrows might be another, going through the Massaum ceremony still another, and

197

so on through several difficult and important trials. One who wished to acquire great spiritual power might make an effort to pass one of the ridges each year for four years; but it is to be understood that the passage of one of these ridges called for much physical effort and was very costly.

It was felt that persons who had been through the important ceremonies—as Medicine Lodge makers, those who have taken part in the Massaum ceremonies, and others—should be treated respectfully, even reverently, by all. They must not be addressed flippantly, nor should jokes be made about them or at their expense. They on their part should be dignified. They were not expected to hold aloof from others, but their conduct should show that they felt the responsibility of their position. If they were joked with or treated with slight respect, they made a little prayer to the Great Father—Heammawihio.

TANNING THE WOLF SKIN

Of tabus for women some had to do with the dressing of hides. Women might not dress the hides of bear, beaver, wolf, or coyote; such hides were usually dressed by captive women of other tribes, or, in early days, sometimes by men. Women believed that if they should dress a bear-skin the soles of their feet would crack, and hair would grow over their faces. They also feared that they might become "nervous," like a bear. In several other Plains tribes the women fear to dress a bear's hide.

Since wolves were common and desirable as food, and since their hides were useful, it was worth while that these should be tanned. There was a woman's society whose members after certain ceremonies were freed from the tabu attaching to the skins of wolves and coyotes, and were at liberty to dress the hides. It was believed that any woman who should dress a wolf's hide without going through these ceremonies and so joining this society would become palsied. Many women underwent this ceremony, which was neither difficult nor costly.

The man who directed the ceremony by which women were freed from the operation of this tabu was a member of the Young Wolf Medicine Society. On determining when the ceremony should be performed, he sent a crier through the camp, announcing that any woman who wished to join this society should come to his lodge, which for the purpose consisted of two large lodges set up together. Usually there were a number of candidates. Before the ceremony began, a wolf-skin had been placed on a bed of white sage in the back of the lodge, behind the fire. The man sat on his bed, at the south side of the lodge —the left side of the entrance. When the women came in, they wore their ordinary clothing, save that their feet were bare. Each woman wore her knife, as usual, and each carried in her right hand a filled pipe, and in the left hand a gift. In recent times this gift was often calico, though it might be almost anything; but in old times parfleches were not uncommonly given. The women passed one by one before the master of ceremonies, and each offered to him the pipe which she carried. He smoked, thus agreeing to take charge of her initiation, and she placed the gift on the ground before him. After all had done this, they sat down and let their dresses fall to the waist. The master of ceremonies then proceeded to paint them, first the right foot from the ankle down; then the right hand from the wrist down; then the left foot, and the left hand. Next a circle—the sun— was painted on the chest, a crescent moon over the right shoulder blade, and the face from halfway up the nose down to the throat. Only red paint was used.

Sometimes the wolf-skin which lay behind the fire was an old one; sometimes one from a recently killed wolf was used. On the feet and nose, the skin was painted with red paint, and a streak of red paint ran from the nose to the tail. On the right shoulder was painted a half-circle—a half-moon—and between shoulders a circle—a sun. The master of ceremonies took the knife belonging to the first woman, rubbed its sides and back with a bit of charcoal, and returned it to the woman, who cut a little hair, or a little skin and hair, from the right shoulder of the wolf-skin, held it toward the sky, and then dropped it on the ground behind the wolf's shoulder. Then she cut a piece from the right side of the rump, held it toward the sky, and put it on the ground behind the right hind leg. She did the same to the left hip and to the left shoulder. Finally she cut a piece from the wolf's withers, and held it up and placed it on the ground as before. Then she left the lodge and stood outside. Each woman did the same thing, until all had left the lodge, when they formed in a line, standing abreast, and from within the lodge the master of ceremonies instructed them to go outside the camp, passing through the opening in the circle on the east side, then turning to the right to go south, then west, then north, and then east. This they did. When they reached the south side of the circle they faced south, held up their hands toward the south and howled like a wolf. Then going on, they stopped at the west side, held their hands toward the west and again howled, and at the north side and the east side they did the same. Then, having completed the passage about the outside of the camp, they returned through the opening in the circle to the lodge of the master of ceremonies, where he awaited them. As they passed through the center of the circle they stopped and again howled like a wolf. When they had entered his lodge, the master of ceremonies took a bundle of white sage and passed it over the parts where each woman was painted, thus ceremonially "wiping off" the paint. The women then left his lodge, went to the river, and washed off the paint. After this ceremony had been performed, these women might at any time stretch and dress wolf-hides.

TANNING THE WHITE BUFFALO HIDE

Though they were extremely rare, nevertheless white buffalo sometimes occurred in the herds that formerly covered the plains. Yet they were so unusual that although the Plains Indians spent most of their lives hunting the buffalo, on which they lived, very few men have seen more than two or three white buffalo. With the Cheyennes, the skin of an albino buffalo was sacred and might not be used for any purpose, but should be hung up as a votive offering to the maiyun. In later years, however, such skins were occasionally sold, for, with increasing intercourse with white men, old beliefs and customs became weakened, while the luxuries to be purchased from the white man were more and more desired.

When a man shot a white buffalo he did not touch it, but, leaving the arrow in the body, at once set out to look for some old man who possessed the needed spiritual power. If the buffalo had been killed with a gun, the man who was to perform the ceremony over it must have killed an enemy with a gun. If it had been killed with an arrow, the man to perform the ceremony must have killed an enemy with an arrow.

When the proper person had been found and brought to where the white buffalo lay, those who had gathered there moved the carcass until its head faced the east, and then rolled it over and propped it up on its knees and belly. The man who had killed it then pulled a tuft of hair first from the right shoulder and dropped it on the ground; then he pulled hair from the right rump, then from the left rump, from the left shoulder, and from the withers, each time dropping the hair as the wolf's hair had been placed on the ground in the women's ceremony with the wolf-skin.

After this had been done, the men took hold of the body, and, after making four motions, turned it over on its back, rolling the carcass toward the north. It was then disemboweled and skinned. The skin of the head must be taken off by a man who had counted coup on and had scalped an enemy. The meat was left on the ground.

The hide was taken to camp with appropriate ceremonies. The skin might be placed on the horse which was to carry it only by a man who in battle had taken a captive and carried him off on his horse. If such a man could not be found, then the hide might be placed on the horse by a man who in battle had picked up some dismounted friend or fellow tribesman and carried him off on his horse to safety.

The owner of the hide walked back to camp, leading the horse which bore it. When the company reached the village, the hide was to be taken off the horse by some man who had pulled an enemy from his horse, and, finally, some man who had counted a coup inside an enemy's lodge carried the white buffalo hide into the owner's lodge, and, passing to the left of the fire, placed the skin on the ground behind the fire.

The crier was now sent through the village to shout an invitation to all the men who had counted more than one coup to assemble at the lodge where the hide was. After they had entered the lodge and were sitting all about it, the woman entered who was to dress the hide. She passed around behind the fire, and sat down behind the buffalo-hide. She dropped her dress to the waist, while the master of the ceremony painted her whole trunk to the waist with white clay paint. He wiped off the paint from a circle on her chest to represent the sun or the morning star, and from a crescent on her back, over the right shoulder blade; then, drawing his hands down over the body, he made vertical stripes on the white paint with his finger nails. At the woman's waist, in front, was tied a small bundle of white sage, and similar bundles were tied over each hip— over each kidney—while to the hair behind each ear a bunch was tied which stuck up like a little horn on either side.

After its blade had been rubbed over with charcoal, a knife was handed to the woman. She held the knife with the forearm horizontal, and the blade pointing upward. The man sitting next the door on the left side of the circle related the various coups he had counted, and at each coup recounted the woman cut a hole in the border of the hide for a pin to pass through in stretching it.

The man next in the circle then counted his coups, and for each coup recited the woman cut one hole in the margin of the hide, and so the counts went about the circle. About the head five holes were necessary, and in the head only a single hole could be cut for each man who spoke, no matter how many his coups.

After a sufficient number of holes had been cut, the woman began to flesh the hide, but only about its border. As she took off each piece of flesh, a coup was counted for it, one coup by each man on each piece, beginning again at the left of the circle.

After the border of the hide had been fleshed, a man who had dragged an enemy out from a lodge took up the hide, and, counting a coup on it before he left the lodge, carried it outside. The woman then took the skin to the center of the camp and spread it out. The men went with her, and the skin was laid on the ground flesh-side up and spread out with its head toward the east. Beginning at the right shoulder, facing the east, a warrior counted a coup, and the woman drove a pin through a hole in the border of the hide at this point. Then she moved to the right hip, then to the left hip and the left shoulder, and finally back to the root of the tail. At each of these points a coup was counted on a pin, which was driven through a hole in the margin of the hide for its preliminary stretching. Thus five of these pins were driven and five coups counted. The woman then drove the rest of the pins and stretched the hide in the usual manner, without further ceremony. When this had been done, she took the flesher and, when ready to begin the work of fleshing, a man who had captured a female enemy in a fight counted his coup, and the woman fleshed the hide.

Later, when the hide was to be thinned down, another man counted a coup before the work of thinning began, and when the robe was ready for tanning a man was called who had been on a successful war-party which had returned without losing a man. He counted a coup over the hide, and when he had done so the work of dressing it began. The ceremony was performed with deliberation, and occupied a whole day. All this work was done in the presence of old men who possessed spiritual power. They sat about and watched it, to see that everything was in accordance with the prescribed fashion.

In 1873 Wolf Chief was hunting with Many Magpies—a famous Southern Cheyenne, perhaps better known as Heap Of Birds—when he killed a white buffalo. Wolf Chief witnessed the ceremony of tanning its hide. It was dressed by Flat Woman, the mother of Wolf Chief. The man who owned the robe selected a middle-aged or an old woman who possessed spiritual power, and who was known to be a good tanner, to dress the hide.

Wolf Chief said that two or three generations ago it was the law that a man who had previously killed and counted coup on an enemy dressed in a scalp shirt and leggings, when he himself was dressed in similar clothing, might count many or perhaps all of the coups required in the white buffalo ceremony.

Some Cheyennes declare that the other buffalo avoided white buffalo, and say that the horses used in running buffalo were always dark-colored, as buffalo seemed to be afraid of a white horse. What seems more probable is that dark-colored horses were used in running buffalo because less conspicuous than white ones and not likely to be noticed so soon.

CONTRARY SOCIETY

The Contrary Society with its many members appears to have no connection with the Contrary warrior who carries the thunder-bow, yet it bears the same name; its members act as he does by contraries, and it has some relation to the thunder. Members of the society—people who greatly fear lightning and thunder, most of them old men and old women—take part in a ceremony which is held at irregular and infrequent intervals. In this society by their actions and words members attempt to reverse things, to do the opposite of what they are supposed to do; they back into and out of the lodge; and sit on the ground upside down, that is to say, with head and body on the ground and legs in the air. They are fun-makers, and their absurd actions are enjoyed and applauded by the people.

It is believed that the Contraries can do much for the sick. If one of them touches a sick person, or jumps over him, it is a great help to him. Sometimes on the occasion of these ceremonies they lift up the sick and then put them down, or sometimes lift them up and hold them head downward.

In the so-called Crazy, or Animal, Dance—*Massaum*—members of the Contrary Society take the part of the hunters who carry four arrows and simulate killing the pretended animals in this dance.

A feature of the ceremony referred to is the boiling of a kettle of meat, which is an offering to the thunder. From this boiling pot, men and women snatch pieces of meat with their bare hands. The society employs a certain plant which, having been prepared by the priest in charge of the rite, is rubbed over the members' hands. This is supposed to protect the hands from being scalded when they take the meat from the kettle.[5] The meat may be removed only with the naked hand. People who join this society, through fear of the thunder, after pledging themselves to go through the ordeal, must pay the priest for his instruction.

When the time for the ceremony has been determined on, some old woman, who has taken part in it on a previous occasion, is sent to call those who have pledged themselves. She backs into the lodge where one of these resides, and says, "I have not come after you." The person addressed knows that the ceremony is about to be performed and that he must attend. When the one who is to offer this sacrifice takes the pipe to the priest in charge of the ceremony and asks for instruction,

[5] Dr. Melvin R. Gilmore, of the North Dakota State Historical Society, tells me that the leaves of the prairie mallow, when chewed, yield a mucilaginous fluid which, when rubbed on the hands, forms a coating enabling one to plunge the hands quickly into hot water without being scalded. This is used by the Arikaras to protect their hands in similar ceremonies. The Cheyenne plant is *Dasiphora fruticosa*. See plant list, p. 176.

the pipe is reversed; that is, the stem is fixed in the bowl of the pipe and the hole which commonly receives the stem is filled with the smoking material.

This is a detailed account of the ceremony as I witnessed it years ago.

About the middle of the afternoon a Contrary lodge was put up toward the south side of the great camp circle, and so east of the Issiwun lodge. The covering of the lodge was inside out, the lodge-poles on the outside, and the smoke-hole was turned the wrong way. Before it—to the east—a kettle was set up, and a fire built under it. The setting up of the lodge was done slowly, and the kettle was put out two hours after the lodge was erected. The kettle hung from four sticks, coming together above it, instead of the usual tripod. Shortly after the kettle was hung, an old woman came out of the lodge, ran forty yards to the east, stopped, raised her right hand, and prayed; she then ran to the south and did the same; then to the west, then north, and again east, each time as she stopped holding up her hand and praying.

As the sun got low (at 6 P.M.) a naked man, his body painted white, some red paint on neck, breast, and arms, his breechclout ragged, a bunch of sage tied in his white-painted hair, and a collar of sage about his neck, backed out of the lodge, walked about, and then lying down on the ground close to the lodge, rested his feet and legs against its wall, his back and head resting on the ground, thus reversing the position of one who should sit down on the ground and lean his back against the lodge. After resting there for a short time, he rose, walked about, and backed into the lodge. Not long after, he backed out of the lodge and went to the fire and fed it.

An old woman, quite naked, except for a short ragged breechclout or apron, and about her head a red fillet in which a bunch of sage was stuck, and painted white over the whole body, backed out of the lodge, and walked to the fire to feed it. In her mouth she held a bone whistle, which she blew almost continuously. After feeding the fire, she walked to the south, held up both hands in prayer; then to the west, to the north, and to the east. After she had prayed to the four directions, she walked to the door of the lodge, and stood before it dancing, jumping up and down a little, so that her whole body shook; and then turning, she backed into the lodge.

Long before this, a great crowd of persons had collected about the lodge, but no one approached it nearer than fifty or sixty yards.

An old woman, fully clad, now came from this crowd, and going to the lodge entered it backward.

The white-painted man now backed out of the lodge, and, bent forward, walked about near it, pulling up weeds. As the root of each plant left the ground, the man fell over backward and turned a somersault. These antics were greeted by the spectators with much laughter. He walked all around the lodge, and out pretty near the crowd, and jumped over one of the persons nearest the lodge.

A woman, fully clad, came out of the lodge, and walking south, disappeared into the crowd.

A man, wrapped in a sheet and wearing trousers, came from the lodge, walked over to the kettle and looked into it from the four directions.

A woman, painted white as before, and naked except for the ragged cloth around the hips and a cloth around the breast, backed out of the lodge, went to the edge of the circle south of it, and talked to the people there.

A man, Big Knee, painted half red and half white, the red yellow-spotted and the white red-spotted, came out. The woman and the man began to pull weeds backward; that is to say, to back up to weeds and pull them from between their legs; and then went into the lodge.

A man, red-and-white painted, with his hair hanging over his face, looked out of the lodge toward the east. He retired into the lodge again, and a woman looked out.

An old woman (Wolf Running Together Woman), clad, came out of the lodge, followed by two naked women and three naked men. They faced south, and all held up their hands and prayed. Then they faced to the west and prayed. Then they gathered near the fire and marched north, and prayed; and then east and prayed. Then they marched up to the fire, and stood there looking east. The clad woman danced clumsily, hopping on one leg and kicking out with the other. Then she changed legs, still hopping and kicking. Then they went to the lodge, and all entered backward, except the clad woman. A man raised the lodge-skins, and partly backed out under the side of the lodge, danced a step or two, and then went in. Wolf Running Together Woman came out in the usual way; the others all backed out. Drumming was heard from within the lodge, and all those in front of it danced irregularly, no two alike. All blew on their bone whistles. The men went to the kettle and passed their hands over the bail and rim, and then left it, while the others continued to dance. Chief Killer butted backward into the hips of Wolf Running Together Woman, who in turn butted against him, and kicked out backward. Then all entered the lodge backward.

A fully clad man, Sore Eye, came out of the lodge, walked over about the kettle, spat ceremonially on his hands, and rubbed them four times over the supports, chain, and bail of the kettle. The purpose of this was said to be to cool the cooking food. The others came out and danced four times about the kettle. Wolf Running Together Woman dipped her hands in the soup, and later Chief Killer did the same, and rubbed his hands together as if enjoying it. There was more or less byplay of quarreling and kicking among the dancers, which caused the spectators to laugh heartily.

All went into the lodge again. Turtle, fully clad, came out of the lodge, and went about the kettle. He placed his hands on the ground to the east, south, west, and north of the kettle, in order, and after each placing them on the ground, passed

Mrs. J. E. Tuell

MEDICINE LODGE
RAISING THE CENTER POLE

the hands over the chain and bail of the kettle, to cool the soup. All the dancers backed out of the lodge, dancing, and went about the kettle north to east, to south, to west. It was noticed that their hands seemed dark-colored, possibly painted with some mixture to protect them from the heat of the fluid in the kettle. They dipped their hands in the kettle, and rubbed the soup on their chests, making motions of delight, and held their hands up to the sky as if praying. All reëntered the lodge.

Tall Red Bird, fully clad, came out to cool the soup, from the four directions, by spitting on his hands, like the others, and passing them over the supports, bail, and chain, and by shaking the kettle. He dipped his hands in the soup, and rubbed them together with a motion of washing the hands. Then he went to the lodge door, returned, fussed about the kettle, and then entered the lodge.

Drumming again began within the lodge. A man clad in undershirt, drawers, and a green cap, came out and cooled the soup by shaking the kettle, from the four directions, as he passed once around it.

All came out of the lodge, Wolf Running Together Woman leading; she held her hands to the sky. They danced about the kettle, and dipped their hands in the soup four times, and then returned to the lodge, Chief Killer entering last.

The drumming began again. All came out and faced north, side by side, holding their hands toward the sky. They danced twice about the kettle, and then all went to it, dipped their hands in the soup, and held them toward the sky. Then they returned to the lodge, and entered it with much byplay, amusing to the onlookers.

Sore Eye came out and cooled the kettle as he had done before, and then went in again.

Again the drumming began. All backed out, dancing, passed around the kettle from the north, approached it from the east, dipped their hands in the pot, held them up to the sky, and then took out pieces of meat. They ran swiftly to the spectators and gave pieces of meat to them; then ran back to the kettle and dipped bunches of white sage into it, and whipped themselves over the body with the bunches wet with the soup. Then they went back to the lodge. One of the old women held her hands toward the sky; then holding the bunch of sage up above her head in her right hand, she held the other hand toward it. Then all entered the lodge, and the spectators dispersed. Later, a Contrary, unpainted except for his face, blessed a woman (Rambling Woman) who approached the lodge, by passing lightly over her clothing and hands, from above downward, a wisp of white sage dipped in the soup. The woman faced east, and after he had finished, the man gave her a slight push, and she walked to the east on the north side of the kettle. Later, several women with dishes went near to the lodge, and sat about it. Before seating themselves, they went to the door and bowed low. Soon after this the performers came out, with the paint washed off and wearing their ordinary clothing.

When the dancers ran toward the spectators with pieces of meat, they ran very fast, and in a threatening manner. If the persons they were approaching rose to their feet to run away, or even showed signs of alarm or shrinking, the dancers threw at them the pieces of meat they were carrying. If, however, the person sat still, and reached out his hand to take the meat from a dancer, it was given to him, and he might eat it, and it would bring him good fortune.

MEDICINE LODGE

THE midsummer ceremony of many Plains Indians, which is commonly called the Medicine Lodge, bears its own name in each tribe by which it is practiced. The term Sun Dance comes from the Sioux, since they call one feature of the occasion "sun-looking dance," or the dance where they look at the sun. To fix their gaze on the sun and the moon, to which they look for help, is a practice common to many tribes, but this and the suffering that goes with it are not a part of the Medicine Lodge ceremony, but, wherever it is done, this is in each case the payment of an individual vow. The sufferer who swings to the pole by himself out in the hills still keeps his eyes fixed on the sun.

In early times, and in certain places as late as 1875 or 1880, the most striking thing about the Medicine Lodge was the so-called torture, which most often took the form of swinging to the pole or dragging skulls. In this suffering the practice was for the man—in fulfilment of some pledge that he had made— to have the skin pinched up on the right side and the left side of the breast, a knife run through this skin, and then a wooden skewer passed through each incision, which skewers were tied to the end of a rope fastened to the center-pole of the Medicine Lodge. The man danced at the length of this rope from the pole, and from time to time threw himself backward, striving to tear loose from the rope by breaking the skin. The dragging of skulls was a similar performance. The skin over both shoulder blades was pierced, skewers were passed through and tied to short ropes, to which buffalo-skulls were attached. The sufferer then walked and ran about the camp-circle in the effort to

211

break the skin through which the skewers were passed and free himself from the skulls he was dragging.

This torture was long supposed to be a part of the ceremony of the Medicine Lodge, and government officials, missionaries, and some ethnologists, have taken it for granted that this was a necessary part of the ceremony. To the civilized eye the acts were so striking that they obscured the real ceremony, which has thus always been misunderstood.

Civilized man usually assigns to primitive people under his observation those motives and modes of reasoning that he himself would employ under like circumstances, but often the motives of the savage and his reasoning may be wholly different from those of civilized man, and he may be governed by impulses that the latter would not at all understand. The difficulty of getting at the basic motive for any act by the old-time Indians is very great, and years of association, study, and inquiry may be needed to discover the real facts in such connection.

It was the practice of the primitive Indian, when he found himself in situations of difficulty or danger, to promise to sacrifice to the great powers, in case these powers would help him, something that was very precious; and what can be more precious than a man's own body and blood? Such sacrifices are confined to no race, creed, or sect. From earliest times this has been a means of invoking the help of the powers that rule the universe. The parallel between Old Testament sacrifices and those of the Indians is close. Analogous offerings are made by Christians at the present day.

In the old war times it was common practice, if a man greatly desired some success, or if he found himself in some dangerous situation, or supposed he was threatened by misfortune, to make public promise that he would swing to the pole, would drag skulls, or would make some other offering—which he named—to the great powers, in the effort to gain their favor. Such a pledge was almost always kept. Failure to fulfill it would incur the contempt of the whole tribe and would bring inescapable misfortune. Unless the man making the vow specified a definite occasion when he would perform the sacrifice, he was at liberty to choose his own time. He might declare that he would swing to the pole in the Medicine Lodge, or that he would perform the same sacrifice alone in the hills. If he had declared that he would suffer at the Medicine Lodge, it was expected that he would do so at its next following performance, but this was not necessarily done; if not, people would feel that he might have reasons of his own for deferring the matter.

I have pointed out that the sacred influences of the Medicine Lodge, like those of some other important ceremonies, extend through the entire camp and last throughout the ceremony.[1] These influences make the occasion one particularly favorable for the performance of any spiritual and sacred operations of which prayer is especially a part. As in the case of the renewing of the medicine arrows, the time is one especially auspicious for the mixing of secret medicines and for the making of shields. The period of the Medicine Lodge was favorable to the performance of good deeds, and an appropriate time to pay vows. The various performances so vividly described as shocking by persons who have witnessed the old-time Medicine Lodge, or Sun Dance, were the carrying out by individuals of certain previously made promises of self-sacrifice.

Those who were to undergo the suffering of swinging to the pole or of dragging skulls were pierced for the skewers by their instructors—the men who, under present-day conditions, merely paint them. There were different ways of piercing the candidate. Sometimes he knelt on the ground while his breast was being pierced, or he might lie on his back; when the skin of the back was pierced, the candidate sometimes knelt, and sometimes lay on his face. The skewers and the strings with which they were tied to the rope were prepared by the instructor, while usually the young man himself furnished the rope,

---

[1] *American Anthropologist*, N. s. vol. XVI, p. 249.

which very likely had been used before for this purpose and was now borrowed.

Besides the work of piercing the candidate and instructing him in certain ritual and certain acts that should be performed, the instructor did everything in his power to help the young man to success, encouraging him to persevere in his difficult task, going through many motions of rubbing, holding, and shaking, with the purpose of making the young man courageous, long-winded, and enduring. Sometimes, if the novitiate was unable to tear the skewers from his skin, the instructor would add his weight and strength to the pull on the rope to complete the breaking away of the skin. Very often the candidate succeeded in breaking loose; sometimes he did not do so. To fail was no disgrace. The public regarded the matter as distinctly his affair, and while eager to encourage him to carry through successfully what he had undertaken, did not comment adversely if he had not the strength to break away, nor the endurance to carry the ordeal to the end.

All these things have to do with long ago, and are no longer performed in public, though, as I shall show farther on, young men who desired to offer this sacrifice to the powers have done so within the last few years. The strongly religious character of the Indian, and his simplicity, tend to keep alive in him these notions which in others we call primitive, but which we regard as wholly natural if they are found in the sacred books in which we believe.

It was the law in olden times, now abandoned, because no longer practicable, that the formal ceremonies of the Medicine Lodge should last for eight days. The preliminary exercises occupied four of these days, and on each one of these four the camp must be moved—a shorter or a longer distance. Usually, in these old times, the moves were very short, and after the Indians had been obliged to abandon their old free ways and were settled on reservations, this moving of the camp during the first four days was discarded and its place taken by certain symbolic acts which represented this moving.

If while the tribe was assembling in the great camp it became known that the Indians of a certain group were coming and were near at hand, the chiefs might decide that on their arrival a feast should be given them. Young men were sent about the camp, each carrying a bundle of sticks, of which one was given to each woman from whom a contribution of food was expected. Each one receiving a stick would furnish some food—meat, bread, coffee, or berries. The women receiving the sticks cooked the food with apparent pleasure, and, when ready, put it in a clean new dish, combed their hair, and dressed themselves nicely, preparatory to taking the contributions to the feast. From all parts of the camp women were seen going toward the appointed place, carrying the food and chatting gaily with each other. Sometimes more than one stick was given to a family, but by inadvertence. The giving of two or more sticks called for no more food than a single one.

I have seen several kinds of these sticks. One of them was about fourteen inches long, was painted green, and had a deer-skin fringe about the end not held in the hand. Another was twenty or twenty-four inches long, painted blue, with three crow-feathers at the end. Another, about eighteen inches long, painted green, had hawk's down-feathers on the end. Still another, fifteen inches long, was painted red, and was adorned with a bit of fur about the end, from which down-feathers hung. The custom of sending about these sticks at such a time and for such a purpose is very old. Such sticks are merely the counters for the hand game, but in their ornamented form are modern, having been trimmed in this way by the ghost dancers since about 1890. This association gave the sticks a sacred character, hence they were handled reverently.

Each candidate who had promised to make a Medicine Lodge —called here Medicine Lodge maker—was obliged to secure the direction and assistance of some man who had already made a Medicine Lodge, and in the same way any young man who decided that he would pay his vows and undergo the suffering of swinging to the pole or of dragging skulls, must enlist the services of one having had a like experience. These instructors were paid for the assistance that they gave.

The candidate for instruction asked the aid of his instructor, or painter, in the usual ceremonial fashion, offering him a filled pipe before preferring his request. The older man might accept the pipe and smoke it, thus pledging himself to do whatsoever might be asked of him, or he might inquire of the young man what favor was desired. In any event, if he smoked the pipe he pledged himself to accede to the young man's request. To take part in these ceremonies for the first time thus involved not only some physical suffering, but considerable expenditure as well.

When the instructor was asked for his help, he usually talked very seriously to the candidate, warning him that the step contemplated was of great importance and would cost him some suffering, and that he should not undertake it without careful thought, nor unless he had made up his mind to carry it out to the end.

Each instructor had sole charge of the Medicine Lodge maker who asked his help and who accepted no instruction from anyone else. The instructor had nothing to say about any Medicine Lodge maker other than the one who asked his help. The instructor of the man who had vowed the Medicine Lodge was the leader of the instructors and gave the signal for the performance of the various acts of the ceremony. Each instructor had an assistant, who performed the actual operations for him. Thus, each Medicine Lodge maker had an instructor, and each instructor called on some man to assist him, but always one who had already made a Medicine Lodge.

Usually the candidate tried to select for his instructor a man who had not very often filled this office, for it was believed that every time a man acted as instructor he parted with a certain portion of the spiritual power acquired when he first made the Medicine Lodge, so that finally his power became less and his helpfulness to the candidate was slight.

It was law that the instructor must receive from the Medicine Lodge maker at least the same payment that he himself made to his instructor when he was making the Medicine Lodge; but the candidate, if he desired to do so, might pay to his instructor gifts of greater value than those the instructor had made when he passed through the Medicine Lodge. If the candidate did this, later in life when he was asked to become an instructor he would receive from the candidate who might then offer him the pipe, gifts at least as valuable as those which he himself had made. If the Medicine Lodge maker was poor, he was obliged to call on his relatives to contribute property to help him make the large payments needed. Much later, when as instructor he received his payments from candidates, he returned to these relatives the equivalent of their contributions.

If, subsequent to his making the Medicine Lodge, an instructor married, the wife had no share in what he received; but an earlier wife, even though divorced from him, came into the Medicine Lodge, assisted him to instruct, and claimed and received half of what he got. If the man who was about to make the Medicine Lodge had more than one wife, he was at liberty to select the wife he wished to assist him.

The ceremonies were in charge of one or more soldier bands. If the man who made the Medicine Lodge belonged to a soldier society, that society had general charge of the ceremony. From this it sometimes resulted that several soldier bands might be in charge of a Medicine Lodge, the different Medicine Lodge makers belonging to different soldier societies. Men of the different soldier bands sang for the dancers on each of the four nights, and each morning the crier called through the camp what soldier band was to sing that night. It is said that the women belonging to a soldier band did not, on this occasion, sing with their own band, but with one of the others.

On the day before the first operation connected with the Medicine Lodge all the soldier bands paraded about the camp. Two braves were chosen to lead this parade, and two to lead each soldier band. In the parade the soldiers went first, followed by the chiefs, and after the chiefs came the boys of the camp, all on horseback. As the parade moved, the different soldier bands sang their songs. Often a similar parade took place after the ceremonies were concluded.

In preparing for this ceremonial march the soldiers gathered by bands on the south outer side of the opening of the circle, marched to the opening, into it, and turned south, marching around the camp, close to the lodges, south, west, north, and east, passed out of the opening, turned to the north, and going north, west, south, and east, entered the circle and dispersed. As elsewhere said, no Dog Soldier might stop and dismount to recover anything he might lose. For this reason the Dog Soldiers were followed at a little distance by a man who looked over the ground and picked up and brought with him any article that might fall from a Dog Soldier's person or from his saddle.

On the day before the erection of a Medicine Lodge it was customary for one or more of the soldier bands who had charge of the proceedings to go out and kill a jackrabbit, the skin of which was needed in the ceremony. Formerly it was required that the rabbit should be run down on horseback and killed with a stick or a club. He who was lucky enough to kill it expected to have good fortune and to count a coup when he next went to war. The strips cut from the rabbit's fur are ceremonially tied on the buffalo-robe worn by the lodge makers. Some of the Indians suggest that the use of the rabbit in this ceremony refers back to that traditional time when the Cheyennes are supposed to have lived in the North and to have subsisted chiefly on rabbits.

Several constructions or shelters were used in conducting the ceremony of the Medicine Lodge. These were the gathering lodge, the "only" lodge, the medicine lodge proper, and one or two shades, shelters, or large lodges, for the uses of the soldier bands who had the ceremony in charge.

Before the beginning of the Medicine Lodge ceremony those people most deeply concerned, that is to say, the priests and old men, and the Medicine Lodge makers, with their instructors and assistant instructors, came together in a lodge which is called the gathering lodge—*tsĭh mōh nō ĭv'*. Here they planned for the ceremony and strove to arrange it in orderly fashion. Though the Medicine Lodge makers were present, they took no part in the discussion: they were present only to learn. The gathering lodge stood on the west side of the camp-circle, just behind where the lonely lodge afterward stood on the inner circle of the lodges.

On the day before. the cutting of the pole and the building of the medicine lodge, the scene of the ceremony was transferred from the gathering lodge to the lone medicine lodge, *nŭkeyūm'*, also called the only lodge. Here came together the priests, the old men who in past years had made Medicine Lodges, those most familiar with the ceremony, and those who were now to make the Medicine Lodge. It was at this time that the Medicine Lodge makers selected their instructors, offered them the pipe, and asked them to teach to each the secrets of the ceremony. The details of this will be told elsewhere.

The last ceremony of the Medicine Lodge that I witnessed, some details of which are here described, began on the Tongue River Indian Reservation, August 13, 1911. It was held in the valley of the Lame Deer River, about half a mile above the traders' store, and so somewhat south of the site of the old camp where Lame Deer was killed in 1877, when General Miles attacked the village. The stream, formerly known as the Muddy, takes its name from that fight. There were three Medicine Lodge makers—Rock Road, Shave Head, and Red Bead.

The instructors were: for Rock Road, Curly; for Red Bead, Wolf Chief; and for Shave Head, Pine (Southern Cheyenne). Soldier Wolf was master of ceremonies. Young Bird, Big Head Man, Frank Standing Elk, and Bull Tongue, a Southern Cheyenne, were the principal assistants.

The Medicine Lodge may be offered by either man or woman. This one had been vowed by Shave Head's wife, but as she could not dance with the men, Shave Head took her place.

Of the Medicine Lodge makers, Shave Head was the leader. The other two joined him in order to "stay in his lodge," as the saying is. The usual number of Medicine Lodge makers is two or three. Once in Oklahoma there were four, but this was thought to be wrong; there should not be more than three. Rock Road and Red Bead had also vowed a Medicine Lodge, but the ceremony was spoken of as Shave Head's Medicine Lodge. However, after this ceremony the two other men were qualified to act as instructors in the Medicine Lodge.

The observations which follow were made during five days, of which only three were devoted to the Medicine Lodge, for the last twenty-four hours was divided and reckoned as two days. The days of preliminary instruction with the movings of the camp and the division of the last day may have represented the eight days of former times.

I entered the lonely (or instruction) lodge late in the afternoon of August 13, 1911.

Before the instruction began, one of the instructors took an ordinary stone pipe with a rather short stem, and placing the mouthpiece on the ground before him, the stem being held vertically, he passed his right hand and then his left hand twice down the stem toward the ground. He then gave the pipe to one of the Medicine Lodge makers, who repeated these motions, and returned the pipe. A coal was taken from the fire and placed in front of the instructor, who lighted the pipe and passed it to Shave Head, a lodge maker, who got it going well and passed it to Rock Road, the pipe passing from left to right, and the stem being held toward the ground in passing. The pipe then went back to the instructor, who handed it to the women who were to take part in the ceremony. Each man before smoking moved the mouthpiece of the stem from side to side before his face.

The ritual instruction soon began. This consisted chiefly of a long series of repetitions of ritual, the instructor announcing a sentence and the Medicine Lodge maker repeating it after him. The sentences consisted of a prayer and an offering, and began, "To the bright star, I give my wife [*nāmēh'o,* my beloved one]." Then, in succession, various powers and influences were named, so that the learner repeated the offering to the mountains, buttes, hills, animals, birds, timber, grasses, fruits, medicines, waters, and waters of all colors. Each prayer was recited four times by the instructor, and each time the learner repeated the words.

After this instruction was ended, all smoked another long-stemmed black stone pipe, and in passing this pipe also, the stem was held toward the ground.

For much of Monday, August 14, nothing was done, though the Medicine Lodge makers and instructors spent considerable time in the instruction lodge. Shortly before sundown the Medicine Lodge makers and the instructors left the instruction lodge and walked out toward the east on the prairie, where they sat down in a row, facing east. The three men to the south, sitting side by side, were the Medicine Lodge makers. The men to the north, in order, were Spotted Hawk, Big Head Man, Soldier Wolf, Young Bird, Little Hawk, Cross Wings, Bull Tongue (two Southern Cheyennes), Wolf Chief, Pine (Southern Cheyenne), and Curly. Behind some of these sat the old men, Bull Thigh, Limpy, and Tall White Man. A little fire was built near the south end of the line.

With the ball of his right thumb, Soldier Wolf made smooth in the dust on the ground before him a circle, about four inches in diameter, which represented the earth. Soldier Wolf's office was that of earth maker; he was the master of ceremonies.

For a little time Soldier Wolf was engaged in whittling several pipe sticks. Now Red Bead brought a filled pipe, and squatting before Soldier Wolf and resting the pipe-bowl on the ground, inclined the stem toward Soldier Wolf. Shave Head brought a coal from the fire and placed it in front of Soldier Wolf, who, taking the stem of the pipe in his hand and holding the bowl toward the sky, moved the mouthpiece, with the sun, around and over the dust circle that he had recently made with his thumb. Then Soldier Wolf lighted the pipe, and resting the bowl on the ground, held the stem first toward Shave Head, who smoked, then to Rock Road, and then to Spotted Hawk, both of whom smoked. Then the pipe passed down the line.

The three Medicine Lodge makers now moved a dozen feet to the southeast, away from the line of other men, and sat there on their buffalo-robes. Another pipe had been lighted, without ceremony, and the two pipes crossed one another as they passed along the line, one going north, the other south. Presently Red Bead brought a filled pipe to Little Hawk, who, after making the circular motion with the stem pointed to the ground, as had been done before, lighted the pipe and gave it to Red Bead, who pressed the stem first to the right shoulder, then to the left shoulder, and passed his hands down over the stem twice, the right hand first. This ceremony represented a moving of the whole camp.

During this time the lonely or instruction lodge had been moved forward so that it stood within the camp-circle. This does not mean that the lodge was taken down, but the instructors and other principal men surrounded the lodge and, a single man grasping each pole close to the ground, the whole lodge as it stood was lifted and carried forward bodily fifteen or twenty feet.

All returned to the lodge and Rock Road was called over

north to Curly, and to Rock Road was given a bundle of sacred things, which he took on his left arm in the fold of his buffalo-robe. This bundle had belonged to Box Elder, long dead, who had received it from his father.[2] It is not known how long it has been in the tribe. Besides the straight pipe, it seemed to contain chiefly braids of red-painted sweet grass, with some buffalo-wool.

After Rock Road had received the bundle, the three Medicine Lodge makers and their instructors left the lodge, moved out about thirty yards farther, put down their things, and sat down. This represented another moving of the camp. After remaining seated a short time, they arose, and, carrying their pipes and offerings, returned in single file to the ceremonial lodge and paused before the door. Curly, one of the instructors, wore a buffalo-robe, and the others blankets. Rock Road was naked except for breechclout and moccasins; Shave Head had on breechclout, leggings, and moccasins; and Red Bead a red shirt, leggings, and moccasins.

Wolf Chief took up a buffalo bull's skull which had been placed outside the lodge on the south side, carried it around to the door, stopped there, moved the head four times toward the door, and the fourth time went in with it. It was carried around the south side and placed in the back of the lodge, facing the east. The three Medicine Lodge makers now entered the lodge, Rock Road first, Shave Head next, and Red Bead last; Curly and Wolf Chief followed, and then Pine, carrying a rifle which he had received in part payment for instructing the pupil.

The three Medicine Lodge makers sat next to the door on the southeast side of the lodge, being now naked except for breechclout and moccasins. Soldier Wolf, who sat next to (west of) the three Medicine Lodge makers, again made in the dust with his thumb a circle which represented the earth. Big Head Man

[2] Box Elder, known also as Maple, and his father, Horn, were famous men among the Northern Cheyennes seventy-five or a hundred years ago.

sat to the left of Soldier Wolf, Young Bird next, Wolf Chief next, Pine next, and then Curly. The last three were the instructors.

Red Bead left the lodge and soon returned carrying a peeled stick four feet long, which he handed to Soldier Wolf, who broke the stick into halves, and with a new knife cut one of the parts in two. Before beginning to cut, he made four motions with the knife. He began to make pipe-sticks. When these were finished, Soldier Wolf rose, went and stood before Curly, and held his hands—the edges together—before the face of that instructor, who spat on them ceremonially. While Soldier Wolf was working, Red Bead, who sat nearest to the door, went to the fire, took a coal from it, carried it to his seat, put the coal on the ground and from it lighted a pipe, pointed the stem to the ground, and then passed the pipe to Rock Road, who smoked and passed it to Shave Head, when it was returned to Red Bead. Only the three Medicine Lodge makers smoked this pipe. Before each of them on the ground lay his pipe and tobacco-sack, the bowl of the pipe pointing to the east.

When Soldier Wolf had finished the pipe sticks, he soiled them with dust gathered from the ground, and placed them just outside the circular flattened space before him. Meanwhile Shave Head had been filling a catlinite pipe, the stem of which was painted red. He handed it to Soldier Wolf, who placed it upright on the ground between himself and the circle representing the earth, with the bowl pointed to the west. He wrapped buffalo-wool pulled from the robes of the Medicine Lodge makers about the larger ends of the two pipe cleaners, and placed them by the pipe. Red Bead went out and brought in a peeled stick, forked at the end, with which he took from the fire a coal which he put in front of Soldier Wolf, outside of the smoothed circle. Soldier Wolf pointed the mouthpiece of the pipe toward the earth and then lighted the pipe. He then moved the mouthpiece around the circumference of the smoothed circle, and resting the bowl of the pipe on the ground,

PAINTING FOR THE MEDICINE LODGE

offered the stem to Shave Head, who smoked, Soldier Wolf still holding the pipe. Soldier Wolf smoked and passed the pipe to his left-hand neighbor, and the pipe went around, the stem in passing always being directed toward the ground. Red Bead now filled a pipe, and walking across the front of the lodge offered it to Lone Elk, who lighted it at the fire without ceremony, and passed it to Bull Tongue, who sat immediately to the left of the buffalo-skull. Bull Tongue smoked and passed the pipe to his neighbor.

Soldier Wolf took up the pipe that had been smoked out and had been lying on the ground before him, held the stem to the ground, rubbed his hands down the stem four times, and then took off the bowl. He placed bowl and stem on the ground, took one of the prepared pipe-cleaners, then the bowl again, and cleaned it. The stem was then held vertically, mouthpiece toward the ground, the bowl put on, and he rubbed his hands four times down over the pipe and stem, and returned the pipe to Shave Head.

Rock Road is a Dog Soldier, Red Bead an Elk Soldier, and Shave Head a Chief Soldier. Tall White Man went out of the lodge and cried four times in a loud voice, directing the Dog Soldiers to come and practice. He then returned. Again he went out as before, and called the Elk Soldiers and the Chief Soldiers to come and practice.

Young Bird scraped the soil from under the left-hand side of the buffalo-skull to make it rest evenly, then spat ceremonially on his hands and made the ceremonial motions. Tall White Man again went out, and again called the soldier bands, directing them to bring with them a drum.

Young Bird called Shave Head over to the buffalo-skull, and Shave Head, kneeling by the side of Young Bird, who guided his right hand, very slowly and reverently drew a line of yellow paint from between the horns down to the end of the nasal bones. He next made the ceremonial motions over arms, legs, and head. After this was ended, Soldier Wolf lighted another pipe, and called Shave Head over to smoke it. Shave Head passed first his right hand down and over the hand of Soldier Wolf, who held the pipe, puffed vigorously until the pipe was going well, then as Soldier Wolf took it away from his mouth he passed his left hand over Soldier Wolf's hand and arm, and drew both his hands toward his own mouth. He retained the last puff of smoke in his mouth, and holding his hands together before his mouth, blew the smoke into them and passed them ceremonially over his arms, legs, and head.

Always before lighting a pipe, Soldier Wolf held the mouth-piece close over the symbolic earth circle before him, and passed it about the circumference. After each pipe had been smoked, the pipe was placed upright between Soldier Wolf and the smoothed circle of dust. After cleaning the pipe, Soldier Wolf always emptied the ashes from the pipe into the middle of the circle. Before rubbing his hands down the pipe, Soldier Wolf placed them on the ground. First the right hand was placed on the ground, then rubbed down over the whole pipe, and again placed on the ground and rubbed down over the pipe, and so with the left hand. Then the right hand was again placed on the ground and passed with a circular motion over the opening of the pipe, which was directed toward Soldier Wolf.

Shave Head now filled another pipe and placed it upright before Soldier Wolf. He had some difficulty in balancing it, and Soldier Wolf after passing his hands from the mouthpiece toward the bowl over the stem, settled it firmly in place, wedging it up with earth where necessary. The pipe and the cleaners lay between Soldier Wolf and the circle in the dust before him. Soldier Wolf delivered a long address of advice to the young men who were about to take part in the coming ordeal.

A drum was brought in and put down near the door on its north side. Long intervals of waiting followed, during which nothing was said or done. Many of the men, young and old, appeared to be praying—looking toward the earth or sitting with closed eyes. Presently Soldier Wolf lighted another pipe, which Shave Head set going with the same ceremonies as before. Four drummers sat close by the drum, and on the north side of the lodge were twelve or fifteen other young men, members of the different soldier bands.

The red-painted pipe which was placed before Soldier Wolf was given to the earth maker, represented by Soldier Wolf.

The drumming and singing now began, and four wolf songs were sung. At a change in the air the Medicine Lodge makers and the soldiers all stood up and danced, blowing their eagle-bone whistles in time to the drumming. The dancers did not move their feet, but merely bent the knees slightly, rising and falling in time to the song. At a pause in the dance, Soldier Wolf ceremonially cleaned his black smoked-out pipe. The red-stemmed pipe still lay before him. Shave Head, by direction of Soldier Wolf, offered a pipe to the drummers, the music ceased, and all the dancers sat down. In starting the dance again, the drummers sang four songs before anyone got up, and then at the change of the air after these songs, all arose and danced. From time to time food had been brought in, until now there was a large pan of crackers and one of dried meat, and two kettles of coffee. Soldier Wolf now ceremonially lighted the red-painted pipe which Shave Head commenced to smoke as before.

More soldiers had come in to join the dance, until there were about twenty-five of them present, besides a number sitting outside the lodge for whom there was no room. The dancing began again, but during the first dance only the soldiers stood; when the second song began, however, the Medicine Lodge makers rose and joined them. The hair of the Medicine Lodge makers was unbraided. At the close of each series of dances Shave Head offered a pipe to the drummers. When the fourth pipe had been offered the ceremonies closed for the day—about 10 P.M.

In each dance the soldiers danced four times, dancing to

227

four songs. There were thus four complete dances, and sixteen songs and sixteen individual dances.

FIRST DAY

Before daybreak of this first day, the scout chosen for the purpose set out from the camp, ceremonially found the tree which was to be used for the center-pole of the Medicine Lodge, returned, and announced its discovery. This tree might be ceremonially discovered only by one who, as a scout in the old war times, had discovered the enemy, and returning, had announced that fact. The actual selection of the tree for the pole was made several days before its ceremonial discovery. The scout who found the pole on this occasion (1911) was Little Hawk, son of Gentle Horse. He had discovered Crook's troops before the Rosebud fight, June 17, 1876.

Since the old-time wars ceased long years ago, few if any men survive who can fulfill the conditions demanded for the office of discovering the center-pole for the Medicine Lodge. Twenty years ago, among the Southern Cheyennes, but two men remained who possessed such experience—Wolf Face and Mad Wolf, aged men and tried warriors, each of whom had found camps of the Pawnees and had been in the heavy fighting of the years 1852 and 1853.[3] The naked body of Wolf Face showed five scars which, from their position and size, represented serious wounds. Among the Northern Cheyennes a few years later only two or three men were left who could perform this duty.

The man who found the pole, when he returned to report its discovery, imitated, as nearly as he could, the acts he performed when he had returned from his actual scout and reported the discovery of the enemy years before.

Wolf Face, whom I saw come in to announce this discovery in 1902, entered the camp-circle just before sunrise through the opening to the east, in the manner of a scout of the olden

[3] The Fighting Cheyennes, pp. 75-92, New York, 1915.

time. As he had been on horseback when he discovered the enemy on the occasion which this occurrence represented, so he was mounted now. He rode into the circle, changing his course and zigzagging as he rode, howled like a wolf, and went through all the formal acts of a scout bringing news of the enemy. He shouted out his discovery four times.

In the center of the camp-circle the chiefs had gathered and were waiting for the announcement, and so soon as it had been made, the old crier began to pass around the camp, shouting his directions to the soldiers to get together and go out to cut the pole. Before long they began to ride up and to gather by bands not far from where the chiefs sat, their numbers continually increasing. Soon they rode out of the camp-circle to cut the center-pole, and to bring in the posts and rafters which would form the framework of the lodge.

The ceremonial cutting of the cottonwood for the center-pole was done by some man who had struck an enemy with a hatchet. As he prepared to cut the tree, he walked up to it, made four motions toward the trunk with his hatchet, and recited his achievement. The tree was then felled without further ceremony. It is said that in olden times, before the tree was actually felled, certain men marched about it singing.

On this occasion the soldiers began to return with the material early in the morning. Some of them held long straight willow branches with tufts of leaves on their ends; these represented lances. Many carried on their backs frames of willow twigs shaped like shields, the leafy ends of the twigs hanging down to represent feathers. Other bundles of twigs represented bows and quivers. Some men wore wreaths or bonnets of willow twigs about their heads, others were crowned with chaplets of vine leaves, from which long trailing leafy sprays hung down behind like the "tails" of war-bonnets. The horses wore collars of willow and cottonwood twigs. Each returning soldier band came on in a close body, pairs or trios of men dragging with their ropes cottonwood poles, either rafters or posts. At a point

229

seventy-five or a hundred yards before they reached the place where a heap of buffalo-chips had been piled, they dropped their ropes, charged upon the pile, and touched it with the sticks in their hands. They then rode back, picked up their ropes, and dragged the poles to their places—where the lodge was to be built—and leaving them there, rode to the opening of the circle, out of it, and about the circle.

In ancient times the center-pole was brought first into the camp, but of late years the rafters and posts have been brought in first. Formerly the center-pole was dragged in by the horsemen with ropes, but recently it has been hauled in on a wagon, as also have been the branches used in the ceremony, which are brought by the women.

Between the opening of the circle and the point where the coup was to be counted, those who were bringing in the center-pole stopped four times. At the fourth stop the center-pole was dropped, its butt lying toward the east.

After the men, came the women with the branches; they were on foot, surrounding the wagons and singing as they went. They also were crowned with chaplets of willow twigs and held similar twigs in their hands.

After all the material for the Medicine Lodge had been brought together a sham battle took place, in which the young men and the boys took part. Most of them were on foot, and many carried the imitation weapons of willow which they had brought in a short time before. Six or eight men, however, were permitted to go into this fight on horseback. The footmen divided into parties, usually by soldier bands, and indulged in the kicking game, the kickers springing into the air and kicking at the opponent with both feet. Sometimes in sport the willow weapons were used; but the young men were careful in using them, no severe blows were given, and all were good-tempered.

Soon after all the material for the lodge had been brought in, the soldiers with axes began to notch the rafter poles, about two feet from the butts, so that when put in position they should not slip along the cross-pieces. Two elderly men began to dig the hole for the center-pole, loosening the soil at first with a root-digger, and taking it out with a horn spoon.

Of the soldiers who worked about the lodge, each band had its appointed station. The Elk-horn Scrapers and Bowstring Soldiers were on the south side of the lodge, while the Fox Soldiers and Dog Soldiers were on the north side. While the older men were digging the hole for the center-pole, which was always half an arm stretch, or three feet, deep, the soldiers all about the lodge, with iron bars, were digging holes for the up-rights, setting the posts, filling in the dirt, and tramping it down about them. This was done more rapidly than the dig-ging of the single hole in the center, and without ceremony.

All this is of the Southern Cheyennes in 1902.

At the ceremony in Montana in 1911, on the day when the material for constructing the Medicine Lodge was brought in, only a few old men were in the instruction lodge early in the morning when I entered.

The assistant instructors, who performed the actual work, were Big Head Man, Bull Tongue, and Young Bird. Instruc-tors and assistants alike were thoughtful, silent, and reverent, much of the time praying silently with closed eyes or with their hands over their faces. After food had been served and eaten, the dishes were passed out through the door by the younger men.

After a time, discussion arose as to whether it was proper in this ceremony to use the bull's skull that had been selected for it, since this skull had already been used in a ceremony con-nected with the sacred hat (Issiwun) several years before. White Bull declared that it might be so used, provided it were purified by having a certain song sung over it. Meantime, with a stout pointed stick, something like a tent-pin, Wolf Chief was breaking up and removing the ethmoid bones of the skull, which he placed temporarily in front of the nose.

The red-stemmed pipe which stood before Soldier Wolf had

carved on the upper surface of the stem, near the bowl, a bull's head, above this a turtle, farther toward the mouthpiece a lizard, and close to the mouthpiece a deer's head. It was often lighted by Soldier Wolf and passed along the line of instructors.

The assemblage was now waiting for those who had been sent to bring in the grass to be placed in the buffalo's nose. This is a water-grass or sedge (*Carex nebracensis*). Meantime the older people were conversing and describing to the present instructors the ways of the Medicine Lodge in old times. A man handed in through the door a "possible sack," two jack-rabbit-skins and a tanned deerskin. Pine opened the sack and from it took other hare-skins—one or two in winter pelage. Other deerskins and hare-skins were brought in and examined by the instructor, and two of each were chosen. From the possible sack Wolf Chief took strips of sinew, red-dyed horsehair, and eagle-feathers. He opened a bundle containing down-feathers of eagle, tail-feathers of flickers (*Colaptes*), and skins of the redheaded woodpecker. All these birds and animals belong to this ceremony.

It was about this time that the soldiers returned to the camp, dressed in green willows or cottonwood or hop vines. On this later occasion, instead of having a sham battle as in the South, they charged around the camp, one group just within the circle following the course of the sun, and firing guns. The Dog Soldiers—to which Rock Road belonged—started first to ride about outside of the circle, and before starting to ride about inside the circle the Elk Soldiers—Red Bead's soldier band—waited until the Dog Soldiers had got outside. They rode in opposite directions and thus passed each other about halfway around the camp opposite the opening of the circle, one band riding outside and the other inside the circle. After this parade was ended and all had returned, the Dog Soldiers and the Elk Soldiers busied themselves in taking down two lodges to be used for dancing and eating places for the two bands. Somewhat later the Chief Soldiers did the same. The lodge covering for each of these shelters, tied to its single pole, was carried across from the place where the lodge had stood, by two men on horseback, and the poles were carried in the same way.

While this was going on, the assistant instructors and their helpers in the ceremonial lodge were busied with various tasks —cutting rabbit-skins into strips and cutting strings of deerskin or strips of rawhide, while Young Bird was sorting out the grass for the buffalo-skull's nose, placing the heads of the grass all in one direction.

Rock Road, who had been absent from the lodge, now brought in a carbine, and a bow-case and quiver containing the bow and arrows. These he handed to Soldier Wolf, who passed them to Young Bird, who put them behind him. Shave Head brought in a rifle. The guns were put behind the Medicine Lodge makers.

Tall White Man was now cutting wide strips of rawhide, which the Medicine Lodge women would use as belts, such as they used to wear in olden times. Bull Tongue was making up plumes or bundles of feathers, each usually of four eagle down-feathers tied together, to which was added later a strand of red-dyed horsehair, and the whole was tied with a deerskin string. One of the feather bundles was now passed to White Bull to be ceremonially completed. In bygone years, in a fight with the Snake and Ute Indians, he had worn such a feather bundle on his head, and during the fight had killed and scalped a Snake and a Ute. The counting of this coup over the plume rendered it specially effective. This particular plume was of three down-feathers, one stouter than the other two, from which the vanes and a part of the shaft had been removed, so that it was short. With these were tied five dried heads of a certain grass, and the lower mandible and throat skin of a redheaded woodpecker. The whole was bound with a deerskin string, both ends of which were left long. If the strings on a plume were not long enough, sometimes a long deerskin loop was tied lightly with sinew to the lower end of the plume.

233

Big Head Man counted a coup over another of the feather plumes. On the north side of White River he saw three persons traveling on the prairie, and killed and scalped one of them. The final operation in finishing these plumes is with a knife to trim off the end of the quills square, but this may not be done until after the coup has been counted.

These feather plumes are for attachment to the bone whistles of the dancers. Long deerskin strings were now prepared, to make loops by which the whistles should hang around the dancers' necks. After these had been prepared, the feather plume was bound to the end of the whistle with a short piece of sinew taken from over the shoulder blade of the buffalo (now a beef). They need also for this ceremony a piece of fat from the right side and from the right shoulder of the buffalo.

Before trimming a feather plume, Big Head Man counted another coup: "On the other side of the Big Horn Mountain, I was sent out to look for enemies and found them. I reported them to the camp, and the following morning we went out and charged them. I killed one, and when I scalped him I did it in this way."

Young Bird continued to arrange the grass for the buffalo-skull, while Big Head Man and Bull Tongue began to sew up skirts, or tunics, of dressed deerskin for the three Medicine Lodge makers. A buffalo-robe was brought in for Bull Tongue, but before it was given to him it was ceremonially treated, one of the instructors biting off a piece of root, blowing it out on his hands in the prescribed way, making the ceremonial motions and then purifying the robe by spitting on it in five places—the right shoulder, the right ham, left shoulder, left ham, and the middle of the back, just behind the shoulders.

Rock Road made a short address, declaring that the ceremony of the Medicine Lodge was undertaken for the benefit of the whole people. It was to insure a good harvest of all the fruits of the earth, as corn, berries, and roots. He asked that it be closely watched and a good report made on it.

The grass which was being prepared for insertion in the orbits and nose of the buffalo-skull should all have been brown-headed grass (*Carex*), but because this was hard to find, they put in some common slough grass to make the bundle the right size. Certain old men, as Bull Thigh and White Bull, said that this might be done, since slough grass grows near the stream. From this it was inferred that the use of the grass is a prayer for an abundant supply of water. The grass was tied in bundles with sinew, then was doubled back from the middle of the bundle outward and the heads brought down to the butt, so that the head of each blade of grass almost reached its own butt. This gave a thick, circular-ended bundle of grass, hollowed out in the middle.

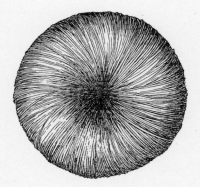

The assistant instructors now began to attach square strips of hare-skin on each corner and to the middle of each of the buffalo-robes to be used by Medicine Lodge maker and instructors. These strips were twice pierced, a deerskin string put through the two holes and tied, and the two ends then passed through holes in the buffalo-robe and tied. The flesh-side of the hare-skin lay against the fur-side of the buffalo-robes.

Using clay taken from tin dishes, the assistants now began to whiten the feather plumes. Before taking the clay in his fingers the assistant made four motions toward the clay, and taking some up with the fourth he rubbed it on the sinew binding and the feathers. When this had been done, three piles, each consisting of a tunic, a feather bundle, a whistle, and a rawhide belt, lay toward the middle of the lodge between the instructors and the fire. A bundle of white sage was afterward placed on each of the piles.

The assistants now whitened the fur-side of the buffalo-robes, drawing rough lines from the head to the tail, from each hind quarter diagonally to each fore quarter, across the back, and drawing on the right side a circle which represented the sun. An armful of white sage in bloom was brought in, which the assistants, Big Head Man, Bull Tongue, and Frank Standing Elk, tied in bundles. Long strings were left hanging from the bundles. Big Head Man consolidated his sage bundles by biting them, to bring the stems close together. The instructors did little or no work, but seemed carefully to watch their assistants, who conversed and joked with one another. The instructors were serious and silent.

At about ten o'clock the Chief Soldiers came into the camp and were heard singing outside.

Meantime, the bundles of grass of a proper size for the buffalo's orbits were made in the same way as those for the nose.

Now Bull Tongue tied on Red Bead's head a plume of feathers, touching the bundle to the right forehead, the right side of the head well back, the left side of the head well back, and the left forehead, and having moved it all around the head touched it again to the forehead and then tied it to the scalplock. Red Bead now turned his back to the assistant, and the doubled buffalo-robe, flesh-side out, was laid on his shoulders. He pulled it up, so that it fell hair-side out. On this robe were the five pieces of hare-skin as described, on the quarters and in the middle of the back. While this was being done other assistant instructors put deerskin strings on the ends of the rawhide belts.

Soon after the Chief Soldiers came in, there was a parade of the chiefs riding slowly and singing within the circle of the camp. This took place about ten-thirty. Soon after this the lodge was set up to serve as a shelter for the soldier bands; it was of many poles over which were spread two large lodge coverings.

About this time, in the instruction lodge, Young Bird, after he had tied up his hair, with four motions placed the grass bundles in the orbits and nose of the skull, filling the right orbit first. He then took two sacks of paint, one of red and one of black, and painted the skull. He drew a line of black from between the horns of the skull down the median line of the face to ends of nasal bones. Filling a piece of fat with red paint, he slowly pulled off small fragments of the fat with his fingers and smeared a line down the middle of the face next to the black line just drawn, and then painted the whole right side of the face red. He walked around behind the skull and painted a red line down the left side of the face just to the left of the median black line, and then painted the whole left side red. Under the left orbit he painted a black crescent moon, the opening looking backward, and under the right orbit a red circular sun.

There seemed some difference of opinion as to whether this painting was in all respects as it should have been, but the matter was finally settled by the statement that this was the painting used in the South.

A cottonwood stick about four feet long, pointed at one end and tapering for about half its length until it was perhaps an inch and a quarter in greatest diameter, was now brought in and placed on the ground on the west side of the skull. This stick represented a root-digger. At its thicker end four notches were cut an inch and a half apart, each notch at the end toward the point of the stick being cut in at right angles to the axis of the stick for half an inch, and the wood shaved away with a

237

constantly diminishing thickness toward the butt of the root-digger, until the next notch was reached, like this:

Parallel to the root-digger lay an arrow, and a foot south of the arrow and close to the root-digger was another arrow, without head or point. At the points of the root-digger and the arrow lay a buffalo-chip.

About noon the occupants of the lodge began to eat, Spotted Hawk serving the food. Before anyone began to eat, Soldier Wolf called Shave Head before him and gave him a piece of meat, which Shave Head, breaking into four pieces, offered to the four sides of the mimic earth—the circle in the dust—before Soldier Wolf.

After all had eaten, Young Bird very carefully, and with four motions, took up the arrow lying by the root-digger and carried it, point held downward and close to the ground, to the opposite or south side of the buffalo head and eighteen inches distant from it. Then he slowly reversed the arrow so that the head pointed upward and the feather end rested on the ground. Shave Head, called over, went to Pine, who, having bitten a piece of the root tied to the corner of the buffalo-robe, spat ceremonially on Shave Head's hands. Shave Head then squatted close to Young Bird, who, taking his hand and making with it four motions, caused him, with the forefinger of the right hand, ceremonially to paint the east side of the arrow. In the same way he had him paint with the forefinger of the left hand the south side, with the right hand the west and north sides, and again the east side. Then Shave Head returned to his place and Young Bird applied the actual paint to the arrow and put it back in its place, reversing the former motions. Now Young Bird took the root-digger and with four motions lifted it, butt upward, over the skull and rested the point on the ground. Red Bead, called over, was instructed as Shave Head

238

had been, and ceremonially painted the root-digger as Shave Head had the arrow, but Red Bead actually painted the lower two feet of the root-digger red and then retired. Shave Head, called over, painted a black ring about the root-digger just below the notches, and Young Bird completed the black painting on and above the notches without ceremony. The notched parts of the root-digger, and an inch below them, were black and the remainder (except half an inch without paint at the tip) was red. Young Bird now put the root-digger in its place.

He then took the slab of back fat from which little pieces of fat had been pulled for use in this painting, and spread it before him on a bed of the butts of the grass cut from the stuffing of the skull's nose and eyes. To the right of the piece of fat he placed a new knife, for in the Medicine Lodge all knives used must be new. From this piece of fat Young Bird cut a circular piece four inches in diameter, and called Red Bead. As before, Pine spat ceremonially on Red Bead's hands, who made the ceremonial motions, and then went to the side of Young Bird, who caused him to anoint his fingers with red paint. Young Bird took Red Bead's hand, forefinger extended, and drew the forefinger across the circle of fat from north to south and then sent Red Bead back to his place. Young Bird painted the fat with black paint on the east side and red paint on the west side without further ceremony, and then with the knife made in the fat a crescent-shaped cut in the middle of the circle about at the line of juncture of the red and black paint.

Big Head Man went to Pine, and the ceremonial motions were performed and Big Head Man placed himself on Young Bird's left. With four motions and very slowly Big Head Man took up the red-painted arrow, drawing the point along the ground till it was in front of him, and then pointed the arrow-point at the line between the black and red painting, and prayed long and loud. His right hand held the arrow below the feather; the left hand was lower and near the point. The prayer ended with a war-cry, and as he uttered it he thrust the arrowpoint through the fat and into the earth, and left it there. He then did the same thing, without the prayer, with the root-digger, drew the circular piece of fat about a foot above the ground on both arrow and root-digger, lifted both slowly, turned them around, points to the west, rested the points on a buffalo-chip, and left them there.

Now, from a bundle lying at the south side of the skull Young Bird with four motions took a straight redstone pipe, with a stem, and pipe-stick, both painted red. He took also a very old piece of buffalo sinew, from which he slowly tore four narrow threads, each of which he tapped four times on the pipe end of the stem. From a little sack, also taken out of the bundle, he took a tuft of buffalo-wool and by pulling it out thin prepared it to wrap about the pipe end of the stem to make this end fit tightly to the pipe. Putting this wool in its place on the stem, he laid the stem aside and with his left hand put the four threads of sinew in the palm of the right hand and rolled them into a ball, tearing them meanwhile into finer threads. This little ball he put on the ground by the buffalo-wool. Rock Road, called over, wearing his robe hair-side out, went to Young Bird and knelt by him. Young Bird went around to Rock Road's right side. Curly, an instructor, bit a piece of the root tied to the buffalo-robe and spat ceremonially on Rock Road's hands. Rock Road dropped off his robe, which Young Bird arranged, so that a corner of it lay on the ground close to the pipe. He then called for Rock Road's tobacco-sack, and taking from it a little tobacco, put it on the corner of the robe. Taking Rock Road's hands in his own, he moved them slowly down over the pipestem and with four motions caused him to pick up the pipe and to move it slowly back over the stem to the mouthpiece and then to the robe, where it was placed standing upright. He then caused Rock Road to pick up the little ball of sinew, to hold it above the pipe, and with four motions downward and one motion moving it around the bowl, to drop it in. Now he picked up the pipe stick, and with the circular motion around

HAIL PAINT OF THE MEDICINE LODGE

the pipe and four motions, began to ram down the ball of sinew. The pipe was filled in the same way. Four pinches of tobacco were inserted alternately by right and left hand, with the same motions. Between the introduction of each two pinches of tobacco, two with the right hand and two with the left, the pipe was moved with a circular motion over the tobacco lying on the robe. The pipe stick was now picked up with four motions and the tobacco in the pipe was rammed with four motions. The remainder of the loading of the pipe was performed without ceremony. When the pipe bowl was filled, the instructor took Rock Road's hands and caused him to pass the filled pipe over the stem from the mouthpiece to its place, where it was put on the ground.

Young Bird took Rock Road's hands and moved them down over the stem to the pipe end, and caused him with four motions to wrap the buffalo-wool about the pipe end of the stem. Rock Road now went and stood before Pine, and the ceremonial motions were performed. Young Bird took the candidate's hands and passed them down over the stem and caused him to grasp the pipe and lift it a very short distance toward the stem, when it was put on the ground again. This moving was done four times, and the fourth time Rock Road fixed the pipe on the stem and took his hands away, while Young Bird took the pipe and fixed stem and bowl securely together. He then rubbed white sage over his hands and went back behind Rock Road to his place, and Rock Road returned to his place. The loaded pipe and the pipe stick remained on the ground southeast of the nose of the buffalo-skull while Young Bird tied up the bundle from which the various things had been taken.

There was now a short recess, when all left the lodge.

When they returned, the wives of Red Bead, Rock Road, and Shave Head came with them, and these women sat in that order from south to north, south of west of the buffalo-skull. Curly sat next them to the south and Young Bird next to him, then Wolf Chief and Soldier Wolf. As different people entered there was some little change of position. Pine seated himself between Curly and Young Bird, and Young Bird changed his place so as to sit next Red Bead's wife.

Frank Standing Elk, after his hands had been ceremonially spat on by Young Bird, handed Young Bird some bundles of white sage. Presently Big Head Man knelt on the ground before Shave Head, and Frank Standing Elk before Rock Road. The women were told to remove their outer garments. Red Bead's wife took off three dresses—one each yellow, red, and plaid—and still had one left. Women handed in possible sacks through the door of the lodge, and Shave Head's wife passed a porcupine comb up the line to Red Bead. The instructors now took from the Medicine Lodge makers' heads the feather plumes that had been tied to them. Big Head Man stirred a vessel which held white clay paint and water. Red Bead's wife now removed the upper part of her last dress as far down as the waist and raised the skirt nearly to her waist. Two twisted deerskin strings were passed by Big Head Man from Shave Head's wife to Frank Standing Elk. With a porcupine comb, Big Head Man and Frank Standing Elk, who stood close before the partly naked woman, brushed her hair. The other women removed their clothing in the same way, and the women tied up their dresses with the protective strings so that they held about the waist.

Now Bull Tongue painted the legs of Red Bead with white clay, streaking the paint by drawing his finger nails down over it. This is said to be a prayer to the snake. Afterward his face was painted and streaked in the same way. Now all the Medicine Lodge makers removed their moccasins. Frank Standing Elk painted Red Bead's wife with white clay, first drawing a line of white down arms and legs, and a circle on the chest, and then smearing the paint over the whole trunk and streaking it with the finger nails. In combing the hair and in applying the paint four motions were made before beginning. Then four streaks of white clay were drawn across the smoothed hair.

242

All the women were painted alike. Bull Tongue painted a black circle about Red Bead's right ankle and wrist, and left wrist and ankle, a black sun on the chest, and a black crescent moon on the right shoulder blade. The same painting was followed with the women, but when the shoulder blade was painted the women did not get up and turn around, but leaned forward. Red Bead was painted also black around the face from chin, in front of ears, over forehead and down to the chin again, and a black cross was made on the bridge of the nose. From the inner side of the black circle surrounding Red Bead's face four black projections were marked, one on the forehead, one over each cheekbone, and one on the chin, thus:

Red Bead now stepped into a deerskin tunic, which reached from waist to the ground, and was tied about the waist with a red and white cord and tassel. Meantime, the women's hair was tied up at the side, somewhat in the old-time fashion. Red Bead put on a long strip of cloth, hanging down from his waist in front, and another hanging down behind, the two representing a breechclout, and a long bundle of sage was tied about each ankle and wrist in the ceremonial order. Bundles of sage were tied to the wrists and ankles of the women, and long narrow bundles of sage were tied in their hair, at each side of the head, above and behind the ears. Except for their dresses drawn about their waists, the women were now naked.

When Big Head Man had finished painting Shave Head's wife, he went over to Shave Head and combed his hair ceremonially with a porcupine comb, while Frank Standing Elk did the same to Rock Road. As the painting began, Shave Head tied up his hair. A feather plume was now tied in Red Bead's head, and when the dressing was at an end, Red Bead thanked Bull Tongue for what he had done by passing his hand over him, and made a prayer. Big Head Man whitened Shave Head's tunic with white clay, and Frank Standing Elk did the same to Rock Road's tunic, and the two put them on, and then assumed the imitation breechclouts, before and behind. Now the whistles were put over the men's heads with four motions, the feather plumes tied in the heads of all, and their hair was let down, while four sprigs of sage were stuck—in front, on both sides, and behind—in the belts of Shave Head and Rock Road. The women, who had drawn their dresses down over their legs, now handed out to the assistant instructors shawls, blankets, moccasins, a quilt, and a gun. Shave Head's wife paid Big Head Man. The instructors had received their pay the day before.

After eating, the Medicine Lodge makers took their pipes and tobacco-sacks and smoked, and the assistants gave the women buffalo-robes and put the robes about the women with the rawhide belts. An instructor consecrated a pan of water by spitting ceremonially over it, and the women, one after another, went over to the pan and after making four motions toward it with the face, each drank, the wife of Shave Head first, of Rock Road second, and of Red Bead last. Pine now passed behind the skull and was about to drink, but was laughed at by all present. He had made a mistake; it was not his time to drink. Meantime the women were putting on their moccasins and standing up.

Young Bird took the root-digger and the arrow from their former place and moved them to the south side of the skull, the points directed to the east. Pine spat on the hands of Shave Head's wife, and with four motions she lifted the buffalo-skull from the ground and, stooping and walking very slowly, carried it to the north around the fire and out of the door, the other women following. In taking up the skull, Shave Head's wife made a mistake as to where to place her hands, but before she lifted the skull this was corrected. The Medicine Lodge makers followed the women, passing about the lodge to the north side of the fire and then out. As he passed the pan of consecrated water, Shave Head and Red Bead each drank—his last drink —but Rock Road did not drink. Wolf Chief spat on Red Bead's hands and gave him the old medicine—the straight pipe and its stick, and the root-digger and the arrow. The other Medicine Lodge makers carried the buffalo-chips, paint, and other sacred things. As they passed out, each instructor drank of the consecrated water.

Very slowly and reverently Shave Head's woman carried the skull down toward the partly erected medicine lodge—almost to the brush-pile. On the way she stopped four times, and finally with four motions put down the skull. Wolf Chief took from Red Bead the medicine, and the pipe, which he placed on a buffalo-chip south of the skull, where also the root-digger and arrow were placed, pointing diagonally a little northeast. The women sat down on the ground just behind the skull, the Medicine Lodge makers well to the south of them, and the instructors and old men between. Now from south to north, passing in front of the line of sitting people, came a man carrying an offering and a little child to be blessed, and following him was a long procession of people with offerings, many of the women and men being accompanied by small children. Some men and women offered their babies to the Medicine Lodge women, who held them in their laps, blessed them, and prayed over them.

The three Medicine Lodge makers now rose to their feet and followed Bull Tongue about the medicine lodge as marked out by the uprights for the frame, which had already been set in the ground. He led them in single file outside of the lodge, around from west to north, to east, to south, and when they reached the rafter on the south side each man, with four motions, placed his foot on the rafter. After stepping on the southernmost rafter they kept on again around the lodge, placed the foot on the northern rafter and walked four steps on it. On the second round they went through the center of the lodge and, ceremonially stepping on the center-pole, walked four steps on it from butt toward fork, and then stepped off and walked back to the instructor Pine, who spat first on the hands of Bull Tongue and afterward on those of all the Medicine Lodge makers. Now Bull Tongue, followed by Shave Head, who carried a sack of red paint and some fat, and by Red Bead, who carried black paint and some fat, again went around the medicine lodge sunwise. Stopping at the eastern rafter, it was painted by Shave Head with a band of red eight or ten inches wide about twelve feet from the butt. Four motions were made before the paint was applied, and the paint was rubbed on four times. The southern rafter was painted red in the same way. The Medicine Lodge makers following the instructor came back to the line of people, walked behind the skull and then again around the medicine lodge, stopping at the westernmost rafter, which Red Bead painted black as the others were painted red. The north rafter was also painted black by Red Bead. Each rafter was measured by Bull Tongue, and the paint—about one foot wide—was applied at a distance of two arms' spans of Bull Tongue from the butt of the rafter.

The four men now returned from the north through the middle of the lodge, and Red Bead painted about the center-pole a wide band of red, and immediately above this band of red Shave Head painted a wide band of black. Then the four returned to the line where the instructors sat. Pine again spat ceremonially on the hands of Bull Tongue and of the three Medicine Lodge makers, and Bull Tongue walked over to the pile of green cherry and cottonwood brush, which was to be tied up and put in the fork of the pole.

Instructed by Bull Tongue, Shave Head and Red Bead each with four motions picked up a branch of brush, and with four motions—that is, pointing the branch at the fork of the pole twice on the north side and twice on the south—moved it to its place, where Red Bead held it. After that the brush was placed in the fork without ceremony. Cherry brush was put in first, but on top was some cottonwood brush, and Bull Tongue tied the whole bundle firmly together and then lashed it to the fork of the center-pole with the long, pliable strip of water-soaked rawhide cut in the morning in the ceremonial lodge. The passing of the line back and forth was begun very slowly and ceremonially around the brush and the fork of the pole, but it was finished without ceremony.

While the painting of the poles and the binding of the bundles of brush were being done, the soldier lodges were being taken down and the soldiers by companies were arming themselves with lodge-poles—sometimes tied together to form shears —with which to raise the center-pole and the rafters.

Bull Tongue and Shave Head now returned to the line, and after the hands of both had been ceremonially spat on by Pine, Bull Tongue held Shave Head's hand in his own and caused him, with four motions, to pick up and carry the root-digger and the arrow thrust through the fat to the brush tied in the fork of the pole, and with four motions to push the two into the bundle. Meantime, Spotted Hawk, Lone Elk, Frank Standing Elk, and Tall White Man were tying in bundles the offerings that had been made to the skull and which now were placed in the fork of the pole. The Medicine Lodge makers then returned to their places. The bundle of brush is called the Thunder's nest (*Nŭno'maēh'whĕts*).

After the offerings had been tied in place and all had returned to their positions in the line, Wolf Chief and Pine called forward the Medicine Lodge women and seated them to the south of the skull in this order: Red Bead's wife to the north, Rock Road's wife next, and Shave Head's wife next—farthest to the south. The last two were then moved back, and Red Bead's wife was flanked on the right by Wolf Chief and Pine. Red Bead's wife held the straight pipe in her right hand.

Spotted Hawk, Lone Elk, and many women, including Wind

Woman, went to Pine, who spat ceremonially on their hands and they made the ceremonial motions. Orders were called out to the soldiers to prepare to raise the center-pole. An old man came up to the line and gave to each Medicine Lodge maker a piece of tobacco cut from an old Hudson's Bay "carrot." The instructors now began to sing, the women joining them, and the soldiers crowded about the pole which was lying on the ground. At the close of the song the soldiers uttered yells and bent down, seized the tree, lifted it a little way, then pushed it forward and let it down. At the end of the song some men howled like wolves, and all shouted the war-cry. The instructors sang again, and again at the end of the song the pole was lifted, pushed forward, and dropped. This occurred a third time, and at the close of the fourth song, its butt being over the hole, the pole was raised high and the shears placed under it, and it was lifted higher and higher until the butt slipped into the hole. The horizontal cross-pieces were raised and put in the forks of the wall posts. The twenty-eight rafter poles extending from the fork of the center-pole to the horizontal poles on the outside were now put up without ceremony. Red Bead's woman now moved back so as to sit in line with the other Medicine Lodge women, and presently the Medicine Lodge women and the instructors moved ten feet or more back from the skull. Meantime, the soldiers with rawhide thongs had lashed the rafters to the horizontal poles and were covering the medicine lodge with canvas lodge coverings. At this time also the instruction—the lonely—lodge was taken down.

The sun had fallen well toward the western horizon—it was about five-thirty—when Rock Road's woman, instructed by Pine, took up the buffalo skull, and stooping forward, very slowly carried it around the north side of the medicine lodge and into it. On the way to the door she stopped four times, and at the entrance again stopped and moved the skull forward four times, making the motions of entering, going in at the fourth motion. She passed very slowly around to the west side of the medicine lodge, and with four motions placed the skull on the ground, facing east, at some distance behind the center-pole. The other women, the lodge makers, and the instructors followed her. The three women sat down behind it, and their bodies were wiped off with bundles of sage which, together with the rawhide belts that they had worn, were put on the ground west of the skull. The instructors took off from the Medicine Lodge makers the anklets and wristlets of sage and caused the three to sit in front of the instructors to the northwest of where the women were. They also took the feather plumes from their heads, removed the tunics they had worn, and the men were then wiped off with sage. The tunics and the other things were put on the ground back of the skull. On the ground south of the skull were placed an unpainted, long-handled fire-spoon of cottonwood and four rattles with some sacks of paint. Now, while some rawhides were being brought in, the women and men went out, the women having resumed their dresses, but wearing the buffalo-robes over them. The Medicine Lodge makers soon returned.

A number of the chiefs and old men now gathered about the drum, just south of the entrance, and began to drum and to sing. All the Medicine Lodge makers sat down at the back of the lodge in the southwestern part. Presently the Medicine Lodge women returned and seated themselves behind the skull. After an interval of singing by the chiefs, shots were heard, and presently the Elk Soldiers marched into the lodge—one of them on horseback. A little later the Fox Soldiers came in, and still later a few of the Crazy Dog Soldiers. There were present of these soldiers about forty-two men elaborately dressed, some wearing war-bonnets and six of them on horseback. They ranged themselves about the lodge and sang and danced.

Presently Bob-Tailed Bull and White Hawk made speeches; a little later Crazy Head and Bob-Tailed Bull directed the horsemen to dismount, and the horses were taken out of the lodge. Porcupine and Lone Elk selected for their achievements two men from the Fox Soldiers and two from the Elk Soldiers, to be honored. These men were addressed at some length; they were urged to continue to set a good example, and to be patriotic and helpful to the people—to teach the young to live well. Their names were called out and they were pointed to as examples of well-doing.

One of these men was Black Horse, an elderly and crippled warrior who was a great fighter in the decade between 1870 and 1880. Another one was Ridge Walker, much younger, and notable for his industry and his success in cultivating the ground. The men who had been thus honored danced to the door and back again.

The relatives of these men expressed their sense of the honor done them by bringing forward various gifts which they presented to them. Then Porcupine and Grasshopper made each a speech, and the soldiers formed by companies to leave the lodge. They advanced four times to the door, stopped there, and retreated three times, passing out the fourth time. The men whose names had been called were the last to go out. The lodge was now deserted by the public.

Old women then brought in back-rests, quilts, and blankets, and began to prepare beds for the Medicine Lodge women, who left the lodge for a moment and then returned and sat down on the south side, waiting for the beds to be arranged. Besides the women, there were in the medicine lodge only the Medicine Lodge makers, three instructors, and two or three old men. A large fire was kindled in the southeast corner of the lodge, not far from the door.

The women who contribute the beds and linings and shades for the Medicine Lodge women, and put them up, will receive these articles again when these Medicine Lodge makers and their wives become instructors. If before that time the women who have contributed shall have died, the heirs of each will receive the things back from the Medicine Lodge makers when these have become instructors.

A woman receives a present for taking down—changing—the beds for the Medicine Lodge women; but if she is well-to-do, she may perform this service if called on to do so, and give to some other person the presents which she receives. In some cases the beds are changed at each painting. They must be changed at least four times during the Medicine Lodge.

After the soldiers had left the lodge, those young men who had been considering the suffering in this Medicine Lodge—dancing, so-called, or perhaps swinging to the pole—thought over the matter for the last time, and each, when he determined to carry the thing through, repaired to the lodge, taking with him the various articles required for the occasion. As yet the young men were not painted.

Each young man who intended to dance was obliged to go to someone who had previously suffered in the Medicine Lodge, and ask him for help. This consisted in painting him, caring for him, and telling him what he should do. For this service he gave the instructor a present. The number of men that danced was not large. It might be twenty, it might be fifty. Each had some special purpose in dancing: either he was paying a vow, or was imploring a blessing, or was suffering in order to show loyalty to a member of his soldier band, or to some close friend, who was paying his vow. During the four days and four nights of this dancing the sufferer might not eat or drink, and he would have little rest. On the first night of their dancing, the young men prayed four times, holding their hands toward the sky and bowing down and placing the hands on the earth four times. Then they lay down to rest and slept through the night. When so resting during the Medicine Lodge, they lay with their heads toward the center-pole, resting on beds of white sage, with a pillow of the same. To some of the young men, however, their female relations had already brought blankets or quilts. Standing in the ground by each man's head was a forked stick two and a half or three feet long, on which he hung his whistle when he was not using it. Often some charm, as the image of a

251

swift lizard to be worn about the neck, was also hung there. These lizards can go without water for a long time, and the images are worn in order that the dancer may be able to endure thirst. Also the lizard sometimes raises itself on its four feet and stands still in the sun for a long time, looking. It is watchful.

Gradually people began to return to the lodge. Fifteen or twenty dancers, now painted white, sat about waiting. After a time a crier called out summoning the Dog Soldiers and the Elk Soldiers.

Presently Bull Tongue and Young Bird spread out a folded rawhide and tried to crush it flat so that it might be used as a drum. More women came in, carrying quilts and bedding which they gave to those who were to dance. These were gifts to pay to their instructors, and were not for the dancers' use. South of the skull and of the Medicine Lodge makers sat a group of old people and instructors who presently began to sing old-time songs. The first song was without drumming accompaniment. Bull Tongue took Shave Head out to the hide which had been left near the fire, and taking Shave Head's hands in his own, caused him to make four motions toward the hide, grasping it with the fourth motion. He then directed him where to go, and Shave Head carried the hide with four stops to the skull and then very slowly to the group of old people, where he put it on the ground. They afterward drummed on it when they sang. At the end of each song, an instructor prayed briefly in loud tones.

After this singing an order was called out, and all intending dancers rose to their feet, keeping on their blankets or shawls about the waist. Their bodies, arms, and faces were painted white. Each had a whistle about the neck and an eagle down-feather tied in the head. On all the hair was hanging loose.

Now the fire was built up and it was much lighter. The dancers stood for a few moments, seemed to arrange what they had on, and then sat down. At an order, however, all dropped their blankets, rose, and stepped forward. They were about to practice the dance for the morrow.

The old people sang and drummed on the parfleche, and at certain intervals the dancers blew a long blast on the whistles and raised their right hands. Then at a signal they walked out from their places in a serpentine fashion to the other side of the lodge. Bull Tongue led them, and they all imitated his motions and followed where he walked. Standing close together on the other side of the lodge, they rushed more than halfway round the lodge, repeated the blast on the whistles and the raising of right hands. Then Bull Tongue walked back outside the circle of dancers, who followed him back to their original places. Standing there, they blew nine blasts on the whistles and after each blast raised the right hand. Then, as before, the dancers left their places and walked back on the outside of the circle to the north side of the lodge, where they blew nine blasts and after each blast raised the left hand. The leader then turned again and walked east outside of the line, the dancers following until all were once more in line. When facing the outer or north side of the lodge they blew five blasts and at each interval raised the left hand—five times. Now Bull Tongue, turning about, walked inside the line, back again, and the others followed him and again faced outward, and when they stopped they blew seven blasts and with each blast raised the left hand. Again turning, Bull Tongue walked inside the line and the others followed and again faced out, then eight blasts were blown and the left hands raised eight times. Bull Tongue now turned toward the center of the lodge, followed by the others, and when the line had straightened the dancers stopped and faced outward. This was followed by seven blasts on the whistle and seven raisings of the left hand. All now faced about and edged from side to side to make room for each other, and then they blew six blasts and after each blast raised both hands. They now faced outward, blew eight blasts and eight times raised both hands. Facing about again they repeated this, each one of the eight whistles being followed by the raising of both hands, and facing outward, again repeated this. Now they faced inward, moved backward away from the center-pole for room, grasped hands, and swung them forward and backward in time with short whistle blasts, swinging alternate arms. A long song was now sung, and when it was ended the dancers walked about the outer edge of the lodge and returned to their places. The rawhide which had been used as a drum by the old people was taken back to its place near the skull without ceremony. The dancers put their blankets about them and went out, and Bull Tongue busied himself in folding the rawhide. In all the marching and countermarching above described, Bull Tongue led the dancers and the three Medicine Lodge makers closely followed him.

Under instruction by Bull Tongue, Red Bead now ceremonially carried the rawhide from behind the skull to the drummers at the door, who, when it was thrown down before them, yelled and cheered. On the way to the door Red Bead made four stops.

Now the drummers began to pound on an ordinary bass drum and to sing. The fire was replenished. After four short songs the dancers rose and for a while performed the usual dance practiced in the medicine lodge, which was then repeated. An old woman outside the lodge sang a strongheart song urging the dancers to have courage even though they should be tired and hungry, and the drummers cheered the song. After another short song the dancers sat down. Braided Locks, rising from his seat among the old men about the drum, walked out toward the fire and counted a coup, telling of an occasion when he had taken a hundred horses.

At the starting of a familiar Medicine Lodge air the dancers rose and danced as before. At the close of four short songs the dancers sat down and the day's ceremonies were ended.

Bobtail Horse counted a coup, telling of a fight near the Shoshoni Agency in Wyoming. The dancers began to prepare to sleep on their beds of white sage, and everyone not officially connected with the ceremony departed.

SECOND DAY

On Wednesday, August 16, the crier aroused the camp with his calls, before 4:30 A.M. Twenty-five minutes later the first dance was in progress, the older men drumming. There were forty-four dancers, mostly young men in apparently good physical condition, though some were so fat that it was obvious that they could not hold out to the end. Most of the dancers wore their hair long, but some were schoolboys whose hair had been cut. There were only half a dozen male spectators within the lodge, but outside were a number of women, relatives of the dancers, who joined in the singing. The dancers stood in a rather close half-circle, the Medicine Lodge makers being about halfway down the half-circle, and south of the center-pole. Just before sunrise the dancers stopped and sat down, and took the feathers from their heads and the whistles from their necks. The instructors went outside, and soon the dancers followed. The sky was overcast, hence the dancers did not go outside and stand in a line facing the east to sing to the sunrise.

On another occasion on this day, in 1902, just before sunrise all the Medicine Lodge makers, their women, the instructors, and some of the dancers went out through the door of the medicine lodge, formed in a long line facing the sun, and as it rose sang, holding out their hands toward the sun and then making the ceremonial motions over arms, legs, bodies, and heads. Then returning to the lodge, the Medicine Lodge makers washed off their paint by rubbing each other with little wisps of white sage dipped in water and used as sponges. This salute to the sun was omitted in 1911, as just said.

By 7:30 A.M. all the dancers had returned and were lying on their beds, some sleeping, others talking and joking or smoking. Some of the young men were smoothing their hair with combs made of porcupine-tails, others were filling pipes.

The assistant instructors, Bull Tongue, Big Head Man, and Frank Standing Elk, made hoops for the altar, peeling and shaving down red-willow sticks, which they bent and then pressed both ends in the ground so that the stick formed a half-circle. An oldish man was whittling out the long slender wooden pins to be used later in connection with the altar. Soldier Wolf sat near at hand talking and giving directions. On his right was Cross Wings. The Medicine Lodge makers and the Medicine Lodge women were not in the lodge, but soon entered. To an upright piece of iron standing in the ground north of the center-pole was tied a small package of medicine done up in red calico. From time to time a woman entered, walked to a dancer, and handed him something. These were wives or relatives bringing articles that had been asked for. One woman brought the tail of a mule-deer.

Presently the Medicine Lodge makers taught by their instructors, measured and marked and then began to dig, about eighteen inches in front of the nose of the skull, a rectangular hole in the ground. The hole was dug ceremonially by Shave Head, who moved a new knife over the place in the four directions, while the actual digging was done by Big Head Man and Young Bird without ceremony. The soil taken from the hole to a depth of six inches was placed on a piece of calico, slowly carried to the foot of the center-pole, and deposited there.

At about eight o'clock, the Medicine Lodge makers and the Medicine Lodge women, with the instructors and some elderly men, left the lodge and assembled about fifty yards east of the door. Bull Tongue with an unused axe began to cut out a rectangular piece of sod from the prairie. He outlined the piece, fifteen inches long and nine wide, its greater length being east to west, and east and west of this he cut two other rectangles six inches long and nine inches wide from north to south. The cut lines at the east and west ends of the smaller rectangles met the sides of the larger one.

ALTAR IN MEDICINE LODGE

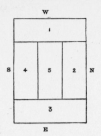

With a spade Bull Tongue deepened the lines, cutting through the grass-roots. In working he followed the sun. The work was hard and the sweat dropped from his face; finally he gave the spade to Young Bird, who used it for a time, and then taking the axe, inserted the blade in the cuts, pressing it down with his hands. Young Bird made little progress with the axe, and Bull Tongue busied himself in sharpening the spade with a stone. Bull Tongue at length loosened the sods with the spade, beginning at the east side of the rectangles, and following around to the south, west, and north. At first only the outside sods were loosened; the large middle one was last to be freed, when it was lifted a little and allowed to fall back into its place. Now the instructors, followed by the Medicine Lodge women, went to Pine, who spat on their hands.

An instructress, holding the hands of Rock Road's wife, caused her with four motions to lift the sod on the eastern side of the rectangle. She carried it upside down very slowly, followed by the instructor Curly, to the medicine lodge, while the other women sat down to wait. Rock Road's wife entered the medicine lodge without stopping, went around the south side, stopping four times on the way, and under Curly's direction stopped south of the skull, and with four motions put down the sod southeast of the nose of the skull. The sod rested on the ground, roots up. Rock Road's wife walked behind the skull, around on the north side of the lodge, and out of the door. An instructress and Shave Head's wife carried the most southerly sod, the instructress turning it over on the woman's hand.

Pine, wearing a buffalo-robe, followed Shave Head's wife as she went forward very slowly and stooping over. Like her predecessor she made four stops within the lodge and placed the sod south of the horns of the skull, then passed behind the skull and went around and out. Red Bead's wife now did the same thing, using four motions in taking up the most westerly sod. Wolf Chief followed her, and she passed around behind the skull and placed her sod north of the horns, about eight inches from the skull. Rock Road's wife, an instructress standing at her right hand, took up the northerly sod and carried it in, as before followed by Curly; she passed around behind the skull and deposited the sod north of its nose. The central sod was lifted from its place by the four women, but was carried by Shave Head's wife, who was followed by the other Medicine Lodge women, they by the three instructors, they by the Medicine Lodge makers and the old men. In taking up this sod, the instructress took the hands of the three women and with four motions pressed them on the sod. The sod was carried as the others had been and deposited back (west) of the skull, almost between the horns. They called this ceremony "cutting the earth."

This placing of the sods represented an act of the Creator when He made the earth. The women carried the soil as He carried it. The sods represented the ground which supports us, and the five brought in and put about the buffalo-head were prayed to, that all fruits, grass, and roots, and all things from the earth may be abundant. They wish to make their prayers to fresh earth. The grass held in the nose of the skull—which represented the buffalo's mouth—was put there to feed the buffalo, because buffalo eat grass. Thus the operation of bringing in these sods and placing them about the buffalo-skull expressed reverence for the earth. Prayers were made for the growth of berries, roots, and grass, as well as of cultivated crops, and the prominent part taken by women in this earth worship may be supposed to refer to the work of women in caring for and harvesting these crops.

Bull Tongue, Big Head Man, and Young Bird now spent some time in breaking up and arranging the sods to their satisfaction, and in making a little wall or ridge on three sides of the skull. This was the beginning of what I term the altar. The wall was open toward the east, but continuous as a rough rectangle on the other three sides.

When this wall had been completed, a bunch of small brush (*Symphoricarpus*) was brought out. Bull Tongue and the three Medicine Lodge makers went to Pine, who spat ceremonially on their hands. Bull Tongue then led the three Medicine Lodge makers back, and taking their three hands in his, with four motions caused them all three to take up a spray of brush, to carry it to the altar and thrust it in the ground at the eastern corner of the south side of the altar. Rock Road thrust in a second twig at the west end of the south side, and Red Bead one each at the west and east ends of the north side. Then all three united in placing a spray at the middle of the west side. When this had been done, Bull Tongue, Big Head Man, and Young Bird completed the sides of the altar, thrusting the stems of the plant in the ground without ceremony.

A crier shouted out and a few moments later several Crows, men and women, entered and offered gifts to the Medicine Lodge makers, twenty-five cents to Shave Head, and quilts to the others.

Meantime a coal from the fire had been placed before the nose of the buffalo-skull. Now large straight cottonwood branches—almost small trees—were brought into the lodge by Bull Tongue and Young Bird, and thrown on the ground south of the center-pole. They had been cut for at least a day or two, for their leaves were somewhat withered. With an unused hatchet Bull Tongue trimmed the lower twigs from these branches, shortened them to the proper height by cutting off the butts, and sharpened them. While this was being done She Bear made a speech, and Two Moon a prayer or speech.

Two straight choke-cherry trees, ten or twelve feet high, were now brought in and by Bull Tongue were trimmed and prepared like the cottonwood branches. Big Head Man presented to Pine a sharpened box-elder stick four feet long, which represented a root-digger. Pine handed it back to Big Head Man, who placed it on the ground east and a little south of the skull's nose. Now the Medicine Lodge women reassumed their robes and belts, which they had laid aside—perhaps on account of the temperature, for it was very hot. An instructress rose and with the three Medicine Lodge women, directed by Wolf Chief, passed out to near the nose of the skull, lifted the four-foot stick from the ground with four motions, carried it to the altar, and thrust it in the ground at the four points where the large branches were to stand, thus ceremonially planting these branches. With an ordinary crowbar Big Head Man made the holes at the four corners where indicated, beginning at the southeast corner. Meantime Bull Tongue was arranging the large brush for its use. Shave Head, followed by the other two Medicine Lodge makers, went to Curly, who spat on their hands, and one after another they made the usual motions. The three then followed Bull Tongue to the place near the center-pole where the large bushes lay, and Bull Tongue, standing on the right of Shave Head, the others clinging to Shave Head's arms, caused the three ceremonially to lift one of the cherry bushes, and with four motions to set it in the hole near the southeast corner of the altar, where Bull Tongue wedged it in place. Shave Head alone without ceremony took up a large cottonwood branch and planted it in a hole just southeast of the recently placed cherry. Again without ceremony, but slowly and reverently, he lifted the other cherry tree, carried it around behind the altar, and planted it, and did the same with the other cottonwood. These two stood in the same relation as those previously planted, the cherry just north of the east end of the altar on the northerly side, and the cottonwood a foot to the north of this. Bull Tongue and Big Head Man settled and wedged the trees in their places so that they were firm.

On another occasion, some years before, these branches were planted by the Medicine Lodge women, not by the men.

Curly spat on Bull Tongue's hands, and he with Big Head Man and Young Bird, followed by the three Medicine Lodge makers, repaired to the rectangular hole in front of the nose of the skull. A bundle of white sand done up in a cloth lay east of the hole. It was opened, and Shave Head was instructed by Bull Tongue how to sprinkle the sand in the hole, covering the bottom. The sand was taken up with four motions, handful by handful, and scattered smoothly. After Shave Head had done this ceremonially the instructors finished the work.

At a request from Bull Tongue, Shave Head brought out a pipe-cleaner and put it on the ground, and with it was shown ceremonially by Bull Tongue how to make the trails for the colored paint on the white sand. Shave Head was caused to draw with the point of the pipe-cleaner a shallow furrow in the sand from east to west on the south side of the sand surface, another to the north, and then another and another until four furrows had been made, about two inches apart. The three Medicine Lodge makers then drew nearer to the hole. Shave Head, the others holding his arms, took in his hand a pinch of black paint which he scattered along the south furrow in the sand, from east to west. From another sack, another lodge maker took red paint, which in the same way he sprinkled in the second furrow. The Lodge Makers then retired to their places, and Bull Tongue sprinkled yellow paint in the third furrow, and Young Bird, white paint in the northernmost of the furrows. South of the white furrow, little pinches of white paint were dropped at intervals on the sand, and yellow, red, and black pinches of paint were dropped south of each similarly colored furrow, then other pinches of paint were dropped on the north side of the various furrows, so that on each side

261

each furrow was bordered by a succession of dots of its own color.

The Lodge Makers now approached the hole, and Shave Head, the others aiding him, picked up a slender peeled cornel twig, which he bent into a half-hoop and slowly passed over the hole, till he reached the end toward the buffalo-skull, when an instructor thrust both ends into the ground. Over this half-hoop another similar but longer twig was placed in the same way, the two hoops standing just west of the end of the hole. Another, longer, and a fourth still longer, were placed over the first two, so that now there were four hoops standing one above another. These represented the rainbow—the trap which catches the rain.

At a call from Bull Tongue, Shave Head brought over the eighteen pins made by the oldish man. Some were wholly peeled and some still carried the bark for about an inch at the unsharpened end. Shave Head then passed behind the altar and met Big Head Man, who gave him several articles, including two sacks of paint, red and black. Finally, Big Head Man took back the articles and himself brought them around, and Shave Head returned to his seat.

The pins were set in the ground in two rows alongside the rectangular hole, nine on each side, the partially unbarked ones to the south of the hole, the peeled ones to the north. Shave Head, very slowly and with four motions, the other Medicine Lodge makers holding him, took up a pin and thrust it into the ground on the south, with four motions, and so with three others, and the instructors set the rest. The instructors then opened their bundles of paint and prepared to paint the pins. They painted those to the south red, on the peeled part, and black on the unpeeled portion. The fat used in painting those to the south was the fat of eagles, and following the painting those pins were dressed with eagle-down colored black on the black portions and red on the red parts. The pins to the north were painted white, with white clay in water, and were ornamented with white eagle-down. The four hoops above the rectangular hole—the earth—were painted in this order: the lowest red, above that black, above that yellow, and the topmost white; each was dressed with down of its own color. The cherry and cottonwood trees to the south of the altar were painted red below for about two feet from the ground, and above that black, and were ornamented with down colored as the paint was colored. The trees to the north were painted white and had white down on them. This down is supposed to be the down of eagles, and is so in part, but it is mixed with the winter pelage of the prairie rabbit, which, as already suggested, is an important animal in this ceremony. The eagle-down is called thunder feathers and represents the feathers of the thunderbird.

About noon, the first party of dancers came out of the Medicine Lodge and went about among the people within and without the lodge choosing their instructors, that is, the men who should paint them and care for them during the trial they were about to undergo. Certain old men were thought to possess special powers and their help was often desired by more than one dancer, so that three or four young men might choose the same instructor. Some time after noon, long lines of women and children, dressed in their finest clothing and carrying food and presents, began to come toward the medicine lodge. There were offerings of many kinds; but food, carried in kettles and in pans, was brought by almost everyone. One woman carried on her back a trunk, on top of which were tied two or more quilts. When brought into the lodge the relatives of each dancer put down their food as nearly as possible in front of him.

By two o'clock all the food had been brought in. The painting had begun as soon as the instructors were selected, and by this time most of the dancers had been painted. Not a few of them were helping the women by carrying about the food and putting it in its proper place.

Led by the Medicine Lodge makers the dancers now began

to make the usual sacrifices, dipping sprigs of sage into the kettles of food and carrying them around the lodge, making offerings to the four cardinal points, represented here by the painted rafters, to the altar, and various points on it, and to the center-pole.

This took a long time, and until understood was very confusing. When the sacrifices had been completed, the food was all removed by the women.

There was much variety in the fashion of the dancers' painting. Yellow was a common ground color, often with grasshoppers on the forearms and upper arms, and on each side of the front and back of the body. The sun was painted on the chest and a crescent moon on the left shoulder blade. The dancers so painted wore sprigs of sage in the belt. Pink, black, or white was sometimes a ground color.

All through the afternoon the dancing went on. At intervals the paint was washed off, new paint was applied, and more food was brought in, to be removed again after the formal sacrifices had been made by the dancers. On the other hand, food was eaten by the old men and by dancers' instructors. But by far the greater part of the food was carried out again and consumed by the spectators. By its passage through the medicine lodge this food had acquired a sacred character and one who ate it was benefited far more than by eating common food. A spiritual benefit was received by one who ate it, and, as I have elsewhere noted, an effort was made to have everyone in the camp share this benefit by eating of this food. The same belief is held by the Blackfeet.

THIRD DAY

This day (Thursday, August 17) the ceremonies began a little later. Owing to the delay in starting the Medicine Lodge, the instructors the night before had directed the dancers to dance all night, and counted this night-dancing as a day, so that this day was reckoned as two days and closed the Medicine Lodge.

Before nine o'clock, many armfuls of slender willow twigs had been brought into the Medicine Lodge and distributed, and the instructors of the dancers were now preparing the willow wreaths, wristlets, and anklets, and getting ready to paint their men. These willow twigs had long and very narrow leaves, and seemed almost like the twigs of the weeping willow. After a time the paint had been washed off from all the dancers, and the repainting began. Young Bird painted Red Bead with a band of red, half an inch wide, about the body below the ribs and around the arm just below the elbow, a sun on the chest, and a crescent over the right shoulder blade. From the red sun on the chest, red lines ran down to the hip-bones and up to the shoulder on each side. The forearms and legs were red. He painted a circle of red around Red Bead's face over the forehead close to the hair, down in front of each ear, over the cheekbone and to chin, and so around. Outside this red, and touching it, was a black circle. The trunk was painted black. Shave Head by Little Hawk, and Rock Road by Frank Standing Elk, were painted as Red Bead was painted. A number of the dancers on the south side of the lodge were being painted in similar fashion; others on the northwest side of the lodge had bright yellow as a groundwork, those on the northeast side were painted wholly black except for a red line above the wrists and a red crescent over the left shoulder blade. Some of the instructors of the dancers were occupied in tying up small bundles of sage with sinew.

Presently the Medicine Lodge women came into the lodge painted red—the color being mixed with fat—with a black circle about the wrists and a black sun on the chest, a red circle about the face with blue on the forehead and cheeks. The paint on the men was mixed with water, not fat.

To the willow wreaths which were being made were tied—in such a way that the plumes stood erect—two eagle down-feathers, a strand of yellow-dyed horsehair, and some wood-pecker feathers, and to one wristlet was tied an eagle's feather and to another a mule-deer's tail. The yellow-painted men on the northwest side of the lodge were variously ornamented. Some had a dragonfly on upper and lower arm, and on right thigh and lower leg, and on right breast. A curved line—prob-ably a crescent moon—showed on the right shoulder blade, two dragonflies to the left of this, and on the chest a sun, all in black. Some had a white prairie lizard, head upward, on

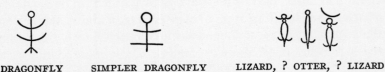

DRAGONFLY   SIMPLER DRAGONFLY   LIZARD, ? OTTER, ? LIZARD

upper and lower arms, thighs and lower legs; a crescent over the right shoulder blade, and lines about wrist and ankles, all white.

Soldier Wolf opened a bundle which had been just brought to him and which was full of bright green fresh sorrel. He gave little bunches of this to several of the dancers to chew.

A yellow-painted dancer had red lines about wrist and ankles, a red sun on chest, and on either side a simpler dragon-fly than the one just mentioned as on the back. A crescent was on the right shoulder blade, and on the opposite side, two lizards lower down than the crescent, and what was perhaps an otter between them.

The instructors of the Medicine Lodge makers—who, of course, were not painting their men—had stripped off their clothing and were combing and wrapping the hair with strips of cloth. On the left arms they carried bundles of willows.

On the dancers near the Medicine Lodge makers, the men who were painted as the Medicine Lodge makers were painted, the sun was green and the face within the surrounding red border was also green. Red Bead's painting was changed after Young

Bird began, and the lines running down and up from the sun toward hips and shoulders and down the upper arm were made blue. On the forearm and down the forearm to wrist and to a line about that, this blue changed to black, and a black line ran outside each leg from the waist to the ring about the ankle. The crescent on the shoulder blade, except its border, was blue, and his instructor dotted the trunk with blue spots representing hail, the paint being applied with the end of the finger.

The wholly black-painted men at the northeast side of the circle had small dark blue dragonflies painted on the outside of arms and legs, four rows of four each, one above another on the arms, and three or four rows of from three to five each on the legs below hips, down to ankles. Three men on the west side of the lodge were simply painted red all over, with black wrist lines and a black curved line—crescent moon—over the right shoulder blade. They had a black sun on the chest, and above this in outline the front view of a man with outstretched arms wearing a bull's horn war-bonnet and a fringed scalp shirt.

The faces of the men who had the white-painted lizard showed this paint: a white line running back from each corner of the mouth, a white line double-crossed over each cheekbone, a short green vertical line at the outer corners of the eyes, and a green cross-mark halfway up the forehead above the nose.

In the southwest corner of the lodge, half a dozen young men who had chosen White Bull as instructor were painted blue, with white dots (hail) on the lower face; white and green lines on body and arms, sometimes shaped like an arrowhead; red lines about the wrists, and long red lines from ankles and wrists upward, ending in a fork, meaning lightning. Each of these dancers had the tail of a mule-deer tied to his willow shoulder belt below the left arm. The tail of a black-tailed deer was tied to the anklet on the left leg of one hail-painted man and an eagle-feather to the right anklet of another. Some men were painted red over the whole body, with black hands and feet, a narrow blue line with four interior projections about the face, and small blue lightning lines running down from the outer corners of the eyes.

The legs and arms of the pink-painted men were splashed with red of a darker shade, this color being applied by dipping a sprig of sage into the paint dish and slapping the wet sprig against the flesh. When the painting was finished the dancers picked up the paint dishes and put them at the foot of the center-pole. Red Bead's face was not now painted, but the faces of Shave Head and Rock Road were dotted with blue paint.

The painting having been completed, the Medicine Lodge makers assumed their tunics, and the instructors—not their painters—put on them the willow shoulder belt, the wreaths, and the wristlets. To Red Bead's shoulder-belt was tied on the right side an eagle's down-feather. The Medicine Lodge makers now went out and the dancers put their shawls or blankets about the waists. The necks and chins of the hail-painted men were all black up to the red line which surrounded the faces.

Food was now being brought in by the relatives of the dancers and put down before themselves, and before no one else.

Now certain dancers went about the lodge and offered filled pipes to older men who lighted them, and smoked and passed them back to the young men, each of whom smoked ceremonially, passing his hands over the old man's hands and arms, and after returning the pipe to him blew the last puff of smoke into his own hands, and made the ceremonial motions over his own body. This was to ask the old man's pity, help, and blessing. Meanwhile Crazy Head sang an Issiwun song, at the close of which wreaths were put on the heads of four of the dancers.

Soldier Wolf, who had carried the pipe throughout the ceremony of the Medicine Lodge, was supposed, on the last day of the ceremony, to carry with him the bones of some dead enemies. Lying on the ground to his right were some small bones of a dog, which represented these.

268

Certain sacred songs were sometimes sung for the young men who were having the wreaths put on them. Magpie Eagle sang a song belonging to the sacred hat ceremony for the benefit of such a young man, and the instructor, Little Yellow Man, who stood on the right and in front of the dancer, moved the wreath in time to the song, and as the song ceased put it on the dancer.

Big Head Man, flanked by Bull Tongue on the left and by Pawnee on the right, sang with them an Issiwun song, and they put wreaths on three hail-painted men. The wreaths were moved four times about and over the head, and the fourth time were put on the heads and pressed down.

The faces of the black-painted men, with blue dragonflies, were bright red with a black line around each. The blue dragonflies were scattered thickly over the body.

White Bull, rising to his feet, made a speech in which he said that the people depended greatly on the jackrabbit. Recently a man presented him with a rabbit, but when he saw it he recognized that it was a tame rabbit and useful only as representing so much food.

A little girl brought in a bunch of mint and presented it to one of the Medicine Lodge makers. It was divided, some going to the instructors, some to the Medicine Lodge women, and some to the Medicine Lodge makers. The eating of the sorrel, and of a sort of bitter root that was given to Red Bead, was to stimulate the flow of saliva, relieving the dryness of the mouth and helping the endurance.

Lightning-painted men did not wear willows. Their wreaths, anklets, and wristlets were of sage. Five lightning-painted men came and offered the pipe to Soldier Wolf, squatting in front of him and beyond the pipe which, with the pipe sticks, lay between Soldier Wolf and the circular bare spot before him. He pointed the pipe to the pole and to the south. One of the young men brought a coal from the fire and Soldier Wolf lighted the pipe, pointed it to the four directions and to the buffalo-skull,

and rested its bowl on the ground for the men to smoke ceremonially. These young men had a white-edged crescent moon
painted under the left arm and a sun under the right arm, a
deer-antler on each side of the back, and under the eyes a long
lightning mark. This same pipe was passed to Magpie Eagle,
and to certain dancers who smoked without ceremony.

Three more lightning-painted men brought a pipe to Magpie
Eagle and one of them went for a coal. Magpie Eagle had
trouble in lighting the pipe, but when it was going freely he
held it to the pole, to the four directions, to the altar (or the
skull), and to the ground, and then had the young men smoke.
The top of this pipestem was carved. Near the mouthpiece was
a snake, below this another snake, then a turtle, a lizard, and
perhaps an imaginary animal—an otter with forked tail. Magpie Eagle, after resting the pipe-bowl on the ground, pressed
his right hand on the ground and passed it up the pipe on that
side, repeating the performance with the left hand. He again
repeated this with the right hand and the left, and then moved
the left hand in a circle about the bowl. Then he handed the
pipe back to the young man, put his hand over the young man's
hand, pressed the hand four times, and then took his hand
away.

The dancers now brought food, which they offered to the
older men, who before eating gave the young men little pinches
to offer in sacrifice. Those who received such morsels from
Soldier Wolf pressed their hands four times on the pipe lying
on the ground before him and made the ceremonial motions.
The sacrifices were then put on the ground north of the pipe.
All the dancers had sprigs of white sage in their waists, usually
behind the body.

Now began the offering of food to the powers.

In the sacrifices of food made in this Medicine Lodge it was
required that five kinds be sacrificed, and to this was added the
corn, making six sacrifices. The offerings were meat, choke-
cherries, sarvisberries, flour cakes fried, crackers, and corn.

The rite of sacrificing went on for a long time, the men marching in long lines about the medicine lodge, offering these six sacrifices, one by one, to the four directions, the four corners of the altar, the center-pole, and perhaps to other things.

When the sacrifices had been completed the women began to take out the food, and for a long time there was much tumult and confusion. The men kept shouting orders and the women kept getting more or less confused, but at last it was concluded. This was after midday and the dancing was soon to begin.

Among the dancers were two or three who believed in the modern Ghost Dance, and who to some extent tried to adapt this ceremony of the Medicine Lodge to that religion. In front of each of these stood in the ground small cedar trees hung with pieces of calico. The most modern Ghost Dance painting—which was adopted by these young men—was a groundwork of bright yellow, with white lines running from either side of the waist behind up to the shoulder and down the arms to the wrist, and in front from either side of the waist to the shoulders and down the arms. Down the middle of the back was a line to the waist, and on either breast was a short vertical line. All these were white. The side lines ended above in green balls, the front and back lines were interrupted by green balls at the short ribs and the joints of shoulders, elbows, and wrists. On the chest was a green sun.

The black-painted men with blue dragonflies wore sage wreaths, wristlets, and anklets, and had orange-colored eagle down-feathers tied to the back of the sage wreaths.

Big Head Man now spat on the hands, both sides of the back, and the soles of the feet of his man, and blew strongly and spat on the back of the neck just above the shoulders and on top of the head. In spitting on hands and feet the usual ceremonial order was followed—right foot, right hand, left hand, left foot. Meantime, Curly was instructing Rock Road in the ceremonial filling of the straight pipe; they were almost in the altar on its south side.

The straight redstone pipe had been taken from the Box Elder bundle and placed within the altar south of the buffalo-skull. Curly very slowly and reverently, and with four motions, reached into the altar, took up this pipe, drew it forth, and with four motions placed it on the ground south of the excavation before the buffalo-skull. The stem lay east and west, the bowl pointing toward the center-pole. The pipe-cleaning stick was placed by the pipe.

Curly took a strand of sinew and tore from it a shred which, with four motions, he put on the ground before Rock Road, on whose hands he spat and who made the ceremonial motions. Then Curly tore off four more shreds of sinew and caused Rock Road, with four motions, to place the first shred across his left hand near his body, the second across the hand over the fingers, the third nearer the body parallel with the first one, the fourth on the fingers within the second, and the fifth on the middle of the hand. Then Curly showed Rock Road how to turn over the ends of these sinews and to work them between the hands into a little round ball, which Curly then placed in the bowl of the straight pipe and caused Rock Road to ram down with the pipe-stick, with four motions.

Curly took the hands of Rock Road, reached them over the stem of the pipe, and caused him with four motions to grasp the pipe-cleaning stick and to pass it east, south, west, and north, around the stem and then to put it on the ground. Rock Road spread out the corner of his buffalo-robe and, directed by Curly, took from a tobacco-sack four pinches of tobacco, which he put on the corner of his robe north of him. Then with four motions he took a pinch of the tobacco, put it into the pipe from the east, picked up the pipe-cleaner, rammed down the tobacco with four motions, put down the pipe-cleaner, and put into the pipe a pinch of tobacco from the south, another from the west, and another from the north. After each pinch of tobacco was placed in the pipe, the pipe held upright, the bowl pointing toward the sky, was moved around the tobacco,

MEDICINE LODGE

DANCERS WITH WHISTLES

over it, and then lowered toward the ground. When the pipe had been filled, it was again rammed with the pipe-cleaner, and Curly passed to Rock Road a piece of fat with which he fixed the tobacco in the filled pipe. When this had been completed, the bowl was held over the mouthpiece of the stem and slowly moved along the stem toward the west, and then was placed on the ground. Curly painted red the end of the stem which fits into the pipe. He tore off from his robe a little bunch of buffalo-wool, gave it to Rock Road and guided Rock Road's hands, holding this tuft in both hands, along the stem from the mouth-piece to the pipe-end of the stem about which Rock Road wrapped the wool. Then Curly took both Rock Road's hands, moved them down over the stem from mouthpiece toward the pipe until they were over the pipe, caused Rock Road to grasp it, and with four pauses to move the pipe nearer to the stem, and then with four motions to place it on the ground. Then Curly fitted the pipe to the stem, and it was held upright, the mouthpiece resting on the ground. A piece of fat with some red paint was placed on the Lodge Maker's hands; he rubbed them together, and then, instructed by Curly, moved one of them up and down over the pipe on the four sides, and then up and down the stem, thus painting both stem and pipe. Then taking the stick and the stem of the pipe in both hands, Rock Road and Curly crept to the edge of the bower and placed the pipe there on the south side of the skull, the stem to the west.

The straight pipe is called the Medicine Lodge pipe, and is one of the most revered objects used in the ceremony. It is smoked only three times during the ceremony, the first time in the lonely lodge, the second time as the center-pole is raised, and the third time during one of the paintings toward the close of the ceremony. There are believed to be only two of these pipes left in the tribe. This pipe is used also in the Massaum ceremony.

Bull Tongue and Young Bird were engaged in folding a raw-hide in the middle of the lodge southeast of the center-pole,

273

after finishing which they left it there. Shave Head now went to Pine, and standing in front of him extended his hand, on which Pine spat ceremonially. Shave Head took up the fire-spoon, drew a coal from the fire and carried it, slowly and stooping, to the front of the altar south of the nose of the skull. With Bull Tongue at his left, directing him, they made a little fire southeast of the buffalo's nose. Then Bull Tongue caused Shave Head ceremonially to lift the rawhide and carry it to the rectangular hole dug in front of the buffalo's nose, move it up and over that hole, then take it back and carry it around behind the altar, and around on the north side of the pole and beyond the fire to the drummers, where with four motions he threw it on the ground among them. They all yelled and beat on it with their sticks.

The young men who had not yet chosen instructors now arose, and began to pass about the lodge and to offer pipes to different old men, asking them to act as instructors. The young men brought from the fire coals with which to light the pipes. Old men who consented to help them lighted the pipes and smoked, and then each offered the pipe he had been smoking to the young man who had brought it to him. The young man passed his hand over the old one's in thanks, and took four draws on the pipe, blowing the smoke into his own hands, and made the ceremonial motions. All this took a long time.

Presently some of the old men who were to act as instructors and painters for the younger men, advanced to the Medicine Lodge women and sat down before them. The women and the instructors touched the tip of the forefinger to the tongue and to the ground, and again to the tongue, and the women spat ceremonially into the joined palms of the men, who made the ceremonial motions.

One of the Medicine Lodge makers with a wooden fire-spoon six feet long lifted a coal from the fire and slowly carried it over behind and northwest of the altar. Another Lodge Maker did the same.

The elderly instructors had now distributed themselves about the lodge, and each had seated himself behind the young man he was to have in his charge. The dancers made the ceremonial motions before they sat down to be painted. Then, sitting with their backs toward the center of the lodge, they combed up their hair and tied it out of the way on top of the head, and the old men began to paint them. Before this was commenced, a woman began to paint one of the Medicine Lodge women, who was naked to the waist. On this last day until this woman began, no painting could be done.

Before beginning the actual painting, the instructor passed his right hand up the young man's right arm from wrist to shoulder and placed it on his breast; then he passed the same hand over the left arm in the same way, then he placed both hands on the head, then passed the right hand up the right leg from ankle to thigh and rested it on the breast, and passed the same hand up the left leg and placed it on the breast. When these motions were concluded he began the painting. In this first painting were used two tones of yellow, one rich and the other pale. Many of the men, after being painted over the whole body, were streaked, the painter drawing his finger nails over the color, which was applied with water. Some men were painted green, with round white spots on the wrists and under the shoulder blades.

The wristlets of white sage, worn on the day the medicine lodge was built, were placed on the ground about the center-pole, where the earth taken from the hole in front of the buffalo's nose had been put. In old times, little images of buffalo and of other food animals used to be put about the center-pole, and there they used to make little buffalo wallows with the thumb, the purpose of this being that buffalo and all game might become abundant.

Women now began to enter the lodge, bringing in dishes of food, armfuls of quilts and blankets, white sage for the beds, and various ceremonial objects. After the painting was completed, each young man deposited his paint-cups at the foot of the center-pole. The painting was various. Usually there was a crescent moon under the right shoulder blade, but sometimes a cluster of dots, which were said to represent stars. Green or blue stars were painted on the face, sometimes from the ear to the mouth, sometimes across the face above and below the mouth. The Medicine Lodge makers and their wives had a black line from the parting of the hair over the forehead, down the nose to the chin, and on the chin a black spot an inch and a half in diameter; these also were painted red over the bodies, and the men wore under the right shoulder blade a crescent moon in black. Some young men had a cluster of green stars in the middle of the chest, bands of black about ankles and wrists, with a black line around the face, over forehead, cheeks, and chin, and from this oval, four inward projecting points of black, one under each eye, and one under each corner of the mouth. After being painted, each young man took from the forked stick which stood in the ground before his bed, his bone whistle, ornamented with a single eagle down-feather, and hung it about his neck.

The women of the camp now brought in a great quantity of food, together with other offerings, and the Medicine Lodge makers, and later the other persons who were paying vows in the medicine lodge, walked about making ceremonial sacrifices of food, which cannot be given in detail. They sacrificed at the foot of the center-pole, under four painted rafters, and at the foot of each white-painted cottonwood branch, near the buffalo-skull. The offering of these sacrifices took a long time, and after they were completed all the food was taken out again, no one except a few old men having eaten anything. Horses were led into the lodge to be given away and then led out again, and an old man made a speech, telling to whom and for what purpose the horses were being given. Most of them had been presented to men who were to pierce the ears of children.

Soon after this the singing began again, and then the dancing, but it did not last long. An hour or two later the dancers were sitting down, with their paint washed off, and with their teeth were stripping fine willow twigs, to be used as wreaths, wristlets, and shoulder belts. Later there was repainting and dancing, with frequent intervals for rest.

The dancers now all rose to their feet, and going to the fire secured coals which each put on the ground in front of his bed. Their painters bent over, lifted up the blankets on which they had been sitting, and put on the ground fresh stems of sage, then arranged anklets, moved their hands over the back, and pressed the legs and wrists. Then the drums sounded and the singing began. Each instructor tended his pupil carefully. Almost all the dancers held in the left hand the tail-feather of a war-eagle. In each man's head at the back was a dried head of a certain kind of grass, the wearing of which kept the man from getting tired. As they danced, some of the men looked up at the sun, others looked at the bundle of brush on the center-pole. One or two of the instructors rose to their feet, and by speech and gesture told their men how and at what they should look. Two dancers, Walking Calf and Fighting Bear, wore no vegetable ornament whatever. Walking Calf carried a pipe.

They now danced to four songs, each song being divided into four parts, and with a brief intermission between the parts of each song. After this was over the dancers went out of the lodge, washed off their paint, and then returned. In the repainting, the Medicine Lodge makers had the trunk black with white hail marks, a green red-edged crescent on the right shoulder blade, a green red-edged square with the corners up and down on the chest, lines of green running from the sides of the square down toward the hips and up to shoulders and down the upper arm to meet red bands about the arm above the elbow. Below the red bands the forearm was white except for a black line continuing down to a black wrist band. One Medicine Lodge maker had the green replaced by blue, a red line about the body above the navel; a black line continuing the green or blue hip-line went down the outside of the leg to a black line around the ankle. The legs were splashed with red by a sprig of sage. The men in the northwest part of the lodge, who in the morning were painted yellow with white swift lizards, were now white with green swift lizards, their faces green, painted with marks like those of the morning, but the cross-lines on the cheekbones were yellow. A crescent moon, the concavity upward, showed on the forehead above the nose, and wide but short up-and-down marks at the outer corners of the eyes.

The yellow-painted men on the northeast side of the lodge had many large red oval marks, two inches long and one inch wide, on the chest. On the left shoulder blade was a small black

crescent, a black mark like this (which Soldier Wolf

said signified a man) above each shoulder blade and above each breast, black wrist and ankle rings, and running up four inches from the wrist on the outer side of the arm a mark like this

 . The Medicine Lodge makers, and the hail-painted men

near them, retained their willow ornaments. The yellow-painted men with red spots took up again from a pile of white sage articles at the foot of the center-pole their wreaths, wristlets, etc., that they had deposited there. During an intermission the beds of the Medicine Lodge women were taken down.

The dancers who had been painted yellow with large black dragonflies were now again painted yellow with a row of figures running down the arms which represented buffalo-tracks. These were painted by Grasshopper. The marks did not greatly resemble buffalo-tracks, but looked more like two pears with long

stems placed side by side. The white-painted men at

the northwest corner of the lodge were now painted with a green lizard over each breast. The dancers painted like the Medicine Lodge makers—that is, hail-painted—had the faces painted green surrounded by a red line and outside that line white hail dots all around the face. Two men whose faces earlier had been red-painted surrounded by narrow blue lines with lightning marks under the eyes still wore this face paint, but the body paint was changed to yellow, with red wrist and ankle lines, a red moon on the right shoulder blade, and a red sun on the chest.

By four o'clock in the afternoon most of the dancers whose painting had been completed had gone out, and some were returning. Spotted Hawk came into the lodge carrying three small rattles, and gave one to Bull Tongue and one to Young Bird, keeping one himself.

Some dancers in the southeast part of the lodge were hail-painted, but each had a blue red-edged crescent on the right shoulder blade, a square on the chest, blue lines leading to shoulders and hips from the sides of the squares, and blue faces. White Bull's novices had the trunk painted black, with white on top of the shoulders and on the neck, the white running down to a point in front and behind. Their faces were yellow, with a black or blue line around them, and lightning marks running down from the eyes, the fork at the lower end; a yellow sun under the right arm, and a crescent moon under the left; dashes of yellow over the black of the body; the forearms yellow, with zigzag lightning running down to the root of the forefinger.[4]

[4] Bull Thigh said that the yellow-painted men on the north side wore a device of their own which was given them in dreams by the Great Power. This was true also of some of the men on the south side of the lodge. The "hail" paint is the old Cheyenne painting for the Medicine Lodge. All these other modes of painting are modern.

The four lines of paint in the rectangular hole before the buffalo-skull—red, black, yellow, and white—represented the four trails that lead to the Medicine Mountain—meaning, of course, the mountain in the Black Hills where Sweet Medicine is reputed to have been given the arrows and where live the maiyun.

Food was now brought in again.

The first trails made that morning and that afternoon were termed "dog trails." Three hail-painted men, after receiving bits of food from Soldier Wolf and pressing the pipe, deposited these morsels at intervals from the door to the center-pole. This may have been a sacrifice to the dog, since the Cheyennes' first beast of burden was a dog; or perhaps the reference may be to Sweet Medicine's dog. All the dancers, one after another, were making a sacrifice before Soldier Wolf's pipe, which represented the straight pipe—the first pipe ever given to them.

A yellow-painted dancer with a red sun on his breast, on the south of the lodge, had tied in his head a bear-claw and the rattles of a snake. This was probably Plenty Crows' painting.

It should be noted that the men who were painted with the crescent moon on the left shoulder blade were painted by instructors who had made the Medicine Lodge as single men. As already said, however, such a man was obliged to borrow a woman to help him.

The Ghost Dance dancers—the most modern of all the painting—were now red with white lines and balls as before, except for the color; but only a single line passed down the outside of the arm and a ball was at the shoulder. They had a moon with rays of light on the cheeks; a very small crescent moon

on the lower eyelid; a square, angle up, on the chest,

with a line at right angles to each side—said to represent a morning star.

The food now was removed and was taken out easily and fast.

All the dancers now went to the fire for coals, and each instructor made for his man a smoke of sweet grass, and began to prepare his pupil for the last trial. He freshened his stand-

They were straight, and the man who participated in the ceremony was regarded as pledging himself thenceforth to live a straight life, to do nothing wrong.

ing place, rubbed his hands on the ground, and then on the feet, hands, thighs, knees, back, and finally on the forehead of the pupil. He also blew strongly on various parts of the body, chiefly on the calves, back of the knee-joints, loin, and back of the neck. He also placed a sprig of dried grass in the hair. Young Bird called out to the singers asking them to begin. The instructors pointed out to their men what they should look at. At last, in unison as the singing began, the instructors grasped the votaries' arms and waved them toward the pole in various ways until the pupil had learned how to do it. They directed their gestures to the pole or to the sky.

Without the Medicine Lodge old women were singing strong-heart songs to encourage the dancers not to succumb, but to endure to the end. The hail-painted men stretched out first the right arm and waved that from side to side, then the left arm and waved it similarly. The three dancers who carried the slender willow twigs with red and yellow calico tied to them were brought around near to the door from their places on the north side of the lodge, and danced there, facing the pole, a little within the circle. These men were painted by Limpy, and were to sacrifice the calico.

During a pause in the singing White Bird arose and counted a coup, describing how he went to the Elkhead and brought back forty or fifty horses.

The dance was now soon to end, and Little Hawk called out, "Those who are wearing the old Cheyenne paint are not to wash it off; others may do as they please!" All the dancers except those wearing the Cheyenne paint were now wiped off with sage, but first they took their wreaths and the sticks on which their whistles and other things had been hung, and deposited them at the foot of the center-pole. Most of the dancers who did not wear the hail paint left the medicine lodge wrapped in blankets.

Crazy Head stripped down to his breechclout and was painted by Bull Tongue with a white sun on his chest, rabbit-ears on wrists and ankles, lower face and head all white, a cross on his forehead, and a crescent moon on his right shoulder blade. All these were large and coarse.

With four motions Crazy Head took a bundle of sage from a bed and with four motions put four handfuls of it on the ground, southeast of the pole and again southwest of the pole, went around behind the altar and put down four handfuls northwest of the pole and again four handfuls northeast of the pole. Spotted Hawk picked up all the forked sticks from the pole and leaned them against the choke-cherry tree at the southeast corner of the altar where the fire-spoon had already been put, and also deposited there the rawhide belts worn by the Medicine Lodge women. Meantime Crazy Head put down another four handfuls of sage between the pole and the altar.

Crazy Head led out two hail-painted dancers, those whom he himself had painted, and placed them near the sage lying on the ground northeast of the pole. With four motions the first man put his right foot on it and the other stepped on it beside him. Women brought in quilts and blankets, and wrapped them around Crazy Head. As the song began, Crazy Head and the young men danced toward the pole, waving the right arms as they advanced, and then danced back, waving the left arms as they retreated, and moved to the southeast bundles of sage and danced there. At each dancing the quilts and clothing wrapped around Crazy Head dropped off and were gathered up and carried around behind him. The three moved around behind the altar, more clothing was wrapped around Crazy Head, they danced there, the clothes fell off, and so the three proceeded until they had danced from all the piles of the sage toward the pole and back again, waving the right arms as they advanced, and the left arms as they retreated. Standing on the sage between the pole and the altar, they danced toward the altar and back twice. One of the pupils with his right foot knocked down a pin and put his foot on it, and the other put his foot on it. The three now retired, passing north of the pole to their places.

Big Head Man was now painted by Spotted Hawk in the same manner as Crazy Head had been painted. He took sage and put it on the ground as Crazy Head had put his, in five bundles, close to but east of Crazy Head's beds. He called out three men, and repeated what had been done before. The first time they danced twice to the pole, but after they had danced twice to the pole from the four directions, in dancing from center-pole to altar, they advanced and retreated four times, and knocked down three of the sticks.

After his return to his place Big Head Man was wiped off with sage with four motions.

Pine was next painted as the others had been. Wolf Chief made a sage bed between the pole and the altar, and Shave Head and Pine danced on the south side of the altar and again behind it. Pine was not wrapped about with clothing and bedding, though these things were carried around behind him. They danced twice to each of the three sides of the altar, and when in front of it, with their backs to the pole, they danced four times toward it. Shave Head with his foot pushed over a stick or two.

Curly, unpainted, danced in the same way with Rock Road about the altar at the south side, the southwest corner, behind and at the northwest corner. At the third dance and the fourth Curly was wrapped up in quilts, bedding, calico, etc.

Wolf Chief performed the same ceremonies with Red Bead. Clothing was wrapped about Wolf Chief on each occasion, and Red Bead kicked over the last of the white sticks.

Little Hawk shouted an order. Pine, carrying a peeled willow twig about six feet long, to the small end of which was tied an eagle down-feather, went close to the center-pole and stood east of it, and all the hail-painted dancers rose and followed him, ranging themselves on either side of him, north and south. The song and drum sounded, and after a moment of dancing all danced a little way toward the door and then stopped and danced in one place, then danced forward again nearly to the door, where they stopped and danced. The third time forward they reached the door and stopped and danced a little, and then, at the fourth start, rushed out of the door, thirty or forty yards onto the prairie, and ran around in formation and returned into the lodge to the pole. Pine, who was leading, reached the pole first, and the others, as they came rushing in, looked like demons in their paint. They now formed again, ran around the pole and out to the southwest side of the lodge, going a shorter distance; returned and ran around the pole four times and went out to the northwest; turned and came back and ran around the pole four times and (by error) went out the northeast side and back. Pine ran hard, and kept back the others by waving his twig, that is, his lance, in front of them. They then went to their places and washed. The Medicine Lodge was finished. The end came between sundown and dark.

In old times, instead of an eagle down-feather on the end of the long slender pole there was a scalp, and to be touched by this scalp was very unlucky.

THE Massaum ceremony, also called the Animal Dance, Buffalo Dance, Crazy Dance, and Foolish Dance, appears to be an ancient rite. It is sometimes spoken of as the ceremony during which people act as if they were crazy or foolish. *Massaum* is related to the word *massa'ne*, foolish or crazy, and is interpreted as the lodge of the crazy, or the lodge of the "Contraries." The Massaum ceremony is said to have been brought to the tribe by one of the two similarly dressed young men who went into the earth and brought out food—the one who represented the Tsistsistas. The Great Power had taken pity on these two men, one named *Mŏt sĭ ĭ'- ŭ ĭv*, a Cheyenne, and the other, *Tŏm sĭ'v sĭ,* a Suhtai. The name of the Cheyenne means Sweet Root Standing, or Sweet Medicine Root, while the Suhtai culture hero is variously called Rustling Corn Leaf, Listening To The Ground, or Erect Horns. To his own tribe Sweet Medicine Root brought the medicine arrows; while to his, Listening To The Ground brought the buffalo cap. He brought the Suhtai the ceremony of the Medicine Lodge. All these mysteries and ceremonies came to these men from within the earth; and all they learned about them and afterward taught to the tribes was the instruction that they had received from the spirits whom they encountered in the mysterious underground lodges they had entered.

In this ceremony there are suggestions of an old story found among certain Plains people, in which the animals and the people strove in a great race or other competition to see whether in future the people should eat the buffalo or the buffalo should eat the people. Yet the priests of the Massaum ceremony declare that this rite has no relation whatever to that contest.

Other traditions without any particular point are told concerning this ceremony, which in old times appears to have been performed, in part at least, for the purpose of bringing food to the camps in time of scarcity. The ceremony is a sacrifice offered specifically for the benefit of the man who has pledged himself to perform it, but is also for the general benefit of the whole tribe. The offerings are made to the earth, the obvious source of subsistence. As so often explained, the earth supports us, produces food for the animals on whose flesh we depend, and also the berries and the roots which we eat. Out of and over it flows the water we drink. Above all things, therefore, the earth is to be propitiated. The powers through whom the earth continues to exist and who live within it must receive reverence and sacrifice.

Black Horse told me in 1911 an old story about the origin of this ceremony, which seems to refer to a time before the Cheyennes had seen buffalo. He said:

One morning, many generations back, our great-great-grandfather was out hunting, looking for deer, which in those days were our food, for then there were no buffalo. He saw three deer run up on a hill, and then pass on over a wide level prairie. He followed them, hoping that he might kill one.

As he went on, suddenly he saw five buffalo coming over a hill from the west. They went down to a stream and stopped and lay down. He could see the steam coming from their nostrils as they breathed. It looked as if they had been running hard. As he looked at them, he thought, "Well, here are buffalo."

Presently he raised his head and looked about, and saw four buffalo coming toward him from the north and running down to the first ones; they stopped there, and lay down with them.

Not long after that, three buffalo came from the south, and later two from the east. All of them stopped with the first buffalo.

Soon after this, great herds of buffalo began to come from all directions, and after that the people had always plenty of buffalo.

At the same place animals of all kinds gathered, and in commemoration of this gathering the people instituted this Massaum ceremony. In ancient times the buffalo would appear to them in two or three days after the conclusion of the ceremony. In this ceremony were formerly used a pair of buffalo-horns taken from a hermaphrodite buffalo. These buffalo horns have been lost.

This tale suggests that the ceremony began soon after the Cheyennes reached the country of the buffalo. White Frog, who had served as the chief priest of the ceremony on seven different occasions, did not know the story told by Black Horse.

The Massaum ceremony was often vowed during a war journey. The leader, anxious for the success of his expedition, or for the health of someone left at home, or for the general good of the tribe, might say, *"Nāh mēh' ā ī' wāk ū* (I give woman I promise)." The sacrifice was for the general good, but the man who vowed it received the greater benefit.

The Cheyennes declare that the ritual of the ceremony and the different operations which they perform are as nearly as may be what they were told to do by the older people who instructed them in its performance. These instructions have come down from generation to generation. The priests have tried to preserve the ritual, but portions of it have been lost and the meanings of certain words have been forgotten.

FIRST DAY

The ceremony lasts over four nights. On the first day the pole for the lodge is erected and the covering is put on.

In the center of the principal lodge in the ceremony, where the yellow wolf is painted, stands, as a center-pole, a straight green cottonwood trunk, about twenty-five feet high and four inches thick at the butt end, trimmed of its branches to a height of fifteen or twenty feet, but with the topmost twigs and leaves still clinging to it.

The first apparent act of the ceremony was the selection by the chief priest (in this case White Frog) of the tree to be used for a center-pole for the lodge in which the ceremony was to be held. When he chose the tree, which he did in company with the man who had pledged himself to carry through the Massaum ceremony, together with the man's wife and his own wife, he offered a prayer in which he addressed the trees and all vegetation, saying: "Today we are here to do what those two men of ancient times told us we ought to do, and today we ask you for a tree to take the part in our ceremony. I beg that all the trees and grass and fruits may thrive and grow strong, and I ask that if we do not perform the ceremony just as it ought to be done, you will pardon us for the mistakes we make." When this prayer had been recited, *Mih nio nŭhk* (thirteen-lined spermophile), the man who was offering the sacrifice, holding the pipe, repeated after White Frog the precise words of his prayer.

After this had been done, Mihnionuhk, commonly called Frank Little Wolf, ceremonially chopped down the tree; that is to say, he made four motions with the axe toward the tree trunk, striking it with the fourth motion. The tree was now felled by the women without further ceremony, but to the accompaniment of a slow, solemn, and droning song which sounded much like the humming of wind through the branches of trees.[1]

When the pole had fallen, the branches were trimmed off to the required height. Then with four motions the women lifted it from the ground and after three false starts set out to drag it to the camp. After they had passed into the opening of the camp-circle they stopped three times and at the fourth stop left the tree with the butt-end lying close to where it was to stand.

Now White Frog, after making the ceremonial motions, took the hands of Frank Little Wolf and his wife (*Ē' kō mĭ'na*, Shell Woman), and caused them to dig, ceremonially, five holes in the ground at the place where the pole was to stand. They

[1] White Frog, explaining these matters to me, made a prayer to all the spiritual powers, asking them to pardon him for revealing these things to an enemy, that is, a stranger—myself.

A DANCER IN THE MEDICINE LODGE

made the motions of digging a hole to the southeast, southwest, northwest, northeast, and one in the center of this square. Then without further ceremony the young man began to dig the hole from the center hole outward. In digging this hole he used a crowbar and made an excavation two and a half feet deep, removing the earth with his hands, and putting it on a blanket.

A little to the southwest of where the hole was being dug, sat seven men, who at intervals sang, and while they were singing six women and one man lifted the pole and with four stops carried it a little nearer the hole, finally placing it on the ground so that the butt of the pole was at the edge of the hole. There the pole was left, and without order or ceremony the persons who had been carrying it returned to their places.

White Frog's first wife (*Man ho ah* ?, Island Woman) with an unused axe now chopped from the butt of the pole a slanting section. Meanwhile Bobtail Horse with the end of a long rope lashed together two lodge-poles near their smaller ends, in the form of a pair of shears, to be used in raising and guiding the pole at a point higher than men could reach. Crane, Big Nose, Flying By, Medicine Top, and Wolf Chief looped a guy-rope about the upper end of the pole to steady it. Now the smaller end of the pole was lifted from the ground; the "shears" were placed under it; it was raised, held by the guys, and the butt fell into the hole. Frank Little Wolf rose from his seat, went to the blanket, and from the four directions deposited in the hole four handfuls of soil taken from the blanket, then returned to his place and sat down. Bobtail Horse now replaced the remaining earth by handfuls and tamped it down with a bar, while Medicine Top followed him around the pole, stamping down the soil with his feet.

After a time White Frog's wife took two lodge-poles from a pile of sixteen lying southwest of the pole, and placed them on the ground near the standing pole, butts to the northeast. She then took two lodge-poles from another pile lying northwest of the standing pole and placed them, butts to the northwest, west

289

of the pole, their smaller ends crossing the smaller ends of the first two lodge-poles. The four were then lashed together. This is the usual method by which a double lodge is put up by the Cheyennes; that is to say, four poles are always tied together, whereas in erecting a single lodge only three poles are thus tied.

The four lodge-poles were now raised by nine old women. They were spread at the butts, carried easterly, and moved over the green standing pole so that the pole passed as nearly as might be against the crossing lodge-poles. Standing in an ordinary lodge the pole would have passed up through the midst of the smoke-hole. This done, the remaining lodge-poles were leaned against the forks, as in the ordinary raising of a lodge. The whole number of poles was twenty-seven. Two lodge coverings were now put on the poles without ceremony.

It has been said that White Frog was the chief priest of the occasion. Bobtail Horse was the master of ceremonies, receiving instructions from White Frog, and seeing that these orders were carried out. He was spoken of as the servant.

The great double lodge now stood on the grass of the prairie, facing eastward, and was without a door. Those who entered it got down on hands and knees and crept under the lodge covering, but a little later, as the covering stretched, it was practicable to raise it and to enter by stooping close to the ground.

The various operations had occupied the greater part of the day, and evening was now approaching. After dark a fire was kindled in the lodge, between the center-pole and the door, and a little later the ground within the lodge was leveled off smooth (*ĭ hy ŭk' a o mā' ĭn ĭ*, "smoothing off the earth"). The growing grass was removed and a circular space, in the center of which stood the green cottonwood pole, was dug out about twelve feet in diameter and three inches below the level of the prairie. In dry weather this had the effect of giving the lodge a flooring of light, fine dust. All around the circumference of the lodge a space about five feet wide between the border of the dug-out circle and the circumference of the lodge was left un-disturbed, and on this was spread a bed of stems of white sage, except at the point where the people entered, where there was merely a path of dust about two feet wide.

In old times, in every lodge in any camp where people re-mained more than a night or two, the grass was removed, the middle part of the lodge dug out, and a bed of sage spread around the margin. Water was frequently poured on the dust, so that the floor soon became so hard that any litter could be swept into the fire with a brush of feathers or of sage.

The fire between the pole and the doorway side of the circle —east of the pole—might be built of any kind of wood except pine or cedar. In this case the wood used was box-elder. All this work was done before midnight.

SECOND DAY

At daylight on the second day of the ceremony (August 21, 1911) certain sacred objects, among them a buffalo-skull, were brought into the lodge.

The wife of the man who was offering the ceremony, accom-panied by Island Woman, White Frog's wife, went out of the lodge to get the buffalo-skull and passed around to the south side of the lodge where the skull lay. While she went out to fetch this sacred object everyone in the lodge was silent. When she had reached the skull and had grasped the horns, she cried out, "I have my hands on it!" White Frog then started a song, and as the people in the lodge sang, the woman began slowly to walk toward the door. When the singing ceased she stopped and rested the nose of the skull on the ground. When another song began she raised it up and slowly came forward, Island Woman instructing her as she went. At the close of the second song she stopped again, started at the third, and at the end of the fourth song stood at the door. Before entering she made four motions forward with the skull, going in with the fourth.

She walked around the south side of the lodge, stood back of where the skull was to rest—at the west side of the lodge—and then with four motions placed the skull on the ground, the nose directed eastward. Frank Little Wolf, sent out to bring in a wolf-hide, entered the lodge without ceremony and walked around it rapidly. As he placed the skin on the ground north of the buffalo-skull, the chief priest said to him, "If it has come in quickly, it will go out slowly."

On the south side of the buffalo-skull was a bundle recognized as the one used in the Medicine Lodge, which is said to have come down from Box Elder (*Mĭtskĭm'*), the important medicine man so often referred to. It contains among other things the straight pipe used in the Medicine Lodge, some red-painted braids of sweet grass, a beaded deerskin sack which holds yellow paint, a sphere of buffalo-dung, and a small bundle of old buffalo-sinew done up in red flannel. None of these things could be seen at this time. Behind the skull lay a buffalo-chip; in front of the skull, resting on the dust of the circle, was a bundle of white sage, the butts of the stems toward the south, and between the sage and the pole, about three feet from the nose of the buffalo-skull, was a Greek cross (said to represent the thunder and the lightning) marked in powdered gypsum with the arms four or five inches long and directed toward the four cardinal points. At the point where the arms of the cross would have met, a small circular hole an inch and a half wide and two inches deep had been dug out and the powdered earth taken from this hole had been piled up in four little mounds between the arms of the cross. The mounds to the southeast and southwest were sprinkled over with black paint, the other two with red paint. These four mounds represented the four hills supposed to hold up the earth, in each of which lives one of the powers of the four directions. The spirits who inhabit them watch the earth, hold it up, and keep it safe. At a height of six or seven feet above the ground around the lodge-covering were tied five bundles of sage which were roughly opposite the little mounds of earth between the arms of the cross and represented them, and were also under the four poles that were tied together, and one bundle—that to the west—is said to stand for the center-pole—the sky.

On the canvas at the back of the lodge—its west side—at the height of a man's head, was drawn the figure of an unclothed man five or six inches high, the head wearing horns, suggesting a bull's head war-bonnet. The whole body except the face was spotted with black dots; the feet were represented by claws—

the talons of a hawk or an eagle, thus: . This figure

represented a spirit watching. White Frog said it was like the picture of a saint or an angel such as we see in churches.

Early in the morning of this second day of the ceremony the only persons present in the lodge were White Frog and his wife and Bobtail Horse. Soon after, the wife of Frank Little Wolf and then her husband, both wearing buffalo-robes, came in.

Standing upright in front of Bobtail Horse was an ordinary redstone pipe resting on the bed of sage stems, and outside of the pipe, toward the circle of bare earth, was a small, circular, flattened space, smoothed out in the dust by the man's thumb, which represented the whole earth. Close by the pipe lay a pipe stick, wrapped at the larger end with buffalo-fur. This pipe was the one offered to the underground people to smoke during this ceremony; any pipe may be used.

Lying south of the center-pole, on the dust-covered floor of the lodge, was a short stick of choke-cherry, eighteen inches long, split in four at one end, and under certain circumstances used as fire-tongs. For about two inches from the split end, the stick was peeled; then the bark was left on for two inches, and removed for another two inches, and so on to the end, thus,

Another double tongs of the ordinary form, unpeeled, rested on the bed of sage north of the pole. This partially peeled stick was a constant reminder to the priest to pay close attention to the ritual of the ceremony and to omit nothing. The stick had been given to White Frog by the four powers who control the four directions. It was placed there in open sight for the priest to look at, and was supposed constantly to repeat to him, "Tell me everything that you know about this ceremony."

The following sketch gives an idea of the ground-plan of the lodge and the relative positions of things in it. The important people were on the south and southwest sides of the lodge.

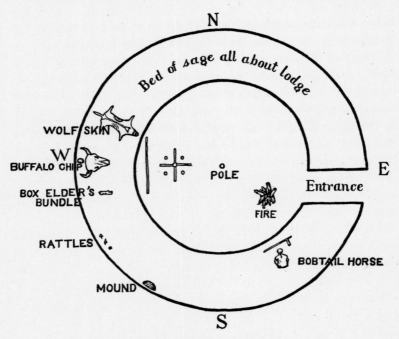

PLAN OF MASSAUM LODGE

To the southwest of the buffalo-skull and close against the lodge covering lay five or six small rattles.

For the greater part of the morning nothing particular took place. People passed in and out, and there was some conversation. About noon Frank Little Wolf brought into the lodge another wolf-skin, which was placed on a quilt north of the first skin. Soon after this a filled pipe was offered to White Frog, who smoked it and passed it along. After the pipe had been partly smoked out, White Frog called Frank Little Wolf to him and directed him to smoke. After doing so he passed his hands ceremonially over the pipe, put it down, and made the usual motions with his hands over his own body. Then he took up the pipe and retired to his place.

White Frog, after tying up his braids, passed around the lodge from the south side across the door to and behind the buffalo-skull, moved the buffalo-chip from behind the skull to the foot of a lodge-pole, moved the Box Elder bundle to the south, and placed fresh sage where the bundle had been. He moved the wolf-skins to one side, north; then shifted the buffalo-skull a little to the south, and with his fingers made a mark in the dust on either side of the skull. He moved the skull to the north and west, quite out of the way, took up a short-handled, new axe and began to chop out the soil, to make a bed in which the skull was finally to rest. When he had loosened the soil, he took it out with the right hand, by single handfuls, placing the earth on a blanket at his right. After digging out the bed to a depth of three inches, and once or twice fitting the skull into it, it seemed to satisfy him, and he moved the blanket west to the edge of the lodge covering, and there emptied the dirt. Then he returned to the bed and continued to work at it, taking out more earth, deepening the trench, fitting the skull twice more, and again emptied the soil off the blanket. Then spitting ceremonially on his hands, he made the ceremonial motions, and after passing each hand over arm and leg, placed that hand on the middle of his chest. Then taking the skull by the horns from behind, with four motions he set it in the trench.

295

He moved the wolf-hides back to their places, and then went around the lodge to his place and sat down.

It is said that the buffalo-skull is placed in a bed dug in the ground because originally the buffalo came out of the earth. This is no doubt a reference to the coming of the buffalo out of the earth after the visit of the two culture heroes to the old woman in the hill.

Now took place some discussion about the preparation of the wolf-hides for the use to which they were to be put, the softening of the hides of the heads, and preparing them for painting. Water was applied to the flesh-side of the wolf-heads, and they were worked over and pulled about so that they might be ready to take their shape, a little later.

Lying on the south side of the lodge were five miniature wheels (ahkoiyu), little models of the wheels used in the game of the same name played by the Cheyennes. These wheels are very old and, like the straight pipe, have come down from ancient times. Later they are to be attached to the wolf's hide. In the ceremony the wheels are called *hotū'a,* bulls. The buffalo-skull is the principal hotua, and the wheels represent other buffalo.

After White Frog had worked for some time at softening the head skin of one of the wolves, the wheels were painted yellow and put aside. Then White Frog painted Frank Little Wolf red, and Island Woman painted the wife red. As already said, the chief priest may not touch the wife of the candidate. About the ankles and wrists of the woman were painted black rings. After these young people had been painted, they rubbed their hands over the partly peeled stick lying in the inner circle, thus painting it red.

THIRD DAY

On the morning of the third day (August 22) Box Elder's bundle had been moved in close to the buffalo-skull. The wolf hides had been folded and lay in bundles south of the skull, with the heads toward the fire. From the east arm of the white cross, extending toward the center-pole, was a line of eight coals three or four inches apart on which sweet grass had been burned. Of these coals the most easterly was less than two feet from the pole.

When Frank Little Wolf entered the lodge he went to White Frog, held his hands toward him, and White Frog spat ceremonially on them. The young man made the ceremonial motions, concluding them by pressing each hand alternately on his chest and finally holding both hands together on the chest, the right hand above. His wife now produced two good pieces of red calico, and without ceremony placed the wolf-hides on them. Some little time was given to instruction, White Frog announcing that at the time of this ceremony the camp should be very quiet, and no one should move about on horse-back. On the fourth day, when the wolf goes out of the lodge, everyone in the camp is supposed to be in his lodge. If anyone is outside the camp and sees that the wolf is going to pass between him and the camp, he will run hard toward his lodge so as to reach it before the wolf passes.

Bobtail Horse said:

The cross marked on the ground was given to us long ago, and the tree in the center of the lodge is the object to which we pray. When we pray to that we pray also to all trees, shrubs, grasses, berries, fruits, and everything on earth that grows out of the ground. The old-time people knew better than we do how to perform these ceremonies. We have forgotten much and sometimes do things in the wrong order. The buffalo-skull should have been dressed—painted— before the trench for it was dug. We are obliged to think, discuss, and argue for a long time before we can decide what to do and when to do it.

The hole surrounded by the four little mounds represents the whole world, and by making it we offer a prayer that the earth and the tribe and all people may be blessed. This is a prayer for health, long life, good living, and kindly feeling toward each other. The earth

297

is sacred and must not be disturbed, injured, or interfered with. The one who taught us this ceremony dug this hole to show us that we must not be afraid of the earth and that we may live on it without fear of harm. We believe that the earth will protect us as it supports us.

Shortly after this speech was ended, Frank Little Wolf took a pipe, filled it, and gave it to a man to light. He received it in the ceremonial way, holding the stem—bowl resting on the ground—in both hands, the right hand above the left. The man who returned it grasped Frank Little Wolf's right hand, which held the pipe, with his own left hand and gripped it four times—gave four pressures. Sometimes the left hand of the giver wholly enclosed Frank Little Wolf's hand. Before returning the pipe, the last man who smoked rubbed the pipestem— bowl on ground and directed toward the center of the lodge— alternately with right and left hand four times upward and once over the end of the bowl. Before each motion the hand was placed on the ground.

Frank Little Wolf's wife now smoked ceremonially a pipe which had just been lighted by White Frog. She passed her hand over his hands, and when she had finished smoking passed her hands up the pipe, blew the last puff of smoke into her hands, and made the ceremonial motions. All these things were done slowly, quietly, reverently.

About noon White Frog and Iron Shirt were working with cups of water on the heads of the two wolf-skins, continuing to soften and to pull them into shape. The water was applied to the flesh-side of the skin with sprigs of sage. After this work was finished, the skins were placed on beds of sage a little distance apart, and Iron Shirt sat between them. White Frog sat near Iron Shirt and was nearly behind the buffalo-skull.

Food was now brought in by some of the old women, and two dishes of dog meat were carried back to White Frog and placed behind the skull. White Frog selected pieces of the meat for sacrifice, from which he caused Frank Little Wolf to pinch off five small fragments, including the tip of the tail. White Frog first spat on the hands of Frank Little Wolf, who performed the ceremonial motions, and then went to the door and deposited one fragment at the outer edge of the bed of sage, three others at intervals between the door and the fire, and one at the very edge of the fire, and then returned to his place southeast of the skull. These sacrifices of meat were placed on the sun's trail and were intended as food for the sun.

White Frog now dipped five sprays of sage in a vessel of stewed choke-cherries toward the four directions and in the center of the pot, and after the hands had been spat on and the usual motions made, Frank Little Wolf took the sprays and deposited one hanging over the edge of the little bank about the dug-out circle under the easternmost sage bundle, one under the southernmost sage bundle, went back around the lodge and placed one under the west bundle, one under the north bundle, and one at the foot of the pole, and returned to White Frog. The same ceremony was now performed with five pinches from a loaf of bread, the pieces being put down on the bed of sage about four inches back of the sprigs of sage with the choke-cherry sacrifice. Five grains of corn were pinched from an ear held vertically by White Frog, one grain each from the east, south, west, north, and the top—the last to represent the center. These grains of corn were put down at the foot of the four lodge-poles, toward the four cardinal points, and one at the foot of the center-pole. These last sacrifices were made to the four directions. It is the purpose to feed the spiritual powers, and after these powers have eaten as much as they wish, the people eat what the spirits have left.

Now, Frank Little Wolf carried back the dishes of food to White Frog's wife at the door and returned to his place. While White Frog made a long address the food was passed and all ate.

After they had eaten, and while they were smoking, White Frog again spoke at length, and then he and Iron Shirt once more set to work softening the skin of the wolf-heads. Presently White Frog, with a bunch of sage dipped in a dish of yellow paint mixed with water, began to paint the skin he was working on, while Iron Shirt for some time continued to soften the other skin, but later painted the flesh-side with white paint.

FOURTH DAY

The following morning (August 23) operations in the Massaum Lodge began about seven o'clock. On the ground between the nose of the skull and the center-pole lay a second row of eight coals, parallel to the first row. Sweet grass had been burned on these.

White Frog at once began to fill the nose and eye-sockets of the buffalo-skull with grass of the same kind and in the same manner as was done in the Medicine Lodge. The reason given for doing this was that the old people taught them to do it in this way. The grass used was a species of brown-headed *Carex*.

During the previous night the softened heads of the wolf-skins had been pulled and pinched into a likeness of heads, the nose and ears fixed in position, and the skins had been placed on their beds of red calico, with their heads to the fire, north of the skull. Late the night before, the wife of Frank Little Wolf had been painted with three black vertical streaks on each cheek and a streak down the middle of the forehead from the hair to the nose. This had mostly worn off.

An elderly woman, the wife of Limpy, whose face was painted with a broad streak of red down the forehead to the root of the nose, and whose chin and cheeks were painted red, was sent out to call in certain persons who were to take part in the ceremony. She acted as a messenger for this lodge.

White Frog passed behind the buffalo-skull from the south, moved the wolf-skins a little toward the north, and placed the yellow-painted one on a blanket covered with red calico. White Frog sat down northwest of the skull, spat on his hands, and made the ceremonial motions. Meantime, Frank Little Wolf was filling a pipe, which he lighted without ceremony, except that as usual he pointed the stem to the ground. White Frog began further work on the head of the yellow wolf. After a time he moved six small graniteware bowls out northwest of the skull, and from a seventh bowl poured a little water in each. An armful of white-sage stems was brought to the door of the lodge, received by Frank Little Wolf, and put close to the lodge covering, immediately behind the skull. The fox-skin and a sack of paint were placed on it.

The fox-skin used on this occasion should have been *wūh'kis,* the kit fox (*Vulpes velox*). This species has been exterminated or perhaps never was found in this particular region, and in its place was used, for the first time, the skin of a gray fox (*Urocyon*)—which the Cheyennes call timber fox, or timber swift—brought up from the South by Bull Tongue.

There are said to be two kinds of timber swift, one quite black, the other lighter. Tall White Man, the priest who had charge of the fox-skin, announced to the camp that he intended to use the blacker fox. This might be done, the old people said, provided a horse was given to the maiyu—that is, to the priest who represented the fox. If the blacker fox had been used it might have been employed again at subsequent ceremonies without so large a payment. However, after all, the lighter-colored skin was used—but it was that of a gray fox.

White Frog now spat on his hands, made the usual motions, opened the sacks of paint, and began to mix the paint. The seven dishes used as paint-pots contained, when White Frog had finished his manipulations, black, blue, white, yellow, and red of two shades, and clear water. White Frog stirred the water into the color with a doubled stem of sage; meanwhile a small sack of black paint and a cup piled high with pounded charcoal and blue clay were brought to the door, received by Frank Little Wolf, and taken around to the back of the skull and there placed on the ground.

After mixing his paints, White Frog continued to work on the

301

head of the yellow wolf, stretching and shaping it and painting it with yellow paint. Bobtail Horse, Wolf Chief, Medicine Bull, and Little Sun entered the lodge at intervals and sat down, most of them to the south of, and near, the door.

White Frog made a long speech to these auditors, asking for their advice as to how he should begin the ceremonies, since some of the various actors had not yet come. At times the lodge became very smoky, and more than once Frank Little Wolf blew the fire to flame through a pipestem. In this, as in many other ceremonial lodges, it was not permitted to blow the fire directly with the mouth; to do so would cause a high wind.

To the pile of sacred objects at the south side of the skull had been added two more little wheels, ahkoiyu. These appeared to be old, and were tied to bunches of buffalo-hair. Besides these there were two buffalo-horn tips, three or four inches long, scraped smooth, with holes for strings at the base of each.

A dish of wet blue clay was passed into the lodge and received by Frank Little Wolf, who handed it to White Frog. He, after biting at the root tied to the corner of his buffalo-robe, spat on his own hands, then on those of the wife of Frank Little Wolf and of his own wife, and all made the ceremonial motions. White Frog's wife moved to the south side of the skull, and Frank Little Wolf's wife came to her side and both knelt on the ground, Frank Little Wolf's wife being to the west, or toward the lodge covering. Frank Little Wolf took his position between White Frog and White Frog's wife; *i.e.*, east of the latter. Island Woman with both her hands took both the hands of Frank Little Wolf and his wife, and with four motions moved them over the front of the skull; then, freeing the left hand of each, she moved the right hands down and with four motions pressed them on the skull above and within the right eye-socket. Then after moving the hands twice around (over) the skull sunwise, they were pressed on the skull inside the right horn, then they were moved twice around that horn and then pressed on the skull inside the left horn and moved twice around it;

then pressed over the left eye, moved twice around (over) the skull, and finally rested in the middle of the forehead between the eyes. After a pause the hands were placed between the horns and moved a distance of about two inches toward the nose, then placed at the base of the left horn and moved across the base of right horn, or from north to south. The hands were now released and the young people went to their places. This was the ceremonial painting of the buffalo-skull by the wife of the man who was offering the sacrifice. The motion across the skull between the horns and in the middle of the forehead represented the painting of the morning star.

Now White Frog took a ball of red paint and with four motions touched with it various points on the skull in this order: the ends of the two premaxillaries, a point over the right eye, inside the right horn, inside the left horn, over the left eye, and last of all the skull between the eyes. In other words, he followed the motions of the hands of the young people. Then without further ceremony he painted the whole face of the skull with dry red paint. The borders of the premaxillaries and of the orbits were red, painted with red clay. A little paint was smeared on the grass in the nose and eyes of the skull, but it seemed to be by accident. Above the red color which ended just back of the horn cores, the skull was painted black with charcoal and fat.

After this painting had been completed, White Frog spat on the hands of Frank Little Wolf and wife, who made the usual motions. Then on the red of the painted skull he drew two lines running from the black within each horn core toward the nose. The longer of these lines was about three inches in length and commenced three inches within the horn; the shorter line started about two inches from the horn and was two inches long. On the southerly, longer line White Frog began the painting with four motions, but he painted the other line without ceremony. These finished, he drew with four motions a line of black along the inner borders of the nasals from end to base.

He called up his wife, and Frank Little Wolf and wife, and spat on their hands. After they had made the ceremonial motions, his wife took the right hands of the young people and caused Frank Little Wolf's wife to hold a piece of blackened fat close to and touching the south side of the skull, just below the eye-socket. She did the same on the north side, but with red paint, touching the cheek just below the eye. Then White Frog, the others having retired, did the actual painting, a black sun on the right cheek and a red crescent on the left cheek. Before painting either side he spat on his hands and made the motions; then he held the paint in front of the skull's nose and moved it around to the southerly or right cheek. Before painting the northerly or left side, he held the paint before the skull's nose, and moved it around over the south side, over the south horn, the back of the skull, and the north horn to the north cheek.

The young people were again called up. White Frog spat on their hands. He caused Frank Little Wolf to take his wife's right hand, which held a bit of blackened fat, and with four motions to move it down to the right horn of the skull and a little way around the tip of the horn, smearing some paint on it. White Frog painted this tip, the southerly one, black. In the same way the woman with four motions touched the tip of the left horn, the northerly one, with a bit of red paint, and then retired. White Frog painted the tip of this horn red. White Frog took a long blade of stiff grass, and breaking it in two places, less than an inch apart, brought the longer ends together so that the grass formed a long triangle with a narrow base and two equal long sides, and with this he measured in the four directions from a central point at the base of the nasals of the skull. After the usual ceremonial blowing on the hands of the young woman, she, by his direction, split off and handed to him a thread from a strap of sinew. He used it to bind together the two long sides of his grass triangle, which was to serve as a pattern.

Again he called up the young people, and after the pre-

MEDICINE LODGE

AWAITING THE RISING SUN

liminary ceremonies placed Frank Little Wolf's hand on top of the young woman's; with four motions Frank Little Wolf took the triangle of grass and with four motions placed it on the upper nasals of the skull, the narrow base toward the east. Then he lifted it up and reversed its position, placing it above the nasals, the base to the west. Again he changed it, placing the base to the north, and then changed it again and put it down with the base to the south. Then the young people retired.

White Frog now placed the grass pattern on the skull, base to the east and two inches above the end of the nasals, and with a sage twig dipped in blue paint drew a blue line marking out the complete triangle. Reversing the triangle so that its base was west and its apex at the apex of the blue triangle just drawn, he drew another triangle. The base of the pattern was now turned to the north, the apex meeting the apices of the two outlines already drawn, and another was drawn, and finally the pattern was again reversed so that its base was south. Thus something like a Maltese cross, or cross pattée, was made, the morning star.

Everything within the outlines so drawn was now filled in with blue. All the triangles were painted in the same way in the order in which the outlines had been applied. The painting was done very slowly and carefully. When it was finished, White Frog moved back to a point northwest of the skull and for several minutes prayed silently, with head bowed on his crossed arms resting on the knees.

The ceremonial painting of the buffalo-skull is a most important matter, and ought to be done according to the prescribed order. Nevertheless, a mistake was made on this occasion, for the sun was painted on the skull at the wrong time. The morning star should have been painted on the face of the skull before the sun was painted on its side, for the reason that the morning star precedes the sun; that is to say, rises before the sun rises. The error was not discovered until after the ceremony was over.

Shortly after noon, food was brought in, and by 1.30 all had eaten. Neither White Frog nor his wife, Frank Little Wolf nor his wife, nor Bobtail Horse ate or drank during the ceremony. Grass (the brown-headed *Carex* used in the skull) was brought in and two piles of it were placed on the ground, one of them behind (west of) the skull. The tips were toward the south and the butts toward White Frog. The other bundle was placed nearly north of the skull on White Frog's left, or east of him.

Someone in the lodge pointed out that in this lodge things went by sevens. Seven people took part in the ceremony; there were seven onlookers, and seven paint-cups, six of which held different colored paints and one clear water. The reason given for this was that the priest had conducted this ceremony seven times. If he had conducted it eight times there would have been eight of each.

Mrs. Frank Little Wolf had painted herself—a streak of green paint down the forehead to the nose and on down to its end, and two vertical green streaks on the cheeks.

White Frog was now sorting out the grass lying behind the skull, clearing it of dry stems and putting it on the bundle which lay to his left. After an interval he raised this bundle and jogged it on the ground to get the butts even.

After White Frog had ceremonially spat on the hands of Frank Little Wolf's wife, she took up a strap of sinew and with four motions tore off a thread and handed it to White Frog and then without ceremony continued to tear off threads. White Frog passed these through his mouth and then through his hands, and when they were softened applied the first one to the ends of the bundle of grass, then tying the sinew tightly about the bundle, near the butts. Next he tied the grass with another sinew above this, and again midway of the grass. It was thus tied in three places. Then he doubled the grass over on itself and again tied it three times over the same places where the sinew had passed before. It was now a long bundle, about fitting the sewed muzzle of the yellow-faced wolf, into which he thrust and then withdrew it. In the same way he now prepared a similar bundle, which he tied to the first one a little back of its end, and by bending over and tying, gradually completed a bundle of grass which had roughly the shape and size of a wolf-skull. This he enlarged and gradually changed, fitting it to the wolf's head until it filled it. Toward the end he abandoned all ceremony and added to the bundle new handfuls of grass so as to make it large enough to fit, and rammed it into place with a stick. Almost an armful of long slough grass was now passed by White Frog's wife to Frank Little Wolf, and by him to his wife, and by her was put down behind the skull, the butts directed toward White Frog. Iron Shirt now came around behind the skull and sat to the north of White Frog, all the sitters in the lodge moving forward to allow him to pass behind them. He began to work on the gray wolf.

White Frog, having inserted his bundle of brown-headed grass in the yellow wolf's head, stuffed slough grass in about it and worked on the head, pushing, pressing, and modeling it so as to make it resemble a wolf's head. Iron Shirt turned his wolf-hide flesh-side down, the head pointing to the southeast, pulled out the legs, and with a spray of sage tips as a brush, dipped in a bowl of white clay and water, ceremonially touched the fur-side of the skin on the left fore leg, the left side of the neck, right fore leg, right side of neck, and end of nose. He then passed the brush down the skin from the point of the nose to the root of the tail, and touched the right and left hind legs. Now, turning the hide flesh-side up, he plentifully applied his gray paint first to the head and then the neck. He began to prepare sinew threads torn from a strap of sinew, for the purpose

307

of sewing the mouth and throat of the wolf, and was constantly losing his threads among the sage at his knees. White Frog spat on his own hands, made the ceremonial motions, and began to gather nice sprigs of sage. He put his wolf-skin, flesh-side down, on a blanket. The head now looked fairly like a wolf's. While the men were working on the wolf-hides, a tall sunflower stem, about five feet long, carrying all its leaves and a single terminal flower, was brought into the lodge.

White Frog, spitting on his hands, and making the ceremonial motion every time he touched the wolf-skin, anointed the fur with the black paint made with blue clay and charcoal, smearing the color on the parts in the following order: the left fore foot, the right fore foot, the right hip across to left shoulder, the left hip across to right shoulder, nose to tail. Then, after spitting on his hands, he lifted the wolf's head with four motions and put the blanket under it. Then he smeared the whole head as far back as the ears with the same black paint.

Now spitting on his hands, with four motions he dipped a brush of sage tips in the pot of yellow paint and with four motions, holding the brush above the fur, drew the brush from the right hind leg to the middle line of the back and moved it about there (a sun); then, from the left fore leg to the same place, from the right fore leg and left hind leg to the same place; then the brush was moved along the right side of the body from neck to tail; then along the left side of the neck and body; then down the middle line of the back from between the ears to the tail.

Having accomplished this ceremonial painting, he now began to smear the yellow paint on the fur in the following order: the right hind leg, left fore leg, left hind leg, and right fore leg, on the right side of neck and body, and on the left side of neck and body; then down the back of the neck, and generally wherever there was a space of the fur that was not covered with paint.

After ceremonially spitting on his hands, White Frog now

turned up the tail and posterior end of the wolf-skin, passed west of it, and continued his painting from the north side. The whole fur-side was smeared with the paint, the throat and ears being the last parts painted. After this was finished, he wiped his hands on sage stems and then proceeded again to go over the head with black paint.

At five o'clock White Frog had finished his painting and had returned to his seat on the south side of the lodge. Iron Shirt had finished sewing the lips of the gray wolf and was again painting the flesh-side of the head and neck. Those engaged in the ceremony declared that nothing more would be done during the night. I left the lodge.

FIFTH DAY

On Thursday, August 24, at seven o'clock, White Frog was already ceremonially painting the head of the yellow wolf in the Massaum lodge.

During the night there had been singing and some offering of sacrifice, for a line of eight coals on which sweet grass had been burned lay to the south of two similar lines already mentioned as lying between the cross and the center-pole.

The blue clay with which the yellow wolf's head was painted had dried to a gray color, and White Frog was painting the head with narrow cross-bands of different colors, working back from the nose. The first band, about an inch from the nose, was irregular, black, and about a quarter inch in width. The next, an eighth of an inch farther back, was white; then, touching each other, came narrow bands of red, blue, yellow, red, black, blue, white, red, blue, yellow, white, red, yellow, black, white, yellow. This last bar crossed the lower corner of the eyes. It was followed by lines of blue, black, white, and red. From the end of the nose the third blue line and the fifth red line ran zigzag across the muzzle, and so occupied three or four times the width of the other lines. Above the red zigzag came yellow, blue, black, white, red, yellow, blue, black, white, red, yellow, this last line with projections all along it toward the ears. These projections looked like mountains. White Frog began to paint each band low down on the north side and drew the bands over the head toward the south.

On top of the wolf's head, behind the gray clay, was painted a wide black band which ran nearly from ear to ear and sent out branches to the front and rear of each ear. Down from the ears running toward the throat was a band of red.

The wife of Frank Little Wolf stripped her dress down to the waist, pulled it up to the thighs, and sat facing east, White Frog's wife sitting in front of her. The older woman spat on the young woman's feet and she made the ceremonial motions. Then White Frog's wife painted her right leg and right arm, then left arm and left leg from thigh down, with red paint. White Frog took part of a white tanned deerskin, cut off a piece, and passed it out to a woman, who was preparing whistles for use. It was to make strings to hang them about the neck.

Sand Crane came about the lodge, passing behind the skull, and taking up the gray wolf-skin, went out. On his way he took up two of four stout unpeeled cherry sticks, five feet long, that had been handed in and lay near Bobtail Horse, and carried them away with him. He was taking the skin out to Iron Shirt to work on. Sand Crane returned, offered his hands to White Frog, who spat on them, and Sand Crane made the motions. White Frog then bit off a piece of the root tied to the corner of the buffalo-robe and gave it to Sand Crane, who went out.

Frank Little Wolf's wife's body and face had been painted, and after her hair had been combed with a porcupine-tail comb, the hair was painted red. Black lines were painted about right ankle and wrist, and left wrist and ankle, in that order.

In response to a request by his wife, White Frog made from a spear of yellow dry grass a small triangle like the one used in painting the cross on the buffalo-skull; he handed it to his wife to be used in painting the face of Frank Little Wolf's wife. White Frog explained to his wife that the narrow base of the triangle was to come beneath the nose, outside of each eye, and next to the hair on the forehead, the apices of the triangles to meet over the root of the nose. His wife received and tied the triangle and began to do the painting. She started wrong and was corrected.

White Frog continued to paint cross-bands on the yellow wolf's head. The yellow line with the projections was probably intended for a zigzag line. Back of this line came narrow bands of blue, black, red, yellow, white, red, blue, white, black, red, white; this last line was rather wide and reached the base of the ears. Then came narrow lines of yellow, red, black, and white.

Bobtail Horse now took the two stout cherry sticks already mentioned and ceremonially prepared them for use. Beginning with four motions of the knife, he squared their ends and then with four motions cut off a portion, so that they were about thirty inches long.

As Sand Crane was about to paint Frank Little Wolf, White Frog's wife spat on the hands of both the men, who made the usual motions. Sand Crane went to the fire and brought a coal, which he put down in front of Frank Little Wolf, and tearing off a bit from a plait of sweet grass, sprinkled it on the coal and passed his hands through the rising smoke, and then passed the hands over Frank Little Wolf in the usual order. Then Sand Crane proceeded to paint the young man's legs and arms with red paint in the usual order.

While this was going on, Tall White Man entered the lodge and asked for the fox. Frank Little Wolf rose, went to the back of the lodge, got the fox-skin, and carrying it in both hands brought it around the lodge and offered it to Tall White Man with the head directed toward the south. Tall White Man at first refused to receive it, but when Frank Little Wolf turned it so that its head pointed north, he accepted it and carried it out of the lodge. This was a mistake. The young man should have carried it head toward the door; *i.e.*, entering, turning south and going round the lodge, the head to the north.

The upper half of the face of Frank Little Wolf's wife was now being painted blue by White Frog's wife with the symbol of the morning star. Besides the blue cross already mentioned, the color covered the lower half of the upper lip, the chin, and lower cheeks, while two vertical lines as broad as a man's finger passed upward in front of the ears and parallel. She now resumed her dress.

In preparing to paint Frank Little Wolf's face, Sand Crane began by pressing the base of the palm of his right hand against the chin, the forehead, the right side, the left side, and then upon the nose. After that he painted the whole face. He combed the young man's hair ceremonially, making four motions with the comb, and then gave it to the young man, who thereafter did the work himself. Sand Crane painted black in the usual order the ankles and wrists, painted on his chest a black circle representing the sun, and on the right shoulder blade a black crescent moon opening upward.

The head painting of the yellow wolf having been finished, White Frog spat on his hands, took a bowl of carmine paint and a long bunch of sage, and painted the fur of the wolf with a long crescent opening downward—a rainbow—running from behind the fore leg down the right side to flank, or just in front of the hind leg on the south side. Then going around behind the wolf-skin he painted the north side of the skin in the same way. Returning, he drew down on the south side a second broad red streak, also in crescent form above the first one and reaching from just behind the fore leg down to the flank, and the same on the other side. Thus, there were two parallel crescent-shaped smears—rainbows—on each side of the skin. White Frog now painted a red line down the back a little to the south of the median line of the back, which line, just before it reached the end of the skin, curved a little to the south and reached the border of the skin three or four inches south of the tail. He

312

then again spat on his hands and painted a corresponding red line on the other side of the median line of the back, the line just before reaching the tail curving to the north and terminating at the border of the skin three or four inches north of the root of the tail. These are explained as being lightning trails.

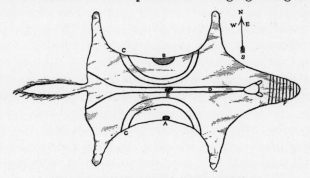

PAINTING ON SKIN OF YELLOW WOLF

A, Sun; B, Moon; C, Rainbows; D, Lightning Trails; E, His Heart.

While this was in progress, Sand Crane was painting Frank Little Wolf's face with the blue morning star symbol.

White Frog's wife tied a bundle of sage to the right-hand braid of the hair of Frank Little Wolf's wife, selecting for this purpose four strands of sinew, which she took up from the ground and put down in another place, each with four motions. She placed the bundle of sage with four motions on the sinew and tied the first sinew; the second and third were tied without ceremony; the fourth she put aside and began to select sinews from another bundle. Meanwhile, White Frog had painted a black round spot—the sun—near the middle border of the south side of the wolf's hide, another one in the middle of the lightning lines of the back, and a red crescent—the moon—on the north border, a little nearer the fore leg than the hind one. The black spot in the middle of the back they call *hĭ'st hē' wā*, his heart. With red paint he ceremonially painted—not touching the hide—across the skin from the right hind leg to the left

313

fore leg and from the left hind leg to the right fore leg, stopping a moment each time over the black heart spot in the middle of the back. This having been done, he painted red the lower part of the right hind leg and the lower part of the left fore leg, and then the lower right fore leg and the lower left hind leg.

While this was being done Frank Little Wolf and his wife had put on their finest clothing, moccasins, leggings, etc. Only the paint on the faces was to be seen.

White Frog now wiped his hands with sage, suggesting that the painting of the hide was completed. He took up the bundle of five little wheels (ahkoiyu), four of them plain and one orna- mented, and a wad of buffalo-wool. He placed the four plain wheels before him in a row from north to south, and behind each wheel put a little wad of buffalo-wool. The ornamented wheel had a beaded rim and was slightly larger than the others, and this one he presently put in the middle of the line with two plain wheels on either side. A wad of buffalo-wool lay west of each wheel. He now spat on his hands and from a sack took some yellow paint, which he placed on the palm of the open right hand, fingers directed southward, and he held it before the eyes of Frank Little Wolf and his wife. White Frog then with the yellow paint painted each plain wheel, beginning with the one to the south. The ornamented wheel was not painted. Again beginning at the south, he painted all the wads of buffalo- hair.

White Frog spat four times on the end of the handle of a new knife, rubbed the sacred root four times down its back, then cut a number of deerskin strings, long and short, and painted them with the wet yellow paint. While this was being done, some people entered the lodge, and a cotton shirt was placed over the head of the wolf, completely covering it. White Frog now tied one of the small deerskin strings to each wad of buf- falo-hair and put each one back in its place west of its wheel. Pausing now, he made a long address. After this had been fin- ished, he tied the four buffalo-hair wads to the four plain wheels, thrusting the strings through the strands of netting in the wheels, apparently at random. Last of all he tied its wad of buffalo-hair to the ornamented wheel. Now, with an awl, on which he spat four times, he pierced from the outside the hide of the wolf over the right hip, and with four motions thrust through the hole one string of a plain wheel and pulled it through. The other awl hole was then pierced, the other string put through, and the two strings tied. The hide was not turned over, but the tying was done by feeling. The same thing was done with the left shoulder, high up.

Meanwhile Bobtail Horse was ceremonially tying bundles of sage to the larger end of each of the sticks he had prepared, and parallel to the sticks. He put five bundles on the first stick, each with four motions, and tied them with five sinews. The second stick was treated in the same way. Meantime, White Frog had tied his wheels on the wolf-skin in the usual order, the ornamented one being put on last in the middle of the back over the black spot at E. When Bobtail Horse had finished tying the sage on the sticks, he cut off the high blossoming heads of the sage—three or four inches—which projected above each stick.

The seven old women, known as Young Wolves, had now gone out.

Bobtail Horse now passed the sticks to the back of the lodge, where they were put next to the lodge covering behind the buffalo-skull. White Frog was now engaged in ceremonially punching with an awl a hole from side to side—south to north—in the end of the wolf's nose. This done, he began to tie together with a sinew some heads of sage. A woman brought in four large buffalo-chips and handed them to White Frog's wife, who received them and put them in a pile south of Box Elder's bundle.

White Frog, having spat on his hands, took a long thistle-stalk surmounted with a blossom, and the blossom of a sunflower, and placing on the ground a few stems of sage with the

315

heads directed southward, put the sunflower with them, the flower directed south. The tips of a few stems of sage and the thistle bloom were placed beside them, but with the heads pointing north, and the bundles were tied together with five sinews; thus one set of blooms pointed north and one south. The work was done between the buffalo-skull and the yellow wolf-skin. Now the sinew ends were cut off, and also the heads of the sage, so that the sunflower and the thistle blossom formed the two apparent ends of the bundle. The stems of sage remaining in it as supports were painted with yellow paint. The ends of a single sinew string were left long for tying this bundle to the wolf's nose, which after some difficulty was done, the sinew being passed through the hole from south to north. The sunflower exercises a good influence and the rough thistle a bad one. As the man who wore the wolf-skin walked about camp outside, the sunflower was always directed toward the center of camp and the thistle toward everyone outside of camp —whether they be the men of the tribe or enemies.

White Frog now painted yellow the sticks prepared by Bob-tail Horse, after four times passing the hands over them, without paint, up from the ground on either side, the right hand first. Afterward he painted the lower end of each with red paint and put one stick on either side of the wolf.

Spotted Elk, who was to wear the yellow wolf-skin, had entered the lodge some hours earlier, and had seated himself north of skull. When he entered he was clad, but a little later removed his clothing and now wore only moccasins and a breechclout.

White Frog now prepared to paint Spotted Elk yellow. Passing behind the buffalo-skull he came around north of it and spat on the hands of Spotted Elk, who made the usual motions. Then White Frog ceremonially passed his hands over Spotted Elk's body in the usual order, and then without ceremony proceeded to paint him in the order: right leg, right arm, left leg, and left arm. Then he painted his body, beginning on the middle of chest, and this was followed by streaking all the paint with the finger nails.

Before painting the face, White Frog spat on Spotted Elk's hands, and Spotted Elk made the ceremonial motions. White Frog touched Spotted Elk's face ceremonially, and then began to paint. He painted red the feet, ankles, hands, wrists, and lower part of face to cheekbones on sides; a black disc—the sun—on chest, and a black crescent on the shoulder blade. The body was yellow, as said. The red on feet, hands, and mouth represented blood where the wolf had been eating.

A crier was now heard shouting through the camp that the wolf was coming out.

Frank Little Wolf's wife, White Frog's wife, and Frank Little Wolf had their hands spat on. White Frog caused the young people with four motions to take up the wolf, holding to the fur in the middle line of the back, and by four motions to lift it and to start toward the door on the north side of the lodge. Here with the skin four motions were made, and at the fourth motion the head reached the door of the lodge and was thrust partly out, looking to the east. For a moment it was held there and then drawn back, then thrust out again a little farther, and withdrawn; the third time it was thrust out farther; then the fourth time it remained out long, and the fifth time, with four motions, it was slowly and reverently carried out and placed on a travois, which stood in front of the lodge, the head facing to the east. It took some little time to arrange it.

Now, a number of children, led by their parents and carrying offerings, came up in front of the lodge, approaching from the south to the south side of the travois, and placed their offerings on the travois, or White Frog's wife tied them to the hide. The children who brought offerings were chiefly little girls and very small boys; the little boys might place their hands on the wolf-skin, but the little girls might not do so.

Now a great number of people, practically the whole tribe,

very silently came to the lodge and stood at a distance, the men all together on the north, and the women by themselves on the south. They stood there for some time regarding the wolf, most of them silent or praying in low tones.

After an interval, perhaps half an hour, the wife of White Frog, with Frank Little Wolf and his wife, lifted the skin from the travois as before, and brought it back to the lodge, entering with four motions, and carrying the skin around to its place, north of the skull, depositing it there and covering the head as before. The offerings remained attached to the hide.

Wounded Eye was already in the lodge, and soon afterward Bull Tongue entered. White Frog's wife was now engaged in painting the face of an old woman—one of the Young Wolves —as the face of Frank Little Wolf's wife was painted, with the morning star symbol.

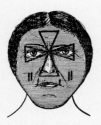

These women, called Young Wolves, constitute a society who imitate the painting of the Massaum ceremony, paying a horse or other good property for the right to do so. They were not in any way connected with the sacrifice, but were onlookers.

Medicine Bull, after having had his hands spat on, took up Box Elder's bundle from the south side of the skull and opened it before White Frog, taking from it the straight pipe, the pipe stick, a wad of buffalo-wool, a piece of sinew, and some old plaits of sweet grass. He stripped off a thread of sinew and put it on the ground before Frank Little Wolf, whose hands were then spat on by White Frog. Medicine Bull split off other threads of sinew, five in all. Then he spat on his hands and, guiding the young man's hands with his own, caused Frank Little Wolf to pick up and deposit each sinew in the palm of his own left hand, the tips of each of the five threads being between the different fingers. Under instruction, Frank Little Wolf made a ball of these threads of sinew, rubbing the ball together between his palms. Medicine Bull picked up the straight pipe, held it before the young man, and caused him to drop the ball of sinew into the pipe; gave him the pipe stick; had him move it with a circular motion about the pipe hole, ram down the wad, and then holding the pipe in both hands, put it with four motions on the ground. From a tobacco-sack Medicine Bull now took tobacco which he placed on one corner of the buffalo-robe. He then spat on his hands and after making the ceremonial motions caused Frank Little Wolf, with four motions, to take up the pipe and then, first with the right hand and afterward with the left, alternately, to put four pinches of tobacco in the pipe. Then with his right hand he took the pipe stick, made four circular motions around the opening of the pipe, and gave the stick to Frank Little Wolf, who then with four downward motions rammed the pipe. Medicine Bull next handed the young man a piece of fat with which he fixed the contents of the filled pipe. Medicine Bull now took the young man's hands and caused him to move out the pipe held in both hands along the pipestem and with four motions to place the pipe on the ground. Medicine Bull, after spitting on his hands, took up from its place the buffalo-wool for wrapping the pipe end of the pipestem, and Frank Little Wolf wrapped it about the stem.

Now took place the ceremonial approaches of the stem to the pipe. Medicine Bull spat on his own hands; took Frank Little Wolf's hands; caused him to lift the pipe and to bring it nearer to the stem. This was done with four motions, and before each of the four motions the hands were spat on. At the fourth motion the young man affixed pipe to stem and handed the pipe to White Frog, who rubbed it down and placed it on the ground.

Frank Little Wolf's wife was called to bring a coal from the fire, which she placed near the bowl of the pipe. Medicine Bull ceremonially took red paint and put it in Frank Little Wolf's hand, then sprinkled sweet grass on the coal, and handed the pipe to Frank Little Wolf, who, holding it upright, the stem on the ground, rubbed it alternately with right and left hands, twice with each, from the ground up, and also rubbed it, as he held it in each hand, with a twisting motion with right and left hand alternately, thus painting it. The pipe and stick were now placed on the sage before the buffalo's nose, bowl of the pipe and point of the stick directed to the north. The young people moved over next to the skull, passing behind the skull and to the north of it.

A little bed of sage was now placed before White Frog on the bared circle to the northeast of the buffalo-skull. It was therefore almost in front of the nose of the yellow wolf. Four little bundles of sage were placed on the ground within the circle to the north of the pole, reaching with three-foot intervals between them from near the skull toward the door. Frank Little Wolf now brought a coal and placed it in front of the nose of the yellow wolf. White Frog called on his wife, who was now on the opposite side of the lodge, to bring him a piece of the sacred root. Having bitten a piece of it and spat on his hands, he called up Spotted Elk and put on him the yellow wolf-skin. The head fitted over Spotted Elk's head, and the hide over his back, the tail hanging down behind. A bone whistle hung from Spotted Elk's neck.

The travois before the lodge had been removed. White Frog tied strings attached to the hide about the arms, thighs, and across the breast of Spotted Elk, in the usual order. He caused Spotted Elk to kneel, spat on Spotted Elk's hands and on his own, took a piece of root from the ground, moved it four times toward the handle of one of the sticks and toward Spotted Elk's mouth, into which at the last he put it with four motions. This was repeated toward the other stick with another piece of root,

MASSAUM CEREMONY
YELLOW WOLF ON TRAVOIS

and then the two walking-sticks were given to Spotted Elk. White Frog spat on his own hands and pressed them on Spotted Elk's breast, went to his place, took up one after another a number of rattles, each of which he shook a few times. Those who were to use the rattles spat on their own hands. White Frog now made a speech of instruction to Spotted Elk, telling him what he should do. He was told to stop at the opening of the circle and give a long whistle, on the south side to stop again and give a long whistle, and so on the west and the north sides of the circle. All these things he did as instructed. The rattles were passed, White Frog retaining one, which was red-painted. He sang, and the others joined in.

At the second song Spotted Elk rose to his feet and prepared to step off, making four motions with the right foot, before placing it on one of the sage bundles within the circle, and then walked around the north side of the lodge, putting his right foot without further ceremony on the bundles of sage in the circle, walking around the north side of the lodge to the door. There he stopped and four times put his head out the door, whistling each time.

The song which was being sung was now interspersed with imitations of howlings of the gray wolf, and while this was going on Bobtail Horse wept bitterly, sobbing like a child as the tears rolled down his cheeks, and other men seemed much moved. No doubt it was the memory of the old buffalo days that caused this emotion.

The fourth time Spotted Elk put his head out he walked on, and set out walking a little north of east toward the border of the camp. As he walked he stooped forward, and used the sticks held in each hand as supports; in other words, as the fore legs of the wolf he represented. He went straight to the opening of the circle and there turning to the right went about the outside of the circle.

A little later, the gray wolf, represented by Head Swift, who had been dressed by Iron Shirt, came out of a small lodge, the door of which faced west, near the edge of the camp-circle to the east of the Massaum lodge. He walked around the lodge to the east, and then sunwise inside the circle of the camp to the opening of the circle. From the nose of the gray wolf-skin hung a scalp; a long squared strip of buffalo-skin with the hair on, cut from an old robe, was attached to the gray wolf-skin behind the ears, and passed down the middle line of the back to and beyond the tail, so that the strip dragged on the ground. To the sides of this buffalo-skin, between the ears and shoulders of the wolf-skin, were tied the pair of smooth polished buffalo-horn tips—earlier seen in the Massaum lodge.

After a long wait, during which the two wolves had thus circled the camp, the yellow wolf, Spotted Elk, was seen entering the opening of the circle to the east, where he had gone out, and returning to the lodge. At its door he stopped, and at a call from White Frog entered without ceremony and walked around the north side of the lodge and seated himself near the skull. The gray wolf, Head Swift, was seen coming, but his progress was slower.

Meanwhile, thirty or forty feet east of the Massaum lodge some women—the Young Wolves—were putting up a high shade of two lodge coverings, each supported by half a dozen lodge-poles and open to the east. Others, old women, were planting in the ground two lines of small cottonwood branches from eight to fifteen feet high, which formed two diverging wings, running from the shade in a general northeasterly and southeasterly direction and widely opened to the east. The sharpened butts of the branches, which were freshly cut, were thrust in holes in the ground.

When the gray wolf reached the Massaum lodge it was seen that his whole body was painted white, the paint being vertically streaked with the finger nails. As he advanced he whistled, and at length entered the lodge without ceremony. As he walked he supported himself with walking-sticks, but these were peeled and painted white. The offerings of calico and other things were still attached to both wolf-skins when their wearers returned.

Now Frank Little Wolf, who had left the lodge, carried around the south side of the shade another old buffalo-skull and put it down about midway between the north and south ends of the shade and five or six feet east of the lodge covering. In carrying the skull he walked very slowly and stooped forward. The Box Elder bundle was carried from the Massaum lodge by Frank Little Wolf and put down south of this skull, and the pipe placed in front of the bundle. Two buffalo-chips and two parfleches were put behind the skull.

The two wolves now went out of the Massaum lodge and around the shade, entering from the north side and sitting down on the north side of the shade, that is, north of the skull. Frank Little Wolf's wife and the old men followed the wolves out of the Massaum lodge, entered the shade from the south side, and sat on the south side of the skull.

Now appeared two men, the fox, Whistling Elk, and his leader, Crane. Tied on his head the man representing the fox wore a tanned skin of the timber swift, that is, a gray fox.[2] The flesh-side was painted yellow and the back blue, and the hide was quite complete and heavily haired. The wearer was painted yellow, his arms dotted on the outside with circular blue spots as large as a silver quarter dollar. His leader, also yellow-painted, carried a staff with green leaves tied to the end. These men made their appearance running swiftly and irregularly, this way and that. The fox followed every turn of his leader, who was one of the most graceful men I ever saw. The hair of each was loose and flowing.

I have not seen the preparation of the fox-skin, but Tall White Man, the priest of the fox, told me that the fox-skin must remain for four nights in the Massaum lodge. On the morning of the fourth day a crier, who received his orders from the Massaum lodge, went about the camp, shouting out

[2] *Urocyon cinereo-argentatus scotti.*

to all those who were to paint themselves to represent the different animals, to make ready to come out.

Frank Little Wolf had had set up a lodge in which the fox was to be dressed (*i.e.,* painted). He made inquiry as to who was the proper person to dress it and learned that it was Tall White Man. Frank Little Wolf himself went to see the priest, whose first question was, "Have you chosen the man to wear the fox-skin?" The young man said that he had chosen Whistling Elk, and in reply to another question said that Crane was to be the leader. Tall White Man then asked, "Where have you put the lodge?" Frank Little Wolf pointed it out, and the two went over and found there the man who was to wear the fox. After Tall White Man went in, Crane entered.

Tall White Man told these two men to remain in the lodge while he himself went to the Massaum lodge to get the fox-skin.

When the fox was taken into the lodge where it was to be painted, it was carried in from the south side of the door and around on the south side of the lodge to the back of the lodge, and placed on the ground with its nose pointing to the fire. After putting the skin down on the ground, Tall White Man took it by the tail and drew it back toward the lodge covering. He prepared five bundles of sage and put them on the ground, four of the bundles lying toward the four directions and one where the skin was first put down. In all the bundles the heads of the sage stems were directed toward the fire. On top of the bundle representing the middle—about where the fox-skin had been—he made a bed of sage for the skin to rest on.

He then picked up the skin, grasping it by the head and the root of the tail, moved it forward, and put it down on the bed of sage without ceremony. Then he drew out the right (south) fore foot, and straightened it, then the right hind foot, the left hind foot, and the left fore foot. Tall White Man had asked for and received from Frank Little Wolf yellow paint and blue paint to dress the fox. He drew a line of blue paint down the middle line of the back from the tip of the nose to the end of the tail. About opposite the heart on the right (south) side was drawn, also in blue, a small disc about the size of a quarter of a dollar, representing the sun, and on the left, or north side, a crescent, symbolizing the moon. All the rest of the fur was dotted with yellow paint. From each foot up the leg ran a slender line of blue paint, meeting the blue line which extended down the middle line of the back. To a stick, hardly larger than a match, attached to the fox's nose were now tied a blue hare-bell and the single leaf of a thistle.

The man who was to wear the fox-skin was now painted yellow over his whole body, feet, and hands. From the right ankle up outside the leg and running up the body to the shoulder, and then turning and running down the outside of the arms to wrists, were pairs of dots of blue paint larger than the tip of a man's thumb. This painting was repeated on the left side. Under the eyes and on the nose he was painted black with charcoal. Crane, the man whom Whistling Elk was to follow, was painted yellow over his whole body, without blue dots, but with the same black on his face. The stick that Crane carried was painted yellow and had four small bundles of white sage, each three or four inches long, tied to the end nearest his hand.

Before they went out of the lodge, the stick was placed on the ground on the north side of the lodge. He who was to wear the fox-skin walked behind the fox and sat down north of the skin and therefore southwest of the cane.

Tall White Man now took up the fox-skin without ceremony and with four motions put it on the head of Whistling Elk, tying it under the chin, and, with longer strings, under the arms. The nose of the skin was over the forehead, and the stick attached to the nose hung just between the eyebrows. When this had been done, Crane walked around the lodge and sat down by the cane. Both men were squatting on their hams. Tall White Man picked up the cane and offered it to Crane, who with both hands attempted to grasp it, but did not do so, and Tall White Man withdrew it and offered it again. This was done four times,

325

Crane seizing it the fourth time. Crane now tried to rise to his feet three times, and the fourth time did so. Before they started toward the door, Tall White Man told them to step off first with the right foot and then with the left, and four steps, two with each foot, brought them to the door. At the door the right foot was brought up to the left. Crane now put his whistle in his mouth, put his head out of the door, looking toward the south, and whistled. Crane drew in his head, and Whistling Elk put his head out, looking to the north, and whistled. Then Crane looked out to the north, whistling, and Whistling Elk to the south. Then when about to whistle to the east, Crane made two motions to put his whistle out of the door, and then whistled, and Whistling Elk made two motions to put his out, and then whistled. The fox was represented by one person, but his leader shared in his work.

After this whistling, the wearer of the fox-skin fell behind Crane, and the two, in single file, leaped out of the lodge like animals and started straight for the south side of the opening of the camp-circle, but before they reached it, doubled back for a short distance, then ran around inside the circle until they reached the south side, when they doubled back and then started around again. At the west and north sides they doubled back and then started for the north wing of the brush, but before reaching it doubled back four times. When they reached the side of the north wing they ran out to the east end of that wing and lay down under the trees there, after scratching about in the ground a little as foxes would do.

Presently, while these men were running about between the wings and close in front of the shade, the fox was called by White Frog and came close to the shade and squatted for a moment in front of the buffalo-skull. He was then called to one side in front of White Frog; his hands were spat on, and the fox-skin was taken from his head and ceremonially placed on the buffalo-skull, flesh-side down and head pointed to the east.

Frank Little Wolf sat west of the skull, his wife at his left,

White Frog next to him to the south, and the others in a half-circle beyond, to the south. The men sat away from the lodge coverings, and the old women sat behind them.

About 3.30 P.M. White Frog, spitting on his hands, untied the strings by which the yellow wolf-skin was fastened to Spotted Elk's body and took the skin off. A little later, Iron

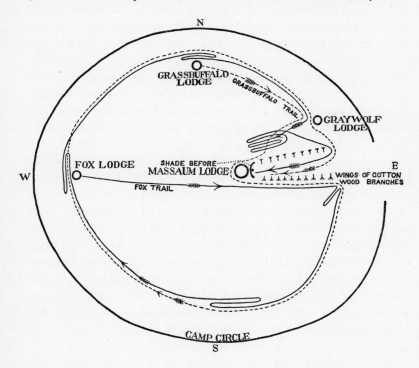

Shirt, after his hands had been spat on by White Frog, took the gray wolf-skin off Head Swift; the offerings were removed from the wolf-hides and put in a pile on the north side of the buffalo-skull. The two wolf-skins were placed on the ground, heads to the east, where the wearers had been sitting, and the walking-sticks of each laid on either side the skin.

When the fox-skin had been taken from the head of Whistling Elk, the grass buffalo—thirteen women, two little girls, and two men—left their lodge on the north side of the circle. All the women wore elaborate hanging headdresses of slough grass and carried in their right hands wreaths with strings across them. The little girls wore similar headdresses. The men were painted dark gray above, the legs below the knees yellow, with a red sun on the chest and a red crescent moon on the left shoulder blade. They carried in their right hands bunches of buffalo-hair. They walked down the trail made by the fox, but turned off where he doubled four times, walked around behind the shade toward the south side of the opening of the camp-circle, and followed the trail of the fox—which was also the trail of the gray wolf—around to the north side of the opening of the circle and then southwest between the wings. At the southeast side of the circle they marched around a sick man who had come out from his lodge and was sitting on the ground, and at the southwest side of the circle they marched around, prayed over, and so doctored, another sick man.

Now from the southwest part of the camp came four men, led by Young Bird, representing elk. Their lower legs, arms, and shoulders were painted black, and the rest of the body yellow. On the head they wore wreaths of white sage and carried in the right hand long willows with leaves on the upper end. Stuck in the wreaths of sage were bare twigs eighteen inches or two feet long, which represented antlers. These elk, after showing themselves, went to the southeast side of the camp and circled about a sick woman (Bird Bear's wife), whom they doctored by prayers and by passing their hands over her. At the south side of the camp they stopped near another woman, and again by others, and treated them. All the animal representatives have mysterious power for curing the sick.

While this was going on White Frog and Iron Shirt again put the wolf-skins on their wearers, and White Frog put the fox-skin on the head of the fox.

Now came into the wings eleven men, the first five yellow-painted, the next three red, the next two white, and the last red-painted. They carried long leafy willows. This represented a dream which came to White Bull many years ago, and the animals were white-tailed deer.

White Frog's wife brought out the wife of Frank Little Wolf and caused her with four motions to touch the straight pipe. White Frog's wife then lifted the pipe from the ground and gave it to the young woman, and they carried it out to midway between the wings. The seven Young Wolves followed, and the nine stood there in a close group. Meantime, his leader and the fox had started off on a run, the fox closely following his leader. They went away to the northeast. After a time the two fox men returned, running as usual, stopping, zigzagging, and running irregularly, and went to the southeasternmost tree of the southerly wing and squatted or lay down in the shade.

Seven men, white-painted except as to necks and upper shoulders, ran by the wings on the south side of the shade and up to the lodge, from which the gray wolf had first emerged, and then turned south. These were members of the Contrary Society, represented hunters, and were so called in the Ceremony, *Ēmhŏ'niŭ*. They were the fun-makers or clowns of the occasion. They carried red-painted bows and arrows, which they held and used in a reversed way, and wore breechclouts of gunny-sacking. They acted in an eccentric way, and darted hither and thither, unexpectedly. Their antics were highly enjoyed by the people. They were said to act like lightning in a storm. The Thunder in a storm is believed to have with him people like these, and acting in the same way. They doctor by jumping over people.

The different animals which had scattered now all returned and were gathered in a close group between the wings surrounding the nine women, one of whom carried the pipe.

Now the two wolves started out and slowly walked about these animals. Another group of differently dressed buffalo had appeared, the men black-painted, some of them wearing headdresses made of buffalo-hide with heavy bulls' horns. Others wore on the head wreaths of willow or cottonwood, and all carried wreaths in their right hands. As the wolves slowly walked around these animals, recalling in their actions the precise scenes that used to be witnessed forty or fifty years ago, a buffalo-bull would now and then threaten with the head, charge a little way toward them and then go back to the herd. Among the animals was a naked man, Old Bull, wearing tied to his head the skin of a coyote, which hung down behind. He was very active, running most of the time. The coyote and the fox men ran about the edge of the buffalo herd and even among the buffalo.

Around the outside of the herd, and at a distance, the white-painted men were constantly in motion, pretending to approach the animals and to shoot at them. Sometimes a buffalo-bull would charge toward them.

After some little time all the animals went off by groups and disappeared. The wolves returned to their places under the shade and the nine women to theirs.

After spitting on his hands, White Frog took off from Spotted Elk the yellow wolf-skin, and Iron Shirt did the same for Head Swift. White Frog's wife took Frank Little Wolf's wife to the yellow wolf-skin, lifted it from the ground with four motions, and with four motions put it on the young woman. The gray wolf-skin was now put on Head Swift by Iron Shirt.

Eleven women, nine following White Frog's wife and two Frank Little Wolf's wife, walked to the middle part of the area between the wings, and there walked in a circle. When Shell Woman put on the wolf-skin she became the leader of the animals, controlled them, and now called them in. The two fox men, who had gone off, returned and the grass buffalo now came back. Spotted Elk—not wearing the yellow wolf-skin, but walking with his staffs—and the gray wolf went out and walked about the buffalo. The deer came in and imitated the actions of deer. The coyote came in and with the fox circled the herd on the run. Then came the black buffalo, the elk, the white-tailed deer, and the hunters. The foxes ran as irregularly as ever; the Contraries had their hair brought forward and hanging in tufts over the left eye. One of the black buffalo wore anklets of hop-vines; others had shoulder belts and wristlets of hop-vines. They were painted with discs of white on shoulders, elbows, wrists, hips, knees, and ankles. A song was started soon after the eleven women went out, and when it ended the animals ran off by companies, the black buffalo and the elk last. The elk wore eagle-feathers on the head, one tied on each side and sticking up through the branched antlers of wood.

Now the wearers of the wolf-skins came in and were relieved of all their paraphernalia, and the foxes ran off out of the south end of the wings and then returned and sat under the tree.

The yellow wolf-skin was again ceremonially put on Frank Little Wolf's wife, and the eleven women once more started out to the point between the wings and walked about in a circle. The foxes had disappeared. They now returned. Presently the grass buffalo came in through the opening of the wings. Some of the women had white flowers stuck in the grass headdresses, as if for horns. The coyote returned, as did the deer, elk, and black buffalo. Spotted Elk, the yellow wolf, left the shade and began to circle the herd, and the gray wolf did the same. The hunters (Contraries) were active, and much laughed at. There were men who wore yellow feathers in their hair, war feathers; others had otter-skin head-wrappings. The otter men had red crosses on the right shoulder blade. This was from a dream about the otter.

After a time the animals again dispersed, but the foxes remained. The women with the wolf-skin returned to the shade. Iron Shirt took the gray wolf-skin off Head Swift, and White Frog's wife took the yellow wolf-skin from Shell Woman.

After an interval White Frog and Iron Shirt again put the wolf-skins on their men. The fox and coyote went off before this began and returned about as the operation had ended.

331

Frank Little Wolf's wife took up the pipe and, the women following her, all went out and walked about between the wings. Now came the grass buffalo, followed almost at once by all the other animals. The yellow wolf first, and soon after the gray wolf, left the shade and stalked about the herd.

Presently the wolves returned to the shade; the white-painted hunters ran away; the animals walked off to the opening of the wings, and then the grass buffalo returned part way toward the shade, while the others stood about and whistled.

A lodge-pole was brought up in front of the shade. White Frog and wife showed Frank Little Wolf and wife how to take up the lodge-pole with four motions, and with four motions to thrust it through a sheet of dried meat.

White Frog placed four buffalo-chips on the ground in front of the shade so as to form a small rectangle. He called Spotted Elk and spat on his hands, and then Spotted Elk, with four motions, placed his right hand on the northwesterly chip, and then his other hand, and his feet on the three others. He was thus standing on all fours, head to the west, in a very uncomfortable position. He still wore the yellow wolf-skin.

With four motions the lodge-pole with meat attached was raised north of Spotted Elk and fastened there, leaning against the front of the shade. The fox men were constantly running about. The man wearing the coyote-skin, with four motions, after four trials, crept under Spotted Elk's belly, and the swift fox, after running under the pole bearing the sheet of meat and jumping at it four times, at the fourth jump snatched the meat and carried it off. All this should have been done.

The priest who had instructed the fox had told him that in trying to secure the meat he must jump three times, and the fourth time must seize it. The man who had charge of the pole from which the meat hung raised it three times so that the fox missed, but on the fourth trial he caught the meat. It was the law, and the fox was so instructed, that the fox should watch the coyote, who ought to have made three beginnings to crawl

332

under the wolf and to have gone under it at the fourth endeavor. Each time the coyote made a beginning to crawl under the wolf it was the duty of the fox to jump for the meat, but on this occasion a mistake was made, such as is not known ever to have occurred before. The coyote actually crawled under the wolf four times.

The securing of the meat by the fox represents the getting of buffalo; that is, the procuring of food. According to rule, the Contraries should have snatched the meat from the fox, but on this occasion they did not do so. After the meat was taken by the fox, he ran around to each group of animals, and then ran back to the shade and threw the meat among the singers.

The coyote having crawled under Spotted Elk four times, after the fourth passage White Frog went to Spotted Elk, lifted him up, and took away the chips on which he had been resting. The operation of creeping under the yellow wolf is called "passing through" and marks the end of the ceremony.

The animals now gathered in a group between the wings, and the women and old men who had been sitting under the shade walked toward them. Now the animals by groups marched off to go to the stream. The wolves went on the north side of the procession; the deer led; the grass buffalo and the black buffalo were in the center. They went outside the camp-circle and marched east and around to the south toward the stream. Most of the camp followed, marching on either side and behind the company, but no one in front of it. On the hills round about were groups of brightly clad women and children, who stood and watched the procession.

Presently, when the head of the column was within a quarter of a mile of the stream, at a call all the animals broke into a run and raced to see who could bring back to the woman— Frank Little Wolf's wife—a drink of water in his mouth. After all had disappeared over the hill, Eugene Standing Elk and two others were seen running back. Eugene reached the woman first and gave her a drink from his mouth, and the two other men gave water to Frank Little Wolf in the same way. All now marched on to the stream where all drank, and many went into the water and washed themselves.

When the start was made by the different people to get water, each man strained hard to be the victor. It was believed that the first man going to the stream, getting water, and giving it to the woman, had the best prospect of counting a coup when next he went to war. In this case the winning man was a Chief Soldier; his victory gave the luck to his band. This victory was won by an unfair trick, however.

Afterward the procession reformed, and with less order marched back as it had come, the old men singing.

The Contraries still pretended to hunt, and the black buffalo charged out on them and occasionally caught and killed one. Every now and then a buffalo-cow seemed to be hit with an arrow and staggered about and was supported by a bull which tried to hold her up and help her. The march continued back to within the wings, and from this point, almost at once, the animals dispersed, going off by bands. The old men, Frank Little Wolf and wife, and the two wolves entered the shade, the wolves sitting at the extreme south. Bobtail Horse lighted the sacred pipe which he received from Frank Little Wolf's wife. It was smoked out, and the ceremony was ended.

INTERPRETATIONS

The different groups of animals which appear in this ceremony come from different lodges scattered all about the circle of the camp. On this particular occasion the animals seen were buffalo, elk, deer, wolf, coyote, and fox, but other animals might and should have been there, as, for example, horses, cranes, antelope, bears, mountain-lions, bands of wolves and coyotes, blackbirds, and a red fox.

In old times many species were represented, and the people standing for each imitated the actions of that species. The bear used to go stealthily about, trying to approach near enough to some animal to make a rush and catch it; the mountain-lion would creep and creep and then make a long jump—perhaps twenty feet—and catch a young boy, a calf. The lodge of the yellow wolf, called also the eating wolf (*Mēh' wā wōh' nē*), was the most important of all the lodges, and it was here that the most important ceremonies already detailed were performed. The lodge of the gray wolf, called also the horned wolf (*Ē wĭs' sī wōh nē*), was the next in importance.

The men who were in charge of all the different groups of animals that were to take part in the public ceremonies must send word to the chief priest of the wolf lodge and ask from him permission to take part in the ceremonies.

These different groups of animals usually had their origin in a dream. Some man may have dreamed that he saw some animal—a deer, a buffalo, or some other mammal or bird—acting in a peculiar way, and that this animal gave him the power to perform certain mysterious (supernatural) acts. He announced to some close friend or relative, perhaps to some member of his soldier society, that this power had been given him, and the two talked the matter over. Perhaps the friend may have agreed to assist him who had the dream. Other people were taken into the confidence of the dreamer, and at length a little group of people was formed who would help the man in what he was to undertake. No doubt different motives influenced the various people who joined the group; these may have been their friendship for the man, or a belief that their action would bring them health or other good fortune.

The man who had dreamed may perhaps have felt that he had been given the power to shoot and wound a man so as to cause blood to flow from his mouth, and then to heal the wound; how to prepare for such an act, and what ceremonies to perform to achieve success. The ceremonies attached to the different groups, their dress, and their painting were determined by the dream of the man who organized each.

It may have happened that more than one man had dreamed

335

about buffalo, elk, or deer, in which event there may have been two or more groups representing those animals.

The man who wore the wolf-skin selected his own successor. Formerly American Horse wore it, and he chose Spotted Elk to follow him. Spotted Elk had worn it four times.

Mrs. J. E. Tuell

MASSAUM CEREMONY
YELLOW WOLF GOING OUT

THE CULTURE HEROES

THE entertainment of the Cheyennes was chiefly social, and consisted largely of narratives of adventure, of accounts of the achievements of mythical heroes, of explanations of natural phenomena, and of tales about animals which in ancient days seem to have been half beast or bird and half human. An opportunity may occur some day to publish these stories, but they are far too voluminous to be printed here.

Many of the Cheyenne tales closely resemble those of other Western Algonquians, especially those of the Blackfeet; and Cheyenne men to whom some of these Blackfeet stories—especially those about Napi—have been read, say, "Why, those are our own stories with the names changed a little."

It may be said, however, that of the tales found among the Cheyennes, the creation story and the stories of the culture hero are obviously the most important. These alone will be herein incorporated.[1]

Since the Cheyennes, as before stated, are made up of two related tribes—Suhtai and Tsistsistas—they have two culture heroes and two mysterious objects which these personages brought into the tribe. These two objects—the medicine arrows (Mahuts) and the buffalo hat (Issiwun)—are equally reverenced by all members of the tribe, no matter what their descent.

The creation story speaks of a person floating on the water which then covered the whole earth. All about him were swans, geese, ducks, and other water birds. These had already been created, and of their origin nothing is said. The person called

[1] See also *Journal of American Folk-Lore,* vol. xx, pp. 169-194, July-September, 1907, and vol. xxi, pp. 269-320, October-December, 1908.

some of these birds and directed them to look for some earth. One after another the birds dived into the water to try to reach the bottom and find earth; but none was successful until at length a small blue duck[2] that had dived came to the surface with a little mud in its bill. This duck swam to the man, who took the mud from it and worked the wet earth with his fingers until he had made it dry. Then he put little piles of the earth on the water at different places near him, and these became land which spread out and grew and grew until, as far as could be seen, all was solid land. Thus was created the dry land—the earth.

This story resembles other Algonquian genesis myths, but the introduction of the duck suggests an element found in the Arikara creation story.

After the earth had been made, a man and a woman were created and placed upon it. When the creator, Heammawihio, made the man, he formed him from a rib taken from his own right side; and then from the left side of the man he took a rib, from which he created the woman. These two persons were made at the same place; but after they had been created, they were put apart, the woman being placed in the North, and the man in the South. The creator said to them that where he had placed the woman it would be for the most part cold, and the animals and birds where she was would be different from those found where the man was; but that in summer the birds living in the South would go north. The woman in the North, though she had gray hair, was not old, and never grew older. The man in the South was young, and he grew no older. The woman controls Hoimaha, commonly spoken of as the Winter Man, or the storm, the power that brings cold and snow, and also sickness and death. The man in the South, who probably represents the sun, controls the Thunder.

[2] The bird here called duck is described as the coot or mud-hen, *Fulica*, and the identification is made certain by frequent references to the white spot at the base of the bill.

There is conflict between Hoimaha and the Thunder; and the Thunder furnished to the culture hero fire as a weapon to use against cold and storm. Twice a year there is a struggle between the Thunder and the Winter Man—the changes of the seasons. At the end of summer, Hoimaha comes down from the north and drives the Thunder back to the south; but toward spring, when the days begin to grow longer, the Thunder returns from the south and forces the Winter Man back to his place. When the Thunder comes up from the south, he brings with him the rain and the warm weather, and the grass grows and the earth becomes green.

It is suggestive that the paintings on the skin lodges of the Blackfeet in the olden times often showed on a lodge large figures of the male and female of some species of animal, with the male painted on the south side of the lodge and the female on the north side.

Apparently earlier than the culture-hero story is that of Ehyophstah, Yellow-haired Woman, through whose influence the buffalo were first brought to the people. After a time, however, Yellow-haired Woman disobeyed the instructions of her father, and for this reason the buffalo disappeared and were not seen again. Apparently they had been forgotten, and the Cheyennes, who were in some northern country where there were many lakes, depended for their flesh-food on wild fowl and small animals.

The myths which deal with the second coming of the buffalo and the bringing of corn to the people relate that these things were brought by two similarly dressed young men, one of whom was the Suhtai and the other the Cheyenne culture hero. The name given for the Cheyenne culture hero is commonly Sweet Medicine, Sweet Root Standing, or Rustling Corn Leaf; while the Suhtai culture hero is known as Red Tassel (of corn), Erect Horns, or Standing On The Ground. These men met for the first time not long before they, together, brought to the people these good things. In the account here given paragraphs

339

are taken from different versions of the tale to make a connected story. The more extended account is found in the place cited.

In the center of the great camp many people were gathered. Two men were playing the wheel game and others were looking on and betting on the game. From different sides of the camp, two young men approached the group of people and stood watching the game. Presently each saw the other, and saw that he was dressed and painted precisely like himself. For some time they watched each other, and at last walked toward each other, and one said to the other: "Friend, you seem to be imitating me. Are you trying to mock me?" The other replied, "That is just what I was thinking about you; I thought you were making fun of my dress."

"Where did you get your dress?" said one.

"Where did you learn yours?" replied the other.

The man addressed pointed to a great white bluff that could be seen far off, and said, "I learned it in that big hill over there, where there is an overhanging cliff and a stream of water pouring out."

"Why," said the other, "that is where I got mine; the very place you tell of."

Both young men were astonished. One said: "Well, we will let the people know. Let us go together to that place and try to do something for the people—to bring them something that will help them. We are drawing near to that hill and, when the camp reaches it, we will ask an old man to cry out to the people that we are going in there. They can look at us and see us go in."

They went to the old man and told him what they purposed to do, and said to him, "The second camp from here, when we are so close to the butte that a man at its foot can be easily seen, tell the people that my friend and I are going in there to get something."

When the camp had been made near the butte, two lodges

were pitched in the center of the circle and white sage was spread on the floor of each. The people all followed the two young men toward the butte; but when they had come near it, all stopped, except these two who went on.

When they were near the bluff, the two stopped and put their robes on the ground, and walked to the place where the water fell from the cliff. Each one wished the other to go in first, but at last they went in together, side by side, and the people saw them disappear under the water.

When the first man came up under the spring, he saw sitting beneath the hill a very old woman. As he stepped in, she said to him, "Come in, my grandchild," and took him in her arms and held him for a moment, and made him sit down at her left. To the other she said, "Come in, my grandchild," and took him in her arms and held him, and made him sit at her right side. She said to them: "Why did you not come sooner? Why have you gone hungry so long? Now that you have come, I must do something for your people."

Near her stood two earthen jars which she brought out and set before her, and filled two dishes, one with buffalo meat and one with corn. She offered these to the young men, saying, "Come, my children, eat the meat first." They ate it fast, for it was good; but when they had eaten all they could, the dish was still full. It was the same with the cooked corn; they could not empty the dishes. They were full when the young men stopped, and did not show that anything had been taken from them.

The old woman untied the feathers the young men had on their heads, and threw them in the fire. She painted each man with red paint, and on each one painted the sun and the moon, in yellow. Then she stretched her hand out over the fire; and when she took it away, she held two down-feathers painted red, and tied one to the scalp-lock of each young man.

Presently she pointed to her left and said, "Look that way!" They looked, and saw the earth covered with buffalo. The dust

341

was flying up in clouds where the bulls were fighting. Then she pointed partly behind her, and said, "Look this way!" and they saw great fields of growing corn. She pointed again, to her right, and said, "Look that way!" and they saw the prairies covered with horses.[3] The stallions were fighting, and there was much movement. Again she pointed, and said, "Look that way again!" and as they looked they saw Indians fighting and, looking closely, they saw among the fighters themselves, painted just as they then were. The old woman said to them: "You will always be victorious in your fights; you will have good luck and will make many captives. When you go away from here, go to the center of your village, ask for two big bowls, and have them wiped out clean. Say to your people: 'Women and children and all bands of the societies, we have come out to make you happy. We have brought out something wonderful to give you.' Say to your people that when the sun goes down, I will send out buffalo." To each young man she gave some corn and some meat, and told them to carry the corn in one hand and the meat in the other, and to go back to their people. Before they left, the old woman told them that the oldest men and women were to eat first. Then the two young men went out from under the water.

One version says that she gave the meat to Sweet Medicine, and told him that the buffalo would follow him out of the hill; and that she gave the corn to Standing On The Ground, saying that his people should always have it among them.

When the people saw them coming, they sat down in order, waiting for them. The men sat in front, and behind them the women, and then the children. Standing On The Ground first passed along the lines with the bowl of corn, and Sweet Medicine followed with the meat. As they passed along, each person took the left hand full of corn and the right hand full of meat; and all ate. But although so many people ate, the food in the

---

[3] The reference to horses is of course a comparatively recent interpolation, as horses were not acquired until after the coming of white people.

342

bowls did not diminish. At last, when all had been fed, that which remained in the dishes was put before an old man and an old woman, and they consumed it all. After they had finished eating, Standing On The Ground stepped out before the line, and said: "This is what my grandmother told me. She said that we must take care of the corn and not give it away. If we take care of it and plant it and always look after it, there will always be something for us to eat." He told them what the old woman had explained about planting the corn in the spring of the year; and when he had finished speaking, he stepped to one side. Then Sweet Medicine stood up, and said: "Our grandmother will make for us plenty of what you have eaten [meaning the flesh of all sorts of animals]. When you eat these animals you will be healthy; there will be no sickness among you."

Standing On The Ground said: "The reason I gave the old man the corn last is that when the corn has grown ripe it will turn white, and old men have white hair. The men shall plant and cultivate the corn."

Sweet Medicine said, "The reason I gave the meat to the old woman is that the women shall take care of the skins and flesh of the animals, shall cut up the meat, and tan the hides."

The two young men called out and chose two boys whom they sent to the top of a hill to watch to see whether they could see buffalo. That night the buffalo began to come out of the hill—so many that they frightened all the people in the camp and spread over the whole country. In the morning these young men came back and said that the buffalo were all over the land and close about the camp. Then people went out and killed buffalo and brought in the meat; and as the buffalo moved away, the people moved their camp and followed them. In the spring they moved to a good place to plant corn, and planted it for four years; but in the fifth year the Arikaras came to the camp while the Cheyennes were off hunting, and stole the corn.

After that, Standing On The Ground went back to Old

Woman's Water, and went in to see the old woman; and she gave him the sacred hat which he brought to the camp, and about the care of which he advised the people. It was while Standing On The Ground was instructing the young man he had chosen to care for the hat, that someone came into the lodge with a bad cough; and Standing On The Ground told the young man that this was something that could not be avoided. Disease goes everywhere. The sick man said, "You speak the truth; I have many sorts of diseases, and I carry them to everyone."

About Sweet Medicine, the Cheyenne culture hero, there are many stories. He brought the medicine arrows to the Cheyennes, as Standing On The Ground brought the buffalo hat to the Suhtai. Some of the stories say that these two heroes were in the sacred lodge of the maiyun at the same time, and received then the two mysteries which they afterward took to their people. Some of the tales even say that, at this same time, their mysteries were received by the culture heroes of the Sioux and of the Arapahoes.

The spirits which taught Standing On The Ground and Sweet Medicine the secrets of these tribal mysteries are of two classes—the Listeners Above, *Hea'mma măĭyŭn' tsiă'stomŭni,* and the Listeners Under The Ground, *Astu'no măĭyŭn' tsiă'stomŭni.* Those who actually gave the instructions are said to have been the Listeners Under The Ground, who appear to be somewhat more powerful than the Listeners Above. These last are helpers, still with us on the earth, who watch us and see what we are doing, and help us to carry out the instructions of the Listeners Under The Ground.

Sweet Medicine is the culture hero best known among the Cheyennes, and the longest and most detailed stories are told about him. To him is credited the establishment of four of the soldier bands, the other three of which had a later origin. Sweet Medicine instituted also the Massaum or Crazy Dance, and brought the medicine arrows. Standing On The Ground established the Medicine Lodge.

There are many versions of the story of Sweet Medicine, but for the most detailed one the reader is referred to the *Journal of American Folk-Lore,* above cited.

THE STORY OF SWEET MEDICINE

This woman was married. Her second child she called Sweet Medicine. When the boy was a baby, he seemed to know everything that people were saying about him; and when he grew up to be about five years of age, he seemed very precocious. He surprised people by knowing so much. After he had learned to talk, he said: "Father, on your next hunt kill a yellow calf for me. Skin it, taking the whole skin, head and all. I need a robe. I want a robe to wear."

His father brought him in the whole skin of a calf, and his mother dressed it, and he wore it with the hair-side out. The next year he told his father to go and kill him a larger calf, a yearling; to skin it in the same way; and he had his mother dress it with the head on. A year or two later he told his father to select a coal-black buffalo, for he wanted a black robe. The boy had the power to make his father find the kind of robe he wanted. When he got the black robe, he took more pride in himself, and painted with red paint, as was the custom. He was now a good-sized boy.

In early times the people had the power to do wonderful things. They used to make spiritual dances, to show what power they had and what they could do. When they had one of these spiritual dances, they put up a big lodge where the spiritual men were to dance. All around the border of this were drawn small circles, each of which represented the seat of a spiritual man. He sat there facing inward, looking toward the center. All the people sitting at his left hand were under his control as far as the next circle, where sat another spiritual man, who ruled the people to his left as far as the next circle; and so on around,

345

as far as the fifth circle, which was at the northeastern side of the lodge.

Now at this time they were making ready to have a spiritual dance; and when all had been made ready, Sweet Medicine said, "Father, I am going to this dance, to dance myself."

His father said to him: "Son, these people who make these dances have power, and must show what they can do. You are only a boy; you can do nothing."

Sweet Medicine said: "I shall go, anyway, and shall wear my new buffalo-robe. I shall carry your bow, and its string shall be about my neck." His father said, "What are you going to do with a bowstring around your neck?" The boy answered: "I am going to break my neck. Also I must have my buffalo-robe painted red. I wish you to paint me just as I tell you."

His father then painted him from head to foot with red paint; and Sweet Medicine took the bowstring, and himself painted it red. His father asked him, "Son, what am I to do if you break your neck?" Sweet Medicine replied: "After I have pulled my head from my body, my head will fall to the ground, but my body will still stand up. Then you take my body, and lay it down with my head toward where the sun rises; then put my head next to my body, in its place, with the head toward the sunrise. Then cover me with my robe."

When his father took Sweet Medicine to the door of the lodge, a number of people were standing there, looking on. The boy had an eagle-feather in his hair. The people called out, "Sweet Medicine is coming!" and they followed him.

When they had come to the door of the lodge, the father said to the spiritual men there, "My son wishes to dance." Some of the men inside called out, "Yes, come in!" and asked him on which side of the lodge he would sit—the right side, the left side, or the back part of the lodge. He chose the right-hand side. Some of the great men came in after he was sitting, but all noticed him. There was plenty of cooked buffalo-meat in the lodge. Sweet Medicine was then about seventeen years of age.

After a little they started the sacred dance. Sweet Medicine danced the first dance, keeping time with his bowstring in both hands. Some of the men with great power, who were looking on, said to one another, "Sweet Medicine is one of the greatest dancers we have." They had a smoke and another dance; then they all sat until the third dance. Sweet Medicine kept time with his bowstring around his neck; and the first thing they knew, his head fell to the ground. His eyes were open, and he was looking about at the people. His body was standing, his bowstring still in his hands.

All the people outside were frightened; and they called out to one another, "Sweet Medicine has broken his neck!" All the people who were in the lodge sat down, and the dancing stopped.

Sweet Medicine's father took the boy's body and placed it on the ground, and put back the head in its place, lying toward where the sun rises, and covered him with his robe.

After a little time, Sweet Medicine raised the buffalo-robe from his body, stood up and faced the sunrise, and took his robe in both hands and shook it lightly four times toward the sunrise; and when he stopped, a cool breeze came from the north. The people said, "Sweet Medicine has called that wind from the north." Then Sweet Medicine went over and sat down at the right of the door, and rubbed his bowstring down four times. They all feasted.

From that time Sweet Medicine always dressed in the same way. He wore a two-year-old buffalo-robe. At that time the tribe seems to have been moving constantly, and Sweet Medicine appears to have had the power to keep them moving. Once a party of young men came in, and said that at the place whence they had come there were many buffalo. The camp moved over there; but when they got to the place, no buffalo could be found. Then the people began to say, "Sweet Medicine is doing this; he has the power to keep the buffalo away."

One day the whole tribe surrounded the buffalo, and killed

many. The meat was cut up, but they could not bring it all to camp that night. They left some on the prairie where it was killed. The next day they went out to bring the rest into camp, and the great chief went out also to get what he had killed. Many buffalo-calves, and young buffalo, that had been frightened away the day before, had come back to the place.

Sweet Medicine said to himself: "I will go out to this place and find a two-year-old buffalo, to get a robe from. My robe is getting old and worn."

As he was going along through the timber, he saw some buffalo coming, and sat down and waited. Presently he looked up, and saw near him the very one he wanted—a coal-black buffalo. When he got near enough, Sweet Medicine arose, and shot it as it went by. After his arrow had gone into the buffalo, it went only a little way and fell, and Sweet Medicine turned it on its back to skin it. This was apart from the big herd. Some-one who saw him said to another, "Who is that man skinning the buffalo?" The other said, "I do not know." Others said, "That is Sweet Medicine skinning the buffalo." Now, Sweet Medicine was skinning the animal very carefully, so as not to cut the hide, for he wanted a robe without a hole in it. The buffalo was two years old, and he skinned it, head and all. While Sweet Medicine was at work, the great chief walked down toward him, and said: "Sweet Medicine, I am glad that you killed that buffalo. My robe is wearing out, and I want one just like this."

"No, my friend," replied Sweet Medicine, "this is just what I want. My robe is wearing out too. You can take the meat, my friend, if you please; you can see how fat it is. All I want is the robe." All this time he was skinning the animal.

Then the chief said: "I mean what I say. I want the hide." Sweet Medicine laughed, and said, "I will help you to cut up the meat." And now, having cut the hide off, he placed it to one side, and both together began to cut up the meat. After a little while the great chief left the meat, and went over and commenced to scrape the blood from the hide. After scraping away the blood he went over to where the meat was.

While they were butchering, Sweet Medicine had cut off a part of the hind leg, and had cut the tendons about the foot, so that the foot hung loose. While the great chief was stooping over the buffalo, pulling out the entrails, Sweet Medicine struck him on the back of the neck with the foot, and knocked him senseless, saying to him, "Now you may keep the hide."

Someone who had seen it, called out, "Sweet Medicine has killed our great chief!" Those who were near rushed to where the chief lay. They raised him up and poured water on his face, and presently he came to life again. After they had all seen him stand up, word of what had happened was sent to the camp, and all the young soldiers turned out. They began to look for Sweet Medicine. No one knew which way he had gone. Someone said, "He has gone toward the north." So the soldiers started, and spread out in a wide line. After going a little way, some of the young men in the middle of the line found Sweet Medicine's track; but after following it for a time they lost the track; then they scattered, and searched through the timber and everywhere along the stream, but they could not find him. Then some of the people said, "He must have turned and gone back toward camp." So they returned to the camp. They went to his lodge, and searched it. They went to his relations' lodges, and searched them; but his relations said he had not yet come back. Then they put out guards, who should stand all around the camp, and other guards around Sweet Medicine's lodge and his father's lodge to stay all night. But Sweet Medicine did not return.

The camp moved to another place, but still he did not come; and the people thought that he had gone away to some other place. After the camp had been moving for four days, and still Sweet Medicine did not return, some of the people said, "Sweet Medicine must have gone south, and found some other people."

For some days the camp had been moving, when one of the

men who had been out looking for his dogs saw Sweet Medicine sleeping under a tree, in some timber. The man did not wake him, but went quietly around to the camp, and told the people that Sweet Medicine was sleeping on the divide.

All the soldiers of the camp turned out to go to the place and surround it, and kill Sweet Medicine. They crept up close to the place, and then rushed toward him, calling out to him, "Now we've got you!" But Sweet Medicine heard them coming, and awoke, and jumped up and ran away. When he started to run, they called out again, "Now we have you!" But they could not quite overtake him; he kept just ahead of them, and after running a little way, he disappeared behind a clump of trees and brush; and when the soldiers had passed beyond these, they saw him again on the prairie, a long way off.

But he was running as if he were tired, and they thought they would surely catch him. He ran across the ravine, along the stream; and after running a long way, they saw ahead of him a thick growth of trees. He seemed to be running for that, yet making a circle, so as to have easier going. Some of the soldiers cut across to head him off, running over high bluffs and cutbanks. When Sweet Medicine saw that they were going to get to the timber ahead of him, he turned, and, running behind a point of the timber, disappeared; and when they saw him again, he was far off on the hill. The soldiers could not understand how he got so far away so quickly.

He still ran as though he were very tired and could not go much farther. The soldiers followed him on the open prairie; and he turned to a very high hill, which was flat on top, but had very steep sides. He began to climb the hill, going zigzag, back and forth across the face of the hill; and now the soldiers thought that they would overtake him, and said one to another: "Now, we will get him! We will bring him down and punish him! We will whip him to death!" When Sweet Medicine had reached the top of the hill, the soldiers were at the bottom, starting up. They went up, just as he had done; and when they reached the top of the hill, Sweet Medicine was a long way off, going up another high white sandstone butte. When he had reached the top, he sat down. The soldiers did not understand how he had reached there so quickly. They were tired from running; and they sat down, and called over to him, "We will get you some day!" Soon the soldiers stood up, and Sweet Medicine stood up; but the soldiers went back down the hill toward the camp. Sweet Medicine went down from the butte he was on; and the soldiers, looking back, saw him going away from them very quickly. They gave up the pursuit and went back to the camp.

After some days the camp moved again. Sweet Medicine had not been seen, although all the people were looking out for him. When they moved, they crossed the stream and camped on the other side. After they had made camp, one of the young men, following behind, saw a man coming on the trail, and, after watching him, went in and reported that Sweet Medicine was following the trail toward the camp. All the men came together, and, after separating into two parties, they hid themselves on each side of the trail. They said to one another: "Now, he cannot escape! This time we shall surely catch him!" The prairie coming to the stream where they had crossed was level. Up the creek the water was deep, and at the trail and farther down there was a good crossing. Sweet Medicine came to the stream, and took off his moccasins and began to roll up his leggings. When they saw him do that, the soldiers whispered to one another: "Wait until he drinks, and has filled himself with water. We shall now have him between us, and he cannot get away."

Sweet Medicine began to walk across the creek; and when he was in the middle of the stream, he tucked his moccasins under his belt, and began to drink from his hands. After drinking, he took water in his hand and put it on his head to cool himself. The soldiers were not close to the trail, but were near enough to reach it very soon. When they saw Sweet Medicine

351

come out on their side of the stream, the people called out, "We have him now!" Sweet Medicine had turned down the stream; but when he saw the people were after him, he turned and ran up the creek as swift as an arrow. This was the first time the people had seen him running. He ran up the creek, passing all of them; and after he came to the ravines running down into the stream, they saw that they could not catch him, and gave up.

It was nearly a year before he was seen again, and the people now say that he came back to have a little fun with the tribe.

The camp was in a circle facing the sunrise, on the west side of a stream which flowed north. Sweet Medicine came to the river below the camp, and wandered up the bank a long way. His moccasins and leggings were all worn out. He came to a place where he saw his father and mother standing together, outside of their lodge, on the other side of the camp from him. He saw also his brother's wife standing by the lodge. The sun was just going down. Between him and the camp was a large clump of plum-brush. He crept up toward the lodge, behind the plum-bushes. Near them some little boys were playing about; and Sweet Medicine said to the largest boy: "Tell my sister-in-law that I am here, and that I am hungry. Ask her to get me something to eat." The little boy went to the woman, and said to her: "Sweet Medicine is there behind the bushes. He is hungry, and asks you to get him something to eat." The woman said to the boy: "Do not speak the name of Sweet Medicine any more. The people are watching for him." The little boy went back and told Sweet Medicine what his sister-in-law said; and Sweet Medicine said, "I will stay here in the bushes until she gets something cooked for me." He kept the boys playing there near him. After a while he sent the oldest boy to see if the meal was ready; and the boy came back and said, "Your food is ready." Sweet Medicine stood up, pulled his robe over his head, and walked to the lodge without being noticed by any-one, although the whole camp was watching for him. As he

MASSAUM CEREMONY

CONTRARIES

MASSAUM CEREMONY

THE GRASS BUFFALO

approached, his father said to those about him: "Keep still! Do not notice him or speak to him, so as to make anyone look this way." His mother had new moccasins, new leggings, and a new robe, that she had made a long time before to give to him whenever he should come in. His sister-in-law gave him the new moccasins, leggings, and robe, and said: "Put these on right away. The soldiers are looking for you, and say that they will kill you." After he had dressed, he painted himself with red paint, and put an eagle down-feather in his hair. He said to his sister-in-law: "Make a big fire and put the kettle on, and make me some soup, and keep it boiling. I am going to sleep." Before he went to sleep, his sister-in-law brought in a sack of dried meat and gave it to him, saying that perhaps he might need it in his wanderings.

When he had entered his father's lodge, two strange women were there. His father begged the two strange women not to say to anyone that Sweet Medicine was at home, as he was tired and wanted to rest. Just as soon as these women went out, they told everyone they met that they had seen Sweet Medicine in his father's lodge. All this time the kettle was boiling, and it was growing dark.

When the soldiers heard of this, they went about quietly and told one another that Sweet Medicine was in the camp. They surrounded the lodge. The chief soldier kept calling out to the young men to close up, so that Sweet Medicine could not break through the line or get away. They said, "Now we will bring him out and whip him to death!" While they were calling out, Sweet Medicine awoke and heard them, and rose from his bed, and took the kettle of soup and poured it on the fire. The ashes and steam rose in a thick cloud; and the eagle-feather in his hair had the power to carry him up and out through the smoke hole, and set him on his feet outside the ring of soldiers. The soldiers made a charge on the lodge, but they could not find him. He was gone.

Several days after that, a young man who was out hunting

came to the edge of a cutbank; and as he looked down into the ravine below, he saw Sweet Medicine roasting some meat. The young man spoke to him, saying, "You are roasting meat, are you not?" Sweet Medicine did not answer him or raise his head. The man turned and went back to the camp. It was a big village; and all the people were told that Sweet Medicine was down the creek, roasting meat. The place where he had his fire was under a high cutbank, shaped like a horseshoe. In front of it there was timber, and behind and on either side a cut cliff. All the people turned out and surrounded the timber, and closed in toward the cutbank; for there was no way to climb this bank, and they thought he could not escape. They charged toward him, calling out, "Now we have you!" When they came to the fire, no one was there. Sweet Medicine was gone, but no one had seen him go. Presently someone said, "There goes a coyote down the creek." That was all that was seen. When they could not find him, some said, "Let us look for the tracks where he came in." They found a low place where his tracks were seen coming down the stream and to the fire. The tracks came up from the creek to the place where he had built the fire, but they could find none leading away from there. None could say where he had gone out.

The camp moved again; and after traveling about for a time, they camped on another stream, on which there were much heavy timber and thick willows. Under a cutbank, where he could not be seen, where thick willows were all about him in front, Sweet Medicine made a fire. A man saw smoke coming up from the timber, and, going out to find what made the smoke, he peeped over the bank and saw Sweet Medicine roasting meat by his fire. He went back and told the camp what he had seen. All the men went out quickly, and surrounded the timber, where he could not see them. They stole up close to where he was—so close that they could see him by the fire. Then the head man called out to the young men to rush upon him. They said, "We have got him this time, and now we will beat him to death!" When they reached the fire, meat was roasting over it, but no one was near. The only living thing they saw was a great night-owl, which flew up the bank and alighted on top, right over where the fire was. By this time the camp was always on the watch for Sweet Medicine.

The people had moved again, and had been traveling about for more than one moon, when they camped on another stream, which had cutbanks, and thick timber in the bottom. Sweet Medicine was in the timber, near a cutbank which formed a half-circle, where he was hidden from sight; but a man who was out from the timber saw him, and told it in camp, and the soldiers went out and surrounded the place. They thought they would surely catch him this time, as there was no place for him to get away. When they rushed forward, and reached the fire, no one was there. The only thing they saw was a magpie, that flew up in the top of a tree near the fire, and began to call to them. When they found that Sweet Medicine was gone, the soldiers and the people went away; but they said, "We will still keep watch for Sweet Medicine."

Again the camp moved, and after a time stopped on another stream. A man who was out looking around saw, as he was passing a high bank, smoke rising from the timber. He looked over, and saw heavy timber and logs piled up, one on another, and Sweet Medicine roasting meat by a little fire near a cutbank. When the man went to camp and told what he had seen, the head men and soldiers said to one another, "This time we will do differently." They put guards all about outside of the timber, so that when Sweet Medicine came out they could head him off. They charged through the timber, and felt sure they had him now; but when they reached the fire, he was not there, but a timber blackbird flew up into the trees. A man said, "Nothing but a timber blackbird went away from this place."

The camp moved up the stream and camped on the same creek. One day after they had been camped a short time, a man who was out hunting came upon Sweet Medicine roasting a piece of meat by a small fire. The man hurried to camp and spread the news. The head men put double guards around the timber where he was, and then charged in toward the fire. The head men called out: "Close in fast, so that he cannot escape! We have got him now!" When they reached the fire there was nothing there except the fire; but a very red bird flew up and alighted in a tree near by. The people all returned to camp, wondering why they could not get him.

All this was not done in a short time; it took several years. The last few times that Sweet Medicine was seen, he was naked. He must have left his clothes behind him.

After this, Sweet Medicine must have made up his mind to show himself in plain sight of all the people. He dressed himself up, and painted himself all over with red paint. He had buffalo-beards tied to each of his moccasins; they hung down under his heels. A wooden whistle was tied about his neck with a string. Across his forehead he had tied a night-owl skin and feathers. He carried a Contrary bow, with a little red bird tied on the end. He had the Contrary forked stick, with one prong longer than the other. Tied to the bow, in three different places, were five eagle-feathers—two on each end, and one in the middle; and where he held the bow when shooting was tied a bundle of white sage. On each side of his hand hung two dried bear-guts; so that when he came in sight, he was in the very dress of a Contrary. The only thing that was not painted was his bow: this was clear white wood, with a pure white string. He came from the way the sun rises, toward the opening in the circle; but when he was near the opening, he turned to his left hand and went south, to the southeastern part of the camp, where he marked a circle. Then he passed around it to the southwest corner of the camp, and marked another circle; then to the northwest border, where he made another circle; then to the north side, where he made another circle; and then to the northeast side, where he made a circle. All this time he kept blowing his wooden whistle, and all the time he was moving along. All the people were out watching him, but at first they did not know him in this strange dress. After he had reached the northeast side of the camp, they recognized him; and they all said: "Why, that is Sweet Medicine! He is going through too many foolish things. We will rush upon him!" The camp charged on him; and he started off and ran, taking long steps. The people all ran after him; but all seemed to grow tired very soon, and sat down to rest. A great many of them got cramps in their legs, and could not run.

Some time after this he appeared again. This time, when he came in sight, they knew him. He wore a headdress with raven-feathers standing up around the head, and a row of eagle-feathers from the middle of his forehead, over his neck, to the back. He carried a rattle, painted red all over, with antelope-hoofs tied on the handle. About his neck was a string to which was tied a bone whistle. Over his left shoulder, and across his breast, and down on his right side, was a dog rope, which trailed on the ground. It was covered with feathers, in rows, one above another. He was painted red all over. This time he appeared in the same place, and walked around the camp, as he had done before, making the same circles at the same places as before, and blowing his bone whistle all the time. When he reached the place at the northeast side of the camp, where they had chased him away before, someone said: "Here he is again! He is always doing something. Let us try once more to catch him, and whip him to death!" They ran after him; but he went off to the north, running easily. They could not overtake him.

The camp moved, and traveled about for a year before they saw Sweet Medicine again. This time, when he appeared, he had raven-feathers in his bonnet, and the same rattle, but was painted black all over. As before, he came in sight from where the sun rises, and walked toward the circle, and took the same road around the camp as before, making the same turns and the same circles, until he reached the northeast side of the

357

camp, when some of the men said, "There is Sweet Medicine again!" They went after him, but could not catch him; he went off to the north.

It was a long time, more than a year, before Sweet Medicine was seen again. The camp had moved many times, and traveled a long distance. This time Sweet Medicine wore a long war-bonnet with small buffalo-horns on each side, and a white shield with feathers fastened all over it. He was well dressed, with moccasins, leggings, and a deerskin war shirt. In his hand he carried a crooked lance, the handle covered with otter-skin. Two eagle-feathers were tied to the crooked end, and five eagle-feathers at different places along the handle. He came in sight from the same direction as before, and went through the same motions. They let him get to the same point that he had reached before; and then the people said, "There is that fellow again, coming around camp with his work." They all started after him; but he went off easily, and they could not overtake him.

Again he was gone for a long time; and when he returned, it was from the same direction as before. This time he was painted black, with a little red. He had a short spear, which he used for a cane, and on the top of the spear was a place for a hand-hold. He wore a war shirt, the upper half painted black, and carried a bone whistle. About the spear ribbons were tied. The people had never seen ribbons before, and did not know what they were, nor where he got them. He went around the camp, as he had done before, and did the same things, and stopped at the same places. The soldiers chased him away again, but could not get near him.

The next time he was seen he came toward the camp wearing a cap made of the skin of a buffalo's head, with the horns left on, and the skin drawn tight over his head, so that only his face was seen. About his waist was a piece of buffalo-hide for a belt; and a buffalo-tail was fastened behind, hanging down. He was painted with white clay, and had some white clay in his hair, and carried a wooden whistle, which he kept blowing all the time. As before, he came from toward the rising sun, and moved around the camp, making the same circles, until he reached the northeast side; then all the soldiers charged him, and followed him a long way, and then came back.

Sweet Medicine came back a seventh time, from the same place as before. This time he was painted black over his whole body. He carried a bow, like a Contrary bow, painted black all over. He wore the white feathers from under the eagle's wing, and red feathers in his hair. He went around the camp in the same way; and when he got to the same place, the camp went out after him, and he ran away for a certain distance and then stopped; and when he stopped, the people stopped; they did not go after him.

The next morning, after daylight, he came in sight again, dressed in a fine buffalo-robe painted red, wearing fine leggings painted red. A tobacco-sack hung outside his robe, and he was carrying across his left arm a fine pipe. He came from the same direction as before. When he had come near the camp, he went up on a little hill and sat down for a time. Then he went around the camp to the place from which they used to chase him, and turned, and stopped, and then walked back to a little hill just north of the camp. There he sat down. The people in camp were watching him all the time. Then they rushed out toward him, and he arose and walked away over the hill out of sight. The whole camp looked for him, but could not find him. They did not know where he went. At this time he seemed a middle-aged man.

Now, after a time, the chiefs said to Sweet Medicine's brother: "Tell Sweet Medicine that he may come back to the camp now. We will not harm him." So after a time his brother saw the young man, and told him what the chiefs had said; and Sweet Medicine returned to the camp and lived there. But still the people were planning how they could get rid of him.

Now the people said to Sweet Medicine's brother, "You are

359

a chief now; but if you will throw away that brother of yours, we will make you a bigger chief, and all will do just as you say."

Soon after this, Sweet Medicine's brother said to him, "Let us go out hunting!" They went out, and killed a buffalo; and the brother built four fires around the buffalo, to make a smoke, and broke some bushes and handed them to Sweet Medicine, saying to him, "Do you keep walking around the buffalo, and keep the flies off the meat, while I go to the camp and get the dogs, to take the meat to camp."

Sweet Medicine's brother went to the camp, but he did not go back for the meat. The next morning they broke camp, and moved for three days before they stopped. After that they kept moving from place to place.

For two years after they left Sweet Medicine in this place, the camp did not return there. During these two years they never got enough to eat, and were always hungry. During the first year they lived on rabbits that the young men and boys got in the bushes and in the timber. The second year they found a few deer and antelope, and still caught a few rabbits. At length they began to think that Sweet Medicine was the cause of all this suffering, and came to believe that he had the power to keep the game from them. So, after two years more, the camp turned and traveled back to where they had left Sweet Medicine. They did not know whether he was still alive, nor if he was where they had left him; and after they had come within two or three days' travel of the place, they turned and moved south, and went into camp about a half-day's travel from where they had left the young man.

After they had made camp, Sweet Medicine's brother said, "I am going to see the place where I threw away my brother on the prairie." He started; and when he reached the top of a hill, from which he could see the place where he had left his brother, he was not far off, and could see the white bones of the buffalo. As he looked, he said, "There are the bleached bones where I killed the buffalo, and there is where I left my brother." The longer he sat by the hill and looked, the weaker he grew; and tears came to his eyes, for he felt sorry for his brother. At length he went down to the place; and when he came near it, he could see, around the spot where the bones were lying, a circle marked, and the grass had nearly grown over it. As he drew nearer, he saw that there was a deep trail worn in the ground— a trail so deep that a man standing up, with his arms stretched straight up, could not reach the top. As he stopped by this trench, he heard sounds below him; and when he listened, he heard Sweet Medicine saying, as he still walked around below, "I guess by this time my brother is a big chief, and has the power to make them do anything he wishes." Then the brother could see Sweet Medicine still walking, and still carrying in his hand the branches that had been given him to keep the flies off the meat. The branches were yet green, the leaves as green as when his brother had put the branches in his hand.

Sweet Medicine's brother knelt on the ground, and bent his head and looked down, and said to Sweet Medicine, "Brother, will you not look up at me?" He said this over and over; but Sweet Medicine did not look up, nor turn his head, but kept walking in the circle all the time.

Then his brother said, "Let me take one of your hands in mine"; but Sweet Medicine did not answer, nor look at him. The brother began to cry and mourn, saying, "Take pity on me! Take pity on me, and raise your hand to mine!" Sweet Medicine did not stop in his walk. His brother sat there for a time, crying and mourning, and asking Sweet Medicine to speak to him; but at length he went off and left him, and returned to the camp. There he told his mother and father that Sweet Medicine was still out there where he had left him, and alive, but that his brother would not look at him nor give him his hand.

His father and mother set out for the place; and when they had come near it, they began to cry and mourn; and when they

361

reached the place, his father lay down on the ground and looked into the hole, and said, "Son, look up and give me your hand"; and his mother said the same thing. They begged and implored him for a long time, but he did not look at them; and at last his mother said, "Son, just turn your head and look at your poor mother standing here over you." Sweet Medicine turned his head a very little, just enough to get a glimpse of her; and when his mother reached down her arm, he raised his hand just enough to touch her fingers. He did not come out of the hole, nor speak to her; and after a time his father and mother were discouraged and gave up, and went back to the camp.

After that the camp moved. That summer they killed a few buffalo, but not many. They gathered up old gristle and bones that they found on the prairie, and boiled them; and for that whole summer they wandered from place to place, thinking and hoping that they would find something to eat. The young men used to travel far out ahead, looking for game. Sometimes they saw a few buffalo, and the camp would move toward them; but when they reached the place where they had been seen, the buffalo would be gone. All the time they knew why they were starving; that Sweet Medicine was making them wander about in search of food that they never found. It was now autumn.

That winter the snow fell deep. All the food they could find was a few rabbits, skunks, mice, and other small animals. They were obliged to dig in the deep snow for what they had to live on that winter, and the next spring they were starving. The young men went out and found a few antelope, and for four days after this they killed antelope. During that summer they nearly died. They would grow very hungry and weak, and then they would find antelope enough to keep them from dying. All that summer it was like this; and all the winter they nearly starved, and up to the spring.

The fourth year, early in the spring, they were very weak.

The snow had not yet all gone, but lay in drifts in the ravines: but the slough grass and rushes were beginning to grow. The people were living now on the roots of rushes, old rye-grass roots, wild turnips, and other roots, and what flesh and gristle they could get from the bones of buffalo and of other animals which they found on the prairie. That spring was the worst that they had seen; they almost starved to death; most of the women became very thin; no flesh was on their bones. Some of them were so weak that they could hardly walk, but were just able to sit up.

Early in the spring the camp moved, and after going a little way came to a stream and crossed it, and camped on the other side. The same day the camp moved, Sweet Medicine was traveling, and came on their trail. He followed the trail until he crossed the stream; and on the other side he could see the camp,—a big village. Not far ahead of him he saw four boys pulling up flat rushes and long grass on the banks of the stream. They were eating the roots, and piling some up on the bank. As he drew near, the eldest boy looked up, and said, "There is Sweet Medicine." The other boys said, "No, it is not he." But when Sweet Medicine had come closer, all the boys said, "Yes, it is Sweet Medicine."

Sweet Medicine said to the boys, "My young friends, what are you doing?" The eldest boy answered, "We are pulling these flat rushes to get something to eat."

"What does the camp do for things to eat?" asked Sweet Medicine. The boy said: "They go out and look for old heads and bones of buffalo that have been killed for a long time. The meat and sinew on them are so hard and dried up that it takes from three to four days' boiling before they are soft enough to eat, and even then we can hardly eat the meat."

Sweet Medicine said, "Gather some wood. I will build a fire."

After the boys had brought wood, he built a fire with his own hands; and after it was burning well, he cut two forked sticks as long as from his elbow to the end of his fingers. He thrust the two forked sticks into the ground by the side of the fire, about the length of one of the sticks apart, and then said to the boys, "Go into that timber and find an elm tree, and bring me a piece of the inside bark of the elm."

"How large a piece of bark shall we get?" asked the boys.

"Look at those forked sticks," said Sweet Medicine, "and you can guess. Bring a piece that will reach from one forked stick to the other."

The boys went away, and in a little while brought him a piece of bark. Sweet Medicine took it, and placed it on the ground by the two forked sticks, but a little way from them; and then, taking hold of the bark by the two ends as he raised it to place it on the forked sticks, the boys saw that it was fine fresh meat, with fine backfat.

The boys had with them a little parfleche sack; and Sweet Medicine said to one of the boys: "Take the sack and go to the snowdrift over there, and make one scoop with your hands, and get all the snow you can hold in both hands. Make it into a round snowball, and put it in the sack and bring it to me." When the boy returned and gave Sweet Medicine the sack holding the snowball, Sweet Medicine took the sack, and waiting until the meat was good and hot, and the grease began to drip from it, he put the sack which held the snowball right under the meat.

"Now," said Sweet Medicine to the boys, "make a place to eat."

The boys broke some limbs of trees, and placed them on the ground; and Sweet Medicine took the meat from the fire and placed it on the sticks, and cut the meat into four equal pieces, and took the snowball out of the sack; and when he took it out, it was white marrow fat. Sweet Medicine said to the boys, "Sit down now and eat; eat all you can; eat plenty." The boys were glad to do so, and they sat down and ate all they could, but they could not eat all the meat. After they had eaten, and all were satisfied, they said: "Sweet Medicine, what shall we do with the rest of this meat? We cannot eat it all."

Sweet Medicine said: "Take it home with you; and when the people ask you where you got it, say to them, 'Sweet Medicine gave it to us. Sweet Medicine has come back.' Now," he continued, "I have been walking all day, and I am sleepy. I am going over there to lie down under that bent tree to sleep. If the people want me, you may tell them where to find me. If they want me to come into the camp, they will have to move a lodge from the south side of the camp inside the circle, and put it up for me."

The boys went into the camp; and when the people saw them carrying fresh meat, they were astonished, and asked the boys where they got the meat. The boys did not all live in the same place, but lived with their parents in different parts of the village. When the people questioned them about the meat, they answered, "Sweet Medicine gave it to us."

The men said: "Are you sure it was Sweet Medicine? Did you know him?"

The boys said, "Yes."

Everyone that asked them this question wished to taste the meat. The boys gave everyone that wanted it a taste of the meat, and still they had meat left.

The people talked a great deal about this, and presently two men were sent out from the camp to look for Sweet Medicine. While they were away looking for him, the people in the camp moved the lone lodge, which was on the south of the circle, inside the camp, and put it up within the circle, in about the same place where Sweet Medicine had sat in the first medicine lodge when he was a child. They fixed up a soft bed, with high back-rests. The back-rests were made of small willows, painted with the fine stripes, and were covered with soft buffalo-robes, hanging down from the mouths of the buffalo-heads fixed on top of the back-rests. The big chief said: "I will have Sweet Medicine for my son-in-law. I will give him my daughter to

365

keep his lodge, and make moccasins for him. She is the finest girl in the village." The chief took his daughter to the lodge, and left her sitting on the foot of the bed.

When the two men who had been sent out from the lodge to look for Sweet Medicine came to where he was, they found him asleep under the bent tree. He was well dressed, and wore a buffalo-robe, leggings, and moccasins, all painted red. In his hair he still wore the eagle down-feather. One of the men walked up to him and shook him by the shoulder, and said: "Sweet Medicine, our friend, awake! We are sent to bring you to the camp." When they woke him, Sweet Medicine looked up at them with a smile on his face. He was a fine-looking young man. The men walked back with him to the camp, one on each side. He entered the camp from the northeast side, the same place he had been driven away from, and went straight through the camp to his lodge. He went into his lodge; and when inside, he stood straight up. Within the lodge there were some old people; and one of them spoke up, and said, "This is your lodge, and that is your wife," and he pointed to the chief's daughter sitting on the foot of the bed. After a time a great many others came in to see him, for it was a large village.

One of the chiefs spoke, and said to him, "Sweet Medicine, tell us the news; tell us what you have seen during your travels since you left us."

"Yes," said Sweet Medicine, "I have traveled far over the prairie. I have seen other Cheyenne camps, and some camps of the Arapahoes. They are scattered far and wide."

One of the men said, "It is four years since you ran away, and we have been starving all that time."

Sweet Medicine smiled, and said, "Now, I am going to sing for four nights; but I wish to have the camp moved to a level place in the open, and the camp set up in a true circle." The next morning the camp was moved, and put up just as he had directed. His lodge was put up on the south side, near where it had stood before.

That night he began to sing, and he sang for four nights. There were many men in his lodge, and he said to them, "Tell all the people that if they see some straggling buffalo passing through here, they must not disturb them, nor kill them: they are the leaders, and are going ahead of the herd."

The second morning, after he had sung two nights, some old men called out through the camp, "Buffalo are seen near the camp!" The third morning the young men who were out from the camp came in and told the chiefs that they had seen many buffalo coming in from all directions. All this time the people obeyed Sweet Medicine, and did not disturb the buffalo; and all day long the people stood in the camp and watched the buffalo coming in strings, and did not disturb them.

The fourth night the people thought the night was very long, and that day would never come. The fourth morning the buffalo were all around the camp, except on that side where the wind blew from the camp.

Now Sweet Medicine let the people go. He said to them, "Now you may go out and chase buffalo, and kill what you need." The swiftest runners went farthest, and surrounded a part of the buffalo, and then they began to shoot them with their bows and arrows. The young men went around and cut out the tongues and the humps. They were brought in, and laid at the door of the big chief, Sweet Medicine's father-in-law. The tongues and humps were cooked, and taken to Sweet Medicine's lodge, and all the chiefs and old men were called in to a feast. Then, after the chiefs and old men had gone out, another feast was made, and all the young men, married and single, were called in. No one was missed; all were well fed.

During the years that Sweet Medicine stayed with the camp, they had plenty to eat. While he lived in camp with his wife, he took great pride in her. He combed her hair and painted her face, and kept her in fine clothes. They had no children. After he had been with them for four years, one day he said to his wife, "Tell your father that we are going on a journey." When she told her father, he said, "Daughter, where are you going?"

She replied: "Father, you have heard what Sweet Medicine said, that there are more Cheyennes and Arapahoes who are not yet here in our camp. Besides that, there are other peoples."

Her father said, "Daughter, how long will you be gone?"

She answered: "Father, I do not know. I think we shall be gone a long time."

His wife was now making moccasins for the trip. Sweet Medicine said, "We will take with us our big dog to pack our bed."

After she had finished making moccasins, they started with their large dog, and made the trip to the Black Hills.

When they had reached the place to which they were going, they took the dog out to one side of their lodge, a good way off, and made a shelter for the dog, and tied him there. Sweet Medicine left plenty of meat for the dog to eat. He had the power to keep plenty of meat by the dog after he left.

Somewhere in the Black Hills is a very high butte, and on the side of that butte a big, flat, thick rock. Sweet Medicine and his wife went toward that rock; and when they were close to it, the rock moved to one side, and beyond it they saw an opening and a room. They went in. The first thing his wife saw after they had gone into the room was a coyote-skin. When they had passed the coyote-skin, beyond it they saw four arrows lying side by side, feathered with large hawk-feathers, and the arrows all pointing the same way. A little way beyond these were four more arrows, lying with the heads all pointing the same way; these were feathered with eagle-feathers. A mysterious man (maiyu) was there, who said to Sweet Medicine, "Which arrows do you like, the arrows with gray hawk-feathers, or those with eagle-feathers?" Sweet Medicine answered, "I like better those with eagle-feathers."

Outside this lodge there seemed to be all sorts of people. One came in and said, "I heard that there was going to be a meet-

©1914
J.E.Tuell

Mrs. J. E. Tuell

MASSAUM CEREMONY

CARRYING BUFFALO SKULL TO SHADE

ing of mysterious men,—a sacred meeting,—and I came to see. They are going to give power. They are giving power to a *Woh hăs tăt' tăn*—a human being—the Cheyenne man that has come in."

Then other people came into the lodge, and among them a man who sat just inside the door,—a poor, sickly, weakly man. He was coughing all the time. He had a bad cough. If he had not come in, there would never have been any sickness among the people. These persons who came in were spiritual people from above. None of them was ever seen on earth by the Cheyennes.

At that meeting this spiritual man told Sweet Medicine what to do with the arrows, and how to handle them. He said: "These arrows must be wrapped up in a piece of the hide of a four-year-old buffalo. The buffalo must be shot once in the side. If the first shot does not kill it, the buffalo is to be let go, and not shot again. No other kind of hide except this must be used to wrap up the arrows, and it must be gotten just as has been told you."

Of the coyote-hide which they saw when they first went in, a quiver was made in which to keep the arrows. Beside the arrows lay a long stick—a cane to walk with. In early days a good many persons used long sticks to walk with. A spiritual man then painted Sweet Medicine's wife all over with red paint —her face, her arms and hands, and her robe and all her clothing. Then he painted Sweet Medicine all over. His robe, his pipe, and tobacco-pouch, were all painted red. Then the arrows were taken up, the ones that he had selected. The spiritual men who were teaching him took them up and handed them to him. He was taught to have the arrows touch his right shoulder first, then pass straight across to his left shoulder, then down his left side, then straight over to his right side, then straight to his breast. The points were held toward the ground, the feathered ends up.

The woman was lifted to her feet; and the spiritual man put

about her a robe, tying the belt behind. He placed the arrows on the ground, with their points directed toward the rising sun. The woman was made to stand at the points of the arrows, looking toward the rising sun. Then the arrows were lifted high, and touched first to her right shoulder, then across to the left shoulder and down her left side, then across to the right side, then up to her breast. Then they made four motions—one to the left, one to the front, one to the right, and one straight up. These motions are always made to the four points of the compass. With the fourth motion they put the arrows on her back, and then picked up the long stick, and gave it to her for a walking-stick. The door of the spiritual lodge in the big mountain faced toward the setting sun.

They were in this spiritual lodge, under the ground in the big mountain, for four years, and during this time they were being taught by the sacred men. At the end of the fourth year they went out of the lodge, by the door facing toward the setting sun, and went back to where they had left their dog.

When they had reached their lodge, Sweet Medicine gathered white sage, and had his wife make a bed of the sage-stems on which to place the medicine arrows while he packed the dog. After the dog was packed, he took up the arrows and put them on his wife's back, and handed her her cane, and they started to find the people. They got a forked stick; and every night when they came to camp, they thrust this stick in the ground, and hung the arrows on it, and leaned the cane up against it. Each morning before they started, Sweet Medicine painted his wife as she had been painted in the spiritual lodge. Then he put the arrows on her back, and gave her the walking-stick; and they started and walked all day, and at night thrust the forked stick into the ground at their camp, as they had done before. For four days and four nights they did the same each day and night.

The fifth day the woman began to get tired, and was obliged

to sit down and rest. She had to rest four times; and while she rested her husband smoked, smoking four times.

On the sixth morning he dressed (*i.e.*, painted) his wife and himself, and put the arrows on her back, and gave her the cane, and they went on. When his wife stopped to rest, he took the arrows off her back, and he smoked his pipe. Before smoking, he pointed his pipe to the west, to the north, to the east, and the south, then up above, then toward the earth, then to his mouth. He always smoked four times.

That day Sweet Medicine came upon tracks in different places, all going the same way. He said to his wife: "I think we are near the camp. All the tracks are going the same way." They had gone only a little farther when they came upon the main trail, and followed it.

A person who was coming behind with a load of meat said to himself, "There are some persons going into camp late." Presently he had come close to them, and could see that it was Sweet Medicine. Sweet Medicine saw him, and motioned the man to pass on his right side. The man kept on without speaking, and passed them; and when he reached camp he said to the people: "Put up Sweet Medicine's lodge. He is coming, and is bringing something with him."

When the people heard that, they were excited. They put up his lodge in the same place, and made it ready for him. When he came in sight, all the people were out looking at him. He walked straight to his lodge, took the arrows from his wife's back, and hung them above the door. After night fell, he took them in, and they were hung at the back part of the lodge. His wife's mother led the dog away, and the woman went into the lodge. Then all who could get inside went into the lodge, and sat down and began to weep, asking for help.

At length all the people became quiet, and they brought in something to eat. Sweet Medicine said to the people: "Now you see that I have come back. I have been gone a long time, and have been to a place far away, where I have seen many won-

371

derful things. The spiritual men (maiyun) whom I saw at this place gave me medicine to doctor with, to cure you people when you are sick. This food must be well cooked. You must eat nothing raw; all must be well cooked." The people asked him if he would go and eat outside of his own lodge. He replied, "Yes." He added, "There is one thing that must not be done: no one must walk in front of me or in front of my wife."

A man said, "I want you to come to my lodge." Sweet Medicine went, and walked around to the south side of the lodge, and to the back, and sat down. They gave him some buffalo backfat to eat. When they heard that this man had had Sweet Medicine to feast, all who were in the camp wanted him to visit their lodges. Even a little girl said, "I want Sweet Medicine to come to our lodge." All the food he did not eat went to his mother-in-law's lodge. He did not go to all the lodges. Then he went home. Many people went with him, as many as could get into the lodge.

Soon after this they moved camp. Sweet Medicine dressed himself as before, and painted and dressed his wife. He was in front, leading the camp; and his wife, on foot, followed with her mother, carrying her cane, and with the arrows on her back. During the march they stopped four times. He showed his wife's mother how to take off the arrows, and how to put them on when they started. Her mother raised up her daughter with her hands, and put the arrows on her back, and then picked up the cane and gave it to her, and they started on again; and for three days, as the camp was moving, Sweet Medicine and his wife did the same thing each day.

The fourth day they came in sight of a stream; and after they had smoked, they started on, and camped on the creek. While they were putting up the lodges, many men were with Sweet Medicine, smoking. He always had many visitors. He never went into his lodge until everything was hung up. The cane was always taken inside the lodge.

A variety of incidents are related in the numerous versions

of the culture hero story told by the Cheyennes. Some of these are given in the fragment that follows:

Sweet Medicine came into an old woman's lodge in one of the Cheyenne villages. No one knew whence he came. He was a young boy, perhaps eight years old. The old woman had a small lodge. Sweet Medicine went in, and said, "Grandmother, I am very hungry." She said, "My grandchild has come to visit me," and gave him some meat to eat. When he had finished eating, he told the old woman that he was going down to the timber, and walked out of the lodge. When he left, she looked through the door to see which way he went. When he had gone a little way from the lodge, he became a young man; then she knew he was maiyuniv (possessed spiritual power), but she told no one about it.

He came back about sundown, and, when he entered the lodge, he was a boy again. The old woman knew he was the same. She said, "Have you come back again, my grandson?" He answered, "Yes, grandmother; and I am very hungry." She said, "I have nothing but roots to cook for you"; but he replied, "Wait till tonight, and we shall have plenty to eat." She put the roots in an earthen jar and cooked them.

After a time Sweet Medicine said, "Grandmother, hand me one of those old buffalo-skins that you use for your bed." She handed him one, and he spread it out in the lodge, hair-side up, to the left of the lodge as one enters, and said, "Now take it up." When she lifted it, there was a pile of buffalo-meat under it.

Sweet Medicine said: "Grandmother, do not call anybody in. If anybody comes in, it will be good; and I think someone will come in. Someone will smell me. I smell of sweet medicine." Soon after that they heard a woman speaking outside the lodge, who said that the old woman's lodge smelled very good, and as if they had fresh meat in there. By this time part of the meat had been cut up and was hanging over the fire. The woman came to the door of the lodge and looked in. The old woman was cutting up the meat on the right side of the lodge, and Sweet Medicine was sitting on the left of the entrance. The old woman said, "Sit down over there, and I will give you something to eat," and she pointed to where Sweet Medicine was sitting. When she turned around, Sweet Medicine was gone, and there was a buffalo-chip lying on the bed where he had been sitting. As the woman went to sit down, she said, "You have a fine buffalo-chip on your bed." The old woman replied, "My grandson was sitting there: he must have gone out." Then the old woman gave her something to eat, wrapped up in a piece of hide some meat for her to carry away, and told her not to tell anyone about it. She said she did not know how the meat had come there; she had found it in the lodge by her bed. When her friend had gone, she went outside.

There were several girls near by, kicking the playing-balls about, and she watched them for a short time. When she came into the lodge again, Sweet Medicine was sitting in the same place as before. She said: "I put that buffalo-chip farther back from where you left it. I was afraid my friend would sit on it when she came in." Sweet Medicine replied, "That was myself." Then he said, "I am going out to play with the boys," and he left the lodge.

All around, the girls were standing in circles, kicking the balls to one another. Sweet Medicine went among the little boys who were playing, and said, "I will be a rabbit; you may chase me around." They ran after him, and Sweet Medicine, in running away, scattered the counting-sticks that one of the girls had piled up beside her. The girl who was counting said, "If you come by here again, I will hit you with the ball, for you scattered my sticks." He ran by again, and she struck him with the ball. As the ball touched him, he turned into a rabbit and ran off toward the brush. The village dogs chased him, but he got away. The girls were surprised when he turned into a rabbit, and watched for him. They heard someone say, "What are you looking at?" and turned around to find Sweet Medicine

374

standing behind them. They all said, "Why, you turned into a rabbit!" but Sweet Medicine said: "No, I have been standing here all the time. That rabbit must have jumped out of some hole." Then he began to play again. Close to where the boys were playing there was a deep buffalo-wallow. One of the boys would lie in it, and they would throw dirt and sticks at him. Sweet Medicine said, "I will get in, and you may all throw at me"; so he went in and sat down. The boys got all around him and began to throw dirt at him, and it became very dusty. When the dust had cleared off, Sweet Medicine had disappeared. Then they began to know that he was maiyuniv.

That night everybody was talking about what a strange boy he was. Everyone wanted to know where he had come from, and where he belonged.

Next morning two young men were standing on a knoll on the edge of the camp, when another young man came up and stood beside them. The two young men wondered who he might be, for they did not recognize him. All the young men in a village usually know one another, but he was a stranger to them. They said to one another, "Let us find out who he is, and where he comes from." Meantime, Sweet Medicine had walked away over the knoll. The two said, "Let us follow him!" and they went after him. When they looked over the top of the knoll, they saw a coyote trotting off. When they saw it, they thought Sweet Medicine must be sitting in the high grass; so they stepped back, and said, "Let us wait till he comes back." After a time they looked again, and saw the young man walking down below. They saw him going away, and then they went back to the camp; and when they arrived, they told what they had seen, and how Sweet Medicine had turned into a coyote, and that when they looked again, they saw a young man going down to the creek.

One of the women said: "We do not believe you. No one could turn into a coyote and then back again into a man. We must watch him." Then she and a young girl went up on the hill. They watched, and saw the young man coming toward them.

One of them called to him, "Come here and talk with us!" So Sweet Medicine came up and talked with them. When they parted, they said to him: "You must come often and see us. We will be friends, and often have good talks together."

One of them said: "We hear you turned into a coyote, but we do not believe it. Are you trying to make fools of us? We cannot believe you can change like that." Sweet Medicine only laughed at them when they said this to him, and they stood together and talked for quite a while. Then the girls went back to the camp.

There was a big crowd there. They said, "That is the strange young man," for he was not yet known by the name of Sweet Medicine. Then three young men said, "We will see who he is." They went up on the hill to see him; and when they were near him, Sweet Medicine went over the hill again. They ran fast up the hill and looked over, but saw only a swift fox running off. They watched it, but it disappeared, and they saw Sweet Medicine walking up the next hill. When they went back to the camp, everyone said, "We must try to catch him." The men said, "He is afraid of us, but a woman might catch him."

A band of men tried to catch him. When they saw him, they tried to close in around him, but he disappeared as they drew near; and when they went to where he had been standing, they could find no trace of him. They came to where he had been, and saw a weed growing there. They could not see the root of this weed.

While they were looking for him, he went back as a boy to his grandmother's lodge, and again told her that he was hungry. The woman who had seen him on the hill said he was still there, but he was eating in the old woman's lodge. After eating, he said, "Grandmother, I am tired," and he slept a little.

The girl was told that someone had seen a boy go into the old woman's lodge, so she went to find out. She looked in, and saw a young man asleep. She said, "You change many times," and entered and shook him to wake him. When he got up, he was a fine-looking young man. The woman watched him. Then she went out and told the camp that the young man was there, and then went back and asked him his name. Sweet Medicine replied, "You will know later." She went out again; but the people said to her, "Stay in the lodge with him till we can get some people together to catch him." She went in again, and a big lizard lay where Sweet Medicine had been, so she went out again; and as she looked back, she saw the lizard dig a hole in the ground and crawl in, so she said to the people who were coming up, "He is gone again."

That evening she went to the creek with a jar for water. There was a stump standing on the bank. She threw her robe over the stump while she went down to draw water. As she came up, Sweet Medicine was standing there with her robe in his hand, and there was no stump to be seen. Sweet Medicine said: "Why did you throw your robe over me? Take it back." She answered, "You change so often that I hardly know you." Sweet Medicine said: "I heard you say that only a woman was clever enough to catch me, and for that reason I made the change. I shall change once again, and then I will begin to teach your people; after that, I shall be always with them." When she left with her jar of water, she looked back and saw the stump standing where she had thrown her robe over it. She went back and said to the stump, "I think you are fooling me," and pushed it over. It was rotten, and fell easily.

When she had again reached the camp, she told what had happened to her, saying that she had pushed the stump over, and that it was rotten at the root. The women would not believe her, but she insisted that she had talked with Sweet Medicine. One of the women said, "I tried to push that stump over yesterday, but was not able to; its root was very strong." They all went down to look at the stump; but, when they reached the river, they found a big rock lying where the stump had been.

377

That night this same woman went out and looked up on the hill where Sweet Medicine had stood. She saw a little fire there. A weed was growing there, and sparks were coming out of it. She went up to it, and pulled up the root of the weed. She tasted the root, and found that it was sweet. She came back to the camp and told the people that she had found the root where the man had disappeared. After that, they called him Sweet Medicine.

Sweet Medicine went back to the old woman's lodge, and the next day everyone went out on a buffalo-hunt. During the hunt Sweet Medicine killed a yearling calf. He had cut it up, and was taking the meat from the bones, when an old man came up and wanted to take it away from him. They quarreled about the ownership of the calf, and Sweet Medicine picked up one of the shin-bones and knocked the old man down and killed him. Those who arrived at camp first said that Sweet Medicine had killed an old man, and some of the soldiers were told to kill him as soon as he returned. When he entered the lodge, his grandmother said to him, "I hear you killed an old man." Sweet Medicine said, "Cook meat for me, for I am hungry." She put an earthen pot on the fire and began to cook for him. Some of the young men had seen him enter the lodge, and they gathered around it to kill him. They all came close around the lodge. His grandmother went out.

One of the young men looked in and told the others that Sweet Medicine was inside. They gathered close around, and pulled up the pins of the lodge. Sweet Medicine kicked the pot over into the fire; and, as the ashes rose, he went up with them, and all the men could see was a butterfly in the air. "After this," said Sweet Medicine, "the people shall always have weak eyes from these ashes and this smoke."

Sweet Medicine lived with his people for four long, long lives of men. Young people grew up, became old, and died; other young people were born, grew to old age, and died; but still this man lived. All through the summer he was young like a young man; and when fall came and the grass dried up, he began to look older; and about the middle of the winter he was like a very old man, and walked bent over and feebly. In spring he became young again. At last he died, but before he died he talked a long time to the people and prophesied some of the things that would come to them; and he told them, as they were gathered in his lodge, a good many things that it made him sad to repeat, and that the people did not understand.

One man who sat in the circle in the lodge spoke to Sweet Medicine, who for a long time had been sitting in silence with his head hanging down, as if discouraged. He said: "Friend, what is your trouble? Why are you sorrowful?" Sweet Medicine answered: "Yes, it is true I am troubled. Listen to me carefully. Listen to me carefully." He said this four times. "Our great-grandfather spoke thus to me, repeating it four times. He said to me that he had put people on this earth, all kinds of people. He made us, but also he made others. There are all kinds of people on earth that you will meet some day, toward the sunrise, by a big river. Some are black, but some day you will meet a people who are white—good-looking people, with light hair and white skins." A man spoke up, and said, "Shall we know them when we meet them?"

"Yes," said Sweet Medicine, "you will know them, for they will have long hair on their faces, and will look differently from you. They will wear things different from your things—different clothing. It will be something like the green scum that grows on waters about springs.[4] Those people will wander this way. You will talk with them. They will give you things like isinglass [*i.e.*, things that flash or reflect the light, mirrors] and something that looks like sand that will taste very sweet. But do not take the things they give you. They will be looking for a certain stone. They will wear what I have spoken of, but it will be of all colors, pretty. Perhaps they will not listen to what

[4] Cloth was not mentioned, but the reference is no doubt to the thread of cloth, ravelings.

you say to them, but you will listen to what they say to you. They will be people who do not get tired, but who will keep pushing forward, going, going all the time. They will keep coming, coming. They will try always to give you things, but do not take them. At last I think that you will take the things that they offer you, and this will bring sickness to you. These people do not follow the way of our great-grandfather. They follow another way. They will travel everywhere, looking for this stone which our great-grandfather put on the earth in many places.

"Buffalo and all animals were given you by our great-grandfather; but these people will come in, and will begin to kill off these animals. They will use a different thing to kill animals from what we use—something that makes a noise, and sends a little round stone to kill.

"Then after a while a different animal will come into the country. It will have a head like a buffalo, but it will have white horns and a long tail. These animals will smell differently from the buffalo, and at last you will come to eating them. When you skin them, the flesh will jerk, and at last you will get this same disease. At last something will be given to you, which, if you drink it, will make you crazy. These people will have something to give to animals to eat which will kill them.

"There will be many of these people, so many that you cannot stand before them. On the rivers you will see things going up and down, and in these things will be these people, and there will be things moving over dry land in which these people will be.

"Another animal will come, but it will not be like the buffalo. It will have long heavy hair on its neck, and a long heavy tail which drags on the ground. It will come from the south.

"When these animals come, you will catch them, and you will get on their backs and they will carry you from place to place. You will become great travelers. If you see a place a long way off, you will want to go to it, so at last you will get on those animals with my arrows. From that time you will act very foolishly. You will never be quiet. You will want to go everywhere. You will be very foolish. You will know nothing.

"These people will not listen to what you say; what they are going to do they will do. You people will change: in the end of your life in those days you will not get up early in the morning; you will never know when day comes; you will lie in bed; you will have disease, and will die suddenly; you will all die off.

"At last those people will ask you for your flesh [he repeated this four times], but you must say 'No.' They will try to teach you their way of living. If you give up to them your flesh [your children], those that they take away will never know anything. They will try to change you from your way of living to theirs, and they will keep at what they try to do. They will work with their hands. They will tear up the earth, and at last you will do it with them. When you do, you will become crazy, and will forget all that I am now teaching you."

APPENDIX A

THE Cheyenne villages of which we are told by Sioux and Cheyenne tradition and which deserve further study are these:

1. On Minnesota River near Mankato, Minnesota.
2. On the Yellow Medicine, tributary of the Minnesota River.— Williamson and Riggs.
3. On Kettle Lakes, North Dakota, west of Lake Traverse.— Comfort.
4. On Sheyenne River near Lisbon, North Dakota, called by the Sioux, Cheyenne Plantings. Already mapped.
5. On the head of Maple Creek near Kulm, North Dakota.
6. On the east side of Missouri River opposite the farm school.
7. On the east side of Missouri River on the Little Cheyenne River near (former) Forest City, North Dakota.
8. On the west side of Missouri River at junction of Porcupine Creek and the Missouri.
9. Two miles below Porcupine Creek—possibly a part of Porcupine village.
10. At farm school near the Cheyenne Hills.
11. On Grand River, near Sitting Bull's old camp; and
12. (perhaps) On Dirt Lodge Creek, a tributary of Grand River.

Of these, numbers 4 to 11, inclusive, have been called by the Sioux, Cheyenne Plantings, Shahienawoju.

The Cheyennes today tell of villages at the mouth of White River and the mouth of Cheyenne River, on the Missouri.

There seems reason to suppose that the villages just below Porcupine River (8 and 9) were those seen by Lewis and Clark, October 15-16, 1804.

The most northerly identified point on the Missouri below these villages is Stone Idol Creek, which Coues, Thwaites, and Quaife agree is Spring or Hermaphrodite Creek. If we measure off on the Missouri River Commission's map Lewis and Clark's distances above

382

the mouth of Hermaphrodite Creek, we find that they camped October 13 a mile or more above the former Vanderbilt P. O., on the north side of the river nearly opposite—a little below—the farm school village. This is a little above the point where the river after flowing east turns south.

The following morning, October 14, the day on which the sentence of the court-martial was executed, Lewis and Clark left this camp, passed the farm school site—not mentioning Cheyenne ruins or the Cheyenne Hills—which from the farm school site seem to answer very well the description given us next day, October 15, of "curious hills," like a slant-roofed house. They passed the small creek named Eagle Feather Creek on the Missouri River Commission map, and the larger creek above, the modern Blackfoot Creek, which by Coues and Thwaites is considered the Eagle Feather Creek of Lewis and Clark. Clark says they camped in a cove of the bank on the north—starboard—side, and saw ruins on the south side, which, however, were mostly washed into the river. This must have been nearly opposite the mouth of the stream called Four Mile Creek. But we cannot know where the course of the Missouri was at that time, nor where Four Mile Creek entered it.

The day after this, October 15, during the last three and a half miles of the day's journey, they record, in courses and distances,[1] passing a village of the Cheyenne Indians on the south side, below a creek on the same side. This is probably the site at Slobtown, above which there is a creek, which in times of flood carries much water. A Ree Indian was killed near this creek sixty years ago, and since then the Sioux have called it *Palani Wakpala*, Ree Creek. The name is not on any map. The following morning, just after setting out, they passed a circular work where the Cheyenne Indians formerly lived, and just above that saw a creek which they called Chien.

Of these two villages very near together, the upper one, which they passed on the morning of October 16, seems to be the village near Porcupine Creek.

Measurements of the distances between Lewis and Clark's camps on the Missouri River Commission maps bring their camp of October 15 just below the mouth of the Porcupine, but I cannot locate it.

[1] Orig. Journ., Lewis and Clark, vol. 1, p. 195.

If the Lewis and Clark route is figured back from the mouth of the Cannonball down to the mouth of the Hermaphrodite, the distances agree with the Missouri River Commission maps to within two or three miles, as they do when the distances are figured upstream. The bed of the Missouri River is, of course, constantly changing, and the course of the channel may have greatly altered during the past century.

APPENDIX B

THE man who followed his buffalo wife was he who brought to the Cheyennes a knowledge of how to ornament robes and skins with quills. His name is not known. When he returned from the camp of the buffalo, this man brought with him a possible sack and a cushion. After he returned, he took a wife. They had a daughter, and after she had grown up, she married. After this took place the man said to his wife: "I wish you to make a lodge, and to ornament it after these patterns that I have. It is hard to do this, but I will try to show you about it." His wife answered, "Very well, I will stay inside with you, and we will send for women, our friends, to help us."

The man went out and killed thirty buffalo cows, and the woman asked her friends to help her. They spread the hides on the ground, and the man showed his wife and the women invited to their lodge— whom the wife had feasted—how to flesh these hides. At length they had fleshed five hides—one of them a yearling skin. They took the five hides into the lodge and put them at the back, piled up one on another. In the same way, later, they fleshed the thirty skins in lots of five.

After the first five hides had been taken into the lodge, the man drew from the fire a coal, and on it sprinkled sweet grass. On top of the pile of hides lay a stick, and to this they tied the offerings that they were to make to the Great Power. Then the man rubbed his hands four times over the hides toward the fire. The stick to which the offerings were tied was moved toward the door over the smoke (of the burning sweet grass) four times. Then the man said, "Now we shall ornament these thirty hides."

The next day he sent for two old men and two old women, and when they came to the lodge he showed them where to sit: the two men at the south side of the lodge, and the two women on the north

385

side.[1] He held his hands over the burning sweet grass, and rubbed them over his body in the ceremonial way. While doing all this he was praying to the Great Power above, asking him to take pity on him. He said to the old people that the Great Power above had taken pity on him and had told him how to do this thing.

The first hide was that of a black yearling. It was folded once, hair-side out. The man lifted up this hide in his hand and moved it four times over the smoke, and then put the offerings in the fold of the hide. The invited women sat all about the lodge watching him. Now the man took a piece of meat from the pot and from it pulled five pieces and put them in his wife's right hand, which she held out before her, palm upward. He put one piece at the base of the thumb, one at the outside of the palm, near the wrist, one at the base of the fifth finger, one at the base of the forefinger, and one in the middle of the palm. Then he told his wife to place her left hand, palm down, on the right hand, and to hold them together. He took up a lodge-pin and thrust it straight down into the ground, and then pushed his hand toward the west, so as to incline the upper end of the pin toward the west. Then he drew out the pin and thrust it in the hole, and in the same way inclined it toward the north. Again drawing out the pin, he thrust it into the hole and inclined it toward the east, and again drawing it out, toward the south. Then he thrust it straight up in the hole and pulled it out again, leaving the hole empty. Taking a piece of the meat from his wife's hand, he moved it from the east to the hole, and dropped it in the hole; another piece he moved from the south to the hole, and dropped it in; another piece he moved from the west and dropped it in the hole, and another from the north. The fifth piece he dropped into the hole from above. Now the woman put her right hand over the hole, and the man put his on top of hers and across it. As he held his hand there he prayed, asking a blessing of the Great Power. Then the two lifted up their hands, and with his hand the man moved the earth into and over the hole. He took a coal of fire to the door and placed it on the ground and sprinkled sweet grass on it, and told one of the old women to hold her robe over it and smoke it. After she had

[1] Note sex and direction of animals painted on Blackfeet lodge coverings; also the directions—according to one Cheyenne tradition—in which the first man and first woman sat.

ACTORS RESTING UNDER SHADE

Mrs. J. E. Tuell

done this, he said to her, "Now, go about through the camp and call other women." When the women she called had come, they sat in a row in front of the lodge, and she who had called them now came in. She gave the man a bowl of meat from the food which was over the fire.

In their mouths the man and his wife held the root called *mō tsǐn'-ǐsts*.

The women who had been called entered the lodge, went to the wife, and held their hands out toward her, palms up and edges together, and looked away from her. The woman spat the medicine on the hands of each at the base of the thumb and forefinger of the right hand, and then at the base of the forefinger and thumb of the left hand, and then between the hands—five times in all. The women put their palms together and rubbed them, and then made the ceremonial motions. The wife was at the south side of the lodge, and the women passed before her, and on across the door to their places. On the ground in front of the man was a straight pipe, pointing toward the robes, and a bundle of medicine.

The man said to his wife: "Choose some old woman who shall teach you how to put the quills on; I cannot teach you, because I am a man. It must be a woman who shall teach you." Those who were present selected an old woman on the north side of the lodge, but she said, "I know nothing about it." "Well," said the man, "I will teach you myself." He said to the wife, "I wish you to pack up these robes; I will tell you how to do it." He said to the women, "I wish you to pack up these robes; I will tell my wife how to do it, and she will tell you."

All the people in the lodge now unbraided their hair and the man painted them red over their whole bodies. The face too was red, with a black streak each on forehead, cheeks, and chin, and another from the chin to the middle of the lower lip. The woman now passed food, first to those within the lodge and then to those without. The first old woman went out from the north side of the lodge, and all the others passed around the back of the lodge, and went out from the north side of the door. The man's wife did not go out with them; first she put on a robe belted about the waist, and then she too went out of the lodge, and the man told her how to rub the robes. She rubbed the thirty robes. It took her a long time. Now her husband told her to make six large parfleche sacks to put these robes in; they were to put five in each sack. They piled up all the robes, one on top of another, and then cooked food for another feast.

Next day they invited women to come in. They had not yet been painted; only the man and his wife were painted. They again burned sweet grass, and then the women were painted as before.

After this two women stood next to the robes on the north, and two next to the robes on the south, and another still farther to the south. The six parfleche sacks were piled in front of the pile of robes. Now the wife moved her hands four times over the smoke and took up one of the sacks. A woman picked up first the calfskin and put that in the bottom of the sack. Then the four women packed the robes in the six sacks, five in each. The first sack was placed so that the calf's head would face the north. They piled the other sacks on top of this one, and all the heads pointed north.

After this the wife did with the pin just what her husband had done before, offering the pieces of meat. Then she sent an old woman to bring other women to the lodge, just as her husband had done before. The woman went about to call other women, but some were afraid to come; hardly any of them came. Then they ate, and all went out as before.

The next day the man sent his wife to borrow two lodges, so as to make a big lodge, with plenty of room. "Now," he said, "you women must not eat or drink anything." When the big lodge was raised the man still sat in his place on the south side of his own lodge, and his wife, wearing a robe, sat by him. Presently the man arose and went over to where they had put up the new lodge. It had not yet been painted. He took with him his pipe and medicine sack.

His wife did not go with him. She took on her back the first sack which held the calf-robe, and each old woman present took a sack on her back, slipped the rope already tied to it over her breast, and sat down. Then all together they rose, and going around the lodge, following the wife, they went out from the south side of the door. When they reached the big lodge they entered it at the south side of the door, and put down the sacks—first the one which held the calfskin, with the head toward the north, just as before. The wife went to the sacks, took out all the robes, and piled them up as they had been piled before, and sat down in front of the robes. The man went to her and on her right wrist tied a piece of a scalp. She turned about and took the calfskin and spread it out, flesh-side up, the head toward the north. She placed the stick to which the offerings were tied on the top of the pile. She took a handful of brains—tanning mixture— and touched the skin with them four times toward the four directions. Then she drew a line of brains diagonally from the calf's right fore leg to the left hind leg, or from northwest to southeast; then from the left fore leg to the right hind leg, or from northeast to southwest; then from head to tail, or from north to south. Then one of the old women stepped up and rubbed brains all over it. Then all the remaining hides were brained. It took all night. As fast as they were brained, they were piled up on the north side of the lodge, the calf-robe at the bottom, for in all this ceremony the calf's hide was the important one. They finished this work just as daylight came. They propped up in front of the lodge a number of dog travois and made ready to spread the calfskin over the dog travois, toward the fire, hair-side out.

The wife took the calfskin by the head, and an old woman took it by the tail, and the two carried it around the lodge and began to go out on the north side of the door. When they reached the lodge door, they made four motions with the skin, and pushed the door aside; then they moved the head out the door, and pointed the head to the north, and then drew the skin within the door again; again swinging it partly out, its head was pointed to the south. Again it was drawn in, and again swung out to point straight up. Then the two went on out to the most distant of the dog travois, stopping four times on the way. There with four motions they hung up the calfskin.

The pointing of the skin upward meant toward the west, since they could not turn the hide around. The fourth time, when they walked out with it, represented the pointing to the east.

After this had been done with the calf's hide, they carried out the other hides and hung them over the different travois without ceremony. The hair-side was upward, and the thirty hides hanging there looked like a herd of buffalo.

About noon they brought the calfskin back to the lodge in the same way, reversing all the operations, and put it back where it had been taken from, and then brought in all the other hides and piled them up. After this was done, they all ate. The soldier bands were now feasting outside the big lodge. In the lodge where this ceremony was going on no men might be present, except only the man who was the instructor. After they had finished eating, the hides were again packed in the sacks and were placed with the heads toward the north.

The next morning they took the calfskin outside and sprinkled it four times with water on the legs, and then wiped the whole hide three times. Then they twisted and wrung and worked it, and that day finished dressing the calfskin. For the dressing of the other twenty-nine hides, they cooked food and invited the best dressers to come to tan and soften them. After all had been dressed, they were put back in the sacks.

When the time came for ornamenting these robes, they set up another large lodge, and carried the skins to it as they had done before. After the robes had been brought to this lodge, three of them were taken from the sacks and spread out, one at the back of the lodge, and the others close to it, on its north side. They worked on three robes at a time.

The first thing done was to mark out on the robe the pattern which showed where the ornaments were to go. Then with each robe were placed the grass, the bone smoother, the awl, the quills, the sinews, and the white powder to be used with it, and all the robes were then packed away and piled up again. After that the wife went about the village and called the thirty young women whom she had chosen to do the quilling. After all had come, she who was to quill the calf-robe took that out first and carried it away to her own lodge. Each of the others took a robe, until all were gone. When a woman finished the one she was working on, she brought it back to the lodge and put it into the sack again. After all had been finished, they put up another large lodge, carried the robes into it as before, and the last touches of ornament were put on. This was called *hī nĭm' nĭ vā nĭs' to* (pl.) —the last ornaments. It is believed that this is a Suhtai word. The Cheyenne word would be perhaps *hĭt aĭ' ĭsh tŭn i*.

Now the man sent for all his kinsfolk. They spread the folded calf-robe to the left of his seat, and the others all the way to the north around the lodge to the door. In front of each robe was placed a little bundle of sweet grass ready for use. These kinsmen were all sitting about the lodge, a young man sitting on the calf-robe. Now they all burned sweet grass and purified themselves, and then the young man who had been seated on the calf-robe went out first, going around the lodge so as to pass out from the north side of the door. The man next on his left followed him; then the next one; the one next to the door leaving last. This was the end of the ceremony, as described by Picking Bones Woman.

It was the instruction and organization of the quilling society.

APPENDIX C

NOTES ON CHEYENNE SONGS

ALL Indians are musical and some of their instruments have been described. These are generally used for keeping time. Most Indian music, however, is vocal, and men, women, and children sing. In fact, singing accompanies many operations of their daily life.

The Cheyennes have many religious songs—prayers set to music. These may have words or not. Some of them are used by the doctor while trying to heal his patient. There are mourning songs in praise of the dead, and describing the sorrow of the survivors; songs which are lullabies for children or for their amusement. Morning songs are hummed by men just after they have awakened and before they rise. The many dance songs are accompanied by the beat of the drum, which keeps time for the dancers. Besides these, there are songs of love, of war, and of adventure. Wolf songs, so called—said to have been learned from the wolves and perhaps remotely in imitation of the howling of these animals—are songs of travel, of roaming about, and were commonly sung by scouts or young men who were out looking for enemies, since a scout was called a "wolf."

At the present day many of the religious songs have been forgotten except by the oldest men, since, as the old ceremonies are no longer practiced, the young men learn neither the ceremony nor the songs which go with it.

The wolf songs were sung by scouts, or by young men alone on the prairie, whether traveling or looking for enemies, or often, I am told, by men when they felt depressed, downhearted, lonely, or discouraged. It is perhaps for this reason that these songs contain frequent references to the singer's sweetheart. On the other hand, the words of many of them seem to be addressed by a leader to his followers, in order to encourage them. Some of these songs are supposed to be sung by a girl, and addressed to her lover. Of these, one

392

of the most pleasing, as well for its air as for its words, is the one beginning *"Tá mĭs sĭ vá in,"* a translation of which is, "Put your arms around me, I am not looking," and the meaning is, that if the girl saw that her lover was about to embrace her, she would feel obliged to repulse him, but she wished him to put his arms around her, and now that she was not looking, he might do so without fear of rebuke. Another wolf war-song, supposed to be sung by a man traveling about, says: "My love, it is I who am singing. Do you hear me?" Another one, by a leader addressing his followers, says, "Take courage; do not be frightened; follow where you see me riding my white horse." In another song by a leader to his followers, he says, "Friends, take courage, I see my sweetheart." The view is, that the mention of the sweetheart's name may bring him luck.

A man traveling alone, sang, "I do not see my love," and then changing his address, went on, "Come out of your lodge, so that I may see you"; and again changing it, said, as he discovered her, "Aha, I do see you." Still another runs, "My love, come out of the lodge, I am searching for you"; another, "My love, come out into the prairie, so that I may come near you and meet you"; and another, "My love, do not scold me, I love only you." While these songs were commonly sung during a war journey, or even by people who are alone, away from the camp, they were sung also by young men who are sitting on the hills close to the village, and for no other purpose than their own amusement.

Often, young men about to start on a war journey went about the camp singing songs which were recognized as those sung by people about to go to war. They might march about the circle of the lodges, and stopping before certain of them, sing these songs. From the lodge which was being serenaded, contributions to their equipment were handed out, such as two or three pairs of moccasins, a few arrows, half a dozen balls, or a little packet of powder. Such a song is the following, "Call them together before we go away, and we will dance till morning." This might be sung over and over many times as they marched through the camp. A party just leaving the village to go to war, might sing, "I am going to search for a man; if I find him, there will be fighting; perhaps he will kill me." This was sung again and again as they rode over the hills from the camp.

393

A successful war party, returning to the village, sang, just as they descended the hills close to the camp, and until their people came out to meet them, a song of joy and triumph, "I have returned home; again I shall see my love." Or perhaps this, "All have returned alive; you all shall see your sweethearts"; and later, after they had come into the village, and perhaps were marching about it, such a song as this, "In the mountains I met with a man; I charged upon him and fought him and killed him, and took his scalp."

A warrior whose fortune while on the warpath had been bad, and who was therefore angry and discouraged, might sing, "My heart is angry, my love is lost." A dance song sung by the Fox Soldiers society had words which are in praise of youth, and to encourage valor, by pointing out the miseries of old age. They run as follows: "When a man gets old, his teeth are gone. I am afraid" (of that time), "I wish to die" (before it comes).

The doctoring songs are usually short and simple. The words are repeated over and over again, as in this one: "I know myself; I possess spiritual power." Another song, by a woman, says, "I know about things above; I possess spiritual power."

Beside all this, there are various animal songs, some of them religious, others merely invoking good fortune. A certain song, known as the horse song, may be sung over a horse, in order to make him strong, sound, and swift, for a particular occasion.[1]

[1] Twenty years ago I recorded in the *American Anthropologist*, n.s. vol. v, No. 2, p. 312, a number of these songs.

INDEX

[NOTE. In the use of terms bull, cow, and calf, or any part of either, the reference is always to the buffalo.]

INDEX

411

INDEX

INDEX

INDEX

Nivstanivoo, *see* Cardinal points.
Nomadic life, 96-97, 254.
North, beliefs, II, 94, 338-339.
North Dakota, 37.
North Dakota State Historical Society, II, 205.
North Platte River, II, 179.
See also Platte River.
Northern Cheyennes, 1-2, 6-7, 30, 35, 40-41, 46, 59, 88, 92-93, 96, 101, 107, 161, 165. 193, 201, 221, 226, 239, 263, 283, 307, 331, 341, II, 39-40, 44, 49, 56, 68, 70, 72-73, 77, 92, 113, 138-139, 158, 160, 162, 228.
Nose-rings, 61, 79.
No ta min ('facing the north'), a family, 101.
Nov i voos, in the Black Hills, 98.
Num o sin ha nhi a, an Arapaho division, 11.
Nuts, 249.
Nymphea polysepala, II, 173.

Oak, 193-194, II, 39.
Oak, black-jack, 292.
Oaks, 248.
Oath, 75, 162, II, 18, 32-35.
Observation, keenness of, II, 15-16.
Offenses, 98, 131, 252, 349, 358.
See also Homicide, Manslaughter.
Offerings, in Massaum, II, 298-299, 327.
in Medicine Lodge, II, 245, 247, 263-264, 270-271, 275-276.
to Cardinal Points, 146, 222-223, II, 56, 238.
to Earth, 152, 232, II, 286.
to Great Power, II, 385-386.
to Sky, 75, 121, 162-163, 200, 232.
to spirits, 75, 96-97, II, 99.
to spiritual powers, II, 38.
to stars, II, 221.
to Sun, II, 188.
to Thunder, II, 205.
to Yellow Wolf in Massaum, II, 317.
tribal ceremonies as offerings, II, 220, 286.
See also Ceremonies, Prayers, Sacrifices.
Ohk to kun ah, *see* Ohk to unna.

Ohk to o na, *see* Ohk to unna.
Ohk to unna, a Cheyenne division, 89, 90, 95, 101.
Oil, from fishbones, 52.
O i vi man ah, a division, 90, 93-94, 101, II, 164.
Ojibwas, 8, 10, 11, 23, 240, 245, 248, 274, II, 3.
Okandandas Sioux (Oglalas), 31.
Oklahoma, 212, 248, 292, II, 114, 139.
Old Bull, II, 330.
Old Frog, II, 152.
Old woman who lived in a hill, 251, II, 241, *et seq.*, 296.
See also Grandmother and Listeners Under The Ground.
Old Woman's Water, II, 340-344.
Omaha Woman, 110.
Omahas, 9, 180.
O mis sis, a division, 10, 89, 94, 96, 101, II, 62, 72.
Onions, wild, II, 171.
Ono ni o he, Grand River, S. D., 26.
Onosmodium occidentale, II, 185-186.
Ookh to un a, *see* Ohk to unna.
Opuntia (prickly-pear), 298.
Opuntia polyacantha, eaten, II, 180.
Ordeals, 79, 80, 81, 82, 83, II, 113, 115, 144-145, 211-216, 251.
Ordway, Sergeant, 8.
Organized hunts, 261-263.
See Hunts, organized.
Oriole, on Contrary lances, II, 81.
Ornamentation, 89, 99, 135, 142, 147, 159-168, 187-188, 190-198, 201, 207, 209, 210-221, 233, 235, 242-243, 245, II, 135, 232, 390.
Orphans, 63, 73, II, 162-163.
Osage orange, bows of, 173.
Osages, 44, 60, II, 164.
Osmorrhiza longistylis, II, 181.
Otoes, 3.
Otters, 184, 191, 198, 222, 256, 296, II, 24, 58, 74, 104, 133, 270, 331, 358.
Ouify (Omissis), a division, 38.
Ouisay, 38.
Ouisy (Omissis), 10, 88.
Outer Edge Creek, Colo., 99.
Outlaws, 98, 352, 354-357.
Owl, burrowing, II, 83.

419

INDEX

Plaster of Paris, *see* Gypsum, burnt.
Platte River, 31, 39-46, 98, 106, 251, 253, 350.
Pleiades, or Seven Stars, painted on lodge, 234.
Plenty Crows, II, 280.
Plum Creek, Colo., 43.
Plumes, feather, II, 233, 243-244, 265.
Plums, 71, 250, 315, II, 166, 177.
Plum-stones, seed game, 245.
Plunder, II, 36.
Poison ivy, II, 179, 189.
Pole, center, Massaum, II, 287, *et seq.*, 297.
  Medicine Lodge, II, 219, 228-231, 247-248, 264, 270, 273, 276.
Poles, scalp, II, 38.
Police (soldier bands), 337, 352, II, 48, 53-54, 63.
Polygamy, 153.
Pomme blanche, 68, 250, 255, II, 178.
  See also Red turnip.
Poncarars, 31.
Poncas, 356.
Poor Bull, 231.
Poplar, dishes of, 212.
Population (increase), 101.
Porcupine, 47, II, 131, 249-250.
Porcupine Bear, 256-258, II, 52.
Porcupine Bull, 88-89, 283, 288, 290, II, 164.
Porcupine Creek, N. D., 23-24, 27-28, 240, II, 382-383.
Porcupine quillwork, 60, 99, 142, 147, 161-168, 170, 218-220, II, 122, 169, 172-173, 385.
Porcupines, 164, II, 255, 310.
Port Nelson, 8.
Possible sacks, 245, II, 232, 242, 385.
Potatoes, wild, 251.
Potter's clay, 240.
Potters, women as, 239.
Pottery, 24, 25, 49, 170-171, 235-240, II, 134.
Powder River, Mont., II, 45, 148.
Powell, Ed., 304.
Powers, 102, II, 88.
Practical jokes, 124, II, 24, 26.
Prairie-dogs, II, 189-190.
Pretty plant, *see* Tule.
Prickly-pear (*Opuntia*), 111-113, 298.

Priests, II, 10, 16, 84, 116-117, 195, 277-284, 289.
Property, 58, 75-76, 129, 150, 234, II, 76, 160-162.
Prophecies, II, 91, 107, 379-381.
Prophets, 195, II, 112-113.
Protective-string, 131, 145, 224, II, 242.
Prunus americana, II, 177.
Prunus besseyi, II, 177.
Prunus melanocarpa, II, 177.
Psoralea argophylla, II, 178.
Psoralea hypogeæ, II, 178.
Psoralea lanceolata, II, 178.
Pterospora andromeda, II, 183.
Puberty, boys arrive at, 118-124.
  girls at, 129-131, II, 186.
Public opinion, 104, 128, 156-157, 262, 336-342, 349, II, 5, 48-49.
Pueblo Indians, 15.
Puffball, powder from, 148.
Punch, stone, 185.
Punishment, 98, 152, 262, 349, 358, II, 54-55.
  See also Outlaws.
Punk, *see also* Tinder, 54.
Purgatoire River, Colo., 83.
Purification, 147, 149, 197, 199-200, II, 37-38, 56, 62, 81-82, 168-170, 186, 188, 231, 249, 385-386, 388.

Quaife, M. M., II, 382.
Qualities, typified, II, 87.
Quarrels, 99-100, 154-155, 157, 336, 349-353, 357, II, 71.
Quill-cases, 219.
Quilling implements, II, 390.
Quilling society, 147, 159-167, II, 385, *et seq.*
Quillwork, 56, 60, 121, 159-160, 204-205, 207, 211, 224, 243, 245, 346, II, 59, 65-66.
  See also Decorative arts, Ornamentation.
Quirts, 262, II, 55.
  See also Whips.
Quivers, 87, 184, 291.
  See also Bow cases and quivers.

Rabbits, 5, 102, 115, 176, 198, 247,

421

INDEX

Whistling Elk, 196-197, II, 122, 151.
White Antelope, II, 54-55.
White buffalo, 173, 271-272, II, 200-204, 272-273.
White Buffalo Woman, 346-347.
White Bull, 30, 88-89, 110, 215, 278, II, 115, 119-123, 154-156, 231, *et seq.*
White Bull, Mrs., 239.
White Earth River, N. D., 32.
White Elk, 61.
White Faced Bull, 283-289, II, 164.
White Frog, 32, II, 44, 287, *et seq.*
White Hawk, 265, II, 249.
White Horse, 350, 352.
White-horse men (soldier society ?), II, 56.
White, John J., Jr., 196.
White River, S. D., 29, 31, 37, 277, II, 234, 382.
White Shield, 196, II, 149-150.
White Thunder, 48, II, 49, 119.
White Wolf, 100, II, 75.
White Wolf band, 100.
Whitefish, 311.
Whitestone Hills, N. D., battle at, 27.
Whooper, II, 66.
Whortleberry, red, II, 183-184.
Widows and orphans, 336, II, 162-163.
Wild rice, 248.
Wild Horse Creek, Colo., 283.
Wildcats, as food, 256.
Will, Geo. F., 37.
Williamson, Dr. T. S., 16, 21, 27, II, 382.
Willow, II, 142.
Willows, 49, 74, 105, 113, 135, 202, 208, 210, 215, 240-241, 243, 246, 284, 293, 298, 310-311, II, 20, 168, 229-232, 265, 268, 277, 328-329.
See also Red-willow.
Winchell, N. H., 14.
Winds, 196-197, 265, II, 90, 347.
Wind Woman, 196-197, II, 247.
Wings, lodge, 95, 226, 229.
Winnebago, 351-353, 357.
Winter, 129, 258, 312, 314, 319, II, 7, 74, 94-95, 102-103, 339.
Winter Man, II, 338.
See also Hoimaha.
Wisconsin Archaeologist, 48.

Wisconsin State Historical Society:
Collections, 8.
Proceedings, 22.
Wise One Above (Heammawihio), II, 88.
Wistar, I. J., *Autobiography,* 247.
Wives, 91, 127-128, 149, 151, 153-155, 178.
Wohk po tsit ('white crafty'), a family, 100.
Wohk po tsit si ma han, or White Wolf, 100.
Wolf Chief, 71, 199-200, 269, II, 100-102, 196, 204, 220, *et seq.*
Wolf Creek, Okla., 356, II, 35.
Wolf Ear, II, 46.
Wolf Face, II, 228.
Wolf Fire, 301.
Wolf Man, 271.
Wolf Mule, II, 54-55.
Wolf On The Hill (High Backed Wolf), 30.
Wolf Road, II, 24.
Wolf Running Together Woman, II, 208-209.
Wolf Soldiers (Bowstrings), II, 72, 75-78.
Wolf songs, II, 12, 227, 392-393.
Wolf Walking Alone, II, 39.
Wolves, 150, 256, 288, 290, 297, 299, 300, II, 17, 18, 24-25, 66, 74-78, 105-107, 112, 125, 163, 198, 199-200, 229, 248, 287, 292, 300, 307, 321, *et seq.*
Woman, first, II, 338-339.
Woman, status of, 154.
Woman's Heart, 78.
Woman's work, 62-65, 73, 104-105, 108-109, 121-122, 127-128, 159, 206, 209, 212-217, 226, 239-240, 246, 249-250, II, 34, 149, 166, 180.
Women, 58, 103, 127-129, 154-156, 329, *et seq.,* 350-353, II, 44, *et seq.;* 217; 221, 230, 233, 241, *et seq.,* 256-260, 270-271, 274-276, 288, 298, *et seq.,* 367.
Women's societies, 159, *et seq.*
Woodpeckers, 115, II, 109, 232-233, 266.
Wool, buffalo, ceremonial use, II, 223, 224, 240, 241, 314, 318, 319.